Essential Solutions Architect's Handbook

Master cloud and AI innovation
strategies for the future of architecture

Bikramjit Debnath

bpb

www.bpbonline.com

First Edition 2025

Copyright © BPB Publications, India

ISBN: 978-93-65893-595

To View Complete
BPB Publications Catalogue
Scan the QR Code:

Dedicated to

*My son, **Adi**, my wife, **Tanu**, and*
the cherished memory of my beloved mother

Foreword

We are at an inflection point in technology. Cloud computing and artificial intelligence are transformative technologies that are reshaping industries and redefining how we work, build, and innovate. AI enabled applications and intelligent agents are becoming an integral part of our daily lives, assisting with tasks ranging from summarizing emails to guiding complex decision-making processes.

Leading Microsoft across India and South Asia is a privilege, and it gives me a front-row seat to see how the technology landscape is changing. Our industry is moving at a breakneck pace, and the pressure to innovate is unrelenting. Yet, despite our advances, many IT professionals still find themselves confined within specialized technical roles, not fully equipped to connect disparate dots that ultimately define the architecture of a successful organization. It often takes decades to develop both the depth and breadth of expertise needed to architect complex, scalable, and secure enterprise systems. But in today's world, we do not have the luxury of time. External change is outpacing internal learning curves.

The rate limiter is no longer technology itself; it is our ability to evolve. AI is fundamentally shifting the way software is designed, built, and optimized. It is democratizing programming, altering architecture patterns, and redefining best practices across every layer of the tech stack. To stay ahead, technology professionals must move beyond task execution and develop a strong foundation in systems thinking and solution architecture. The ability to design, integrate, and scale AI-driven cloud-native systems is no longer just an advantage. It is a necessity.

This is *Essential Solutions Architect's Handbook* where plays a crucial role. This book is not just about cloud migration, AI architectures, or data strategies. It is about integrating these elements to drive meaningful business transformation. Whether you are a developer aspiring to become an architect or a mid-career professional looking to broaden your expertise, this handbook will equip you with the insights, frameworks, and methodologies needed to think like a CTO and design resilient, scalable, and future-ready systems.

Bikram, the author, has walked this path himself. From a hands-on developer to a technology leader over last two decades, he has built software solutions and helped businesses navigate the complexities of digital transformation. His passion for breaking down complex topics and his commitment to mentoring the next generation of tech talent come through in every chapter. The real-world insights and best practices in this book make it an invaluable resource for technology professionals at any stage of their journey.

I encourage every IT professional, student, and aspiring leader to embrace the knowledge shared in these pages. The future will not be shaped by those who simply keep up with technology. It will be built by those who understand it deeply, think strategically, and lead with vision. This book is your opportunity to step into that future.

Puneet Chandok

President, Microsoft India & South Asia

About the Author

Bikramjit Debnath is the Country Head of Azure Business for Microsoft India and South Asia, where he leads strategy, operations, marketing, P&L, product availability, and market share growth for the public cloud business. With a diverse leadership background spanning sales, strategy, consulting, engineering, and alliance development, he has experience working across both India and the USA. Bikramjit began his career as a developer, designing cloud-native applications and driving digital innovation. Outside of his corporate role, Bikramjit serves as a mentor board member with India Accelerator, the largest startup accelerator in India, collaborating with VC firms to nurture startups. He is also a certified independent director and an industry thought leader, delivering keynotes on cloud innovation and AI. Bikramjit is a professional visual artist and holds an engineering degree in computer science from the University of Kalyani and an Executive MBA from IIM Lucknow.

About the Reviewers

❖ **Apoorv Malmane** is a principal engineer at VMware by Broadcom, where he leads global efforts in network virtualization, cloud infrastructure, and enterprise security. With over a decade of experience driving innovation at scale, he has played a pivotal role in designing, optimizing and securing high-performance virtualized environments for Fortune 500 organizations worldwide. He is widely recognized for his deep expertise in virtualization technologies. His unique solutions have directly influenced product development and improved security posture across global deployments.

As a senior member of IEEE and a technical reviewer, he continues to contribute to the broader engineering community. He has judged prestigious industry awards, served on advisory committees, and delivered technical training sessions across multiple countries, empowering professionals with cutting-edge troubleshooting skills and architectural best practices. He has also contributed to the development of expert-level security certification exams. He is actively involved in mentoring teams, guiding quality assurance efforts, and driving improvements in software reliability.

Malmane's contributions extend beyond engineering execution; he is a thought leader, mentor, and strategic advisor dedicated to advancing the state of enterprise technology and inspiring the next generation of engineers.

❖ **Jasbeer Singh** is a passionate software engineer and a cloud practitioner with more than 12 years of extensive professional experience in the domains of Python development, testing methodologies, system automation, CI/CD, DevOps practices, data warehousing, and framework development. He is proficient in various tools and technologies related to these domains. Jasbeer specializes in building robust and efficient software systems and loves exploring new technologies and sharing his insights. He has reviewed this book, bringing his practical experience and deep understanding of software development best practices to his assessment of the material.

Acknowledgement

I want to express my sincere gratitude to all those who supported me throughout the journey of writing this book.

First and foremost, I am deeply thankful to my family for their unwavering support, love, and encouragement, which have been a constant source of motivation.

I extend my special thanks to my mentors at Microsoft India and South Asia — Puneet Chandok, Dhanniya Venkatasalapathy, Alok Lall, Dahnesh Dilkhush, Irina Ghosh, and Roan Kang. Their belief in my abilities, the platform they provided me, and the example they set as role models in both technical and business leadership truly inspired me to pursue this project despite a demanding schedule.

I am also grateful to the exceptionally talented colleagues, customers, partners, and friends I have had the privilege to work with at Microsoft, Cognizant, and Birlasoft, as well as those I have connected with through various community forums. I have learned invaluable lessons from them, which helped shape many of the ideas in this book. There are far too many individuals to name here, and trying to do justice to each of them would require another book altogether.

My sincere appreciation goes to the team at BPB Publications for their guidance and professionalism in bringing this book to life. Their expertise made navigating the complexities of publishing a smooth and enriching experience.

I would also like to thank the reviewers, technical experts, and editors who provided insightful feedback and helped refine the manuscript. Their contributions greatly enhanced the book's depth and clarity.

Lastly, I want to thank the readers who have shown interest in our book. Your support and encouragement have been deeply appreciated.

Thank you to everyone who has played a part in making this book a reality.

Preface

I began my journey like many of you as a developer, immersed in code, solving problems one bug at a time. However, I soon realized that clean code was only a piece of the puzzle. The bigger shift came when I started thinking like an architect, understanding how systems connect, scale, and deliver business value. Making that transition was not easy, and it is even harder today. I see talented professionals every day trying to break out of their current roles and influence outcomes that matter. Even expert engineers often struggle, not because they lack skill, but because they have not got enough exposure yet to develop the broader perspective that architects bring. In today's landscape, businesses do not just need coders; they need professionals who can design solutions, make smart trade-offs, and drive impact.

This book is for you if you are at that inflection point. *Essential Solutions Architect's Handbook* distills what I have learned into practical tools, mental models, and real-world insights on system design, cloud architecture, data strategy, and AI. Information is not a challenge anymore. Tools can give you answers, but they cannot teach you how to think deeply, see the bigger picture, or make decisions when there is no clear path. It is about building the strategic thinking and architectural judgment that sets great technologists apart. This is the book I wish I had earlier in my career to help connect the dots and lead with clarity and confidence in a fast-moving tech world.

Thanks for picking it up. Let us get started.

Chapter 1: Introduction to Solution Architecture - This chapter explores the foundational role of solution architecture in today's fast-evolving tech landscape. It defines what solution architecture is, why it matters, and how it bridges business needs with technical execution. Covering key concepts, design patterns, and the architect's responsibilities, it also highlights modern methodologies and best practices. By the end, readers will grasp the essentials needed to design scalable, resilient solutions and take the first step toward becoming effective solution architects.

Chapter 2: Cloud Migration Essentials- This chapter provides a practical foundation for understanding and executing cloud migration. It covers key strategies for assessing data center and application estates, building tailored migration and modernization roadmaps, and implementing infrastructure and data migration techniques. Readers will also learn how to design effective cloud landing zones. By the end, you will be equipped to lead successful migration efforts that optimize cost, boost performance, and align with your organization's strategic goals.

Chapter 3: Operational Excellence in Cloud - This chapter focuses on building resilient, efficient, and cost-effective cloud operations. It explores strategies for cost optimization, including FinOps principles, right provisioning, and workload-specific tuning across compute storage, and AI. You will also learn how to design governance and operating models that balance control with agility and how to plan for business continuity and disaster recovery. By the end, you will be equipped to drive operational excellence through smart financial practices, strong governance, and resilient architecture.

Chapter 4: Modern Application Architecture - This chapter covers the essential principles and technologies behind designing scalable, resilient, and modular cloud-native applications. It explores architectural patterns like domain-driven design, microservices, and event-driven systems alongside orchestration strategies using Kubernetes and serverless frameworks. Readers will gain practical insights into API management, observability, runtime optimization, and legacy modernization, equipping them to build agile, secure, and high-performing applications aligned with modern business needs.

Chapter 5: Development Practices and Tools - This chapter focuses on the principles and tools needed to build scalable, secure, and efficient software systems. It introduces core architecture design fundamentals and a practical review checklist to guide sound decisions. You will explore how to integrate DevSecOps and platform engineering for automation and security, leverage CI/CD for streamlined delivery, and assess when to use low-code/no-code platforms. By the end, you will have the tools and frameworks to choose the right development approach for your goals—balancing speed, flexibility, and long-term maintainability.

Chapter 6: Data Architecture and Processing - This chapter explores the foundations of modern data architecture, focusing on how to design scalable, efficient, and real-time data systems. It covers the database landscape, including relational, NoSQL, in-memory, and cloud-native options, and offers guidance on selecting the right OLTP and OLAP systems based on business needs. You will also learn core techniques for distributed and real-time data processing, as well as best practices for cloud data warehousing. By the end, you will be equipped to architect robust data platforms that support analytics, AI, and fast decision-making at scale.

Chapter 7: Data Strategy and Governance - This chapter focuses on building strong frameworks for managing, securing, and governing enterprise data. It introduces core data engineering principles and explores modern architectures like data mesh and data fabric for decentralized and scalable data management. You will learn how to implement effective governance, ensure data quality, and enforce security and compliance through practices like Zero Trust, encryption, and automated controls. By the end, you will be equipped to design a resilient, compliant, and future-ready data strategy for your organization.

Chapter 8: Advanced Analytics - This chapter explores the evolution of data analytics from traditional reporting to today's AI-driven, real-time, and predictive insights. It covers core techniques in modern analytics, introduces augmented analytics platforms that automate insight generation, and explains how machine learning can uncover hidden patterns within complex datasets. You will also learn best practices for data visualization to communicate insights effectively. By the end, you will be equipped to harness advanced analytics and AI to drive faster, smarter, and more impactful business decisions.

Chapter 9: Generative AI and Machine Learning - This chapter dives into the architectures and practices that power today's generative AI systems. It covers foundational concepts like LLMs, SLMs, RAG, LangChain, and Semantic Kernel, along with operational strategies such as MLOps and AI model deployment. You will explore emerging trends like agentic AI and gain insights into open-source models. With a focus on responsible AI, prompt engineering, and real-world application patterns, this chapter equips you to design, scale, and govern enterprise-ready AI solutions.

Chapter 10: Automation and Infra Management - This chapter explores how automation and modern infrastructure management drive reliability, scalability, and operational efficiency. It covers core practices in **infrastructure as code (IaC)**, application definition tools, and observability techniques using platforms such as Azure Monitor and Application Insights. You will also learn how to integrate **site reliability engineering (SRE)** principles to automate operations and maintain system health. By the end, you will be equipped to build resilient, self-managed infrastructure that supports continuous delivery and business agility.

Chapter 11: FinOps Foundations - This chapter introduces the core principles of FinOps, bringing financial accountability to cloud spending while maintaining agility and scalability. It covers how to align finance and tech teams, build accurate cost models, implement governance controls, and drive continuous optimization. By the end, you will understand how to manage cloud investments strategically, avoid overspending, and foster a culture of cost awareness across your organization.

Chapter 12: Security, Privacy, and Ethics - This chapter explores how to secure modern applications and enterprise systems while upholding privacy and ethical responsibility. It covers foundational principles like the CIA triad and advanced frameworks such as

Zero Trust and **Cloud Native App Protection Platforms (CNAPP)**. Readers will also learn about privacy-enhancing technologies, key compliance standards, and the ethical governance of AI, focusing on fairness, transparency, and accountability. By the end, you will be equipped to build secure, trustworthy, and ethically grounded digital systems in an increasingly complex and regulated world.

Chapter 13: Innovation and Future Technologies - This chapter explores the emerging technologies transforming enterprise IT from multi-cloud and edge computing to quantum frameworks, blockchain, and sustainable computing. It examines how innovations like HPC, GPU-based architectures, and generative AI are reshaping industries by enabling real-time intelligence, decentralized systems, and eco-friendly operations. By the end, readers will understand how to harness these technologies to drive modernization, scalability, and long-term innovation in a fast-evolving digital world.

Chapter 14: CTO's Playbook for Transformation - This chapter brings the entire book together through a real-world-inspired transformation journey led by a newly appointed CTO. Structured across 11 practical phases, from diagnosing legacy challenges to enabling AI, security, and future readiness—it illustrates how to apply architecture, cloud, DevSecOps, data, and FinOps strategies cohesively. Readers will gain a step-by-step playbook to align technology with business goals, navigate complexity, and drive enterprise-wide change with clarity and confidence.

Coloured Images

Please follow the link to download the
Coloured Images of the book:

https://rebrand.ly/cds5zmp

We have code bundles from our rich catalogue of books and videos available at **https://github.com/bpbpublications**. Check them out!

Errata

We take immense pride in our work at BPB Publications and follow best practices to ensure the accuracy of our content to provide with an indulging reading experience to our subscribers. Our readers are our mirrors, and we use their inputs to reflect and improve upon human errors, if any, that may have occurred during the publishing processes involved. To let us maintain the quality and help us reach out to any readers who might be having difficulties due to any unforeseen errors, please write to us at :

errata@bpbonline.com

Your support, suggestions and feedbacks are highly appreciated by the BPB Publications' Family.

Did you know that BPB offers eBook versions of every book published, with PDF and ePub files available? You can upgrade to the eBook version at www.bpbonline. com and as a print book customer, you are entitled to a discount on the eBook copy. Get in touch with us at :

business@bpbonline.com for more details.

At **www.bpbonline.com**, you can also read a collection of free technical articles, sign up for a range of free newsletters, and receive exclusive discounts and offers on BPB books and eBooks.

Piracy

If you come across any illegal copies of our works in any form on the internet, we would be grateful if you would provide us with the location address or website name. Please contact us at **business@bpbonline.com** with a link to the material.

If you are interested in becoming an author

If there is a topic that you have expertise in, and you are interested in either writing or contributing to a book, please visit **www.bpbonline.com**. We have worked with thousands of developers and tech professionals, just like you, to help them share their insights with the global tech community. You can make a general application, apply for a specific hot topic that we are recruiting an author for, or submit your own idea.

Reviews

Please leave a review. Once you have read and used this book, why not leave a review on the site that you purchased it from? Potential readers can then see and use your unbiased opinion to make purchase decisions. We at BPB can understand what you think about our products, and our authors can see your feedback on their book. Thank you!

For more information about BPB, please visit **www.bpbonline.com**.

Join our book's Discord space

Join the book's Discord Workspace for Latest updates, Offers, Tech happenings around the world, New Release and Sessions with the Authors:

https://discord.bpbonline.com

Table of Contents

Introduction to Solution Architecture

Introduction

In today's rapidly evolving technological landscape, solution architecture plays a critical role in shaping the future of business and innovation. This chapter will cover the fundamental concepts of solution architecture, including current trends, guiding principles, methodologies, and best practices. However, what exactly is solution architecture? At its core, solution architecture involves designing comprehensive and coherent technology solutions that address specific business challenges or opportunities. Solution architects bridge the gap between business needs and technical implementation, ensuring that all components of a system work together harmoniously to achieve organizational goals. By understanding the essentials of solution architecture, you will be better equipped to create innovative, efficient, and effective solutions that drive success in any technological endeavor. This chapter sets the stage for your journey into the world of solution architecture, providing the essential knowledge needed to excel in this dynamic field.

Structure

This chapter covers the following topics:

- Importance of becoming a solution architect
- Overview of solution architecture
- Goals of solution architecture

- Key components of a solution architecture
- Solution architecture design patterns
- Roles and responsibilities of solution architects

Objectives

By the end of this chapter, you will be able to understand the foundational concepts and principles of solution architecture, recognize the critical roles and responsibilities of solution architects, comprehend various methodologies and frameworks utilized to design solutions that are scalable and resilient, and apply best practices to ensure success.

Importance of becoming a solution architect

Are you a solution architect, or are you aspiring to be one? It is a question that resonates deeply in the hearts of those navigating technology and innovation every day. The digital world around us is evolving at a staggering pace. We are at a transformative juncture in the history of technology. Innovations in generative AI are reducing the floor and raising the ceiling. This means that more people and organizations can start using AI with less expertise or fewer resources. At the same time, the capabilities, potential, and performance of AI systems are rapidly advancing to solve more complex problems and deliver better results at reduced cost. The more sophisticated models will soon simulate IQ and EQ at human parity. They will get better at larger contexts, complex reasoning, being creative in all forms of output, making decisions, taking actions, and interacting with other AI agents. Computers will soon have more sophisticated eyes and ears; they will make better sense of the world and will be able to interact with the world in a way humans do. The new technology capabilities, from silicon to software, are increasing our ambitions and hopes; we are now only limited by our imaginations. Millions of innovative applications will emerge as AI simplifies and accelerates development. This decade will witness not only the birth of new software but also the rejuvenation of legacy systems to reduce technical debt. Since the birth of computers, they had to be explicitly programmed, and for the past 50 years, we spoke to them via keyboard, mouse, or, recently, touch screens. Now, our interaction methods with computers are changing. We will see systems that can interact with us in the same way we interact with other people. Programming and DevOps are changing, and the nature of work is changing.

We are witnessing the beginning of an intelligence revolution. The role of the solution architect has never been more crucial or challenging. Whether you are a seasoned architect or a hopeful newcomer in a large organization or a mid-size startup, supporting existing systems or building new products, you need to be a better system thinker. You need to understand the domain and business processes and have technological foresight. The journey ahead for you as an architect is filled with both uncertainty and opportunity to shape the future of technology and progress.

Overview of solution architecture

Solution architecture is the art of crafting holistic solutions and structural design of the components tailored to meet specific business objectives, challenges, or opportunities. Solution architects design solutions that align with organizational goals, deliver performance, minimize risk, and propel businesses forward.

The designing of solution architecture starts with the goal of building reliable, scalable, secure, performing, cost-effective, and easy-to-maintain systems that maximize the value of the investment. The architects then decide how each component in the system will be designed and how it will behave and interact with other systems. These design choices may follow well-established design patterns, and some trade-offs might be made under various constraints, as shown:

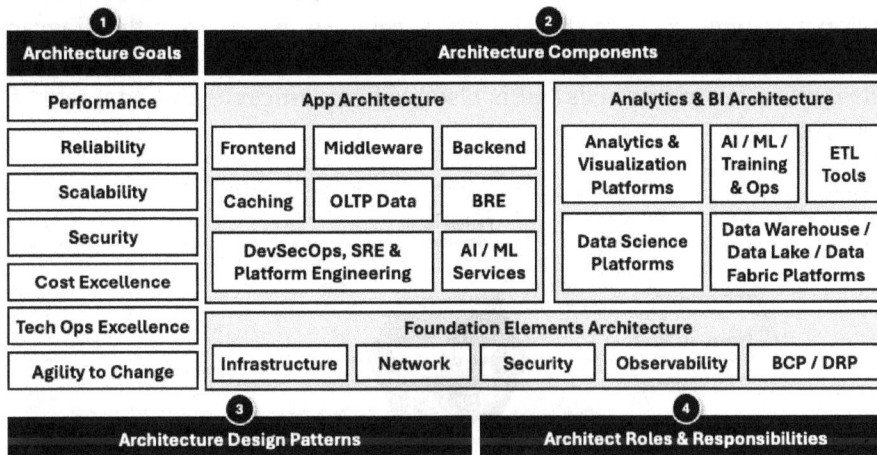

Figure 1.1: *Building blocks of solution architecture*

To design a solution architecture, the following building blocks need to be understood:

- Architecture goals
- Architecture components
- Architecture design patterns
- Architect roles and responsibilities

We will now discuss each of the building blocks.

Goals of solution architecture

The design of solution architecture starts with setting goals to build reliable, scalable, secure, high-performing, cost-effective, and easy-to-maintain systems. The primary goal of a solution architect is to design systems that align with current business requirements while anticipating future needs.

They must ensure that the system has the following:

- Demonstrates resilience and availability.
- Ensures rapid recovery capabilities.
- Achieves desired performance levels.
- Maintains the requisite level of security.
- It is cost-effective and yields a strong return on investment.
- Embraces efficient development practices and operational procedures.
- Offers agility and interoperability, adapting swiftly to changes.
- Integrates seamlessly with pre-existing systems.

To successfully address these business and system requirements, a solution architect must develop a system based on six pillars of excellence, as shown in the diagram below. Each pillar addresses a critical aspect of system design, ensuring that the architecture not only meets current business needs but is also resilient, efficient, and adaptable to future challenges, as shown:

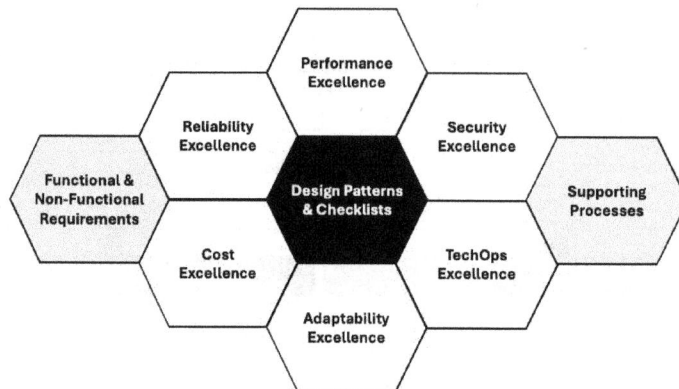

Figure 1.2: *Six pillars of solution architecture excellence*

Let us discuss these pillars in detail:

- **Reliability excellence**: designing for reliability ensures that the system consistently performs as intended under a variety of conditions and delivers the desired level of system uptime, **mean time between failures (MTBF)**, **mean time to recovery (MTTR)**, **recovery time objective (RTO)**, **recovery point objective (RPO)**, etc. A good solution architecture design is coupled with regular system maintenance, disaster recovery drills, and automated failover processes to maintain reliability excellence.

- **Performance excellence**: designing for performance excellence ensures that the system is meeting or exceeding the desired level of response time, throughput, peak performance under stress, and efficiently managing the system load, and resource utilization. A good solution architecture is coupled with capacity planning, performance testing (e.g., load and stress testing), automated resource scaling, and continuous application performance monitoring to ensure performance excellence.

- **Security excellence**: designing for security excellence ensures that the system, data, applications, infrastructure, network, and devices are protected from unauthorized access and threats, and the system has the ability to detect and respond to security breaches and incidents. A good solution architecture is coupled with regular patch management, security audits, continuous monitoring, exposure scanning, security training, incident response testing, etc., to ensure security excellence.

- **Cost excellence**: designing for cost excellence ensures optimized cost per transaction, optimized resource allocation, overall cost efficiency, visibility into **total cost of ownership** (**TCO**), and **return on investment** (**ROI**). A good solution architecture is coupled with budget planning, financial audits, lean resource management, etc., to ensure cost excellence.

- **TechOps excellence**: TechOps excellence in solution architecture integrates DevOps and platform engineering practices to standardize workflows, promote team cohesion, and ensure smooth operations. This pillar prioritizes minimizing process variances and human error to enhance system predictability and customer satisfaction. These practices involve comprehensive observability, automated deployments, and regular feedback loops that ensure operations are both effective and resilient. Platform engineering specifically contributes by creating self-service capabilities and automating infrastructure provisioning, which empowers developers and reduces operational bottlenecks, driving the overall efficiency and agility of the system.

- **Adaptability excellence**: Adaptability excellence ensures that systems are designed to accommodate changes efficiently and integrate new technologies seamlessly to maintain relevance and responsiveness in a rapidly evolving technological landscape. Solutions architects leverage domain-driven, micro services-based, event-driven design patterns along with CI/CD processes to improve time to market for new features, increase the rate of successful change implementations, and improve the system's scalability. These processes allow the teams to respond to new business requirements and technological opportunities promptly.

Each pillar comes with its specific set of risks, best practices, and necessary compromises. Architects must carefully balance these elements to meet the business objectives. While these six pillars form the backbone of a well-architected system, they do not operate in isolation. A strong architecture is not just about optimizing for performance, reliability, security, cost, operations, and adaptability; it also needs a solid foundation and an effective governance mechanism to sustain it over time.

This brings us to two essential aspects that underpin these pillars, *functional and non-functional requirements,* which define the system's core purpose and operational characteristics, and *Supporting Processes*, which ensure that the architecture remains sustainable, secure, and continuously evolving, as follows:

- **Functional and non-functional requirements**: A well-architected system begins with clearly understanding what it is expected to achieve. Functional requirements define the system's core capabilities and what it must do to fulfill business needs. These include specific features, workflows, and user interactions. However, beyond functionality, a system must also meet key operational attributes known as **non-functional requirements** (**NFRs**). These define qualities such as performance, security, scalability, and reliability. While functional requirements shape the system's purpose, NFRs ensure it operates efficiently and withstands real-world challenges. Neglecting them can lead to systems that work in theory but fail under stress, making it imperative for architects to incorporate NFRs as fundamental design principles.

- **Supporting processes**: Beyond technical design, successful architecture requires structured processes to ensure long-term sustainability, governance, and continuous improvement. Supporting processes include change management, IT service operations, compliance frameworks, and risk management strategies. These mechanisms help maintain system integrity, ensuring that enhancements, security updates, and optimizations do not disrupt stability. Furthermore, observability, proactive incident management, and feedback-driven iteration allow the architecture to evolve while aligning with business objectives. Without these processes, even a well-designed system can become inefficient over time, accumulating technical debt and operational risks. Supporting processes are integral components that sustain and enhance the architecture throughout its lifecycle.

Key components of a solution architecture

Solution architecture is composed of several critical components that work together to create a cohesive and functional system. To better understand these components, we can categorize them into three logical groups: application architecture components, analytics and business intelligence components, and underlying and surrounding foundational components. Each group addresses specific aspects of the overall architecture, ensuring that all necessary elements are considered and integrated effectively.

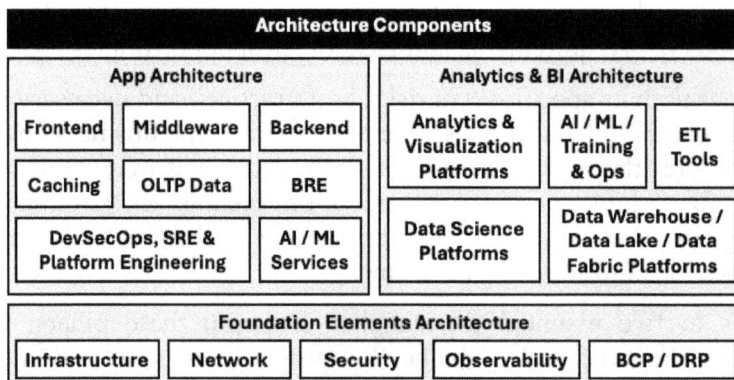

Figure 1.3: Key components of solution architecture

Let us discuss each of these component categories to understand their roles, characteristics, and significance within a solution architecture. The following detailed exploration will comprehensively understand how each component contributes to building robust, scalable, and efficient systems:

- **Application architecture**: It is the system that interacts with the world from here.

  o **Frontend**: The users engage with the system via the frontend, usually the graphical interface, where the architects need to think about behavioral design, accessibility, and cross-platform compatibility. The most common technologies are HTML, CSS, JavaScript frameworks like *React* and *Angular*, *iOS* and *Android apps*, etc. With Gen AI innovations, front ends are transforming to take multi-modal inputs, from natural language to audio and visuals, and we will soon see a lot more innovations here.

  o **Middleware**: Liaison between the frontend and backend, middleware tools manage communication, data, and service orchestration. Middleware ranges from API Gateways, Service Bus, and Event Hubs to Enterprise Message Brokers. It might also leverage **extract, local and transform (ETL)** services, serverless functions, and business rule workflow or orchestration services to perform the job.

  o **Backend**: This is the engine room of business logic and data manipulation layers of the applications. The most common technologies are .NET, Java, Node.js, or Python. Often the business logics are written in PL/SQL, and it runs on database server instead of running on an application server. The backend layer has to also support heavy-duty batch jobs and **robotic process automation (RPA)**, and usually need to integrate with packaged solutions like **enterprise resource planning (ERP)**, **customer relationship management (CRM)**, **human resource management system (HRMS)**, **content management system (CMS)**, **supply chain management (SCM)**, **marketing automation platform (MAP)**, **enterprise asset management (EAM)**, **knowledge management system (KMS)**, **contract lifecycle management (CLM)**, **quality management system (QMS)**, eProcurement, and various SaaS solutions. With the increasing growth of Generative AI, we will see the orchestration layer development at the backend on enterprise data, using **retrieval-augmented generation (RAG)** pattern and technologies like *Semantic Kernel*, *Prompt Flow*, and *LangChain*. The solution architect plays a key role in making this backend layer robust, secure, and capable of handling concurrent processes and transactions.

  o **Caching**: Caching plays a vital role in improving scalability and performance by storing frequently accessed data closer to users, reducing the need to repeatedly fetch it from the primary database or backend services. This leads to *faster response times, lower system load, and a smoother user experience*. Common caching strategies include **in-memory caching** (e.g., Redis,

Memcached) for ultra-fast data retrieval, **edge caching** (e.g., Cloudflare, Azure Front Door, AWS CloudFront) to serve content closer to users, and **database query caching** to minimize expensive database calls. Choosing the right caching approach and tools can drastically improve system efficiency and user satisfaction.

o **OLTP data**: OLTP systems are at the core of transaction management, where database type, ACID properties, and response time are key design considerations. SQL databases or high-performance NoSQL options, along with specialized databases like in-memory databases, vector databases, key-value databases, columnar databases, graph databases, etc., are part of this layer, enabling real-time transaction processing.

o **Business rules engine**: **Business rules engines** (BREs) encapsulate the decision logic separate from the application code, making it easier to change rules without redeployment. They also help to orchestrate complex workflows, often using tools like *Pega, IBM Cloud Pak*, and, and sometime other process and workflow orchestration tools like *Logic Apps, Power Automate* etc. This layer is about agility and maintainability.

o **AI/ML services**: AI/ML services and integration tools are necessary for embedding intelligence into the systems. This layer includes various AI services like text-to-speech, speech-to-text, NLP processing, vision and form recognition, video analyser, cognitive search, conversational AI etc. and tools for custom ML model inferencing.

o **DevSecOps, SRE and platform engineering**: Building a great system is not just about writing good code or designing scalable architectures, it is about making sure that the system is secure, reliable, and easy to operate at scale. That is where **DevOps, DevSecOps, site reliability engineering (SRE), and platform engineering** come into play.

o **DevOps: Speed and automation without chaos**: DevOps is all about removing silos between development and operations so that software moves from code to production faster and with fewer failures. It focuses on automation, **continuous integration and deployment (CI/CD)**, and monitoring, ensuring that teams can ship updates frequently without breaking things. CI/CD pipelines automate build, test, and deployment processes, making software delivery seamless. **Infrastructure as code (IaC)** ensures environments are repeatable and version-controlled, reducing inconsistencies across deployments. Observability and monitoring provide real-time insights into system health, while automated rollbacks and canary deployments minimize risks associated with new releases. With DevOps, the goal is clear, *move fast, deploy often, and keep things stable*. But fast deployments mean nothing if security is an afterthought, which is why we need DevSecOps.

- o **DevSecOps is about shifting security left**: Traditionally, security was treated as a final checkpoint before release, leading to delays, compliance failures, and vulnerabilities that were expensive to fix late in the development cycle. DevSecOps shifts security left by embedding security practices into every stage of development, ensuring that vulnerabilities are caught early, and security does not slow down innovation. Automated security scans run as part of CI/CD pipelines, identifying issues before code reaches production. **Policy-as-code (PaC)** enforces compliance rules automatically, making security governance proactive rather than reactive. Secrets management ensures that credentials never get exposed in source code, reducing the risk of data breaches. Real-time threat monitoring and runtime protection continuously safeguard applications in production. The key principle of DevSecOps is simple, *security should be frictionless for developers.* If security processes create bottlenecks, teams will bypass them. Instead, security must be automated, integrated, and largely invisible until necessary.

- o **SRE: Keeping systems reliable at scale**: While DevOps focuses on delivering software efficiently, SRE ensures that systems remain stable, reliable, and scalable in production. SRE applies software engineering principles to operations, reducing manual toil and improving system resilience. It starts with defining **service level objectives (SLOs)** that establish measurable reliability targets. These objectives are paired with error budgets, which help balance new feature development with reliability improvements, ensuring that teams do not sacrifice stability for speed. Incident response automation helps minimize downtime by quickly identifying and resolving failures, often without human intervention. Self-healing mechanisms proactively detect and fix issues before they impact users, reducing the need for manual firefighting. SRE is about continuously improving system reliability through automation, monitoring, and disciplined engineering practices.

- o **Platform engineering: Enabling developers with self-service**: A strong DevOps and SRE strategy is not enough if developers are spending too much time navigating infrastructure complexity. Platform engineering addresses this by building internal tools and self-service platforms that streamline development workflows, allowing engineers to focus on coding rather than infrastructure management. **Internal Developer Platforms (IDPs)** provide pre-configured environments that developers can use without needing deep infrastructure expertise. Golden paths, or opinionated workflows, ensure that best practices are automatically followed without requiring developers to make difficult architectural decisions. Standardized pipelines eliminate inconsistencies in deployment workflows, enabling teams to deliver software efficiently and predictably. Platform engineering removes operational bottlenecks, enforces best practices, and accelerates software delivery.

      o In a real-world system, these three areas are not separate-they work together. These disciplines work in harmony to automate deployments, embed security into development, ensure system reliability, and provide developers with the right tools to be productive. They help developers with faster deployments, fewer incidents, and a system that scales without breaking down.

- **Analytics and BI architecture**: Here, the system turns data into insights, enabling businesses to explore, understand, and make informed decisions.

      o **Analytics and visualization platforms**: Businesses will need to extract actionable insights from raw data. Solution architects need to design systems that can handle the increasing volume, velocity, and variety of data. With a focus on data quality, security, integration, and ethical usage, data scientists often use tools like *Python* and *R* for statistical analysis, SQL for data extraction, and Excel for preliminary data exploration. Tools such as *Power BI*, *Tableau*, *SAS*, and modern big-data solutions like *Apache Spark*, *Databricks*, *Azure Synapse*, and *Snowflake* enhance visualization capabilities and facilitate efficient data flows across integrated environments. Integrating ML and AI into these systems progressively offers predictive insights and marks continuous advancements in cloud analytics.

      o **AI/ML/training and Ops**: Operationalizing AI/ML means managing data pipelines, compute resources, and model lifecycle. MLOps is the emerging discipline here, blending ML with DevOps principles, and is essential for sustainable and scalable AI solutions. Solution architects should integrate tools and platforms that support version control, model testing, CI/CD, as well as performance monitoring to ensure models remain effective and relevant over time.

      o **Data science platforms**: These platforms serve as workbenches for data scientists, supporting the entire lifecycle of developing, deploying, and monitoring machine learning models. Platforms like *Databricks*, *Anaconda*, *Jupyter*, and even tools like *Databricks* and *Apache Spark* equip data scientists with robust, flexible workflows from initial data ingestion and cleaning through to complex analysis and model deployment, enhancing productivity and cutting-edge analytics.

      o **ETL tools**: They are essential in data engineering as the backbone for managing and processing large volumes of data. These tools perform three key functions: extracting data from various sources such as databases, APIs, and flat files; transforming the data by cleansing, enriching, or restructuring it to align with business needs; and loading it into a target system, such as a data warehouse or analytics platform, for further analysis and reporting. ETL landscape includes a mix of open-source, cloud-native, and enterprise-grade tools designed for seamless data integration. *Airbyte* and *Stitch* are easy-to-use open-source options with pre-built connectors, while **Fivetran** provides an automated, fully managed ETL service. *Informatica PowerCenter* and *Talend* are popular enterprise solutions for complex data transformations. **SQL Server Integration Services** (**SSIS**), a Microsoft tool, is widely used for SQL-based data workflows, enabling data extraction, transformation, and loading within on-premises and hybrid environments. For cloud-native ETL, *Azure Data Factory* offers a fully managed data integration service with support for hybrid and multi-cloud pipelines, while *AWS Glue* and *Google Cloud Dataflow* provide automated ETL capabilities tailored to their respective cloud ecosystems. The right choice depends on factors like ease of use, scalability, and integration with existing systems.

o **Data warehouse/Data lake/Data fabric platforms**: These platforms serve as essential repositories for large-scale analytics and historical data analysis. Key players in this domain include Snowflake, Hadoop, Amazon Redshift, Azure Synapse Analytics, Cloudera, and emerging tools like *Azure Fabric* that can integrate various data management and governance capabilities across hybrid and multi-cloud environments to create a more connected data ecosystem. These platforms and technologies are instrumental in handling vast amounts of data, enabling businesses to derive valuable insights and support data-driven decision-making processes.

- **Foundation elements architecture**: this forms the backbone of any robust solution, providing the necessary infrastructure, connectivity, security, observability, and continuity measures that ensure the system's stability, efficiency, and resilience.

  o **Infrastructure**: Servers, storage, and virtualized resources are the bedrock of your systems. Solution architects will need a deep understanding of virtual machines, container orchestration platforms like *Kubernetes* and *OpenShift*, managed cloud services like *Azure Kubernetes Service* (*AKS*), *Azure Red Hat OpenShift* (*ARO*), *Azure App Service*, and various serverless computing options like *AWS Lambda* and *Azure Functions*. Along with the right computing infrastructure, choosing the right storage and appropriate data caching techniques are critical to ensure cost efficiency and security.

  o **Network**: Crucial for ensuring connectivity and the seamless flow of data across services and users. Solution architects will often use virtual network subnets, network security groups and route tables, public and private IP addresses, **virtual private clouds** (**VPCs**), **content delivery networks** (**CDNs**), **domain name systems** (**DNS**), load balancers, **container network interfaces** (**CNI**) to organize the infrastructure, isolate the network environment & reduce network latency. We will also see more innovations around **software-defined networking** (**SDN**) **and network function virtualization** (**NFV**) to increase network flexibility and manageability.

  o **Security**: Security is an indispensable, foundational element that must be integrated from the outset, not retrofitted. Architects must design systems that protect five key organizational assets, *identity, information, networks, devices, and applications* against external and internal threats. Adopting a *Zero Trust* approach ensures that no user, device, or system is inherently trusted, enforcing continuous verification and least-privilege access across all layers. To build a robust security framework, solution architects should leverage a combination of **firewalls, data encryption, identity and access management (IAM), and cloud-native application protection platforms (CNAPP)** to safeguard infrastructure and applications. Additionally, **security information and event management (SIEM)** systems provide real-time monitoring and threat detection, while **security orchestration, automation, and response (SOAR)** platforms enable automated incident response. AI-driven security insights further enhance threat prediction, anomaly detection, and automated mitigation, ensuring that security remains proactive rather than reactive. A well-architected security model defends against evolving threats and ensures compliance, resilience, and trust in the system.

o **Observability**: You can only manage what you can measure. Observability tools are designed for logging, monitoring, and alerting to get visibility into system health and performance. Solution architects often use **Elasticsearch, Logstash, Kibana (ELK)** Stack, Prometheus, and Grafana. The shift towards service mesh architectures like *Istio* is increasing the need for finer-grained observability at the microservices level.

o **BCP/DRP**: **Business continuity planning (BCP)** and **disaster recovery planning (DRP)** are foundational components of robust solution architecture design, ensuring that critical business operations can continue without interruption and recover swiftly in the event of a disaster or system failure, including hardware failures, cyber-attacks, and natural disasters. This involves the implementation of redundant systems, data backup solutions, and failover mechanisms across geographically diverse data centers to ensure data integrity and availability. Regular testing and updates to the BCP/DRP are essential to adapt to new threats and changes in the business environment.

Solution architecture design patterns

Solution architects face a multitude of concerns; they need to build systems that meet functional needs and also excel in non-functional dimensions, as follows:

- Modular design, interoperability, flexibility/adaptability, upkeep, easy to build, easy to deploy and maintain, monitoring, and visibility into the system.

- Performance, throughput, scalability, cost efficiency, user-friendliness, and accuracy.

- Security, resilience, reliability, fault-tolerance.

While numerous architecture patterns are available, we will focus on the top three most consequential and widely adopted patterns in the field and address the most critical challenges. These patterns represent a synthesis of various design principles, and combinations of these patterns are implemented for complex systems, as shown:

- **Comprehensive cloud-native services architecture**: This pattern encompasses modular services architecture (Microservices, domain-driven design, service-oriented architecture) and cloud-native architectural patterns (Serverless architecture, container orchestration like *Kubernetes*). This cloud-native design pattern follows separation of concern philosophy, and enhances agility, scalability, and operational efficiency. It is ideal for businesses seeking to capitalize on the cloud's potential for rapid deployment, scalability, and resilience.

- **Event-driven architecture (EDA)**: EDA helps systems respond quickly to real-time events by letting different parts of the system work independently instead of waiting for each other. Instead of one service calling another and waiting for a reply, EDA allows *asynchronous communication*, meaning events are sent and handled separately. These events go through tools like *Kafka, RabbitMQ, Azure Event Grid, or AWS SNS*, which pass them to whoever needs them. A key idea in EDA is *Event Sourcing*, where every change is stored as a log of events, so nothing is lost, and you can always go back and see what happened, just like a history book for data. Another common method is **Publish/Subscribe (Pub/Sub)**, where one system sends an event, and multiple others pick it up and act on it without knowing about each other. This is great for things like *live notifications, real-time analytics, fraud detection, and IoT data*. Since systems do not directly rely on each other, EDA makes applications faster, more reliable, and able to handle large amounts of data smoothly without slowing down or failing when demand spikes.

- **API-first architecture**: This pattern encompasses API Gateway, **backend for frontend (BFF)**, and Headless Architectures. This pattern supports easier integration between disparate systems. It promotes a modular and decoupled design approach, which is crucial for multi-platform support.

Roles and responsibilities of solution architects

Solution architects play a pivotal role in driving the success of projects and ensuring alignment between business needs and technical solutions. Here are a few core responsibilities of solution architects within an IT team:

- **Requirement analysis**: Collaborate with stakeholders to analyze business requirements, translating them into technical specifications and architectural designs. This involves understanding the business goals, user needs, and constraints and translating them into actionable plans for development.

- **Solution design**: Create comprehensive architectural designs that address both functional and non-functional requirements, ensuring scalability, performance, security, and maintainability. Solution architects must balance technical feasibility with business objectives to design solutions that meet the needs of the organization.

- **Technology evaluation**: Evaluate and recommend technology solutions, tools, and frameworks that best meet the needs of the project, considering factors such as cost, scalability, and vendor support. Solution architects must stay abreast of the latest technologies and trends to make informed decisions.

- **Implementation oversight**: Provide guidance and oversight to development teams during the implementation phase, ensuring that architectural designs are accurately implemented and aligned with best practices. This involves collaborating with developers, testers, and other stakeholders to ensure smooth execution of the solution.

- **Cross-domain collaboration**: A key role of the solution architect is to drive collaboration across various business domains and between the organization and external partners, including technology vendors, service providers, and industry consortiums. In the age of AI, where solutions often transcend traditional boundaries, solution architects need to establish and maintain an ecosystem of collaboration that encourages the sharing of insights, co-development of technologies, and collective problem-solving. They should also work on building frameworks and platforms that enable such collaborations, focusing on interoperability and integration.

- **Continuous improvement**: Stay informed about emerging technologies and industry trends, continuously evaluating and improving architectural practices. Solution architects must be proactive in identifying areas for improvement and implementing changes to enhance the effectiveness of the team.

Solution architects serve as the linchpin of IT teams, bridging the gap between business needs and technical solutions and enabling the business to stay ahead of the curve.

Conclusion

In this chapter, we covered the foundational concepts and principles of solution architecture. We explored various methodologies and frameworks that are crucial for designing scalable and resilient solutions. We gained insights into six pillars of architecture excellence, reliability, performance, security, cost, TechOps, and adaptability, and we understood how these pillars guide the architectural process to deliver robust and effective solutions. Additionally, we discussed the critical role of functional and **non-functional requirements** (**NFRs**) in shaping system design and ensuring operational efficiency. We also highlighted the importance of supporting processes such as governance, compliance, monitoring, and change management, which help sustain architectural integrity over time. We explored the key components of solution architecture through the domains of application architecture, analytics and BI architecture, and foundational elements of architecture that underpin the entire architectural fabric.

In the next chapter, we will learn about cloud migration essentials. We will explore strategies for successful cloud migration and modernization and learn about the nuances of infrastructure and data migration techniques.

Key terms

- **Solution architecture**: The practice of designing comprehensive and coherent technology solutions that address specific business challenges or opportunities, ensuring all components work together harmoniously to achieve organizational goals.

- **Frontend**: The user interface where users interact with the system, including web interfaces and mobile applications. It focuses on behavioral design, accessibility, and cross-platform compatibility.

- **Middleware**: Software that acts as an intermediary between the frontend and backend, handling communication, data processing, and service orchestration.

- **Backend**: The core of the application where business logic and data manipulation occur, often involving technologies like *.NET*, *Java*, *Node.js*, and *Python*.

- **Caching**: Strategies and products implemented to improve system scalability and performance by reducing load times and enhancing user experience.

- **Online transaction processing** (**OLTP**): Systems that manage real-time transaction processing, ensuring database type, ACID properties, and response time are optimized.

- **Business rules engine** (**BRE**): Software that encapsulates decision logic separate from application code, facilitating agility and maintainability in complex workflows.

- **AI/ML services**: Services and tools for integrating artificial intelligence and machine learning capabilities into the system, including text-to-speech, NLP processing, and custom ML model inferencing.

- **Analytics and visualization platforms**: Tools and platforms that transform raw data into actionable insights, supporting data analysis and visualization.

- **MLOps**: A discipline that integrates ML with DevOps principles to ensure sustainable and scalable AI solutions.

- **Extract, transform, load** (**ETL**): Tools and processes for extracting data from various sources, transforming it to meet business requirements, and loading it into a destination for analysis.

- **Data warehouse/Data lake/Data fabric**: Platforms for storing and managing large-scale analytics and historical data, enabling businesses to derive insights and support decision-making.

- **Infrastructure**: The underlying hardware and virtualized resources, including servers, storage, and container orchestration platforms, that support the system's operations.

- **Network**: Components that ensure connectivity and data flow across services and users, including virtual network subnets, load balancers, and software-defined networking.

- **Security**: Measures and practices to protect systems, data, and applications from unauthorized access and threats, often involving a Zero Trust model and various security tools.

- **Observability**: Tools and practices for logging, monitoring, and alerting to gain visibility into system health and performance.

- **Business continuity planning** (BCP): Planning and preparation to ensure critical business operations can continue without interruption during a disaster.

- **Disaster recovery planning** (DRP): Strategies and mechanisms for recovering swiftly from a disaster or system failure to maintain data integrity and availability.

- **Reliability excellence**: Designing systems to consistently perform as intended under various conditions, ensuring high uptime and rapid recovery capabilities.

- **Performance excellence**: Ensuring systems meet desired response times, throughput, and performance levels, efficiently managing load and resource utilization.

- **Security excellence**: Protecting systems from unauthorized access and threats, detecting and responding to security breaches and incidents.

- **Cost excellence**: Optimizing costs per transaction, resource allocation, and overall cost efficiency, ensuring visibility into TCO and ROI.

- **TechOps excellence**: Integrating DevOps and platform engineering practices to standardize workflows, promote team cohesion, and ensure smooth operations.

- **Adaptability excellence**: Designing systems to accommodate changes efficiently and integrate new technologies seamlessly, maintaining relevance and responsiveness in a rapidly evolving landscape.

CHAPTER 2
Cloud Migration Essentials

Introduction

In this chapter, we will cover the core foundation for understanding and executing cloud migration. We will start with the essentials of cloud migration, including key strategies for data center and application estate assessments. Readers will learn to develop comprehensive migration and modernization strategies and roadmaps tailored to their organizational needs. Topics like infrastructure migration, data migration, and the architecture of cloud landing zones will provide a holistic view of cloud adoption processes.

Structure

This chapter covers the following topics:

- Cloud migration essentials
- Data center and application estate assessment
- Migration and modernization strategies
- Infrastructure and data migration techniques
- Designing cloud and landing zone architectures

Objectives

By the end of this chapter, we will be equipped with the knowledge to navigate complex migration scenarios and apply best practices to ensure success. We will gain an understanding of how to assess your current data center and application estate, develop a strategic migration plan, and execute infrastructure and data migration techniques. This will include insights into designing robust cloud landing zone architectures and leveraging advanced tools for a seamless transition. By mastering these essentials, we will be able to optimize costs, improve performance, enhance security, and support our organization's strategic goals through effective cloud migration and modernization strategies.

Cloud migration essentials

There is no single cloud adoption path that works for every organization, but the main implementation stages of a secure methodology are similar for all organizations and industries, define your strategy, make a plan, ready your organization, adopt the cloud, and govern and manage your digital estate. Microsoft's **Cloud Adoption Framework** (**CAF**) is a comprehensive guide designed to help organizations with their cloud adoption journey.

The following essential cloud migration guidelines comply with CAF best practices:

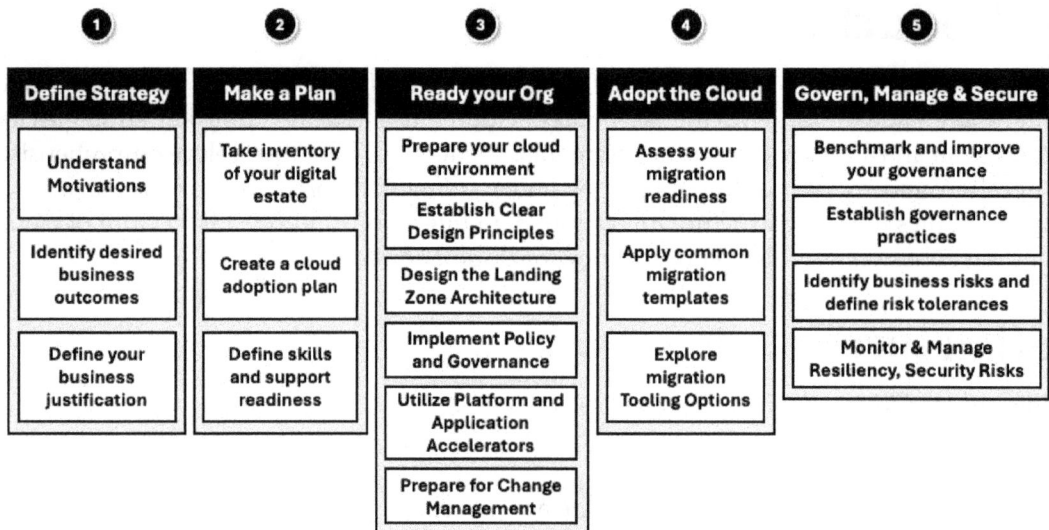

① Define Strategy	② Make a Plan	③ Ready your Org	④ Adopt the Cloud	⑤ Govern, Manage & Secure
Understand Motivations	Take inventory of your digital estate	Prepare your cloud environment	Assess your migration readiness	Benchmark and improve your governance
Identify desired business outcomes	Create a cloud adoption plan	Establish Clear Design Principles	Apply common migration templates	Establish governance practices
Define your business justification	Define skills and support readiness	Design the Landing Zone Architecture	Explore migration Tooling Options	Identify business risks and define risk tolerances
		Implement Policy and Governance		Monitor & Manage Resiliency, Security Risks
		Utilize Platform and Application Accelerators		
		Prepare for Change Management		

Figure 2.1: Phases of cloud adoption as per Microsoft CAF best practices

In the following sections, we will discuss the initial four phases (define your strategy, make a plan, ready your Organization, and adopt the cloud) in this chapter.

Define your strategy

- **Understand motivations:** Understand cloud economics and get the financial and technical tips to help develop your cloud strategy and build your business case. Discover technical and financial flexibility, efficiencies, and capabilities on the cloud that are not possible with On-premises IT infrastructure. Companies are moving to the cloud for several key reasons as follows:

  o **Scalability**: The cloud provides elastic scalability, allowing to adjust IT resources based on demand, enhancing performance and cost efficiency.

  o **Security and compliance**: Cloud providers offer robust security and compliance features, helping companies meet regulatory requirements and build resilience against cyber threats.

  o **Availability**: High availability ensures business continuity for mission-critical systems, maintaining service levels and operational stability.

  o **Reduced datacenter footprint**: Migrating to the cloud reduces the need for extensive On-premises infrastructure, cutting costs and allowing businesses to focus on core activities like application development.

  o **OPEX pricing models**: The cloud offers flexible, pay-per-use pricing, shifting costs from **capital expenditure (CAPEX)** to **operational expenditure (OPEX)**, providing financial flexibility and supporting growth.

  o **Staff productivity**: Cloud migration reduces error-prone maintenance tasks, increasing IT staff productivity, optimization and innovation

  o **Sustainability**: Using sustainable cloud technologies helps companies meet their sustainability goals and reduce their carbon footprint.

  o **Optimization**: The cloud enables workload and cost optimization through advanced management tools, cost-saving offers, and managed services, improving overall efficiency and performance.

- **Identify desired business outcomes**: Establish clear business outcomes that align with your motivations. Identify key stakeholders who will see the greatest value and support the transformation. Clearly define and measure expected changes in business performance, understanding the current challenges or opportunities the business faces. Establish **key performance indicators (KPIs)** to measure success and enable incremental changes. Define how technical capabilities will accelerate business outcomes, prioritize necessary applications, and determine if parts of the solution need rearchitecting or if timelines can be adjusted to prioritize high-impact outcomes.

- **Define your business justification**: Define your business case and create a financial model to project the business impact of your cloud adoption strategy. Creating a business case for cloud migration involves several key components, as follows:

○ Gathering baseline financial data helps understand current costs and forecast On-premises costs if migration does not occur. Your On-premises cost should include the server cost and cost for the building, power, and headcount.

○ The cloud migration scenario forecasts costs and benefits when migrating to the cloud, considering core benefits and optimization strategies like reserved instances and hybrid benefits.

○ A migration timeline and cost estimates guide the process, showing reduced On-premises spending over time.

○ Cloud savings can be achieved through well-architected design for cost excellence, flexible billing models, hybrid benefits, spot virtual machines, reservations, discounts and credits from the OEM, and additional savings plans.

○ Tools like **total cost of ownership (TCO)** calculators, pricing APIs, VM cost estimators, and pricing calculators assist in estimating costs and savings, as shown:

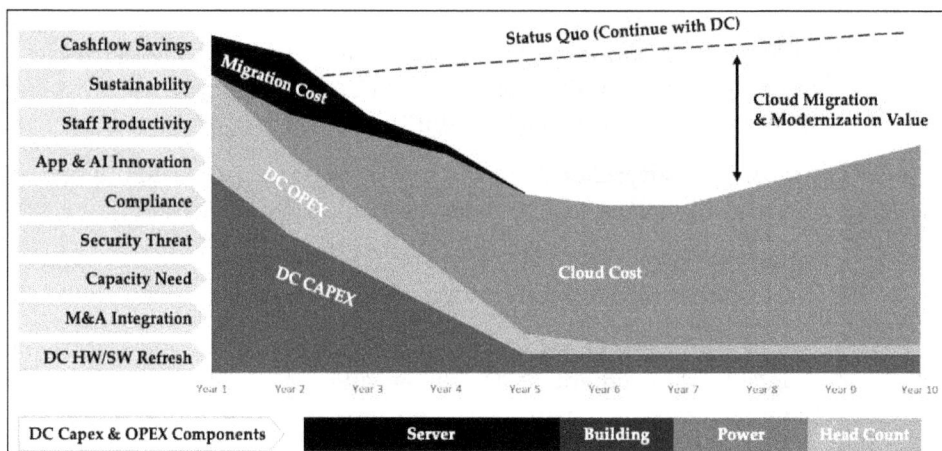

Figure 2.2: Typical business justification model for cloud migration and modernization

Make a plan

Moving to the cloud is not just a technical decision; it is a strategic shift that requires careful planning and alignment across the organization. The first step is to take a detailed inventory of your IT landscape and evaluate the best way to migrate each component. However, for most organizations, this is not as simple as following a checklist. With modern digital estates growing in complexity, traditional methods like decision trees often fall short. Adopting practical, flexible approaches, like workload-driven or incremental planning, can make all the difference.

This section outlines the steps to craft a clear, actionable migration plan. From prioritizing workloads and setting up governance processes to preparing your team for new skills and responsibilities, these strategies will help you tackle challenges head-on and create a roadmap that sets your organization up for long-term cloud success, as follows:

- **Take inventory of your digital estate**: Catalog your workloads, applications, data sources, virtual machines, and other IT assets and evaluate them to determine the best way to host them in the cloud. Cloud rationalization can follow different approaches like *Gartner's 5R strategy, Forrester's cloud migration strategy,* or various other *Cloud Adoption Frameworks.* The traditional rationalization method, using a decision tree for asset classification, is suitable for small estates but impractical for larger ones due to its complexity and time requirements. This process involves detailed inventories, quantitative questions, and qualitative decisions from business stakeholders, consuming significant time and effort. For large estates, rationalization might be highly complex, costly, and time-consuming with low ROI.

  The following table illustrates key discovery and analysis components that help organizations evaluate workloads, dependencies, and cost implications to drive an effective migration strategy:

Discover		Analyse
Servers	App Compositions	Usage & Capacity Planning
Databases	Migration Compatibility	Cost Simulation & Optimization
Applications	End of Support Considerations	Analyze Scenarios
Virtual Infra	Network Config	5R Planning
Dependencies	Security Requirements	Migration Planning

Figure 2.3: Digital estate discovery and cloud migration planning

To address these challenges, digital estate planning can be approached through workload-driven, asset-driven, and incremental approaches. The workload-driven approach assesses security, architectural complexity, operational requirements, financial benefits, and resiliency, requiring stakeholder interviews and anecdotal feedback. The asset-driven approach uses statistical usage data from CMDB or infrastructure assessment tools to evaluate attributes like memory, CPU, storage, and network configurations, assuming an IaaS deployment model.

An incremental rationalization approach reduces risks by staggering decisions, using agentless scanning for initial discovery, streamlining quantitative analysis, and simplifying qualitative decisions. Initial decisions are validated through further analysis, focusing on retiring unused assets for cost savings. This approach starts with an initial cost analysis using the asset-driven method, followed by migration planning with a workload-driven approach to build a lightweight assessment and collaboration. Release planning involves pruning and reprioritizing the migration backlog to focus on the most relevant business impact. Implementation analysis assesses each asset individually and collectively before migration.

Align your cloud strategy with parallel transformation efforts, identifying assets for rehosting, refactoring, revising, rebuilding, or replacing. Select initial workloads based on business and technical criteria to test and build a growth mindset. Prioritize the first 10 workloads for migration, iterating on the approach to refine qualitative analysis and build a migration backlog. This incremental execution speeds up assessment and architecture, enabling faster rationalization and yielding business results sooner.

- **Create a cloud adoption plan**: Create your cloud adoption plan by prioritizing your workloads based on their business impact and technical complexity.

  o **Prioritize workloads**: Evaluate your workloads based on their business impact and technical complexity. Focus on high-impact, low-complexity workloads first to achieve quick wins. Use this prioritization to guide your overall cloud adoption strategy.

  o **Evaluate and document your strategy**: Assess your current cloud strategy to identify strengths and areas for improvement. Document key decisions and plans to ensure all stakeholders are aligned. This will help create a clear roadmap for your cloud adoption journey.

  o **Standardize processes**: Standardize your cloud adoption processes using templates and best practices. This helps streamline migration and deployment activities, reducing the risk of errors and improving efficiency. Consistency in processes also aids in scaling your cloud adoption efforts smoothly.

  o **Develop naming and tagging conventions**: Create a comprehensive naming and tagging convention for all cloud resources. This ensures consistency and makes it easier to manage and locate resources. Clear conventions also help in automating resource management and tracking usage.

  o **Implement governance processes**: Establish governance processes to manage costs, enhance security, and ensure compliance with regulations. Define clear policies for resource usage, access control, and data protection. Regularly review and update these processes to adapt to changing business needs and security threats.

  o **Assess and improve readiness**: Use assessment tools to gauge your readiness for cloud migration. Identify gaps in skills, infrastructure, and processes that need to be addressed before moving to the cloud. Prepare a detailed readiness plan to ensure a smooth transition.

- o **Establish regular well-architected framework review process**: Implement a well-architected framework to guide your cloud operations. Focus on key areas like operational excellence, security, reliability, performance efficiency, and cost optimization. This framework will help maintain high standards and best practices in your cloud environment.

- o **Deploy scalable solutions**: Deploy solutions that can scale with your business needs. This includes robust data management practices and innovative technologies to support growth. Scalable solutions ensure that your cloud environment can handle increased workloads and new business opportunities.

- o **Track organizational roles and responsibilities**: Clearly define and document roles and responsibilities within your organization. Use tools like RACI diagrams to track who is responsible, accountable, consulted, and informed for each task. This promotes effective collaboration and communication across teams.

- **Define skills and support readiness**: Create and implement a skills readiness plan to define support needs, address current gaps, and ensure that your business and IT employees are prepared for the changes and new technologies. As organizations shift to cloud computing, staff roles will evolve, much like previous transitions in IT history. Roles such as datacenter specialists may become cloud administrators or architects. IT staff might feel anxious about needing new skills, but those who adapt and learn cloud technologies can lead this transition. To support this shift, document staff concerns, identify skill gaps, and ensure necessary training. Collaborate across teams to address dependencies and establish new processes. Effective support for these evolving roles requires a team effort and thorough preparation for organizational readiness.

Ready your organization

This section outlines the foundational steps needed to build a strong cloud-ready organization, from establishing design principles to leveraging accelerators and fostering a culture of adaptability and continuous learning.

To ensure a successful migration, organizations must prepare their cloud environment with a clear focus on governance, architecture, and change management. This involves establishing a robust framework that encompasses architectural design, governance, policy implementation, and change management.

The following are the five essential points to guide your organization in designing an effective cloud landing zone:

- **Establish clear design principles**: Establishing clear design principles is crucial for the successful implementation of a cloud landing zone. These principles help guide architectural decisions, ensuring that deviations are well understood and managed. This includes democratizing subscriptions by aligning them with business needs and setting up a suitable management hierarchy. Implementing policy-driven governance helps automate compliance, reduce operational overhead, and provide a secure path for cloud adoption. Maintaining a single control and management plane ensures consistent operations and avoids the complexity of multiple abstraction layers. Focusing on an application-centric service model simplifies governance and operational overhead while aligning with native platform services reduces integration complexity and maintains feature support.

- **Design the landing zone architecture**: The landing zone architecture must be scalable and modular to meet diverse deployment needs. A repeatable infrastructure allows for consistent application of configurations and controls across all resources. Effective resource organization involves creating appropriate management hierarchies and segregating platform services from application services for better operational efficiency. The choice of management approach, whether central, application team, or shared—should be based on the organization's needs and resource structures, ensuring that the architecture remains flexible and adaptable as requirements evolve.

- **Implement policy and governance**: Implementing policy and governance effectively automates compliance and reduces the need for manual oversight, ensuring security and efficiency. By using policy-driven governance, organizations can standardize controls and apply them consistently across the enterprise, maintaining governance and operational integrity. This approach helps streamline the management of resources, reduces the complexity of maintaining compliance, and supports the organization's overall cloud strategy by providing a clear framework for operations and security.

- **Utilize platform and application accelerators**: Utilizing platform and application accelerators can significantly streamline the deployment and management of cloud resources. Platform landing zone accelerators provide a ready-made deployment experience with predetermined configurations that align with the organization's operating model. Application landing zone accelerators help deploy specific scenarios efficiently, ensuring that the application management and governance processes are aligned with best practices. These accelerators enable organizations to leverage infrastructure-as-code implementations, simplifying the deployment process and ensuring consistency across the cloud environment.

- **Prepare for change management**: Preparing for change management involves adapting roles and skills to support the transition to cloud environments. It is essential to address IT staff concerns and identify any gaps in skills or processes. By capturing these concerns and providing the necessary training, organizations can ensure that their staff are well-equipped to manage cloud operations. Documenting and addressing these gaps help facilitate a smooth transition, empowering employees to embrace new technologies and lead the adoption of cloud services within the organization. This proactive approach to change management is critical for maintaining productivity and achieving a successful cloud transformation.

Adopt the cloud

Adopting the cloud is a critical phase in the migration journey, involving the actual transition of workloads to the cloud environment. This phase requires thorough planning, assessment, and execution to ensure a smooth and successful migration.

The following sub-sections outline the essential steps and considerations for adopting the cloud:

Assess your migration readiness

To migrate to the cloud, it is important to take a step back and see where you stand today. This means understanding what your current IT setup looks like, which apps are ready for the move, and what skills your team might need to learn. It is also a good time to think about any risks, like downtime or security issues, and get everyone on the same page, whether it is your IT team, business leaders, or end users.

Using tools like *Azure Migrate* can make this whole process easier and give you a clear picture of how to get started as follows:

Assessment step	Description
Infrastructure assessment	Conduct a detailed assessment of your existing IT infrastructure, including hardware, software, networks, and security protocols. Identify components that are compatible with the cloud and those that may require modifications or replacements.
Application inventory	Create a comprehensive inventory of all applications, categorizing them based on their readiness for cloud migration. Determine the criticality and dependencies of each application to prioritize migration efforts.
Skill gap analysis	Evaluate the skills and expertise of your IT team to identify any gaps that may impact the migration. Provide necessary training and resources to ensure your team is equipped to handle cloud technologies and processes.
Risk management	Identify potential risks associated with the migration, such as data loss, downtime, or security vulnerabilities. Develop a risk mitigation plan to address these challenges proactively.

Assessment step	Description
Stakeholder engagement	Engage key stakeholders, including business leaders, IT staff, and end-users, to gather input and ensure alignment with organizational goals. Communicate the benefits and impacts of the migration to secure buy-in and support.
Readiness tools	Utilize readiness assessment tools to automate and streamline the evaluation process. Tools like *Azure Migrate* provide detailed insights into your infrastructure and applications, helping you plan the migration effectively.

Table 2.1: Assess your migration readiness

Common migration projects

Cloud migration is not a one-size-fits-all journey; it is about aligning your goals with the type of workload you want to move. Whether it is consolidating data centers, modernizing old applications, or setting up disaster recovery solutions, each project type has its unique benefits and challenges.

This section breaks down the most common migration projects, helping you understand their objectives, key advantages, and what to watch out for to ensure a smooth transition as follows:

Project type	Objective	Benefits	Key considerations
Data center consolidation	Reduce the number of physical data centers by migrating workloads to the cloud.	Lower operational costs, improved scalability, and enhanced disaster recovery capabilities.	Network connectivity, data transfer methods, and application compatibility.
Application modernization	Update legacy applications to leverage cloud-native features and improve performance.	Increased agility, better scalability, and reduced technical debt.	Refactoring or rearchitecting applications, integrating with cloud services, and ensuring data consistency.
Disaster recovery and backup	Implement cloud-based disaster recovery and backup solutions to enhance data protection.	Improved data resilience, reduced downtime, and cost-effective storage solutions.	**Recovery time objectives (RTO), recovery point objectives (RPO)**, and data replication methods.

Project type	Objective	Benefits	Key considerations
Dev/Test environments	Migrate development and testing environments to the cloud for increased flexibility and scalability.	Faster provisioning, cost savings, and access to advanced tools and services.	Ensuring environment consistency, managing costs, and integrating with CI/CD pipelines.
Business continuity	Ensure uninterrupted business operations by leveraging cloud infrastructure for critical workloads.	High availability, automated failover, and global reach.	Identifying critical workloads, setting up redundancy, and configuring failover mechanisms.
Specialized workloads	• Transitioning SAP applications to the cloud to enhance performance, scalability, and manageability. • Migrating specialized workloads such as *VMware, NetApp, Oracle,* and *Cray* to the cloud for optimized operations. • Moving **virtual desktop infrastructure** (**VDI**) workloads to the cloud to enhance accessibility and reduce management overhead.		

Table 2.2: Common migration projects

Migration tooling options

A variety of tooling options are available to facilitate the migration process. These tools help in assessing, planning, and executing cloud migrations with minimal disruption and maximum efficiency. Categories of tools include assessment tools like *Azure Migrate*, which provides detailed insights into your existing infrastructure and applications; migration tools that automate the transfer of workloads to the cloud; and optimization tools that help in cost management and performance enhancement. By leveraging these tools, organizations can streamline their migration processes, ensure data integrity, and achieve a seamless transition to the cloud.

Data center and application estate assessment

Modernizing an application estate and transitioning to the cloud is a complex yet critical process for organizations aiming to achieve scalability, agility, and cost efficiency. A successful migration requires a systematic assessment and strategic planning approach to minimize risks and maximize business value. This section outlines the essential building blocks for assessing the data center and application estate, providing IT teams with a clear roadmap to navigate this transformation.

The foundation, comprehensive assessment

The modernization journey begins with compiling a *comprehensive inventory* of all applications, databases, and infrastructure components. This involves cataloging hardware, software, and the dependencies between them to establish a clear picture of the current environment. By understanding how components interact and identifying their utilization metrics, IT teams can ensure no critical details are overlooked.

Categorizing applications based on their suitability for various migration strategies, often referred to as the 6Rs (Rehost, Refactor, Rearchitect, Rebuild, Replace, Retire), is a crucial next step. For priority applications, a deeper analysis is required: source code reviews, mapping interdependencies, and establishing performance baselines. This lays the groundwork for developing detailed migration scenarios with cost and time estimates while also addressing compliance and security requirements. Potential risks, such as downtime, data transfer challenges, and regulatory compliance issues, must be identified and mitigated throughout this phase.

The assessment phase concludes with the development of a *strategic migration plan,* which serves as a roadmap for execution. This plan includes an executive summary, business objectives, data-driven insights, and a gap analysis. A robust business case, incorporating **total cost of ownership** (**TCO**) and cost-benefit comparisons, ensures alignment between technical goals and organizational priorities. Leveraging advanced tools for infrastructure scanning and dependency mapping enhances accuracy and accelerates the process. Engaging stakeholders to validate findings and finalize the strategy ensures readiness and alignment across all levels of the organization.

Building blocks for strategic IT migration planning

With the foundational assessment complete, IT teams can dive deeper into the building blocks that underpin a successful migration strategy.

The following elements provide a structured approach to ensure a seamless and efficient transition:

- **Inventory of assets**: The first building block is a thorough inventory of all assets. This includes both *hardware,* such as servers, storage systems, and networking equipment, and *software,* covering applications, databases, middleware, and operating systems. Each item should be documented with details like make, model, capacity, versions, licenses, and support agreements. Mapping *dependencies* between these components is critical to understanding how data flows, applications communicate, and systems integrate, preventing disruptions during migration.

- **Utilization metrics**: Accurate metrics on resource usage are essential to design a scalable and efficient target environment. IT teams must gather data on CPU, memory, storage, and network utilization, capturing both average and peak usage patterns. Identifying *peak load times* helps ensure that the new environment can handle the highest levels of demand without performance degradation.

- **Application categorization**: The **categorization of applications** is a cornerstone of migration planning. Each application is assessed for cloud readiness and classified into one of the 6Rs:

    o **Rehost (Lift and shift)**: Minimal changes required for migration.

    o **Refactor (Re-platform)**: Minor modifications to enhance cloud benefits.

    o **Rearchitect**: Significant redesign to leverage cloud-native capabilities.

    o **Rebuild**: Full redevelopment using modern, cloud-native technologies.

    o **Replace**: Substituting legacy systems with SaaS solutions.

    o **Retire**: Decommissioning obsolete or redundant applications.

This categorization enables IT teams to prioritize migration efforts effectively while addressing *compliance and security needs* for applications handling sensitive data.

- **Performance and scalability analysis**: Establishing a *performance baseline* is essential to measure the success of the migration. Key metrics include transaction throughput, response times, and latency. *Load testing* validates system performance under various conditions, ensuring the architecture is resilient. Scalability requirements are also defined at this stage, determining whether applications need horizontal scaling (adding more instances) or vertical scaling (increasing resource capacity). Plans for *automatic scaling* ensure that applications adapt seamlessly to fluctuations in demand.

- **Financial considerations**: Financial analysis plays a pivotal role in justifying and planning the migration. IT teams must calculate the TCO for current systems, including hardware, software licenses, maintenance, and energy costs. Projected *cloud costs*, covering computing, storage, data transfer, and management, must also be estimated. Cost optimization strategies, such as right-sizing resources and balancing reserved instances with on-demand resources, help minimize expenses while ensuring the new environment is cost-efficient.

- **Risk and compliance**: Migration involves inherent risks, such as downtime, data loss, and security breaches. *Risk assessment* and mitigation strategies must be documented in advance to address these challenges. Additionally, ensuring adherence to *compliance requirements* is non-negotiable. Implementing measures like encryption, identity management, and access controls safeguards sensitive data and ensures regulatory compliance.

- **Tools and methodologies**: Leveraging advanced tools like *Azure Migrate* and third-party solutions simplifies the migration process. These tools offer features such as automated discovery, dependency mapping, and cost analysis, enabling IT teams to make data-driven decisions. By integrating these methodologies, organizations can streamline assessments, reduce manual effort, and accelerate the migration timeline.

The following is an example of how the final app assessment and migration approach note might look like for a full-service retail bank after following the aforementioned detailed assessment:

Application name	Application treatment	Target service model	Target cloud service	Database treatment	Database (Long term)	Target service model	Target cloud service
Core banking	Rehost	IaaS	VM	Rehost	Replatform	IaaS/PaaS	Cloud DB
Retail mobile banking	Refactor	PaaS	Kubernetes Service	Rehost	Replatform	IaaS	Cloud DB
Trade finance	Rearchitect	PaaS	App Service	Rehost	Replatform	IaaS/PaaS	Cloud DB
Treasury	Rehost	IaaS	VM	Rehost	Replatform	IaaS/PaaS	Cloud DB
Market risk	Retain	On-premises	On-premises	Retain	Retain	On-premises	On-premises
Credit risk	Retain	On-premises	On-premises	Retain	Retain	On-premises	On-premises
Operational risk	Retain	On-premises	On-premises	Retain	Retain	On-premises	On-premises
Financial reporting	Retain	On-premises	On-premises	Retain	Retain	On-premises	On-premises
Supply chain financing	Refactor	PaaS	Kubernetes Service	Rehost	Replatform	IaaS/PaaS	Cloud DB
Loan origination system (Retail)	Refactor	PaaS	Kubernetes Service	Rehost	Replatform	IaaS/PaaS	Cloud DB
Loan management	Rehost	IaaS	VM	Rehost	Replatform	IaaS/PaaS	Cloud DB
Document management	Rehost	IaaS/PaaS	VM/Kubernetes	Rehost	Replatform	IaaS/PaaS	Cloud DB
UPI solution	Rehost	IaaS	VM	Rehost	Replatform	IaaS	Cloud DB

Application name	Application treatment	Target service model	Target cloud service	Database treatment	Database (Long term)	Target service model	Target cloud service
Payment gateway	Rehost	IaaS	VM	Rehost	Replatform	IaaS	Cloud DB
SMS gateway	Replace	SaaS	SaaS	N/A	N/A	SaaS	SaaS
Workflow apps	Rebuild	PaaS	App service	Rehost	Replatform	IaaS/PaaS	Cloud DB
ESB	Rehost	IaaS	VM	Rehost	Replatform	IaaS	Cloud DB
Content management system	Rehost	IaaS/PaaS	SaaS	Rehost	Replatform	IaaS/PaaS	Cloud DB
NEFT/RTGS	Rearchitect	PaaS	App service	Rehost	Replatform	IaaS/PaaS	Cloud DB
Signature verification	Replace	SaaS	SaaS	N/A	N/A	SaaS	SaaS
Debit card management	Rehost	IaaS	VM	Rehost	Replatform	IaaS	Cloud DB
Core banking API	Retain	On-premises	On-premises	Retain	Retain	On-premises	On-premises
Corporate mobile banking	Refactor	PaaS	Kubernetes Service	Rehost	Replatform	IaaS/PaaS	Cloud DB
DevOps tools	Replace	SaaS	Self-hosted	N/A	N/A	SaaS	SaaS

Table 2.4: Sample App Assessment and Migration Approach Note

Migration and modernization strategies

The migration and modernization strategies are based on identifying the best-fit path for each application, considering factors like business impact, technical complexity, and cost.

The following are the key migration paths:

- **Retire and right-size**: Eliminate outdated or redundant applications to free up resources.

- **Low-code/SaaS conversion**: Convert to low-code solutions or SaaS for improved productivity.

- **Containerization and serverless extension**: Optimize and move applications to containers for better agility and resource utilization and use serverless technologies.

- **Lift and shift**: Minimal changes, rehost applications to IaaS.

The following is the app estate transformation approach:

- **Migrate**: Reduce CAPEX and free up data center space quickly by rehosting or replacing with SaaS.

- **Modernize**: Achieve greater cloud efficiency through re-platforming, rearchitecting, or rebuilding applications.

- **Innovate**: Accelerate innovation with cloud-native development, leveraging serverless, microservices, and advanced data capabilities.

Migration strategy decision matrix

This section provides a clear decision matrix to match your objectives with strategies like rehosting, refactoring, or rebuilding, along with the tools and platforms best suited for each approach.

Choosing the right migration strategy depends on your organization's goals, whether it is speeding up innovation, enhancing scalability, or reducing costs, as shown in the following table:

Objective	Rehost	Refactor	Rearchitect	Rebuild	Replace	Options to consider
Deliver new capabilities faster		✓		✓		PaaS, serverless
Provide multichannel access, including mobile		✓			✓	PaaS, serverless
Enable business agility with continuous innovation			✓			PaaS, containers
More easily integrate with other web and cloud apps		✓			✓	PaaS, serverless
Infuse intelligence into processes leveraging investments		✓				PaaS, serverless
Increase agility & support scalability		✓	✓			PaaS, containers

Objective	Rehost	Refactor	Rearchitect	Rebuild	Replace	Options to consider
Free up data center space quickly	✓				✓	VMs, SaaS
Reduce capital expenditure of existing applications	✓				✓	VMs, SaaS
Achieve rapid time to cloud with better service	✓					VMs

Table 2.5: Mapping objectives to cloud migration strategies

This structured approach and template tables provide a comprehensive framework for making informed decisions on application migration and modernization.

Infrastructure and data migration techniques

Migrating infrastructure and data to the cloud is a crucial phase in the cloud migration journey. This section provides a structured approach for evaluating and planning an organization's infrastructure and data migration, ensuring minimal disruption and maximum efficiency.

The following tables outline the key techniques and considerations for both infrastructure or applications and data migration.

Infrastructure and application migration techniques are as follows:

Technique	Description	Use cases	Advantages	Disadvantaages
Rehost	Moving applications from on-premises to the cloud with minimal changes.	Legacy systems needing quick cloud transition.	Quick migration, lower upfront costs, minimal changes.	May not leverage full cloud benefits.
Replatform	Making a few cloud optimizations without changing the core architecture.	Applications needing cloud capabilities.	Improved performance and scalability, moderate effort.	More effort than rehosting, some limitations.
Rearchitect	Modifying the application's architecture to leverage cloud-native features.	Applications needing significant improvements.	Maximum cloud benefits, improved agility, scalability.	High complexity and cost, longer timelines.

Technique	Description	Use cases	Advantages	Disadvantaages
Rebuild	Rebuilding the application from scratch using cloud-native technologies.	Outdated or highly complex applications.	Fully optimized for cloud, future-proofed, highly scalable.	Highest cost and effort, significant time needed.
Replace	Replacing the existing application with a third-party cloud solution, often SaaS.	Non-differentiating applications.	Rapid deployment, lower maintenance costs.	Potential loss of customization, vendor dependency.

Table 2.6: Infrastructure and application migration techniques

The data migration techniques are as follows:

Technique	Description	Use cases	Advantages	Disadvantages
Offline migration	Data transferred physically to the cloud using storage devices.	Large datasets unsuitable for online transfer.	Handles large volumes, reduces transfer time.	Data loss risk during shipping, security.
Online migration	Data transferred to the cloud over the internet or dedicated network connections.	Smaller datasets or continuous synchronization.	No physical shipping, can be automated.	Limited by network bandwidth, higher times.
Hybrid migration	Combines offline bulk data transfer with online incremental updates.	Large datasets needing ongoing updates.	Balances speed and security, minimizes downtime.	Coordination needed between methods.
Data synchronization	Continuous synchronization of data between on-premises and cloud environments.	Real-time data availability needs.	Ensures data consistency, supports active-active.	Requires robust network, complex to manage.
Extract, transform, load	Data extracted, transformed into a suitable format, and loaded into the cloud.	Structured data migration for analytics/warehousing.	Allows transformation and cleaning, supports complex structures.	Resource-intensive, needs ETL expertise.

Table 2.7: Data migration techniques

Infrastructure and data migration is a pivotal step towards leveraging the full potential of the cloud. The right migration techniques can ensure a seamless transition, minimize downtime, and enhance the scalability, performance, and security of applications and data.

This structured approach helps in addressing specific needs, ensuring a smooth migration journey, and setting a solid foundation for future growth and technological advancements.

Designing cloud and landing zone architectures

Cloud and landing zone architectures are foundational for ensuring scalable, secure, and well-managed cloud environments. This section outlines the key components and best practices for designing effective cloud and landing zone architectures, leveraging the Azure Cloud Adoption Framework as a reference model.

A landing zone is a pre-configured, secure, and scalable environment in the cloud that accommodates the deployment and operation of workloads. It incorporates best practices for identity and access management, network topology, resource organization, security, governance, and operational management. The primary goal of a landing zone is to establish a robust foundation that supports cloud adoption and enhances the efficiency and security of cloud operations.

The following table outlines the eight key design areas to ensure a comprehensive and structured approach to designing cloud landing zones. Each area is essential for establishing a secure, scalable, and well-managed cloud environment.

Design area	Description
Enterprise enrollment	Processes and policies for enrolling and managing enterprises within the cloud environment, including subscription and account management.
Identity	Systems and protocols for managing user identities, authentication, and access control, ensuring secure access to cloud resources.
Resource organization	Frameworks for organizing and managing cloud resources effectively, including resource groups, tags, and management hierarchies.
Network topology and connectivity	Design and implementation of network structures, including virtual networks, subnets, and connectivity solutions such as VPNs and ExpressRoute.
Governance disciplines	Policies and practices for maintaining control over cloud resources, including cost management, compliance, and security policies.
Deployment options	Strategies for deploying cloud resources, including automated deployment pipelines, IaC, and manual deployment processes.
Operations baseline	Baseline configurations and best practices for cloud operations, including monitoring, logging, and performance management.
Business continuity and disaster recovery	Plans and solutions to ensure business continuity and disaster recovery, including backup strategies and failover mechanisms.
Design area	Description.

Table 2.8: Cloud landing zone design elements

The following is a detailed explanation of each design area:

- **Enterprise enrollment components**: This section outlines the key components of enterprise enrollment, providing a framework to manage subscriptions, costs, access, and compliance effectively in a cloud environment.

  The following is a tabular explanation:

Component	Description
Subscription management	Processes for creating, managing, and deactivating cloud subscriptions for the enterprise.
Account policies	Policies governing the use of cloud accounts, including security and compliance requirements.
Billing and cost management	Tools and processes for tracking, analyzing, and optimizing cloud spending.
Access controls	Mechanisms for managing user access to cloud resources, ensuring only authorized users can manage subscriptions.
Compliance reporting	Automated tools for generating reports to ensure adherence to regulatory and internal compliance standards.

Table 2.9: Enterprise enrollment components

- **Identity and access management components**: This section highlights the essential components of identity and access management, ensuring secure and streamlined access to cloud resources through robust authentication, authorization, and governance practices.

  The following is a tabular explanation:

Component	Description
Identity provider integration	Integration with identity providers (e.g., Azure AD, Okta) for user authentication and management.
Multi-factor authentication (MFA)	Implementation of MFA to enhance security by requiring additional verification methods.
Role-based access control (RBAC)	Configuring roles and permissions to control access to cloud resources.
Single sign-on (SSO)	Enabling SSO for seamless and secure access to multiple applications and services.
Identity governance	Policies and procedures for managing identities, including lifecycle management and audit trails.

Table 2.10: Identity and access management components

- **Resource organization components**: This section covers the key components for organizing cloud resources effectively, focusing on grouping, tagging, and structuring resources to streamline management, ensure clarity, and optimize cost tracking.

The following is a tabular explanation:

Component	Description
Resource groups	Logical groupings of related cloud resources for easier management and organization.
Tagging strategy	Implementing tags to categorize and manage resources based on various criteria such as department, environment, etc.
Management hierarchies	Creating hierarchical structures to reflect the organization's management and operational structures.
Resource naming conventions	Establishing standardized naming conventions for resources to ensure consistency and clarity.
Cost centers	Defining cost centers to allocate and track cloud spending accurately across different departments or projects.

Table 2.11: Resource organization components

- **Network topology and connectivity components**: This section outlines the building blocks of cloud networking, focusing on virtual networks, secure connectivity, and traffic management to ensure robust and scalable network infrastructure.

The following is a tabular explanation:

Component	Description
Virtual networks (VNets)	Creating secure and isolated network segments in the cloud.
Subnets	Defining subnets within VNets to segment and organize network traffic.
Network security groups (NSGs)	Configuring NSGs to control inbound and outbound traffic to network interfaces or subnets.
VPN gateways	Setting up VPN gateways for secure connectivity between on-premises data centers and the cloud.
ExpressRoute	Establishing dedicated private connections to the cloud for enhanced performance and security.

Table 2.12: Network topology and connectivity components

- **Governance components**: This section focuses on the key governance elements needed to manage cloud resources effectively, ensuring compliance, cost control, security, and adherence to organizational standards.

The following is a tabular explanation:

Component	Description
Policy management	Using policy tools (e.g., Azure Policy) to enforce organizational standards and compliance.
Cost management	Implementing cost management practices to track, analyze, and optimize cloud expenditures.
Security controls	Establishing security policies to protect cloud resources and data.
Compliance audits	Regularly conducting audits to ensure compliance with industry standards and regulations.
Governance framework	Defining a governance framework to guide the use and management of cloud resources.

Table 2.13: Governance components

- **Deployments components**: This section explores the essential tools and practices for deploying cloud resources, highlighting automation, scripting, and validation to ensure efficient and reliable deployments.

The following is a tabular explanation:

Component	Description
IaC	Using IaC tools (e.g., Terraform, ARM templates) to automate the deployment of cloud infrastructure.
CI/CD	Setting up CI/CD pipelines to automate the build, test, and deployment processes.
Deployment scripts	Creating and using scripts for deploying cloud resources and applications.
Manual deployment	Processes for manual deployment of resources when automation is not feasible.
Deployment validation	Implementing checks and validations to ensure deployments meet predefined criteria and standards.

Table 2.14: Deployment components

- **Operations components**: This section highlights the critical components for managing cloud operations, focusing on monitoring, automation, and incident management to ensure the reliability and performance of cloud services.

The following is a tabular explanation:

Component	Description
Monitoring tools	Implementing monitoring tools (e.g., Azure Monitor) to track the performance and health of cloud resources.
Log analytics	Collecting and analyzing logs from various sources for troubleshooting and performance management.
Automated management	Using automation tools to streamline operational tasks and improve reliability.
Performance metrics	Defining and tracking key performance metrics to ensure optimal operation of cloud services.
Incident management	Establishing processes for managing and resolving incidents in the cloud environment.

Table 2.15: Operations component

- **Business continuity and disaster recovery components**: This section outlines the essential components for ensuring resilience and continuity in cloud operations, focusing on backups, disaster recovery planning, failover mechanisms, and defining acceptable recovery objectives.

The following is a tabular explanation:

Component	Description
Backup solutions	Implementing backup solutions to ensure data is regularly backed up and can be restored when needed.
Disaster recovery plans	Creating and maintaining disaster recovery plans to ensure business continuity during unexpected events.
Failover mechanisms	Setting up failover mechanisms to automatically switch to backup systems in case of failures.
RTO	Defining RTOs to determine acceptable downtime durations for different systems.
RPO	Defining RPOs to determine acceptable data loss in terms of time for different systems.

Table 2.16: BC and DR components

Landing zone customer journey

The landing zone journey is a continuous process that prepares your cloud environment for deploying and managing workloads.

It consists of the following four major phases:

- **Bootstrap your environment**: Begin by creating subscriptions, either manually or programmatically, using subscription vending modules.

- **Deploy platform landing zone components**: Utilize accelerator portals, Bicep modules, or Terraform modules to set up the foundational services needed for your workloads.

- **Subscription landing zone vending process**: Implement vending modules to efficiently manage and provision subscriptions.

- **Deploy workload landing zone components**: Use cloud adoption scenarios and accelerators to deploy and integrate application-specific services into the landing zone.

Designing effective cloud and landing zone architectures is essential for successful cloud adoption and operational excellence. By following best practices and leveraging tools and frameworks like the *Azure Cloud Adoption Framework*, organizations can build scalable, secure, and well-governed cloud environments that support their business objectives and innovation goals. This structured approach ensures that cloud resources are managed efficiently, risks are mitigated, and compliance requirements are consistently met.

Conclusion

By the end of this chapter, we covered the foundational concepts and practical strategies essential for successful cloud migration and modernization. We began by understanding the key motivations driving organizations toward the cloud, such as scalability, security, cost optimization, and innovation. We then discussed comprehensive methods to assess data center and application estates, highlighting the importance of strategic planning and careful categorization of workloads. Additionally, we explored various infrastructure and data migration techniques, outlining their use cases, advantages, and considerations. Finally, we examined the critical elements of designing robust cloud landing zones, emphasizing governance, architecture, and change management best practices. Equipped with these insights, you are now prepared to effectively plan, execute, and manage a successful cloud migration aligned with your organizational goals.

In the next chapter, we will explore essential strategies for cloud operations, including cost optimization, robust governance models, and effective business continuity and disaster recovery planning.

Key terms

- **Cloud migration**: The process of moving data, applications, and other business elements from an organization's on-premises infrastructure to a cloud computing environment. This includes the planning, execution, and post-migration management phases.

- **Landing zone**: A pre-configured, secure, and scalable environment in the cloud that provides the foundation for hosting and managing cloud workloads. It includes identity and access management, network topology, resource organization, security, governance, and operational management.

- **Rehost (Lift and shift)**: A cloud migration strategy that involves moving applications from on-premises to the cloud with minimal changes. This approach is quick and cost-effective but may not leverage all cloud benefits.

- **Refactor**: A migration strategy that involves making minor adjustments to an application's code to better suit the cloud environment. This may include optimizing for performance, scalability, and cost efficiency.

- **Rearchitect:** A strategy that involves significantly changing an application's architecture to leverage cloud-native features, such as microservices and serverless computing, to enhance scalability, agility, and performance.

- **Rebuild:** A cloud migration strategy that entails completely rebuilding an application from scratch using cloud-native technologies. This approach maximizes cloud benefits but requires the most time and resources.

- **Replace:** The process of replacing an existing application with a third-party cloud solution, often **software as a service** (**SaaS**). This can rapidly provide new capabilities but may involve trade-offs in customization and control.

- **Hybrid connectivity solutions:** Technologies and methods used to establish secure, reliable connections between on-premises infrastructure and cloud environments. Examples include VPN gateways and ExpressRoute.

- **Total cost of ownership (TCO):** A financial estimate that includes all direct and indirect costs associated with owning and operating an asset over its lifecycle. In cloud migration, TCO calculations help compare on-premises costs with cloud-based alternatives.

- **Infrastructure as code (IaC):** The practice of managing and provisioning computing infrastructure through machine-readable definition files, rather than physical hardware configuration or interactive configuration tools. This approach enables automated and consistent deployments.

- **DevOps:** A set of practices that combine software **development (Dev)** and IT **operations (Ops)** aimed at shortening the systems development lifecycle and providing continuous delivery with high software quality.

- **Compliance automation:** The use of automated tools and processes to ensure that cloud environments adhere to industry standards, regulatory requirements, and internal policies. This helps maintain security and operational integrity.

- **Operational excellence:** A pillar of cloud architecture that focuses on running and monitoring systems to deliver business value and continually improving supporting processes and procedures.

- **Governance:** The framework of policies, processes, and controls that guide and manage the use of IT resources in an organization. Effective governance ensures that cloud resources are used efficiently, securely, and in compliance with regulations.

- **Cost management:** The practice of monitoring, controlling, and optimizing cloud spending to ensure cost-effective use of cloud services. This includes budgeting, forecasting, and implementing cost-saving measures.

Join our book's Discord space

Join the book's Discord Workspace for Latest updates, Offers, Tech happenings around the world, New Release and Sessions with the Authors:

https://discord.bpbonline.com

CHAPTER 3

Operational Excellence in Cloud

Introduction

In this chapter, we will cover essential components necessary for achieving and maintaining high operational standards in cloud environments. We will discuss cost optimization strategies to help readers understand how to maximize efficiency while minimizing expenses. We will also cover the development of robust cloud operating and governance models that ensure compliance and operational control. Furthermore, the chapter addresses critical planning for **business continuity planning (BCP)** and **disaster recovery planning (DRP)**, which is essential for maintaining operations during unexpected disruptions. Practical approaches, combined with theoretical knowledge, will equip readers with the skills to implement frameworks and policies that enhance the resilience and efficiency of their cloud operations.

Structure

This chapter covers the following topics:

- Creating a culture of financial responsibility
- Demystifying FinOps for cost excellence
- Cloud cost modeling and budgeting
- Right provisioning and cost optimization

- Implementing code and compute optimization
- Implementing database optimization
- Implementing Gen AI/RAG optimization
- Implementing storage optimization
- Implementing data transfer cost optimization

Objectives

By the end of this chapter, you will gain a deep understanding of cost optimization strategies, including fostering a culture of financial responsibility, accurately budgeting and modeling cloud costs, and implementing effective cost monitoring and control mechanisms. You will also learn the importance of right-sizing and optimizing costs across environments like pre-production, production, and disaster recovery. Additionally, this chapter equips you with the knowledge to build effective cloud governance and operating models by integrating FinOps principles, establishing governance policies, access controls, and spending guardrails to maintain compliance, operational control, and financial efficiency. Finally, you will master the essentials of business continuity and disaster recovery planning, enabling your operations to remain resilient and efficient during unexpected disruptions while maintaining high operational standards.

Creating a culture of financial responsibility

As organizations increasingly migrate their workloads to cloud platforms, they often encounter unexpected expenses that can significantly impact their budgets. Therefore, adopting effective cost-optimization strategies is crucial. These strategies encompass a blend of cultural shifts, rigorous financial planning, continuous monitoring, and strategic resource allocation to achieve substantial savings while maintaining the agility and scalability that cloud environments offer.

Creating a culture of financial responsibility involves fostering an environment where wise financial decision-making is prioritized and individuals are held accountable for their financial actions. Convey financial expectations to your team to ensure everyone understands the importance of making cost-effective decisions. Share budgets and financial details with all team members to enhance accountability and support a culture of financial transparency. Provide training programs, resources, and support to develop your employees' skills in cost optimization, empowering them to take ownership of such initiatives. Invest in fostering a growth mindset and discovering new cost optimization techniques, promoting ongoing enhancement in your financial practices.

Demystifying FinOps for cost excellence

FinOps, short for financial operations, is an evolving discipline focused on optimizing cloud financial management. This practice emphasizes collaboration among engineering, finance, technology, and business teams to make data-driven spending decisions, ensuring maximum business value from cloud investments. FinOps is more than a methodology; it is a cultural shift that transforms how organizations manage cloud costs by embracing the principles of Inform, Optimize, and Operate.

FinOps is essential for any organization leveraging cloud infrastructure. It provides a structured approach to manage and optimize cloud spending, ensuring investments are made wisely and deliver maximum value. FinOps addresses a critical gap in cloud cost management. FinOps introduces a structured approach to handle the complexities of cloud financial management, ensuring costs are optimized and value is maximized. It is not merely about cutting costs but about fostering a culture of accountability and strategic investment.

The following are the three pillars of FinOps:

- **Inform**: The Inform pillar focuses on improving cost visibility across the organization. It involves detailed cost allocation and chargeback mechanisms. This transparency helps teams understand their cloud expenses and encourages more thoughtful spending. Regular FinOps maturity reviews assess and enhance the organization's cloud financial management practices.

- **Optimize**: The Optimize pillar is dedicated to maximizing the efficiency of cloud resources. This involves implementing cost-saving strategies and optimization techniques, as mentioned in this chapter. The goal is to balance performance and cost, ensuring resources are utilized effectively without unnecessary expenditure.

- **Operate**: The Operate pillar emphasizes governance and continuous improvement. Establishing strong governance frameworks, such as naming conventions and tagging, ensures consistent cost management practices. Regular reviews and updates to KPIs help maintain accountability and drive ongoing optimization efforts. This pillar transforms FinOps into an iterative, evolving practice.

FinOps practices must be tailored to an organization's cloud maturity and specific needs. For organizations at the beginning of their cloud journey, starting with optimization before migration and building a strong foundation for FinOps practices is crucial. In environments with non-optimized workloads, focusing on quick wins, implementing tagging policies, and creating thorough cost reports for visibility is essential. For mature cloud operations in large organizations, ensuring best practices, improving cost visibility, and setting up centralized governance for complex multi-cloud environments is key. Lastly, in cost-driven scenarios, prioritizing quick wins and establishing mid and long-term cost reduction plans while emphasizing optimization over mere cost-cutting is necessary.

Two significant future challenges for FinOps practitioners include the need for dedicated resources and the ever-changing nature of the cloud. Without sufficient budget and commitment to FinOps, organizations will struggle to keep up with rapid technological advancements requires continuous learning and adaptation.

Cloud sustainability and FinOps

Sustainability is a rising concern, and FinOps practices can align with sustainability goals through GreenOps, which focuses on reducing the environmental footprint of cloud operations. Major cloud providers are already incorporating sustainability initiatives, and GreenOps emphasizes waste reduction, carbon emissions reduction, and improved sustainability reporting.

Cloud cost modeling and budgeting

Creating a cost model involves a structured approach to accurately forecast and manage your workload expenses. We can develop an effective cost model as follows:

- **Estimate workload costs**: Assess all potential expenditures and savings associated with the workload. Consider direct vendor costs, operational maintenance expenses, billing model choices, and potential savings from customer or enterprise agreements. By evaluating these factors, you can create a robust cost model that enables precise forecasting and budgeting.

- **Determine cost drivers**: Identify specific factors or variables that influence the overall cost. These drivers can include usage volume, the number of customers served, storage capacity, or any other factors that directly impact resource, service, or operation costs within the workload.

- **Associate costs with business metrics**: Link workload expenses to specific business indicators, such as cost per customer served or cost per transaction processed. This practice provides a clearer understanding of how the workload consumes resources and helps you anticipate costs related to workload fluctuations, ensuring efficient resource utilization based on demand.

- **Negotiate the workload budget**: Use the cost model as a foundation for negotiating your workload budget. Understand that the cost model provides an estimate while the budget represents reality. You may need to negotiate to align the two effectively.

- **Regularly update the cost model**: Keep the cost model current by regularly updating it to reflect the latest data, business conditions, and any changes in the external environment. Engage stakeholders, including product owners and the technical team, in discussions around the cost model to ensure its relevance and alignment with the needs of different teams.

Cloud cost monitoring

Effectively monitoring costs is crucial for identifying savings, ensuring efficient resource usage, and maintaining financial control. We can monitor costs effectively as follows:

- **Enable data collection on all resources**: Collect comprehensive data on all resource usage, including computing and network usage. This granular data collection helps identify inefficiencies, inform resource allocation decisions, and optimize costs to ensure maximum value for your investment.

- **Group cost data for easier analysis**: Organize cost data into meaningful categories such as resources, services, environments, regions, departments, projects, or teams. Grouping data promotes transparency, accountability, and cost awareness, making it easier to manage and analyze costs effectively.

- **Generate cost reports**: Use collected cost data to create detailed cost reports. Cost reports provide visibility into spending patterns, helping you identify areas for cost optimization and make informed decisions. These reports also enable you to allocate costs to different teams, departments, or projects accurately.

- **Assign a resource owner for each cost item**: Designate a **directly responsible individual** (DRI) for each cost item. Assigning a resource owner ensures clear accountability for managing and optimizing the usage and cost of specific resources or services.

- **Establish spending guardrails and governance policies**: Use governance policies to set spending guardrails on various resource aspects, such as types, configurations, tags, location, and data management. Automate these policies to control resource usage, enforce accountability, and eliminate spending on restricted resource types.

- **Define access controls**: Set access controls to ensure that only authorized users can access resources. This reduces the risk of unauthorized resource consumption and usage, helping to prevent unnecessary cost increases.

- **Implement release gates on deployments**: Use release gates as checkpoints or conditions that must be met before proceeding with a release or deployment. These gates ensure that releases are cost-effective and align with optimization goals.

- **Set cost alerts at key spending thresholds**: Implement automated alerts to trigger notifications at key spending thresholds. These alerts notify stakeholders and resource owners when costs exceed predefined limits or when significant deviations from expected spending patterns occur. Utilize budget alerts and forecast alerts to maintain control over spending.

- **Set resource provisioning alerts**: Implement alerts for underutilized resources, orphan resources, and underutilized commitment-based plans. These alerts provide visibility into your spending and enable proactive cost management by highlighting budget issues, cost anomalies, and prepaid plan utilization.

- **Standardize deployments with infrastructure as code**: Use infrastructure as code to manage and control infrastructure resources in a structured and repeatable manner. This approach helps optimize costs by ensuring resources are provisioned and configured according to predefined rules and best practices.

- **Regularly review cost reports with stakeholders**: Conduct regular reviews of cost reports against the budget and cost model with key stakeholders, including finance teams, operations teams, and decision-makers. These reviews help identify cost trends, outliers, and opportunities for optimization, driving cost-saving initiatives.

Right provisioning and cost optimization

Optimizing the cost of workload environments involves a strategic approach to align spending with priorities across pre-production, production, operations, and disaster recovery environments. This process considers availability, licensing, operating hours, conditions, and security requirements.

The following are the key recommendations:

- **Assess the value of each environment**: Understand the broader impact on business, user satisfaction, and alignment with organizational goals. Make informed decisions about resource allocation based on this assessment.

- **Optimize preproduction environments**: Manage resources in development, testing, and staging environments that do not require the full scale and availability of production environments. Reduce costs by using lower-cost resources, regional pricing, turning off unneeded services, and applying discounts for preproduction usage.

- **Optimize production and DR environments**: Production environments often have higher performance requirements and **service level agreements** (**SLAs**) guaranteeing certain levels of availability, performance, or response times. Manage costs by scaling, ensuring redundancy, and selecting appropriate service tiers to meet these requirements. Balance the cost of maintaining a disaster recovery setup to maintain business continuity readiness during disruptive events like natural disasters, cyber-attacks, or hardware failures while being cost-effective with RTO and RPO targets.

- **Optimize cloud features**: Identify and remove unnecessary or unused features to optimize resource utilization and reduce costs. Focus on eliminating unneeded redundancy configurations, networking performance tiers, and premium service tiers. Adjust the size and scale of underutilized resources that are necessary, ensuring they fit actual usage needs. Ensure new components are efficient and essential, preventing unnecessary expenses and resource wastage. Reallocate resources based on the value of application features to users and business goals. Proactively analyze and address inefficiencies to maintain cost-effective operations.

- **Understand various billing factors of resource usage**: Understand billing factors like instance number, time, transaction rates, transaction sizes, number of availability zones, location, storage amount, ingress data, and egress data. Map usage to billing increments using online pricing and total-cost-of-ownership calculators. Validate understanding of billing increments through proof-of-concepts, refining workload design for cost efficiency. Modify services and resource usage to align with billing thresholds, such as compressing data to match transfer rates.

- **Find and use the best rates from providers**: Actively search for cost-effective prices for resources and licenses, considering price differences in regions, pricing models, and special deals. Evaluate and choose between consumption-based (pay-as-you-go) and prepaid pricing strategies based on workload predictability, duration, and utilization consistency. Commit to available discounts based on workload characteristics and usage patterns. Use various licensing programs and options to minimize expenses while maximizing value. Review cost & licenses associated with design, build, and deployment phases, encompassing tools for software development, security, monitoring, and design.

Implementing code and compute optimization

Optimizing code and compute resources is crucial to reduce cloud spending while maintaining performance and functionality.

The following are the detailed recommendations for IT administrators and architects:

- **Instrument code to collect data during runtime**: Implement code instrumentation to gather key metrics during runtime. This data helps identify hot paths and performance bottlenecks, enabling informed optimization decisions. Application performance monitoring tools can provide insights into memory usage, CPU cycles, and execution time, which are critical for cost optimization.

- **Identify and optimize hot paths**: Focus on critical or frequently executed sections of the code that require high performance and low latency. Reduce unnecessary allocations, reuse existing resources, and minimize the size of data structures to improve memory efficiency and overall performance. Use profiling tools to identify these hot paths and make targeted improvements.

- **Evaluate code for concurrent processing opportunities**: Assess the potential for using asynchronous processing, multithreading, or multiprocessing. Implement concurrency to maximize resource utilization and handle more tasks with the same resources, reducing overall costs. Evaluate libraries and frameworks that support concurrency to ensure optimal implementation.

- **Optimize software development kits**: Select **software development kits (SDKs)** that are designed to optimize resource usage and improve performance. Evaluate the features and capabilities of each SDK, ensuring compatibility with your programming language and development environment. Consider SDKs that offer built-in optimizations for common tasks, reducing the need for custom implementations.

- **Evaluate operating system alternatives**: Consider using different operating systems that provide similar functionality at a lower cost. Compare the costs and performance of various operating systems, taking into account licensing fees, support costs, and resource requirements. Ensure compatibility with your applications and infrastructure before making a switch.

- **Optimize network traversal**: Reduce data transfer costs by eliminating unnecessary data transfers and optimizing network protocols. Implement techniques like data compression, connection pooling, and efficient data routing to lower data transfer costs. Use network performance monitoring tools to identify and address inefficiencies in data flow.

- **Optimize data access**: Streamline data retrieval and storage patterns to minimize unnecessary operations. Use data caching to reduce the frequency of database queries and improve response times. Optimize data querying techniques and implement data compression to improve efficiency and reduce costs.

- **Continuously evaluate and optimize architecture**: Regularly review workload architecture to identify opportunities for re-architecting components to use fewer resources. Implement design patterns, adjust configurations, refactor or redesign components, and modify resource sizes to optimize costs. Use architectural review tools and frameworks to ensure continuous improvement.

- **Serverless vs. provisioned compute**: Opt for serverless services when applicable, as they typically offer a pay-as-you-go model where you only pay for the actual usage, thus reducing costs. Example: Azure Functions vs. Azure App Service; AWS Lambda vs. AWS Elastic Beanstalk.

- **Managed Kubernetes cluster optimization:** Right size your Kubernetes cluster and apply power scheduling to turn off clusters during non-peak hours. Use Spot instances for non-critical workloads and autoscaling features to align capacity with demand. For example, **Azure Kubernetes Service (AKS)**, AWS **Elastic Kubernetes Service (EKS)**, and **Google Kubernetes Engine (GKE)**.

- **Analyze usage data to decide on the best scaling model**: Determine the most cost-effective approach between scaling out (adding more instances) and scaling up (increasing resources in an existing system). Use historical usage data to make informed decisions about scaling strategies. Implement scaling policies based on performance metrics and cost considerations.

- **Implement strategies to reduce resource demand**: Use code-level design patterns to minimize resource utilization. Avoid overprovisioning resources and paying for unused or underutilized capacity. Implement techniques like lazy loading, efficient resource management, and load balancing to reduce demand on resources.

- **Optimize autoscaling policies**: Tune autoscaling policies to react to load changes based on defined nonfunctional requirements. Limit excessive scaling activities by adjusting thresholds and cooldown periods. Use autoscaling tools provided by cloud providers to automate and optimize scaling processes.

- **Offload demand strategically:** Distribute or transfer resource demand to other resources or services using caching, content offloading, load balancing, and database offloading. Implement strategies like CDN for content delivery, edge computing, and database replication to offload demand. Monitor the impact of offloading strategies to ensure they are effective and cost-efficient.

- **Set and enforce upper limits on resource spending**: Define an upper limit on spending for specific resources or services to control costs. Establish a budget and monitor spending to ensure it stays within defined thresholds. Use cloud cost management tools to set spending alerts and track expenses in real time.

- **Remove orphaned resources**: Regularly audit and delete orphaned resources such as disks, public IPs, network interfaces, and snapshots. Use tools like *PowerShell*, *Azure CLI*, *AWS CLI*, and *Google Cloud SDK* to identify and manage orphaned resources. Implement policies and automation to ensure resources are properly cleaned up after use.

- **Upgrade virtual machine (VM) versions**: Upgrade VMs to the latest generations to benefit from improved performance, efficiency, and lower costs. Consider using newer CPU architectures like *AMD* or *ARM* for additional savings and performance improvements. Schedule upgrades during maintenance windows to minimize disruption.

- **Right-size virtual machines**: Analyze long-running workloads to ensure resources are appropriately sized. Scale up or down based on CPU, memory, and disk throughput/IOPS usage to optimize costs. Use cloud provider tools to monitor resource utilization and make informed decisions about rightsizing.

- **Standardize VM families**: Homogenize VM families to simplify governance and achieve savings through reserved instances. Choose specific families, VM SKUs, and regions for each environment and enforce their use through policies. Regularly review and update standards to reflect the latest offerings and best practices.

- **Implement VM power scheduling**: Schedule VMs to shut down during off-hours to save on computing costs. Use IaC to automate the deployment and deletion of environments as needed. Monitor power scheduling to ensure compliance and effectiveness.

- **Utilize burstable VMs**: Use burstable VMs that can scale up temporarily during high-demand periods without changing tiers. Ideal for development environments and use cases with fluctuating resource demands. Monitor and manage burstable VMs to ensure they meet performance requirements without incurring unnecessary costs.

- **Leverage reserved instances and saving plans**: Commit to using specific VM families or monetary amounts to receive significant discounts. Ensure a stable infrastructure perimeter and use SPs for flexibility while avoiding premature commitments. Regularly review **reserved instances (RI)** and **saving plans (SP)** usage to maximize benefits and minimize waste.

Implementing database optimization

Database optimization is a critical aspect of managing enterprise applications efficiently. As databases are fundamental in storing, organizing, and accessing information, their optimization directly impacts both performance and cost. With the surge in data volumes driven by big data, data science, and machine learning, optimizing databases has become crucial to avoid skyrocketing costs and ensure efficient data handling. To maintain databases in an optimal state, it is important to align them with appropriate SKUs and sizing and manage licensing and scaling effectively.

The following are some of the key recommendations:

Choosing the right database for your workload

Selecting the correct type of database, relational or non-relational, is foundational for optimization. Relational databases, ideal for structured data, consist of tables with predefined formats, making them suitable for applications where data integrity and compliance are paramount. On the other hand, non-relational (NoSQL) databases offer flexibility in handling unstructured data such as *JSON, BSON,* or *XML* documents, making them ideal for use cases involving large volumes of varied data, like social media or IoT applications.

IaaS database optimization

Optimizing databases in an IaaS environment is essential for balancing performance and costs. This section dives into practical strategies for managing database storage, backups, and clusters, helping you reduce expenses without compromising on efficiency or scalability as follows:

- **Rational database use**: Only store essential data in databases to avoid unnecessary costs. Implement data retention and deletion policies to manage data lifecycles effectively. For colder data, use cost-efficient storage solutions like *Azure Data Lake Storage* or *AWS S3*, which offer different tiers for varied data temperatures. Utilize cache services such as *Azure Cache for Redis* to reduce database load and network traffic.

- **Backup storage optimization:** Store database backups in object storage services like *Azure Blob* or *AWS S3* rather than on disks to leverage cost savings from colder storage tiers. Regularly review backup policies to ensure alignment with **recovery point objective (RPO)** and **recovery time objective (RTO)** requirements. For example, using AWS S3 Glacier for long-term storage can significantly reduce costs.

- **Shared disks for database clusters:** Implement shared disk clusters to lower costs by sharing disk devices among nodes. While shared-nothing clusters offer better scaling and fault tolerance, shared disk clusters are more cost-effective for workloads that do not require multi-region setups or extensive scaling.

PaaS database optimization

Optimizing PaaS databases is about finding the right balance between performance and cost-efficiency. This section covers strategies like rightsizing resources, grouping databases, implementing effective scaling, and leveraging reserved capacity to ensure your databases are both highly performant and budget-friendly as follows:

- **Compute optimization and rightsizing:** Regularly monitor CPU, RAM, disk space, network traffic, and database connections to ensure resources are appropriately allocated. Right size databases by adjusting the compute resources to match actual usage patterns.

- **Database grouping:** Consolidate multiple databases into logical instances or elastic pools to maximize resource utilization and reduce costs. In Azure SQL, use elastic pools to share compute and storage resources among databases, scaling based on demand. Similarly, AWS **Relational Database Service (RDS)** and GCP Cloud SQL allow for efficient database grouping within instances.

- **Database scaling:** Implement both vertical and horizontal scaling strategies to manage increasing workloads. Vertical scaling involves increasing compute resources, while horizontal scaling adds more nodes to distribute the load. Utilize autoscaling rules to automate scaling based on key metrics, ensuring cost-efficiency and performance. Serverless databases, like *Azure SQL Serverless* or *AWS Aurora Serverless*, provide a consumption-based billing model ideal for unpredictable workloads.

- **Reserved capacity:** Utilize RIs and saving plans to achieve significant cost savings for stable, long-term workloads. Both IaaS and PaaS database services offer reserved capacity options, providing discounts for committing to usage over one or three years. For example, Azure SQL, AWS RDS, and GCP Cloud SQL all support RIs, enabling cost-effective database management.

Licensing optimization

Optimizing licensing is a smart way to cut database costs without compromising functionality. This section explains how to maximize existing licenses through **Bring Your Own License** (**BYOL**) models and take advantage of development-specific licenses for cost-efficient testing and non-production scenarios as follows:

- **Bring your own license**: Use existing database licenses to save costs, particularly for high-cost DBMS like *SQL Server* or *Oracle*. Azure supports BYOL for SQL Server, allowing seamless switching between pay-as-you-go and BYOL models. AWS and GCP also support BYOL for major DBMS, leveraging existing licenses for cloud deployments.

- **Development scenarios**: Utilize development-specific licenses and environments to reduce costs. Azure offers Dev/Test subscriptions with lower rates for non-production environments, and Visual Studio subscribers receive monthly Azure credits. SQL Server Developer and SQL Server Express licenses provide free options for development and testing, ensuring cost-effective development processes.

The following are some more data optimization strategies that DBA, system admins, and architects should use:

- **Shrinking relational databases**: Regularly reorganizing or compacting information in databases to free up disk space, especially after large deletions or table drops, can help maintain optimal performance and reduce costs.

- **Shared disk options in public clouds**: Utilizing shared disk options in Azure, AWS, and GCP can reduce costs by enabling shared block storage to be accessed from multiple VMs, reducing the need for redundant storage.

- **Using caching services**: Leveraging cache services such as *Azure Cache for Redis* can reduce database load and costs by handling frequently accessed data in-memory, thus lowering the frequency of direct database queries.

- **Development licenses and personal credits**: Utilizing development-specific licenses and personal credits from Visual Studio subscriptions to test and develop without incurring high costs.

- **Evaluating licensing needs**: Regularly reviewing and downgrading licensing tiers where possible to ensure that only necessary features are being paid for. Using lower-tier licenses for non-production environments can significantly reduce costs.

- **Cluster configurations**: Analyzing different cluster configurations like shared-nothing clusters versus shared disk clusters for high availability and fault tolerance can impact costs and performance.

- **Backup frequency and storage**: Optimizing backup policies, such as using incremental backups, backup compression, and appropriate backup storage tiers, can save costs and ensure efficient data recovery.

- **Data lifecycle management**: Implementing policies for data retention, deletion, and moving colder data to cost-efficient storage solutions can reduce storage costs and improve database performance.

- **Reviewing IOPS needs**: Monitoring and adjusting the **input/output operations per second** (**IOPS**) settings for PaaS databases to ensure they align with workload requirements and can optimize costs related to disk bandwidth.

- **Managing network traffic costs**: Evaluating network traffic costs and optimizing the provisioned throughput to match actual usage can prevent over-provisioning and reduce expenses.

When implemented correctly, these techniques can provide substantial savings and ensure efficient and cost-effective database management.

Implementing Gen AI/RAG optimization

Optimizing Azure OpenAI workloads and generative AI services is essential for reducing cloud spending while maintaining performance and functionality.

The following are the detailed recommendations for IT administrators and architects:

- **Consolidate resources for efficiency**: Consolidate Azure OpenAI workloads under a single subscription to streamline management and optimize costs. Use resource groups for regional isolation to ensure compliance with local data sovereignty laws. Maintain a single Azure OpenAI resource per region to maximize resource utilization and efficiently cater to regional demands.

- **Implement pay-as-you-go and pre-trained unit deployments**: Create PAYG and PTU deployments within each Azure OpenAI resource for models. This allows businesses to scale flexibly, ensuring critical workloads are supported with PTUs and scaling up efficiently during peak periods. This dual deployment strategy helps balance cost and performance based on real-time needs.

- **Optimize compute resource scheduling**: Implement VM power scheduling to shut down VMs during off-hours to save on compute costs. Use Azure automation tools to create schedules that align with usage patterns, ensuring resources are only active when needed. This reduces unnecessary expenditure and optimizes resource allocation.

- **Efficient token and quota management**: Optimize costs and load balancing by managing tokens efficiently. Monitor quotas closely to prevent service disruptions, ensuring consistent uptime for high-traffic applications. Implement backoff strategies for rate limiting to handle peak traffic gracefully, maintaining service performance and availability.

- **Enhance performance with code instrumentation**: Instrument code to collect key metrics during runtime. This data helps identify performance bottlenecks and hot paths, enabling targeted optimization. Use application performance monitoring tools to gain insights into memory usage, CPU cycles, and execution time, facilitating informed decisions for performance tuning.

- **Leverage concurrency and optimize SDKs**: Assess the potential for using asynchronous processing, multithreading, or multiprocessing to maximize resource utilization. Implement concurrency to handle more tasks with the same resources, reducing overall costs. Select SDKs designed to optimize resource usage and improve performance, ensuring they are compatible with your development environment.

- **Optimize network and data transfer**: Reduce data transfer costs by eliminating unnecessary data transfers and optimizing network protocols. Implement techniques like data compression, connection pooling, and efficient data routing. Use network performance monitoring tools to identify and address inefficiencies in data flow, enhancing overall network performance.

- **Streamline data access and storage**: Optimize data retrieval and storage patterns to minimize unnecessary operations. Use data caching to reduce the frequency of database queries and improve response times. Optimize data querying techniques and implement data compression to improve efficiency and reduce costs. Ensure that data storage solutions are scalable and cost-effective.

- **Implement effective autoscaling and load balancing**: Optimize autoscaling policies to react to load changes based on defined nonfunctional requirements. Adjust thresholds and cooldown periods to limit excessive scaling activities. Use **Azure API Management (APIM)** to equitably distribute network traffic and secure API access with APIM policies, ensuring reliable and scalable service delivery.

- **Optimize GenAI services using the RAG pattern**: Enhance AI services by using the **retrieval-augmented generation (RAG)** pattern, which combines document retrieval with generation capabilities. Implement prompt compression techniques to improve latency in generative AI applications. Ensure that AI components adhere to responsible AI practices, maintaining ethical standards, transparency, and data privacy in AI usage.

AI cost optimization based on recent innovations

Based on the latest innovations in models, frameworks, and hardware, this section discusses advanced strategies and actionable insights to optimize cost for AI projects as follows:

- **Model selection and right-sizing**: AI models vary significantly in size, complexity, and resource requirements. Selecting the right model for specific workloads is crucial to balancing performance and cost:

- **Smaller, task-specific models**: Instead of deploying large, general-purpose models like GPT-4o for all scenarios, organizations can achieve greater efficiency by utilizing specialized models tailored for specific tasks. For instance, the Open AI GPT o1 model excels in complex reasoning and problem-solving, making it ideal for applications requiring advanced analytical capabilities. In contrast, the o3 model focuses on enhanced reasoning skills, particularly in coding and mathematical problem-solving, offering improved accuracy for technical domains. For applications where computational resources are a concern, the o3-mini model provides a cost-effective alternative with reduced computational demands while maintaining substantial reasoning abilities. Additionally, the Phi 3 series, including the Phi 3 multimodal model, is designed for media and voice processing tasks, enabling seamless integration of text, audio, and visual data for comprehensive AI solutions. Organizations can optimize performance and resource utilization by selecting models that align closely with specific application requirements, leading to more efficient and effective AI deployments.

- **Quantization and pruning**: Reduce the size and resource intensity of AI models through quantization techniques (e.g., INT8 or FP16). Tools like *NVIDIA TensorRT* and *Azure Machine Learning's* model optimization features enable seamless deployment of quantized models with minimal accuracy trade-offs. Pruning can further eliminate redundant parameters in over-parameterized models, reducing compute costs during inference.

- **Model distillation**: Model distillation is a technique that creates lightweight versions of larger AI models, retaining essential capabilities while reducing computational demands. In the Azure ecosystem, this process is streamlined through integrated tools. For instance, Azure OpenAI Service offers features like stored completions, which allow developers to capture input-output pairs from models such as GPT-4o. These datasets can then be used to fine-tune smaller models like GPT-4o mini, effectively distilling the larger model's knowledge into a more efficient form. Additionally, Azure AI Foundry provides a centralized platform for managing fine-tuning tasks, supporting various models, and ensuring that distilled models are readily deployable across diverse environments. This integration simplifies the distillation process, making it more accessible for applications in edge computing and resource-constrained scenarios.

- **Efficient resource allocation**: Resource allocation is a cornerstone of cost optimization. Modern tools and methodologies ensure that compute resources are used efficiently:

  o **Dynamic autoscaling**: Inference workloads can experience sudden traffic spikes. Use **Azure Kubernetes Service (AKS)** with **Horizontal Pod Autoscalers (HPA)** to dynamically scale compute resources based on load. For OpenAI APIs, implement rate-limiting and batching mechanisms to optimize API call efficiency.

- o **Optimized training pipelines**: Distributed training with PyTorch Distributed or Horovod enables efficient use of multi-GPU clusters for large-scale models. Azure's DeepSpeed library integrates seamlessly with PyTorch to optimize memory usage and training speed for expansive models.

- o **GPU utilization**: NVIDIA's new Hopper architecture GPUs (e.g., H100) provide higher throughput for AI workloads at reduced power consumption. Combined with Azure NDm A100v4-series VMs, these GPUs offer unparalleled performance per dollar for training and inference.

- **Leveraging open-source AI models**: Open-source frameworks and models provide cost-effective alternatives to proprietary solutions while retaining high customization flexibility:

  - o **Meta LLaMA models**: Meta's LLaMA models (e.g., LLaMA 3) are open-source and designed to scale across different use cases. These models are cost-efficient, with fine-tuning capabilities that allow enterprises to adapt them for specialized applications without incurring high training costs.

  - o **Hugging Face ecosystem**: Hugging Face's model hub hosts thousands of pre-trained models, including transformers optimized for specific domains. Combining these models with Azure's Hugging Face partnership enables direct deployment into enterprise workflows with minimal integration effort.

  - o **Collaborative frameworks**: OpenAI's ongoing contributions to frameworks like *Triton* and improvements in their API infrastructure ensure that developers can build scalable solutions with lower latencies and reduced operational overhead.

- **Leveraging new GPU models and AI hardware**: Advances in AI-specific hardware provide significant opportunities for cost optimization:

  - o **GPUs for AI inference**: NVIDIA's Hopper architecture (e.g., H100 GPUs) offers 2x performance gains compared to its predecessors while consuming less power. Azure's ND H100 v5 series virtual machines leverage this hardware to deliver optimized performance for large-scale generative AI workloads.

  - o **Edge AI deployment**: Deploying models on edge devices using hardware accelerators like *NVIDIA Jetson* ensures low-latency inference with minimal cloud dependency, reducing recurring costs.

Implementing storage optimization

Effective storage cost optimization is crucial for managing expenses and ensuring efficient use of resources in the cloud. With the variety of storage options available, ranging from block storage to object storage, it is essential to implement strategies that align with your workload requirements and usage patterns.

Optimizing storage costs is about more than just saving money; it is about striking the perfect balance between performance, reliability, and efficiency. This section discusses the following practical strategies, from provisioning and snapshot management to redundancy and reserved capacity, empowering organizations to reduce expenses and ensure their storage systems are agile, scalable, and aligned with business needs.

- **Thick vs. thin provisioning**: Use thin provisioning to allocate only the necessary storage initially and add more as needed. Apply thin provisioning philosophy to block, file, and object storage to avoid overprovisioning.

- **Snapshot optimization**: Use snapshots judiciously and ensure they are ephemeral. Delete old snapshots once they are no longer needed. Identify and remove orphaned snapshots that are no longer associated with any resource. Separate OS and data disks to snapshot only the necessary data disks. Use incremental snapshots to reduce storage space (Azure, AWS, GCP specifics). Archive snapshots for long-term retention at reduced costs.

- **Storage redundancy**: To optimize costs and meet high availability requirements, select appropriate storage redundancy options. For cost savings, prefer **local or zone-redundant storage** (**LRS/ZRS**) when cross-region high availability is not essential. In Azure, options include LRS, ZRS, GRS, GZRS, RA-GRS, and RA-GZRS. AWS offers default replication, SRR, and CRR. GCP provides regional, dual-region, multi-region, and turbo replication options.

- **Block storage optimization**: Efficient block storage management is crucial for cost reduction while meeting performance requirements. Rightsizing involves analyzing disk performance and capacity to ensure they align with workload needs and downgrading disks if they are underutilized in terms of IOPS and throughput. Snapshot optimization policies should be implemented to regularly delete old and unnecessary snapshots. Ephemeral disks should be used for stateless workloads to save on storage costs. Disk tiering, which involves selecting appropriate disk types (SSD, HDD) based on performance needs, can further optimize storage. Additionally, offloading less frequently accessed data to a file or object storage and using reserved capacity for managed disks where applicable can result in significant long-term cost savings.

- **File storage optimization**: Efficient file storage management is essential for controlling costs while maintaining performance and capacity. Rightsizing involves ensuring that file shares are appropriately sized to meet both capacity and performance needs. Utilizing data temperature tiers, such as hot and cool, based on data access patterns can optimize storage efficiency. Additionally, using reserved capacity options for file storage can further reduce costs.

- **Object storage optimization**: Object storage provides flexibility and scalability but requires careful management to optimize costs. Data temperature tiering should be used to move data to appropriate storage classes (hot, cool, archive) based on access patterns. Implementing life cycle policies can automate data transitions between tiers and ensure data is deleted when no longer needed. Versioning and soft delete features should be limited and tracked to avoid unnecessary costs, while object snapshots should be managed wisely to prevent excessive expenses. Utilizing inventory tools efficiently to collect only necessary metadata can also help control costs. Additionally, using reserved capacity for object storage can result in significant long-term savings.

- **Log storage optimization**: Reduce data ingestion and retention to minimize storage costs. Offload older log data to cheaper storage solutions like object storage with colder tiers.

- **Backup storage optimization**: Backup storage is essential for data protection but can be costly if not managed properly. To optimize backup storage, adjust backup policies to align backup frequency and retention with business needs (RPO and RTO). Ensure selective disk backup by backing up only necessary disks to avoid redundant storage. Choose appropriate redundancy settings for backups based on their criticality and cost considerations. Additionally, using reserved capacity for backup storage when beneficial can significantly reduce costs.

Implementing data transfer cost optimization

Efficiently managing data transfer costs is essential for optimizing cloud expenditure and ensuring smooth operations. Data transfer costs, often referred to as egress costs, can quickly accumulate, especially in large-scale cloud environments where data moves frequently between regions, zones, and services. By understanding the types of data transfer and the key cost drivers, organizations can implement targeted strategies to minimize these expenses.

This section provides an overview of different data transfer types and actionable recommendations to optimize data transfer costs while maintaining performance and reliability.

- **Types of data transfer**: Data transfer types in cloud environments include inbound data transfer, where data moves into the cloud from external sources, and outbound data transfer, where data exits the cloud to external destinations. Inter-region data transfer involves moving data between different geographical cloud regions, while intra-region data transfer occurs between availability zones within the same region. Lastly, internal data transfer refers to data movement within the same cloud environment, such as between services or resources.

- **Key drivers of data transfer cost**: Key drivers of data transfer costs include the volume of data, as the total amount being transferred significantly affects expenses, and the distance of transfer, with longer distances such as inter-region transfers typically incurring higher costs. The frequency of transfers can accumulate substantial costs over time, and the data transfer path within the cloud environment can also impact expenses, especially if it crosses different zones or regions. Additionally, service interactions between different cloud services and the associated data transfers can drive up costs.

The following are the recommendations to optimize data transfer costs:

- **Optimally manage the flows**: Managing data flows can be a real cost drain if not done smartly. This section gives you practical tips to get a grip on your data transfers, cutting down unnecessary flows, keeping transfers within regions, and using caching and compression. It is all about optimizing where your data moves and how much it costs you.

    o **Conduct a flow inventory**: Perform a detailed inventory of all data flows within your environment to understand the purpose, dependencies, and cost implications of each flow. This helps identify high-cost areas and prioritize optimization efforts.

    o **Prioritize flows by value**: Classify data flows based on their impact on business outcomes and resource consumption. Focus optimization efforts on high-value flows to ensure resources are allocated efficiently.

    o **Optimize independent flows**: Analyze and optimize flows that run on separate resources independently. By identifying inefficiencies and optimizing each flow, you can reduce overall data transfer costs.

    o **Separate dissimilar flows**: Run different types of data flows on separate resources to optimize costs. This prevents resource contention and ensures each flow type is managed efficiently according to its specific needs.

    o **Combine similar flows**: Consolidate tasks or processes with similar attributes onto the same resources to eliminate redundancies. This approach ensures more efficient use of resources and reduces unnecessary data transfers.

- **Review data transfer usage regularly**: Monitor and review data transfer usage periodically to ensure alignment with cost and performance goals. Adjust resource allocation and flow management strategies based on usage patterns and cost analyses.

- **Minimize outbound data**: Reduce the amount of data leaving the cloud environment by optimizing application code, using data compression, and eliminating unnecessary external dependencies. This helps lower outbound data transfer costs.

- **Optimize storage and retrieval**: Implement strategies such as retrieving only necessary data, using intelligent tiering, and setting up lifecycle policies to manage data transitions and deletions. These practices reduce unnecessary data retrieval and storage costs.

- **Utilize caching solutions**: Use caching solutions to store frequently accessed data closer to end users, reducing the need for repeated data transfers from origin servers. This minimizes latency and transfer costs.

- **Keep data transfers within a single region or zone**: Avoid inter-region or cross-zone data transfers by keeping data transfers within a single region or availability zone. This reduces the costs associated with long-distance data transfers.

- **Leverage cost allocation and monitoring tools**: Utilize tools for cost allocation, monitoring, and alerts to track data transfer costs and identify optimization opportunities. Regular monitoring helps manage cost drivers proactively and maintain cost efficiency.

- **Automate resource management**: Implement automated shutdowns and resource scaling during off-peak hours to avoid unnecessary costs. Automation ensures that resources are used efficiently, reducing data transfer costs.

- **Compress and deduplicate data**: Apply data compression and deduplication techniques to reduce data size before transferring it. This minimizes the amount of data being transferred, leading to significant cost savings.

- **Design efficient application architecture**: Optimize application architecture to minimize data transfer paths. Consolidate data within the same region and design applications to reduce the traveling path of data, thus lowering transfer costs.

Additional architectural design principles

Effective architectural design can significantly reduce unnecessary data movement.

Let us look at the following additional architectural techniques that can be employed to minimize data transfer costs:

- **Localize data processing**: Process data as close to the source as possible to minimize the need for data transfer. For instance, perform data transformations and analytics within the same region or availability zone where the data is generated.

- **Sharding and partitioning**: Use data sharding and partitioning techniques to distribute data across multiple nodes or regions efficiently. This reduces the need for large-scale data transfers between regions or databases.

- **Strategic data replication**: Replicate data only when necessary for high availability and disaster recovery. Use read replicas to serve read-heavy workloads without transferring data from the primary source frequently.

- **Data aggregation**: Aggregate data at the source before transferring it to reduce the volume of data being moved. Summarize logs, metrics, and other data types to reduce the amount of detailed data that needs to be transferred.

- **Edge computing**: Implement edge computing solutions to handle data processing at the network edge, closer to the data source. This minimizes data transfer to central cloud locations and reduces latency.

- **Efficient API design**: Design APIs to minimize data transfer by optimizing payload size. Use techniques like pagination, filtering, and selective data fetching (e.g., GraphQL) to reduce the amount of data returned in API responses.

- **Compression and encoding**: Apply advanced data compression and encoding techniques to minimize the data size before transfer. Use efficient algorithms and formats that provide high compression ratios without compromising data integrity.

- **Load balancing**: Implement load balancers and proxies strategically to distribute data transfer loads and reduce the need for cross-region or cross-zone transfers. This can also optimize the performance and cost of data transfers.

- **Hybrid cloud integration**: Utilize hybrid cloud architectures to keep data transfers within private networks when possible. This minimizes the need for costly public internet transfers.

- **Multi-cloud data management**: Optimize data placement across multiple cloud providers to ensure that data is stored and processed in the most cost-effective locations, avoiding expensive cross-cloud data transfers.

- **Intelligent traffic routing**: Use intelligent traffic routing to direct data flows through the most cost-effective and efficient paths. Implementing **content delivery networks (CDNs)** and geo-routing can help minimize data transfer costs.

- **Data anonymization and trimming**: Remove unnecessary data fields and anonymize data where possible before transfer to reduce data size and meet compliance requirements without transferring excessive data.

- **Use object storage features**: Utilize features of object storage such as pre-signed URLs for temporary access, multipart uploads for large files, and versioning to manage data transfers efficiently.

Conclusion

By the end of this chapter, we covered the essential components necessary for achieving and maintaining high operational standards in cloud environments. We explored strategies for cloud cost optimization, including creating a culture of financial responsibility, developing accurate cost models, and implementing effective cost monitoring and optimization techniques. We also delved into establishing effective cloud operating and governance models with FinOps principles, ensuring compliance and operational control. Additionally, we discussed the critical aspects of **business continuity planning (BCP)** and **disaster recovery planning (DRP)**, equipping you with the knowledge to maintain operations during unexpected disruptions. By combining practical approaches with theoretical knowledge, you are now equipped to implement frameworks and policies that enhance the resilience and efficiency of your cloud operations.

In the next chapter, we will discuss the essentials of modern application architecture.

Key terms

- **Financial operations (FinOps)**: A set of practices and culture designed to manage cloud spending and maximize cloud investment value through financial accountability and collaboration across teams.

- **Business continuity Planning (BCP)**: A proactive planning process that ensures critical business operations can continue during and after a disaster or unexpected disruption.

- **Disaster recovery planning (DRP)**: A strategy that involves setting up and maintaining systems and procedures to recover and protect a business's IT infrastructure in the event of a disaster.

- **Right provisioning**: The practice of allocating the correct amount of cloud resources to match workload requirements, ensuring cost efficiency without over or under-provisioning.

- **Cost optimization**: Techniques and strategies used to reduce cloud expenditure while maintaining or enhancing performance and functionality.

- **Governance policies**: Rules and guidelines are established to ensure proper management and control of resources, compliance with regulations, and effective operational oversight in a cloud environment.

- **Spending guardrails**: Financial limits and controls set on various aspects of resource usage to prevent overspending and ensure financial discipline in cloud operations.

- **Recovery point objective (RPO)**: The maximum acceptable amount of data loss measured in time before a disaster or disruption.

- **Recovery time objective (RTO)**: The maximum acceptable length of time that a service, application, or business process can be down after a disaster or disruption.

- **Infrastructure as code (IaC)**: The management of infrastructure (networks, virtual machines, load balancers, etc.) using code and automation tools to ensure repeatability, scalability, and efficient deployment.

CHAPTER 4

Modern Application Architecture

Introduction

In this chapter, we will cover contemporary application design principles and practices that are crucial for developing scalable and resilient software. Beginning with an overview of modern architectural frameworks, the chapter delves deep into application definition and development, emphasizing **domain-driven design** (**DDD**) integrated with microservices for modularity and agility. It also explores **event-driven design** (**EDD**) and the orchestration and management of complex application ecosystems, highlighting the role of Kubernetes and serverless computing frameworks. The chapter will further discuss integrating robust service designs, including API management and workflow orchestration.

Structure

This chapter covers the following topics:

- Evolution of architecture
- Essentials of modern application architecture
- Orchestration and management with Kubernetes
- Strategies for runtime and provisioning
- Observability and systems analysis techniques
- Architectural pitfalls and how to avoid them

- Role of AI/ML in modern architecture
- Actionable checklist for architects

Objectives

By the end of this chapter, we will have the knowledge and practical strategies to design, deploy, and manage modern cloud-native applications effectively. We will master the fundamentals of modern application architecture, gaining insights into creating agile, scalable, and resilient systems that adapt to today's rapidly evolving technological landscape. Through DDD, we will align application structures with business objectives, ensuring modularity, adaptability, and clear domain boundaries for optimal scalability and maintainability. We will also help us design reactive, event-driven systems for real-time processing, implement AI-driven techniques for dynamic resource optimization, and orchestrate containers across multi-cloud environments using Kubernetes for high availability and seamless failover.

Additionally, we will discuss serverless frameworks and cost-effective autoscaling strategies for on-demand service delivery. We will embed security and compliance into every layer and apply observability techniques like distributed tracing and anomaly detection to monitor application health and performance. Strategies for modernizing legacy systems and enabling seamless integration with new architectures are covered, along with insights into building architectures that are flexible, sustainable, and ethically responsible. These objectives will equip us to craft scalable, resilient, and efficient applications aligned with modern business demands, leveraging cutting-edge tools and frameworks to navigate complex distributed systems successfully.

Evolution of architecture

The journey of software architecture is deeply intertwined with advances in technology and hardware, as each new paradigm responds to the needs and limits of its time. For those who have witnessed the rise of the internet, the dawn of cloud computing, the mobile revolution, and now the AI era, this evolution tells a story of adaptation and ingenuity. Each shift reflects not only the changing tools but also the underlying societal impact, as innovations shape how we connect, interact, and solve problems.

Mainframe and monolithic era of 1960s-1980s

In the early days, IBM's mainframes dominated the computing world. Machines like the *IBM 360* were massive and expensive, designed to process enormous workloads for corporations and government agencies. These mainframes were tightly coupled with monolithic software built with languages like *COBOL* and *Fortran*. Since hardware was costly, software was architected to maximize efficient resource use, often resulting in massive, interdependent systems.

The limited computing power meant that networking was limited, storage was at a premium, and mainframes were isolated from personal computers. Companies were empowered to digitize operations for the first time, streamlining everything from payroll to inventory. However, the technology was confined to large organizations, with ordinary individuals having little to no access.

Client-server and internet era of 1990s

The 1990s marked a revolution as computers became more accessible, and client-server architecture gained popularity. Networking standards improved, and the advent of TCP/IP and Ethernet allowed for more interactive, distributed systems. Companies like *Microsoft* and *Sun Microsystems* fueled this shift, with Microsoft's Windows dominating personal computing and Sun Microsystems' Java platform enabling cross-platform applications.

With this rise, the internet began to take shape, connecting clients and servers across distances and birthing the WWW. Browsers like *Netscape Navigator* and, later, *Internet Explorer* brought the internet to everyday users, transforming it into an information hub. Hardware advancements, faster CPUs, increased memory, and improved network speeds further fueled the internet's spread.

However, this era's limitations became apparent: systems were siloed, managing interconnectivity was difficult, and scaling was challenging. These hurdles paved the way for cloud computing as companies sought more efficient ways to manage and scale IT resources.

Cloud and mobile revolution in 2000s

The 2000s saw the explosive growth of cloud computing, led by **Amazon Web Services (AWS)**, Microsoft Azure, and Google Cloud. AWS, launched in 2006, was the first to offer on-demand cloud resources, setting the stage for others to follow. Virtualization allowed cloud providers to pool resources, offering flexible, scalable solutions for a fraction of the cost of maintaining physical infrastructure. As cloud adoption spread, software architecture evolved with it, shifting from monolithic to **service-oriented architectures (SOA)**.

Simultaneously, the mobile revolution changed how people accessed information. With the release of Apple's iPhone in 2007 and Google's Android in 2008, smartphones took the world by storm, bringing connectivity to billions. Apps designed for mobile platforms needed new patterns and architectures, leading to the rise of RESTful APIs and responsive design principles. Hardware evolved to meet these demands, with low-power processors and efficient networking technologies like 4G enabling seamless user experiences.

The cloud and mobile era faced its own challenges, latency, privacy concerns, and dependency on centralized infrastructure. These constraints set the stage for edge computing and new, more granular architectures to address latency and data privacy closer to the source.

Microservices, IoT, and edge computing in 2010s

The 2010s brought forward the need for even more modular, scalable software, giving rise to microservices. Companies like *Netflix*, *Amazon*, and *Uber* popularized microservices architectures, allowing their systems to be broken into small, independently managed services. Tools like *Docker* and *Kubernetes* emerged, simplifying containerization and orchestration, while companies like *Red Hat* and *Google* led the open-source movement in cloud-native tooling.

At the same time, IoT devices proliferated, from smart home devices to industrial sensors. This shift necessitated low-latency, high-availability architectures that centralized cloud data centers could not meet, leading to edge computing, where data processing happens closer to the source. 5G networks, which began rolling out toward the end of the decade, further pushed the capabilities of edge, allowing faster, more reliable connectivity.

The need for real-time processing, data privacy, and flexibility marked the next wave of architectural innovation as companies began seeking ways to decentralize, lower latency, and improve data sovereignty. These challenges laid the foundation for the emergence of AI-driven, autonomous, and self-optimizing systems.

AI and quantum era of 2020s and beyond

As we move into the 2020s, artificial intelligence is reshaping the tech landscape. AI's demand for data processing power has pushed hardware design forward, with companies like *NVIDIA*, *AMD*, and *Intel* driving advances in GPUs and AI-optimized chips. Innovations like **Tensor Processing Units (TPUs)** and **Intelligence Processing Units (IPUs)** are creating specialized hardware to handle deep learning tasks, while AI's insatiable demand for data has driven the evolution of storage and networking, with high-throughput databases and low-latency interconnects.

The rise of AI is leading to a shift from *Moore's Law*, the doubling of transistors on a chip every two years, to the *Scaling Law*, which focuses on optimizing AI model efficiency, requiring larger, optimized compute clusters, specialized processors, and scalable data pipelines. To manage this, architectural paradigms are shifting to prioritize models that learn, adapt, and self-manage.

In software, the architecture is moving towards AI-first designs, where applications are built to leverage ML, generative AI, and agentic AI at their core. AI-powered platforms like *OpenAI, Meta, Google, DeepSeek*, and *Hugging Face* make ML accessible for developers, enabling intelligent features across software solutions. AI influences every layer, from *databases* like *Databricks* and *Snowflake* with embedded ML to *networking* enhancements for high-performance, low-latency data flow.

The transition to AI-driven, autonomous architectures represents a convergence of all past paradigms, where hardware, software, and data come together to create solutions capable of self-optimization, real-time learning, and decision-making. The role of architects now includes building for unpredictability, scalability, and adaptability, ensuring that systems can evolve in tandem with societal needs. The journey from monolithic to self-managing architectures demonstrates not just technological progress but humanity's enduring drive to push the boundaries of possibility. The question now is not only what we can build but what we should build, as our designs shape the future of society in profound ways.

Essentials of modern application architecture

In today's rapidly evolving digital landscape, businesses have heightened expectations from their **chief technology officers** (**CTOs**) and IT/engineering teams. These expectations revolve around six core outcomes, agility and speed, innovation, user satisfaction, cost reduction, operational efficiency, and engineer productivity. Concurrently, every digital asset must deliver blazing performance, higher reliability, faster experimentation, stronger security, automated operations, and better cost excellence. These demands highlight the critical role of modern application architecture in determining whether these expectations are met, as follows:

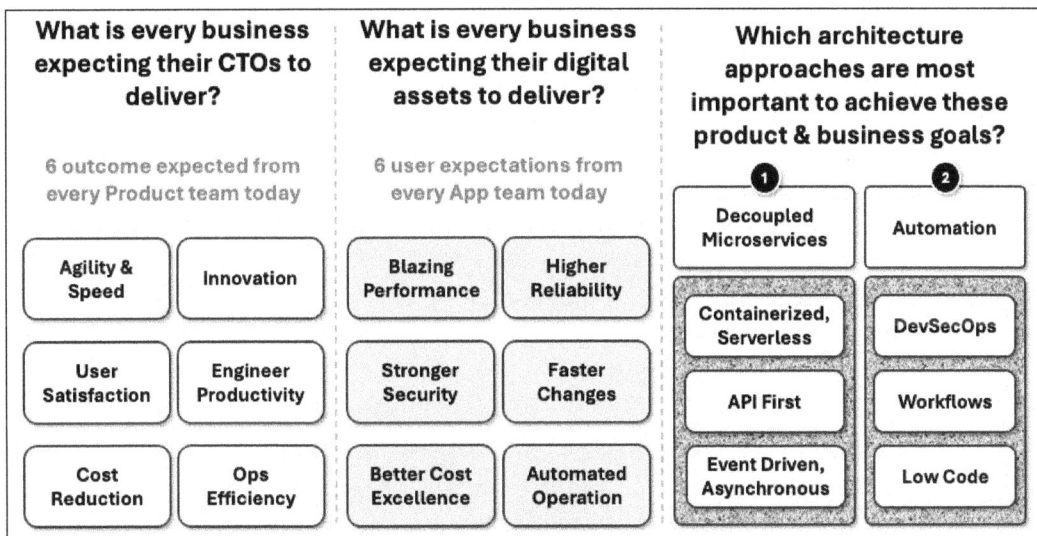

What is every business expecting their CTOs to deliver?		What is every business expecting their digital assets to deliver?		Which architecture approaches are most important to achieve these product & business goals?	
6 outcome expected from every Product team today		6 user expectations from every App team today		①	②
				Decoupled Microservices	Automation
Agility & Speed	Innovation	Blazing Performance	Higher Reliability	Containerized, Serverless	DevSecOps
User Satisfaction	Engineer Productivity	Stronger Security	Faster Changes	API First	Workflows
Cost Reduction	Ops Efficiency	Better Cost Excellence	Automated Operation	Event Driven, Asynchronous	Low Code

Figure 4.1: Expectations from CTOs, digital assets and architecture approaches that can deliver it

A significant portion of achieving these outcomes hinges on architectural and design decisions. Among the various modern architectural approaches, two stand out as particularly crucial: DDD with microservices and EDD. Decoupled microservices facilitate scalability and flexibility, while event-driven architectures support real-time processing and responsiveness. Additionally, leveraging containerized and serverless technologies, DevSecOps practices, and low-code workflows further enhances these architectures, ensuring they meet business demands efficiently and effectively. These strategies collectively enable organizations to build resilient, adaptable, and high-performing applications that align with contemporary business objectives and user expectations.

Principles of application definition and development

To meet the heightened expectations from businesses, the principles of app definition and development must be rooted in API-first and automation-driven methodologies. An API-First approach ensures that all internal and external communications are streamlined, standardized, and well-documented from the outset, promoting consistency and ease of integration. Automation, including DevSecOps and CI/CD pipelines, accelerates deployment cycles, enhances security, and ensures reliable operations. Emphasizing decoupled microservices and event-driven, asynchronous communication enables scalability and responsiveness, vital for modern digital assets. These principles ensure that applications are not only designed for today's demands but are also adaptable for future needs, ultimately driving innovation, agility, and operational excellence.

Integrating DDD with microservices

Integrating DDD with microservices is pivotal for creating scalable, maintainable, and robust applications. DDD focuses on defining and understanding the core business domains and subdomains, ensuring that the system's architecture aligns closely with business objectives and processes. By decomposing the system into decoupled microservices, each representing a distinct domain or subdomain, organizations can achieve higher modularity, allowing for independent development, deployment, and scaling. This approach not only enhances the system's agility and flexibility but also simplifies maintenance by isolating changes to specific services. Moreover, leveraging DDD principles helps in identifying the boundaries and interactions between microservices, ensuring clear API definitions and fostering seamless communication. This synergy between DDD and microservices leads to more resilient and adaptable applications, capable of evolving with changing business needs while maintaining high performance and reliability.

Let us take an example of a shopping cart application with a typical monolithic design. It will have all the functions below in a tightly coupled design, and they will reside within one codebase. This typically will include the following:

- **User interface**: Handles the presentation layer, displaying product catalogs, shopping carts, and user profiles.

- **Business logic**: Manages the core functionalities such as product searches, user authentication, shopping cart operations, order processing, payment processing, and inventory management.

- **Data access layer**: Interacts with the database to perform **Create, Read, Update, Delete** (**CRUD**) operations on various data entities such as products, users, orders, and inventory.

In a monolithic architecture, the tight coupling of all functionalities can significantly hinder agility and speed, as even small changes require extensive testing and redeployment of the entire application. This slows down innovation and reduces the ability to quickly roll out new features, impacting user satisfaction. The monolithic approach often leads to operational inefficiencies, as scaling the application to handle increased load is complex and costly. Moreover, maintaining a single, large codebase can strain engineer productivity as teams experience difficulties in managing dependencies and conflicts.

For instance, if the product catalog requires frequent updates or the payment processing needs enhancements, the entire application must be redeployed, leading to potential downtime and reduced reliability. The lack of modularity also complicates the implementation of automated operations and stronger security practices, as a security flaw in one part of the application can compromise the entire system.

Transitioning to a DDD design with microservices addresses these issues by decoupling the application's components, allowing for independent development, deployment, and scaling. This modular approach enhances agility and speed, as changes to one service do not impact others, fostering faster experimentation and innovation. Microservices can be scaled individually based on demand, leading to better cost excellence and operational efficiency. The isolation of services also improves reliability and security, as issues in one service do not affect others. Implementing principles such as *you build it, you run it* ensures that teams are responsible for the entire lifecycle of their services, promoting accountability and faster issue resolution. Additionally, organizing teams according to the *two-pizza team* rule, where each team is small enough to be fed with two pizzas, enhances focus and collaboration, resulting in higher engineer productivity.

The shopping cart application is decomposed into smaller, loosely coupled services in a DDD approach integrated with microservices. Each service represents a specific domain or subdomain and can be developed, deployed, and scaled independently. This structure promotes modularity, flexibility, and maintainability, as shown:

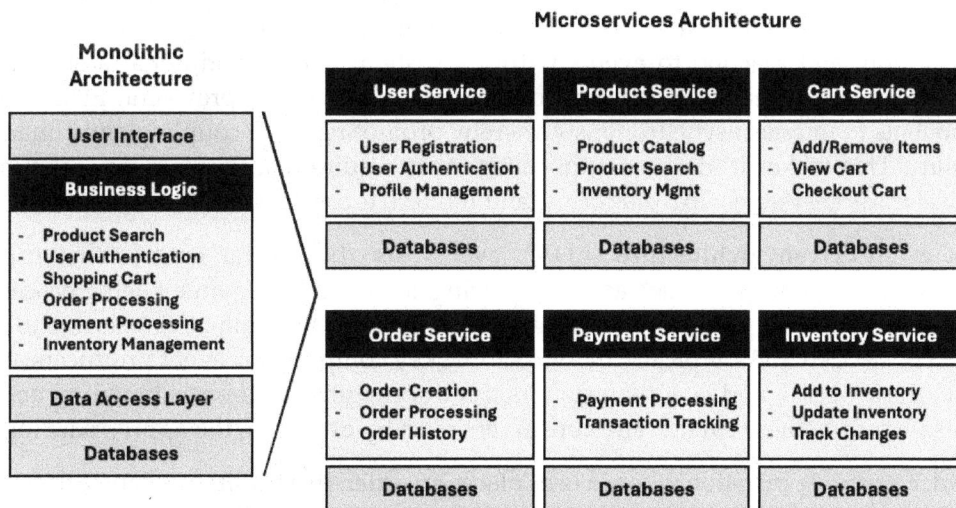

Figure 4.2: Difference between monolithic and microservices architecture

Key domains and their corresponding microservices might include the following:

- **User service**: Handles user registration, authentication, and profile management.

- **Product service**: Manages product catalog, searches, and inventory.

- **Cart service**: Manages shopping cart operations and check out.

- **Order service**: Handles order creation, processing, and history.

- **Payment service**: Manages payment processing and transactions.

- **Inventory service**: Updates and tracks inventory levels.

Each microservice has its own database, ensuring data encapsulation and reducing dependencies, as shown:

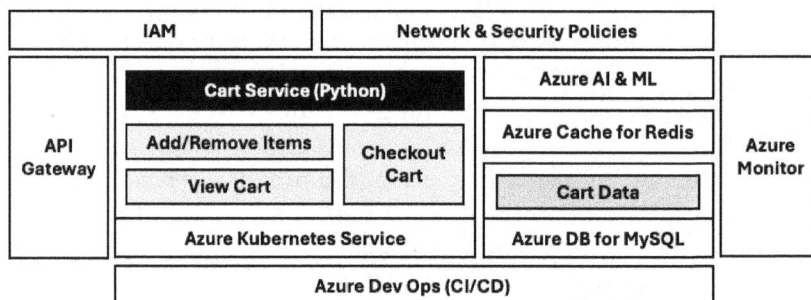

Figure 4.3: *Example microservices architecture of shopping cart application*

Implementing event-driven design

EDD is a powerful architectural approach used to build highly scalable, decoupled, and responsive systems. At its core, EDD revolves around the generation, detection, consumption, and reaction to events within a system. Unlike traditional architectures, where direct communication between components or services is prevalent, EDD enables components to interact asynchronously, thereby promoting loose coupling and enhancing flexibility. This makes it ideal for applications that require real-time processing, such as financial trading systems, IoT platforms, and modern e-commerce systems.

In an **event-driven architecture (EDA)**, events are the central entities that capture significant changes in state, such as a user placing an order, or a payment being processed. These events are then propagated throughout the system, allowing other services to react to them as needed. EDA typically involves three key components: event producers, event routers (or brokers), and event consumers. Producers generate events based on actions, routers distribute these events, and consumers react by executing the appropriate logic.

Consider a retail application where a user places an order. In a traditional setup, this action might trigger a series of synchronous API calls to other services like payment processing, inventory management, and shipping. This tight coupling can lead to performance bottlenecks and decreased fault tolerance. By adopting EDD, the order placement generates an event, such as *order placed*, which is broadcasted to an event broker (e.g., Kafka or Azure Event Grid). Various services, like payment, inventory, and shipping, can independently consume the event and process their respective actions without waiting on each other, improving responsiveness and resilience.

One of the most critical benefits of EDD is its ability to decouple microservices in distributed systems. Since the services interact through events rather than direct calls, they can evolve independently. This modularity enhances scalability, as services can be added, removed, or updated without significant disruptions to the overall application.

There are two popular EDD patterns, *event notification* and *event-carried state transfer*. In the event notification pattern, an event informs the system that something has occurred, but it does not carry the complete state of the event. Instead, services must query additional data if needed. In contrast, event-carried state transfer patterns allow the event to include all the necessary information for a service to react, minimizing dependencies between components and reducing latency.

Advantages of event-driven design

The following are some of the advantages of an EDD:

- **Scalability**: Services can scale independently as they are decoupled from synchronous interactions.

- **Fault isolation**: Failures in one service do not cascade into others, improving overall system resilience.

- **Real-time processing**: EDD supports real-time processing, enabling systems to respond immediately to critical events.

- **Improved developer productivity**: Developers can focus on specific event consumers or producers without worrying about system-wide dependencies.

Payment processing in an e-commerce platform

Imagine the following use case where an e-commerce platform with EDD is at its heart. When a user completes a purchase, an *Order Placed* event is triggered. This event is consumed by:

- A *payment service*, which processes the transaction and emits a *Payment Processed* event.

- An *inventory service*, which updates stock levels based on the order.

- A *shipping service*, which prepares for delivery.

Each service operates independently, processing events as they arrive. The modularity of this architecture allows for better fault tolerance, as issues in the payment service would not affect inventory or shipping. Furthermore, additional services can be introduced later, such as a *notification service* to send users real-time updates by simply subscribing to the same events.

Challenges in event-driven design

While EDD offers many benefits, there are challenges to consider:

- **Eventual consistency**: Since services communicate asynchronously, there may be delays in data synchronization across services, leading to eventual consistency rather than immediate consistency.

- **Complex debugging**: Tracking the flow of events through multiple services can be challenging, especially in large-scale distributed systems.

- **Idempotency**: Consumers must be designed to handle the same event more than once, as events might be re-delivered in case of network issues or system crashes.

By embracing event-driven design, modern applications can become more flexible, responsive, and scalable, aligning with the ever-evolving demands of today's business environments. However, like any architectural decision, it is essential to carefully evaluate the specific use cases and challenges to fully realize the potential of this design.

Orchestration and management with Kubernetes

Kubernetes, commonly referred to as K8s, is the leading orchestration platform for managing containerized applications in today's cloud-native world. As organizations move towards microservices and distributed architectures, Kubernetes provides the automation necessary for deployment, scaling, and operational management. Its role in orchestrating complex applications has made it a cornerstone of modern application architecture. By abstracting the underlying infrastructure, Kubernetes allows developers and operators to define the desired state of their applications, while the platform ensures this state is maintained, even in the face of failures or changes.

In this section, we will explore how Kubernetes fits into the broader cloud-native ecosystem, how it enables serverless computing models, facilitates integration services and API management, and enhances networking through service meshes.

Kubernetes and cloud-native ecosystems

Kubernetes is central to the cloud-native approach, which focuses on building scalable, resilient, and flexible applications designed to run on distributed infrastructures. In a cloud-native ecosystem, Kubernetes enables organizations to run their applications across various environments, on-premises, public cloud, or hybrid. It abstracts away the complexity of managing infrastructure by automating tasks such as container deployment, load balancing, scaling, and recovery, thus allowing teams to focus more on application development and less on infrastructure management.

Cloud-native ecosystems leverage Kubernetes to manage containerized applications in a way that is highly efficient and portable. For instance, using *Kubernetes clusters*, developers can manage the deployment of microservices at scale, ensuring that applications can handle increased traffic without requiring manual intervention. Kubernetes' built-in features, like *auto-scaling* and *self-healing*, ensure applications remain responsive, reliable, and optimized for performance.

Moreover, Kubernetes integrates well with a variety of cloud-native tools like *Prometheus* for monitoring, *Helm* for managing application configurations, and *Istio* for service meshes, making it a key player in the broader cloud-native landscape.

Kubernetes has revolutionized how modern applications are deployed and managed. As applications continue to grow in complexity, Kubernetes enables organizations to maintain agility and operational excellence, ensuring that services remain performant, secure, and highly available.

Serverless computing frameworks and FaaS

Kubernetes also supports *serverless computing frameworks* and **functions as a service (FaaS)**, which have become popular for running stateless, event-driven applications. While Kubernetes traditionally orchestrates long-running containers, it can also be adapted to serverless models through platforms such as *Knative*. Knative extends Kubernetes to manage the lifecycle of serverless functions, allowing developers to deploy event-driven workloads with ease.

Serverless computing frees developers from worrying about infrastructure provisioning, as compute resources are allocated dynamically based on the execution of functions. In this model, resources are consumed only when the function is invoked, optimizing both performance and cost. By using Kubernetes in conjunction with FaaS, organizations can run lightweight, stateless applications that scale automatically in response to events.

For example, an e-commerce site may use serverless functions to handle user-triggered events like *Add to Cart* or *Checkout*, executing them in response to customer actions without needing to maintain persistent servers. Kubernetes, with its ability to support FaaS frameworks, ensures that these functions are automatically scaled and managed, further enhancing the platform's utility in a modern, cloud-native ecosystem.

Designing integration services and API management

A crucial aspect of modern application architecture is the seamless integration of multiple services and APIs. Kubernetes facilitates this by providing robust mechanisms for deploying and managing *integration services* and *API management* solutions, which are essential for communication between microservices or between external applications and internal services.

APIs act as the connective tissue between various services, enabling them to exchange data and functionality. Kubernetes supports the deployment of API gateways, such as *Kong* or *Azure API Management*, which handle authentication, rate-limiting, and traffic routing for microservices. These API gateways enable consistent and secure communication across services, ensuring that requests are processed efficiently and securely.

Furthermore, Kubernetes supports the design and management of *integration services*, which allow applications to communicate across different platforms or environments. For instance, when connecting legacy systems with cloud-native applications, integration services deployed on Kubernetes can facilitate the smooth flow of data between them, translating protocols and managing workflows. Kubernetes' flexibility in deploying these services enables organizations to manage complex, multi-service applications with greater ease and reliability.

Additionally, the platform's declarative approach to configuration allows teams to define API policies and integration workflows as code, ensuring consistency and version control across environments. This enables seamless updates and scaling of services, maintaining system reliability even as integration points evolve.

Utilizing service meshes for robust networking

As applications grow in complexity and adopt microservices architectures, managing service-to-service communication becomes challenging. This is where *service meshes* come into play, and Kubernetes is an ideal platform for integrating them. A service mesh provides a dedicated infrastructure layer for controlling communication between services, enhancing security, observability, and traffic management.

Istio, one of the most popular service mesh frameworks, integrates seamlessly with Kubernetes. It helps manage communication between microservices by handling service discovery, load balancing, encryption, and failure recovery. Istio abstracts these concerns away from the application logic, allowing developers to focus on business functionality while the mesh ensures robust communication.

With Istio, Kubernetes clusters gain additional capabilities, such as *circuit-breaking* (to prevent cascading failures), *traffic splitting* (to enable blue/green or canary deployments), and *end-to-end encryption* for secure service communication. Service meshes also improve observability by providing detailed metrics on service interactions, which helps in identifying and resolving issues related to performance or failures.

In a typical microservices-based application, traffic management and security are critical. Kubernetes, combined with service meshes, ensures that microservices communicate efficiently and securely without manual intervention. For instance, in a financial application where sensitive data is exchanged between services, the service mesh ensures secure communication through mutual TLS, while also monitoring traffic for anomalies that could indicate performance degradation or security breaches.

Strategies for runtime and provisioning

Efficient runtime management and provisioning are vital components of any modern application architecture. In today's cloud-driven environments, organizations must ensure that their applications are not only running smoothly but also optimized for performance, security, and scalability. Strategies for managing runtime and provisioning include careful orchestration of containers, efficient handling of storage needs, and ensuring robust security policies across the network. These elements play a crucial role in delivering high availability and operational efficiency.

In this section, we explore key strategies that enable effective runtime and provisioning, including managing containers and container registries, implementing cloud-native storage solutions, and ensuring security with network policies.

Managing containers and container registries

Containers are the fundamental building blocks of modern cloud-native applications. They package an application's code, dependencies, and runtime into a lightweight unit that can be easily deployed across different environments. However, as the number of containers grows, managing them at scale becomes complex. This is where *container orchestration platforms* like *Kubernetes*, and *container registries*, come into play.

A *container registry* acts as a repository for storing and distributing container images, ensuring that the correct versions of applications and services are always available for deployment. Kubernetes, for example, pulls these images from a registry (such as *Docker Hub, Azure Container Registry*, or *Google Container Registry*) when it needs to deploy or scale an application. Managing container images across multiple environments and teams requires a registry strategy that ensures consistency, security, and version control.

Key considerations for managing containers and their registries include the following:

- **Versioning**: Ensuring that all deployed container images are versioned, making it easier to roll back to a previous version in case of failure or bugs.

- **Security**: Implementing strict access controls and scanning container images for vulnerabilities before they are deployed to production.

- **Automated deployment**: Leveraging **continuous integration/continuous deployment (CI/CD)** pipelines to automate the process of building, testing, and deploying containers.

Containers provide agility and scalability, but without proper registry management, organizations may face challenges in maintaining consistency across environments. By leveraging private registries, implementing automated vulnerability scanning, and ensuring secure image handling, teams can streamline container deployment processes while maintaining control over application lifecycles.

Implementing cloud-native storage solutions

While containers are ephemeral and stateless, modern applications often require persistent data storage. Implementing *cloud-native storage solutions* is critical for managing stateful applications and ensuring that data is accessible, reliable, and secure. Kubernetes offers several mechanisms for managing storage, including **Persistent Volumes** (**PVs**) and **Persistent Volume Claims** (**PVCs**), which decouple storage from the underlying infrastructure, making it easier to manage across environments.

Cloud-native storage solutions, such as *Azure Blob Storage, Amazon S3*, and *Google Cloud Storage*, provide scalable, highly available storage options that can be integrated directly into Kubernetes environments. These services offer a range of storage types, from block storage for databases to object storage for unstructured data, each optimized for different use cases

Key strategies for implementing cloud-native storage include:

- **Dynamic provisioning**: Kubernetes allows for dynamic storage provisioning, meaning that storage is allocated automatically when a persistent volume claim is made, streamlining operations.

- **Data redundancy and backup**: Implementing redundancy policies to ensure data is replicated across multiple zones or regions, minimizing the risk of data loss in case of failure.

- **Performance tuning**: Choosing the right storage class for the application based on performance needs, such as using SSD-backed storage for high I/O applications or standard HDD for archival storage.

Cloud-native storage solutions provide the flexibility and scalability necessary for running data-intensive applications in distributed environments. Organizations can handle large-scale, data-driven applications with greater ease and efficiency by automating provisioning and ensuring that storage is optimized for performance.

Ensuring security with network policies

In any distributed system, security is a primary concern, and network security is particularly critical in cloud-native architectures. Kubernetes provides the ability to define *network policies* that control how pods and services communicate with each other within the cluster and with external networks. These policies are essential for segmenting services, reducing the attack surface, and ensuring that only authorized traffic is allowed.

Network policies are enforced by Kubernetes using network plugins, such as *Calico*, which provide control over network traffic at the pod level. These policies help enforce security boundaries by specifying which pods are allowed to communicate and under what conditions. For example, you might create a policy that ensures only the front-end service can access the back-end database, blocking any other services from making direct connections to sensitive data.

Key considerations for implementing network policies include the following:

- **Pod-to-pod communication**: Defining rules that restrict communication between pods based on namespaces, labels, or network policies, ensuring that only essential traffic flows between services.

- **External access control**: Securing ingress and egress traffic by defining policies that control which external services can access the application and which outbound traffic is permitted.

- **Monitoring and auditing**: Continuously monitoring network traffic to identify anomalies and ensure that network policies are updated as new services or pods are added to the cluster.

By implementing robust network policies, organizations can significantly reduce the risk of unauthorized access and ensure that sensitive data and services are isolated from potential threats. This is particularly important in environments that handle personal or financial data, where compliance with regulations like *GDPR* or *HIPAA* requires stringent network security measures.

Strategies for cost efficiency in provisioning

Provisioning resources in the cloud is often associated with cost, and as applications scale, managing these costs becomes increasingly important. Kubernetes helps optimize resource utilization through its *autoscaling* capabilities, allowing organizations to provision resources dynamically based on actual demand.

One of the most effective strategies for cost-efficient provisioning is to leverage *horizontal* and *vertical pod autoscalers*. Horizontal autoscaling adjusts the number of pods running in response to changes in application demand, while vertical autoscaling adjusts the resources (CPU, memory) allocated to each pod based on its usage patterns. This ensures that applications always have the necessary resources to meet performance requirements without over-provisioning, thus minimizing costs.

Additionally, adopting *serverless computing models* like *Kubernetes*-based serverless frameworks (Knative) can help reduce provisioning costs by automatically scaling resources to zero when they are not in use. This model is especially beneficial for applications with unpredictable or spiky traffic patterns, such as batch-processing jobs or event-driven workloads.

Key strategies for achieving cost efficiency include:

- **Resource quotas**: Setting resource quotas in Kubernetes to limit the amount of CPU, memory, or storage that a namespace or application can consume, preventing runaway resource usage.

- **Spot instances**: Leveraging cloud provider features like *AWS Spot Instances* or *Azure Low-Priority VMs* to provision non-critical workloads at significantly lower costs.

- **Container optimization**: Ensuring that containers are lightweight and optimized for performance, reducing the overall resource requirements and enabling more efficient infrastructure utilization.

Efficient runtime and provisioning strategies are essential for ensuring that modern applications run smoothly and cost-effectively.

Observability and systems analysis techniques

In modern cloud-native architectures, observability and systems analysis are critical for ensuring that applications remain performant, reliable, and secure. With applications now distributed across multiple microservices and infrastructure layers, traditional monitoring tools are no longer sufficient to provide visibility into complex environments. Observability goes beyond simple monitoring by enabling real-time insights into how applications behave in production and how issues can be proactively identified and resolved. Techniques like chaos engineering and continuous optimization play vital roles in making systems resilient and efficient.

In this section, we will explore key techniques for enhancing observability and systems analysis, including applying chaos engineering for reliability and continuous optimization for performance.

Applying chaos engineering for reliability

Chaos engineering is a method of improving system reliability by intentionally introducing failures into the system to observe how it reacts under stress. The goal of chaos engineering is to proactively identify weaknesses and ensure that systems can handle disruptions without impacting end-user experiences. By simulating failure conditions in a controlled environment, teams can ensure that their applications are resilient to real-world incidents, such as network outages, service crashes, or infrastructure failures.

In a microservices architecture, where services are distributed across multiple containers and nodes, even small failures can cascade and cause significant system-wide disruptions.

Chaos engineering helps teams test the reliability of their system under various failure scenarios, such as the following:

- **Killing random services**: Shutting down random microservices to evaluate if the system can continue to function without them.

- **Network latency simulation**: Introducing artificial delays in network communication to assess how services behave when network performance degrades.

- **Resource starvation**: Limiting CPU, memory, or disk usage for certain services to see how they handle resource constraints.

One of the most well-known tools for chaos engineering is *Chaos Monkey*, which randomly terminates instances within a cloud environment to test resilience. By employing chaos engineering practices, organizations can build fault-tolerant systems that are better equipped to recover from unexpected failures.

For example, a streaming service might use chaos engineering to test whether user playback is interrupted when a backend media service fails. By gradually introducing failures, the team can ensure that failover mechanisms and redundancies are correctly configured, allowing the system to maintain uptime during disruptions.

Continuous optimization for performance

In modern cloud-native environments, performance optimization is an ongoing process rather than a one-time effort. As traffic patterns, workloads, and resource requirements fluctuate, organizations must continuously monitor and adjust their infrastructure and application configurations to meet evolving performance demands. *Continuous optimization* focuses on regularly analyzing system metrics and making iterative improvements to ensure that applications remain efficient, responsive, and cost-effective.

One of the key components of continuous optimization is *automatic scaling*. Kubernetes provides tools like **Horizontal Pod Autoscaling (HPA)** and **Vertical Pod Autoscaling (VPA)** to adjust the number of running pods and resource allocations based on real-time demand. This allows applications to scale up during peak loads and scale down when demand decreases, optimizing resource usage and minimizing operational costs.

Another critical aspect of continuous optimization is *performance profiling*. By collecting detailed metrics on application response times, CPU utilization, memory usage, and disk I/O, teams can identify performance bottlenecks and inefficiencies. Tools like *Prometheus* and *Grafana* offer powerful visualization and alerting capabilities, helping teams monitor these metrics in real-time and quickly respond to performance degradations.

Some techniques for continuous optimization include:

- **Load testing**: Simulating high-traffic scenarios to identify the maximum capacity of the system and pinpoint areas where optimization is needed.

- **Resource allocation tuning**: Adjusting CPU and memory requests/limits for containers based on real-time performance data to prevent over-provisioning or under-utilization.

- **Database query optimization**: Analyzing database performance and fine-tuning slow queries to improve response times for data-intensive applications.

By continuously monitoring and optimizing performance, organizations can ensure that their applications remain responsive under varying conditions, ultimately delivering better user experiences and reducing infrastructure costs.

Techniques for log aggregation and tracing

As microservices architectures become more complex, tracking the flow of requests across distributed systems is essential for both observability and troubleshooting. *Log aggregation* and *tracing* are key techniques for gaining visibility into how individual services interact, ensuring that issues can be identified and resolved quickly.

In a microservices environment, each service generates logs that detail its actions, errors, and events. However, managing logs across multiple services and nodes can be challenging. Tools like *Elastic Stack* (*ELK*) or *Fluentd* are used to aggregate logs from different services into a central repository, making it easier to search, analyze, and visualize log data. This centralized log management enables teams to track down the root cause of issues and monitor system health.

Tracing goes a step further by providing end-to-end visibility into how requests travel across services. With distributed tracing tools like *Jaeger* or *OpenTelemetry*, teams can trace the entire lifecycle of a request, from its entry point to its final destination. This helps pinpoint performance bottlenecks and failure points within the application stack, allowing teams to optimize service interactions and improve overall system reliability.

For example, in an e-commerce platform, tracing can help identify why certain product searches are slow by showing the flow of requests through the search service, database, and recommendation engine. If one service is lagging, the tracing data will provide insights into where and why the delay is happening, enabling teams to resolve it efficiently.

Anomaly detection for proactive issue resolution

Effective observability systems not only monitor applications in real time but also proactively alert teams when issues arise. *Alerting* and *anomaly detection* tools provide automated mechanisms for identifying unusual behavior or performance anomalies before they escalate into critical failures.

By setting up *threshold-based alerts* (e.g., CPU usage exceeding 90% or response times above 500ms), teams can be notified as soon as a metric crosses a defined boundary. More advanced *anomaly detection* leverages ML algorithms to detect patterns in system behavior, flagging deviations that may not align with predefined thresholds but could indicate potential problems.

Tools like *PagerDuty, Prometheus Alertmanager,* and *Datadog* enable teams to configure and manage alerts, ensuring that the right personnel are notified when issues arise. This allows organizations to respond quickly to outages, slowdowns, or security threats, minimizing downtime and impact on end-users.

Proactive alerting ensures that issues are addressed before they affect the broader system, improving uptime and reliability. For example, in a banking application, alerting might be configured to trigger when transaction processing times exceed normal thresholds, signaling a potential issue with the payment service before it impacts customer experience.

In cloud-native architectures, observability and systems analysis are essential for maintaining the health, performance, and reliability of applications. These techniques enable teams to detect issues early, resolve them quickly, and keep applications running smoothly, ensuring that end-users experience seamless performance and reliability.

Architectural pitfalls and how to avoid them

In the world of modern application architecture, it is easy to fall into traps that can make systems unwieldy, expensive, or difficult to maintain. This section explores some of the most common architectural pitfalls and problems that architects and developers face repeatedly, often in pursuit of best practices or cutting-edge trends. Each pitfall is paired with practical advice to help readers make informed decisions and design resilient, maintainable systems that avoid these issues.

Pitfall of excessive fragmentation

While microservices architectures offer many benefits, such as scalability, agility, and ease of deployment, they can also introduce a major drawback: excessive fragmentation. In some cases, teams design systems with an overly granular approach, creating dozens, or even hundreds, of microservices, each with a narrowly defined function. The result? High inter-service communication overhead, increased maintenance complexity, and challenges in tracking data flow and dependencies across services.

Consider a retail application that divides functionality into microservices for everything from product cataloging, order processing, and payment, down to minute features like calculating shipping costs or applying promotional discounts. If each function is managed as a separate microservice, the dependencies and data exchanges between services can become overwhelming.

When designing microservices, prioritize bounded contexts over excessive granularity. Group-related functions that align with a single business domain (as in DDD) into cohesive services. Adopting a principle of *macroservices*, where each service is responsible for a broader slice of functionality, can strike a better balance, reducing inter-service chatter while preserving modularity. Avoid creating microservices just for the sake of it; instead, evaluate each service's independence and importance to the business workflow.

Event-driven design challenges

EDD allows applications to handle asynchronous workflows and react to real-time events, making it ideal for modern, reactive systems. However, EDD can make debugging and tracing challenging, especially in large systems where events cascade through multiple services. Tracking down the origin of a fault or understanding the sequence of events can become complex, especially when events fail or do not arrive in the expected order.

For example, in an e-commerce platform, a customer's order triggers multiple events across various services, inventory updates, payment processing, and shipping. If an error occurs in one of these downstream services, tracing it back to the originating event (the order placement) can be difficult.

To manage EDD complexity, incorporate **distributed tracing** and **correlation IDs** across your event-based workflows. Tools like *OpenTelemetry*, *Jaeger*, or *Azure Monitor* can help trace events across services, giving you visibility into each step and enabling faster debugging. Also, establish **clear retry policies** for handling event failures and ensure idempotency in event consumers to prevent repeated processing. By proactively managing these aspects, you can maintain control over asynchronous workflows.

Cost implications of serverless models and autoscaling

Serverless computing and autoscaling are attractive because they reduce upfront infrastructure costs and allow resources to scale dynamically based on demand. However, while serverless functions and autoscaled services offer flexibility, they can lead to unpredictable costs, especially when handling spiky or sustained high-traffic patterns. Without careful monitoring, costs can escalate quickly, outpacing the budget and reducing the benefits of the cloud-native approach.

A media streaming platform implements autoscaling to handle high traffic during peak hours. However, misconfigured autoscaling policies allow for aggressive scaling during a live event, leading to ballooning costs without a proportional increase in revenue.

Carefully configure autoscaling policies to balance performance and cost. Use *cost monitors* and *budget alerts* in cloud platforms to keep track of usage. Establish *scaling limits* to prevent runaway costs and consider mixing serverless and traditional compute resources (e.g., containerized services) for high-demand or long-running processes that benefit from sustained resource allocation. Additionally, conducting regular *usage audits* and adjusting policies based on historical data can help maintain a predictable cost structure.

Over-engineering in the name of future-proofing

Aiming for scalability or future-proofing is crucial, but over-engineering can lead to complex, bloated systems that are hard to maintain, costly to operate, and ultimately less agile. Sometimes, teams overestimate future needs, adding layers of abstraction or extra infrastructure that are either unnecessary or would not be used. This tendency to *plan for the future* can create substantial technical debt and limit agility.

A small SaaS startup builds its application on a complex multi-cloud deployment with advanced load balancing and a global failover system, anticipating rapid expansion. In reality, the company's traffic and resource requirements remain manageable on a single cloud provider, making the initial setup more costly and complex than necessary.

Start small and build incrementally. Use a lean **minimum viable product** (**MVP**) approach, adding complexity only when proven necessary. Regularly revisit architectural decisions and be open to refactoring as real requirements evolve. When scaling is truly needed, adopt *elastic infrastructure* that can grow with demand rather than build out complexity prematurely. Remember, simplicity often leads to better maintainability, reduced costs, and faster development cycles.

Avoiding architectural pitfalls

To help guide your architecture decisions, here is a checklist of best practices to avoid common pitfalls:

- **Right-size microservices** by grouping related functionalities and adhering to bounded contexts, balancing modularity with manageability.

- **Ensure observability in event-driven systems** with tracing, correlation IDs, and monitoring tools to streamline debugging.

- **Optimize serverless and autoscaling policies** by setting cost thresholds, monitoring usage, and mixing compute models to avoid runaway costs.

- **Adopt a lean, incremental approach** to scalability and future-proofing, avoiding over-engineering that can bloat systems and increase technical debt.

Role of AI/ML in modern architecture

Artificial intelligence (**AI**) and **machine learning** (**ML**) are reshaping the landscape of software architecture, introducing new ways to enhance system optimization, performance, and security. As applications increasingly rely on data-driven decisions, integrating AI and ML becomes crucial in driving operational efficiency, improving user experiences, and automating complex processes. This section explores how AI and ML influence modern architecture, from system optimization and hardware advancements to enhanced observability and monitoring.

AI-driven system optimization

AI and ML models can dynamically optimize various aspects of an application's performance, security, and resource utilization, providing an unprecedented level of adaptability. Traditional systems rely on predefined rules for scaling, monitoring, and resource allocation. In contrast, AI-driven architectures use real-time data to continuously learn and adjust system behaviors in response to changing workloads, user interactions, and potential threats.

In cloud environments, AI models can predict demand spikes based on historical data and automatically adjust resources, ensuring consistent performance without manual intervention. Similarly, ML models can learn the baseline performance metrics of applications and identify anomalies that signal issues like server overloads or performance degradation, optimizing resource allocation in real-time.

To enable AI-driven optimization, organizations can use *reinforcement learning models* that learn optimal resource management strategies over time. Pairing these models with *predictive analytics* allows systems to anticipate and prepare for demand, thus optimizing performance, reducing latency, and maintaining cost-efficiency. Tools such as *Azure AI* and *Amazon SageMaker* offer robust platforms for integrating AI models into cloud-native applications, making it easier to incorporate data-driven optimization in scalable architectures.

Emergence of AI-optimized hardware and tools

As AI and ML workloads become more common, new hardware and software tools have emerged to support the computational intensity of these applications. Traditional CPUs are often insufficient for AI workloads, leading to the development of specialized AI-optimized hardware, such as **Tensor Processing Units (TPUs)**, **Graphics Processing Units (GPUs)**, and **Intelligence Processing Units (IPUs)**. These processing units are designed to handle the parallel computations required for AI models, significantly boosting performance and efficiency for tasks like deep learning and large-scale data processing.

- **AI-optimized hardware**: Companies like *NVIDIA, AMD, Microsoft, Google, AWS, and Intel* are leading the charge with processors that accelerate AI applications. **NVIDIA's GPUs**, including the latest H100 and B200 Blackwell architecture-based accelerators, are widely used in ML, enabling faster training and inference for deep learning models. **AMD's MI300 series** provides **high-bandwidth memory (HBM3)** and AI compute cores optimized for both HPC and AI tasks. **Google's TPUs**, specifically designed for TensorFlow, provide high-performance computing for complex neural networks, particularly in large-scale applications. Additionally, **Intel's Gaudi AI accelerators** are emerging as cost-efficient alternatives for AI training and inference workloads.

- **AI frameworks and tools**: Software frameworks like *TensorFlow Extended* (TFX), *PyTorch Lightning*, *JAX*, and *Hugging Face Transformers* support high-performance

AI development by providing tools for data pipeline automation, model training, and scalable deployment. Additionally, platforms like *Azure AI Foundry, AutoGen for agentic development, LangChain,* and *LangGraph* enable developers to build AI agents with reasoning, planning, and execution capabilities. Microsoft's **Azure Machine Learning** and **Azure AI Studio** streamline AI model development and deployment, integrating with **OpenAI APIs and fine-tuning services**. Similarly, **Google Vertex AI and AWS Bedrock** provide comprehensive ML model management, including foundation model customization and inference optimization. These tools allow software development teams to efficiently build, train, and deploy AI applications and intelligent agents into production systems.

- **AI hardware acceleration with CUDA and specialized accelerators**: NVIDIA **Compute Unified Device Architecture** (**CUDA**) and **Radeon Open Compute** (**ROCm**) by **AMD** have revolutionized AI acceleration by enabling highly parallelized computing across GPUs. CUDA has become the dominant platform for AI developers, providing deep integration with ML frameworks like *TensorFlow* and *PyTorch*. Additionally, dedicated AI accelerators such as *NVIDIA TensorRT, Habana Gaudi,* and *Cerebras Wafer-Scale Engine (WSE-3)* offer specialized capabilities optimized for model inference, reducing latency and power consumption while maximizing throughput.

Selecting the right combination of AI-optimized hardware and software tools is critical when designing AI-driven architectures. Consider the model's training and inference needs, data throughput requirements, and cost constraints. Leveraging cloud providers' managed AI services, such as *NVIDIA AI Enterprise on Azure, AWS Trainium,* and *Google Cloud TPU V5e,* can provide scalability without the need to invest in expensive on-premise hardware, making AI accessible for both experimentation and production.

Architecture patterns in Gen AI and Agent systems

Emerging architectural design archetypes for **generative AI** (**Gen AI**) and multi-agent systems are reshaping the development of intelligent applications.

Key patterns include the following:

- **Agentic design patterns**: These patterns enhance AI autonomy and problem-solving by incorporating:

    o **Reflection**: Enabling AI agents to iteratively assess and refine their outputs, improving reasoning and analytical performance. For instance, in a code generation task, an AI agent can generate code, review it, and refine it based on identified errors or inefficiencies, leading to higher quality outcomes.

    o **Tool use**: Allowing agents to interact with external tools or APIs to extend functionality. For example, an AI agent can utilize a database API to fetch real-time data, enhancing its responses with up-to-date information.

- o **Planning**: Facilitating strategic decision-making through goal-oriented action sequences. An AI agent can decompose a complex task into manageable steps, plan the execution sequence, and adjust the plan dynamically based on intermediate results.

- o **Multi-agent collaboration**: Coordinating multiple agents to work together on complex tasks. In a customer service scenario, one agent could handle user inquiries while another processes transaction, working in tandem to provide efficient service.

- **Hierarchical agent architectures**: Implementing layered structures where high-level agents oversee task delegation to specialized sub-agents, improving efficiency and scalability in complex problem-solving scenarios. For example, a top-level agent could manage overall project goals, delegating specific tasks like data analysis or content creation to specialized sub-agents.

- **Decentralized multi-agent systems**: Designing systems where autonomous agents operate without a central controller, enabling robust and adaptable solutions in dynamic environments. In such systems, agents can negotiate and collaborate to achieve common goals, adapting to changes without centralized oversight.

- **Conversation patterns in multi-agent systems**: Effective communication is crucial for coordinated problem-solving in multi-agent systems.

Key conversation patterns include the following:

- o **Request-response**: One agent requests information or action, and another provides the necessary response, enabling straightforward exchanges. For example, a data retrieval agent may request specific information, which a database agent then supplies.

- o **Negotiation**: Agents engage in dialogues to reach mutual agreements, often involving proposals and counter-proposals to resolve conflicts or allocate tasks. This is essential in scenarios where resources are limited, and agents must decide how to share them effectively.

- o **Coordination**: Agents share intentions and plans to synchronize actions, ensuring cohesive efforts toward shared objectives. In a manufacturing setting, multiple robotic agents might coordinate their actions to assemble a product efficiently.

- o **Information sharing**: Agents disseminate knowledge or data to others, enhancing collective understanding and decision-making capabilities. For instance, if one agent learns of a change in the environment, it can inform others to adapt accordingly.

- o **Delegation**: An agent assigns tasks to others, establishing a hierarchical workflow to manage complex activities efficiently. A supervisory agent might delegate specific subtasks to specialized agents to leverage their expertise.

AI in observability and monitoring

Observability is essential in distributed systems for understanding system health, detecting anomalies, and maintaining uptime. Traditional monitoring relies on pre-defined metrics and thresholds, which can be rigid and limited in detecting subtle or emerging issues.

By incorporating machine learning into observability, systems can autonomously learn from historical data, identify patterns, and detect anomalies, providing a proactive approach to monitoring as follows:

- **Anomaly detection**: AI can analyze system metrics, such as CPU usage, memory, network traffic, and latency, to identify anomalies that may indicate potential issues. Unlike threshold-based alerts, which may miss more nuanced patterns, ML-based anomaly detection identifies deviations that reflect subtle performance issues, misconfigurations, or security threats.

- **Predictive maintenance**: ML also enables predictive maintenance by identifying conditions that precede system failures. For example, AI models can analyze disk health, server utilization, and network latency trends to predict when components are likely to fail, triggering preemptive actions to prevent downtime.

- **Log analysis**: Analyzing logs across distributed systems is a time-intensive task that AI can streamline. ML models can identify common error patterns, correlate logs across services, and provide insights that help teams quickly isolate and resolve issues. Tools like *Splunk*, *Elastic Stack (ELK)*, and *Datadog* integrate ML-based log analysis, offering root-cause analysis and trend identification without human intervention.

To incorporate AI in observability, consider using *ML-enabled observability platforms* that integrate easily with existing infrastructure. Platforms like *Dynatrace* and *Datadog* leverage AI for anomaly detection and log analysis, providing real-time insights with minimal setup. For in-house solutions, using open-source tools such as *Prometheus* with custom ML models can give teams more control and customization in monitoring complex systems.

Actionable checklist for architects

As modern applications grow in complexity, having a structured approach is essential to deliver systems that are scalable, resilient, and aligned with business goals. This checklist provides a practical guide for architects to ensure they cover key considerations when designing, deploying, and managing applications in today's fast-paced digital landscape.

Defining core business domains

Understanding and aligning with the business's core functions is foundational to designing effective architectures. By applying DDD principles, you can create services that are tightly coupled with business goals, enabling better modularity, maintainability, and alignment with stakeholder needs, as shown:

- **Identify business domains and boundaries**: Collaborate with business stakeholders to identify key business processes and domains (e.g., sales, payments, inventory). Define boundaries that separate these domains, ensuring each service reflects a specific business capability.

- **Create a domain model**: Develop a shared language and domain model with input from both technical and business teams. This model will serve as a blueprint for how each service operates, interacts, and evolves.

- **Map business goals to service boundaries**: Ensure each microservice or module is responsible for a well-defined business function. Aligning services with business domains simplifies maintenance, supports agile development, and allows for independent scaling and updates.

Choosing the right architecture for performance goals

Selecting the correct architectural style, whether *event-driven, microservices, serverless, or monolithic*, should be guided by the application's specific requirements for performance, scalability, and operational needs, as follows:

- **Analyze workload characteristics**: Determine if the application has real-time, batch, or high-availability requirements. For instance, event-driven architectures work well with real-time and asynchronous processing, while serverless suit variable or event-based workloads.

- **Match architecture with application goals**: If low latency is critical, consider architectures that support fast in-memory processing or close-to-edge computing. Microservices provide flexibility and modularity but may add complexity if overused. Serverless is ideal for functions that do not need persistent resources.

- **Avoid over-engineering**: Consider starting with a simpler architecture, such as a monolith or microservice, and evolve as requirements dictate. Choosing the right architecture from the start helps avoid costly refactoring and unnecessary complexity.

Scalability and fault tolerance

Modern applications should be able to handle variable loads and recover gracefully from failures. Building scalability and fault tolerance into the architecture ensures reliability and performance even under high traffic or unexpected disruptions as follows:

- **Design for independent scaling**: Ensure each service can be scaled independently. This is especially critical in microservices or containerized environments where individual components may experience different traffic patterns.

- **Implement redundancy and failover mechanisms**: Set up redundancy for critical services and establish failover mechanisms that reroute traffic to healthy instances in the event of a failure. Leverage cloud-native features like *auto-scaling* and *load balancing.*

- **Leverage circuit breakers and retry logic**: Use circuit breakers to prevent cascading failures when a service becomes unresponsive. Implement retry mechanisms for transient errors and timeouts to improve fault tolerance and application resilience.

- **Test with chaos engineering**: Regularly stress-test your application using chaos engineering tools like *Chaos Monkey* to simulate failures and evaluate system responses. This ensures the system is prepared to handle unexpected issues in production.

Security and compliance

Embedding security and regulatory compliance into each layer of the architecture is non-negotiable. As threats evolve and regulations become more stringent, a proactive approach to security and compliance helps safeguard data and maintain trust.

The following are the key security and compliance practices to embed into your AI architecture, ensuring data protection, regulatory adherence, and resilience against evolving threats:

- **Apply the principle of least privilege**: Limit access rights for users, applications, and services to only what is necessary. Use **role-based access control (RBAC)** to manage permissions across services.

- **Integrate security early**: Employ **DevSecOps practices** to integrate security checks throughout the development lifecycle, from code review and vulnerability scanning to automated testing.

- **Data encryption and secure communication**: Use encryption for both data at rest and in transit, ensuring compliance with standards like TLS/SSL. Secure API communications with authentication methods such as *OAuth* and *JWT tokens.*

- **Stay compliant with industry standards**: Identify the relevant standards for your application (e.g., GDPR, HIPAA, PCI-DSS) and ensure each component adheres to these regulations. Document security practices and establish regular audits to remain compliant as requirements evolve.

Observability

Effective observability provides insight into system health, performance, and troubleshooting, making it crucial for managing and improving distributed applications. Implementing *monitoring, logging, and tracing* is essential for maintaining visibility and operational control.

The following are the key observability practices to ensure system health, performance optimization, and efficient troubleshooting in distributed applications:

- **Implement distributed tracing**: Use tools like *Jaeger* or *Zipkin* to trace requests as they move through microservices, allowing you to identify bottlenecks and optimize response times.

- **Enable centralized logging**: Centralize logs across services with platforms like *Elasticsearch, Logstash, Kibana (ELK)*, or *Splunk*. This streamlines log analysis, making it easier to detect issues, trace events, and identify root causes.

- **Set up metrics and alerts**: Use monitoring tools like *Prometheus* or *Datadog* to track key metrics (CPU, memory, latency) and set up alerts for threshold breaches. Establish alerting policies based on critical metrics to prevent minor issues from escalating.

- **Leverage machine learning for anomaly detection**: Integrate machine learning for anomaly detection to proactively identify irregularities in system behavior. Tools like *Dynatrace* and *Datadog AI* offer ML-based anomaly detection, which can predict and prevent performance issues before they impact users.

Architectural governance and technical debt management

For seasoned architects, governance and managing technical debt are critical aspects of sustainable architecture.

The following are the recommendations for architectural governance and technical debt management to maintain consistency, control service evolution, and ensure long-term scalability:

- **Governance policies**: Define guidelines for service design, data ownership, and API standards to ensure architectural consistency and avoid sprawl. Establishing a governance model helps ensure services evolve in a controlled way, aligning with broader organizational standards.

- **Technical debt tracking and refactoring**: Include guidance on managing and tracking technical debt as a standard part of the architecture process. Regular refactoring schedules and debt tracking tools (e.g., SonarQube for code quality) can help mitigate accumulated technical debt before it impacts scalability or performance.

Data strategy and data flow management

Experienced architects often emphasize a strong data strategy as core to architecture, particularly as data requirements have evolved with advanced analytics and ML.

The following are the key data strategy and flow management practices to ensure efficient, scalable, and compliant data handling in modern architectures:

- **Data ownership and domain-based data management**: Define clear data ownership by domain, ensuring that each service only accesses the data it requires. Domain-driven data strategy is especially important for architectures involving microservices or distributed systems, where loose coupling and data autonomy are crucial.

- **Data flow and consistency models**: Explain strategies for managing data consistency across distributed systems. For instance, consider when to apply eventual consistency over strict consistency and discuss approaches like the Saga pattern or **Command Query Responsibility Segregation (CQRS)** to handle complex data workflows.

- **Data privacy and sovereignty**: Many architects today are concerned with privacy regulations and data sovereignty requirements. Guidance on implementing region-based data storage, encryption, and data anonymization would provide seasoned architects with insights on meeting regulatory and customer privacy needs.

Resilience and disaster recovery planning

While fault tolerance is covered, a deeper dive into resilience and DR planning will resonate with senior architects who focus on high availability and business continuity.

The following are the recommendations for resilience and disaster recovery planning:

- **Multi-region and multi-cloud resilience**: Include strategies for ensuring availability in multi-region or multi-cloud setups, as many architects face the challenge of providing resilience across geographical regions. Outline considerations for handling regional outages and balancing between cloud providers for redundancy.

- **Automated disaster recovery**: Highlight best practices for automated DR, such as using **infrastructure as code (IaC)** tools to automate failover processes and backup strategies. Discuss tools and processes for regularly testing DR readiness, which is essential for critical systems.

Cost management and optimization

In addition to the brief mention of cost management, a highly experienced architect would benefit from more detailed insights into cost optimization and architectural design patterns to achieve financial efficiency.

The following are the recommendations for cost management and optimization to ensure financial efficiency and cost visibility:

- **Cost observability**: Implement cost observability by tracking and analyzing costs in near-real time, particularly in cloud environments. Use tools like *AWS*

Cost Explorer, Azure Cost Management, or third-party solutions to monitor service-specific costs, detect anomalies, and assess cost efficiency.

- **Cost-aware design decisions**: Provide guidance on cost-aware design principles, such as minimizing data transfer between regions, right-sizing instances, and using spot instances or reserved instances for predictable workloads. Cost consideration at the architecture level helps avoid unexpected expenses as systems scale.

Evolutionary architecture and continuous improvement

A highly experienced architect would expect insights on how to evolve architectures over time and ensure they can adapt to changing business and technology requirements.

The following are the recommendations for building evolutionary architectures to keep adapting to changing business and technology landscapes:

- **Principles of evolutionary architecture**: Discuss patterns for building adaptable architectures, such as using feature flags for controlled rollouts, blue-green deployments, and canary releases. These patterns enable iterative improvements and easier adaptation to new requirements or technologies.

- **Metrics-driven improvement**: Encourage a metrics-driven approach to assess and iterate on architectural performance. For instance, tracking service latency, deployment frequency, error rates, and capacity utilization provides insights to continuously refine the architecture.

Advanced observability techniques

While observability basics are covered, a deeper dive into advanced observability techniques could resonate with senior architects focused on troubleshooting complex distributed systems.

The following are the recommendations to enhance observability in distributed systems:

- **Service dependency mapping and topology awareness**: Enable tools that automatically map service dependencies and visualize system topology, especially in complex microservices or hybrid environments. This allows architects to see how services interact and where bottlenecks or single points of failure may exist.

- **Synthetic monitoring and user behavior insights**: Incorporate synthetic monitoring to proactively test system performance and reliability. Additionally, link observability with user behavior analytics to understand how architectural choices impact user experience in real-time.

Environmental impact and sustainable architecture

With increasing focus on sustainability, experienced architects may appreciate guidance on designing architectures that are not only cost-effective but also environmentally responsible. The following are the recommendations for incorporating sustainability into architectural design:

- **Sustainable design choices**: Discuss strategies for reducing carbon footprint, such as minimizing unnecessary data processing, optimizing resource usage, and avoiding over-provisioning. Architects are increasingly mindful of environmental impact, making sustainability a valuable architectural consideration.

- **Green cloud practices**: Encourage architects to use cloud provider tools to monitor and minimize energy consumption, such as *AWS's Sustainability Pillar for the Well-Architected Framework* or *Google's Carbon Footprint tool*, allowing architects to design with sustainability in mind.

Architecting for collaboration and DevOps alignment

Experienced architects understand that technical success is often a result of strong collaboration and seamless DevOps integration. Including guidance on how to architect with team dynamics in mind helps achieve efficient, cross-functional workflows.

The following are the recommendations to enhance collaboration and DevOps alignment.

- **Collaboration-focused design**: Encourage designs that facilitate cross-team collaboration, such as establishing well-defined service interfaces and communication protocols. Use tools like API specifications (OpenAPI) or gRPC to standardize service communication and ensure clarity across teams.

- **DevOps integration**: Highlight the importance of integrating CI/CD pipelines early in the architecture. Architectures that support DevOps pipelines—through automation, testing, and continuous integration, enable faster delivery and improve reliability. Consider providing guidelines on incorporating GitOps practices, where version control (e.g., Git) manages operational workflows, making deployments reproducible and observable.

Architecting for flexibility and vendor agnosticism

Many experienced architects face the challenge of creating architectures that avoid vendor lock-in, especially in cloud-native environments. Including best practices for maintaining flexibility and vendor agnosticism will resonate well with readers.

The following are the recommendations to ensure architectural flexibility and vendor agnosticism:

- **Avoiding vendor lock-in**: Recommend strategies such as using open-source solutions where possible, designing abstraction layers over proprietary APIs, and deploying multi-cloud strategies where feasible. This provides flexibility in case of cost, policy, or strategic changes.

- **Interoperability standards**: Encourage the use of industry standards (e.g., **OpenTelemetry** for observability, Kubernetes for container orchestration) that enable interoperability across platforms, making it easier to adapt if the architecture needs to be migrated or expanded to new environments.

Business value and impact assessment

An experienced architect considers not only the technical success but also the business impact of architecture. A section on ensuring the architecture delivers measurable business value can enhance the checklist.

The following are the recommendations to ensure architectural decisions drive measurable business value and maintain alignment with organizational goals:

- **Aligning with business metrics**: Define key business metrics (e.g., customer satisfaction, operational efficiency, revenue growth) and create mechanisms to measure the architecture's impact on these metrics. Tracking metrics like time-to-market, error rates, and user engagement can help architects directly link architectural decisions to business outcomes.

- **Feedback loops with stakeholders**: Establish regular touchpoints with business stakeholders to review how the architecture is supporting business goals. This can lead to early detection of misalignment and foster a culture of continuous improvement.

Patterns for governance and compliance automation

Governance is often overlooked in technical architecture but is crucial, especially in regulated industries. Adding a section on governance and compliance automation can provide value for architects managing large, complex systems.

The following are the recommendations to automate governance and compliance:

- **Automated policy enforcement**: Recommend the use of tools like **Open Policy Agent (OPA)** and **Azure Policy** to enforce governance rules automatically. Automating governance can reduce the risk of human error and ensure compliance with standards.

- **Built-in compliance frameworks**: Provide guidelines for integrating compliance checks within CI/CD pipelines to enforce security, data privacy, and regulatory requirements. Automated checks in the pipeline (e.g., for GDPR or HIPAA compliance) help architects ensure ongoing adherence to compliance requirements.

Legacy system integration and modernization

Experienced architects are frequently tasked with integrating new architectures with existing legacy systems. Including a section on best practices for legacy integration and modernization offers practical insights for real-world challenges.

The following are the recommendations to integrate and modernize legacy systems effectively:

- **Incremental modernization**: Highlight strategies like the strangler pattern, where legacy systems are gradually replaced by new components. This allows the organization to modernize while continuing operations without disruption.

- **Data and API modernization**: Provide guidance on wrapping legacy systems with modern APIs or using **extract, transform, load** (**ETL**) pipelines to move legacy data to modern data stores. Ensuring compatibility between old and new systems can enable a smoother transition to modern architectures.

Design for data governance and ethics

With the rise of AI, data governance and ethics are becoming increasingly important, especially for experienced architects working with large datasets or customer-sensitive information.

The following are the recommendations to strengthen data governance and ethical AI:

- **Data access controls**: Implement role-based and context-aware data access controls to ensure that only authorized individuals and systems can access sensitive data. Architectures should enforce strong governance around data handling, particularly for **personally identifiable information** (**PII**).

- **Ethical AI and data use**: For architectures incorporating AI, include principles for ethical AI use, such as transparency, fairness, and accountability. Design models and workflows to minimize biases and provide traceability for data and AI model decisions.

Operational excellence and incident management

Experienced architects often focus on operational excellence and efficient incident management as part of a mature architecture strategy.

The following are the recommendations to enhance operational excellence and incident management:

- **Resilient incident management framework**: Establish an incident management framework that includes automated alerts, escalation procedures, and root-cause analysis tools. Incorporate runbooks that guide teams through common issues, enabling faster recovery.

- **Post-incident reviews and continuous learning**: Emphasize the importance of conducting post-incident reviews and sharing lessons learned across teams. Regular postmortems contribute to continuous improvement, ensuring that the architecture evolves in response to real-world challenges.

Customer-centric architecture design

While technical and business alignment are covered, focusing on customer-centric architecture could add depth. This concept emphasizes designing with the end-user experience and customer value as a core goal.

The following are the recommendations to ensure a customer-centric architecture:

- **End-to-end experience mapping**: Encourage architects to map out the entire user journey across services and interactions. This ensures that every part of the architecture, from front-end latency to backend processing, supports a seamless, responsive user experience.

- **Feedback loops for customer insights**: Integrate mechanisms for capturing user feedback and behavior analytics directly into the architecture. Continuous insights into how customers use the application can help prioritize features and improvements, making the architecture more responsive to user needs.

Advanced data lifecycle and retention strategies

Data lifecycle management is essential for handling long-term data storage, processing, and deletion, particularly as data volume grows. Including advanced strategies for data lifecycle management can help architects optimize storage costs and comply with data retention regulations.

The following are the recommendations to optimize data lifecycle management:

- **Automated data tiering**: Establish automated data tiering based on access frequency, moving data between hot, warm, and cold storage to optimize costs. This is especially valuable for large datasets, where older data can be archived while maintaining fast access to recent data.

- **Data retention policies and legal holds**: Incorporate retention policies within the architecture that specify data retention and deletion timelines. Legal hold mechanisms should be in place for data subject to litigation, ensuring data is preserved when needed without impacting the overall storage strategy.

AI-powered personalization and real-time analytics

Adding a focus on AI-driven personalization and real-time analytics can help architects build systems that respond dynamically to users' preferences and behaviors, enhancing the customer experience.

Here are two recommendations to enhance AI-powered personalization and real-time analytics:

- **Real-time data processing pipelines**: Build data pipelines that can process data in real time using stream processing frameworks like *Apache Kafka* or *Azure Stream Analytics*. This capability enables real-time analytics for applications such as recommendation engines or fraud detection.

- **AI and ML for personalization**: Integrate AI-driven recommendation engines that adapt to user behaviors, leveraging ML models that continuously learn from data interactions to deliver personalized experiences across touchpoints.

Cross-functional architectural decision-making

Adding a section on fostering cross-functional decision-making would provide guidance on incorporating input from different departments (e.g., marketing, legal, and compliance) to make architecture decisions that consider a broader range of business and operational impacts.

The following are the recommendations to foster cross-functional decision-making:

- **Architecture review boards**: Establish cross-functional **architecture review boards (ARBs)** to ensure architecture decisions are made in alignment with company-wide strategies. Include representatives from engineering, security, compliance, product, and other business areas to provide a well-rounded perspective.

- **Shared decision-making frameworks**: Use decision-making frameworks, such as *RACI* or *DACI* models, to clarify roles in architectural decisions. This ensures accountability and avoids miscommunication across departments, which is especially critical in large organizations.

Experimentation and A/B testing

Incorporating systematic experimentation, like A/B testing, within the architecture enables teams to validate features, optimize performance, and continually improve user experience in an evidence-based way.

The following are the recommendations for integrating experimentation and A/B testing into architecture:

- **Integrated experimentation framework**: Encourage architectures to incorporate experimentation frameworks (e.g., Optimizely or Google Optimize) that support A/B testing and feature toggling. This allows teams to test new features or performance improvements with a subset of users, gathering empirical data before full deployment.

- **Rolling updates with feature flags**: Combine feature flags with rolling updates to manage experimental rollouts. Feature flags allow architects to enable or disable features selectively, reducing risk by gradually exposing changes to users while tracking performance and user feedback.

Ethical and social responsibility in architecture

As technology's societal impact becomes increasingly scrutinized, addressing ethical considerations in architectural decisions is crucial. Experienced architects should consider the broader impact of their work on users and society.

The following are the recommendations to embed ethical and social responsibility into architecture:

- **Bias mitigation in AI models**: Encourage ethical practices by implementing processes to detect and reduce bias in AI models, ensuring equitable and fair outcomes for all users. Include diverse data sets, fairness metrics, and bias-detection tools in the design process.

- **Transparent data practices**: Promote transparency in data collection and usage by ensuring that users understand how their data is collected, processed, and stored. Provide clear documentation and make privacy notices accessible to end-users.

Conclusion

This chapter explored the foundational principles of modern application architecture, emphasizing scalability, resilience, and adaptability. We examined DDD for aligning architecture with business goals and EDD for building responsive, decoupled systems. We also covered Kubernetes for orchestrating distributed applications and cloud-native storage strategies for managing stateful workloads.

We discussed AI-driven optimization and observability, leveraging ML for proactive monitoring, anomaly detection, and resource optimization. Security and compliance were emphasized through automated policy enforcement, network policies, and DevSecOps. Additionally, we addressed legacy integration, incremental modernization, architectural flexibility, sustainability, and ethical data handling to ensure alignment with future business and technology needs.

In the next chapter, we will explore development practices and tools, starting with fundamental architecture design principles and an architecture review checklist to reinforce best practices. We will also dive into DevSecOps, platform engineering, and continuous delivery, along with the potential of low-code and no-code development to accelerate software creation and empower non-technical users.

Key terms

- **Modern application architecture**: A design approach focused on building scalable, resilient, and modular applications using cloud-native technologies, microservices, event-driven design, and container orchestration.

- **DDD**: A methodology for structuring complex software systems around business domains and subdomains, enabling clearer alignment between the system's architecture and business goals.

- **Microservices**: An architectural style where applications are composed of small, independent services that are loosely coupled and can be deployed, scaled, and maintained separately.

- **Event-driven design**: A design pattern where system components communicate asynchronously by producing and consuming events, allowing for decoupled and real-time processing.

- **Kubernetes (K8s)**: An open-source platform used for automating the deployment, scaling, and management of containerized applications.

- **Chaos engineering**: A practice used to improve system reliability by intentionally introducing failures to test how systems behave under stress, allowing teams to identify and fix weaknesses before real-world incidents occur.

- **Log aggregation**: The practice of collecting, centralizing, and analyzing logs from multiple services to enhance visibility into system performance and facilitate troubleshooting.

- **Distributed tracing**: A technique for tracking the flow of requests across multiple services in a distributed system, providing insights into system performance and helping to identify bottlenecks.

Join our book's Discord space

Join the book's Discord Workspace for Latest updates, Offers, Tech happenings around the world, New Release and Sessions with the Authors:

https://discord.bpbonline.com

CHAPTER 5

Development Practices and Tools

Introduction

In this chapter, we will cover the essential elements of modern application architecture, emphasizing the principles that contribute to the creation of robust, scalable, and secure systems. We will explore the foundational architecture design principles that guide developers in building efficient software. The chapter also introduces a practical architecture review checklist to ensure designs meet key performance and reliability standards. Additionally, we will examine the integration of DevSecOps and platform engineering practices, which are essential for automating security within continuous delivery and integration pipelines. Lastly, we will discuss the emerging trend of low-code and no-code platforms, which enable faster application development, broadening the scope of who can build applications.

Structure

In this chapter, we will cover the following topics:

- Fundamentals of architecture design principles
- Utilizing an architecture review checklist
- Implementing DevSecOps and platform engineering

- Enhancing efficiency with continuous delivery and integration
- Low-code and no-code development opportunities

Objectives

By the end of this chapter, you will be equipped with the knowledge and insights to design, build, and maintain modern, scalable, and resilient software systems. You will gain a clear understanding of core principles such as scalability, reliability, security, performance efficiency, maintainability, and adaptability and learn how to apply them effectively throughout the software development lifecycle. Discover best practices for scalability and performance, including strategies for handling increased loads, optimizing resources, and implementing horizontal and vertical scaling, load balancing, and caching mechanisms.

You will develop skills to ensure system reliability and security through failover mechanisms, redundancy, automated recovery, encryption, access controls, and secure coding practices.

Additionally, you will master the integration of DevSecOps and platform engineering to standardize environments, streamline workflows, and automate security measures across development stages. You will learn to implement **continuous integration and continuous delivery (CI/CD)** pipelines for faster, more reliable releases and evaluate when to use **low-code or no-code (LCNC)** platforms vs. traditional pro code solutions, leveraging Fusion Development for flexibility and speed.

Finally, you will acquire decision-making frameworks to choose the best architectural and development approaches for specific projects, balancing trade-offs like cost, time to market, flexibility, and long-term maintainability.

Fundamentals of architecture design principles

In this section, we will explore the core principles that serve as the foundation for building modern, scalable, and resilient software systems. These design principles guide architects and developers in making informed decisions throughout the application development lifecycle, ensuring that solutions are not only functional but also maintainable, performant, and adaptable to change.

Scalability

Scalability is the capability of a system to handle increased load without compromising performance. It involves designing software so that it can scale horizontally (adding more nodes) or vertically (upgrading existing nodes). Effective scalability ensures that the system can grow with the business needs without a complete redesign.

The following are some of the best practices:

- *Use microservices architecture* to allow independent scaling of components. Each microservice can be scaled separately, which avoids over-provisioning and optimizes resource usage.

- *Leverage cloud services* that provide elastic scalability to automatically adjust resources based on demand. Use auto-scaling features in platforms like AWS, Azure, or Google Cloud.

- *Implement load balancing and efficient data partitioning* strategies to distribute workloads evenly across servers or nodes, improving performance and availability.

- *Adopt a stateless design* where possible, ensuring that each service instance can handle requests independently, simplifying scaling.

- *Design for geographic distribution* by deploying services in multiple regions to handle global traffic effectively, ensuring low latency for users around the world.

Reliability

Reliability ensures that the system consistently performs its intended function without failures. A reliable architecture can tolerate faults and recover gracefully, minimizing downtime and user impact.

The following are some of the best practices:

- *Design with redundancy and failover mechanisms*, such as using multiple availability zones or regions to handle failover scenarios without service interruptions.

- *Use distributed databases with automatic replication and recovery* to ensure data is always available, even if a part of the system fails.

- *Implement monitoring and automated alerting* for proactive maintenance using tools like Prometheus, Datadog, or Azure Monitor to quickly detect and address issues.

- *Adopt circuit breaker patterns to prevent cascading failures*, allowing the system to isolate faults and recover without affecting other components.

- *Plan for graceful degradation* so that if parts of the system fail, core functionality remains accessible to users.

Security

Security is paramount in modern applications, especially with the rise of cyber threats. Architects must design systems that protect data, maintain integrity, and prevent unauthorized access.

The following are some of the best practices:

- Apply the principle of least privilege in access controls to ensure users and services only have the minimum permissions necessary for their tasks.

- Use encryption for data at rest and in transit to protect sensitive information.

- Regularly update and patch software to address vulnerabilities, leveraging automated patch management tools where possible.

- Implement secure coding practices and conduct regular security audits, including code scanning and penetration testing.

- Adopt **multi-factor authentication** (**MFA**) and identity management solutions like OAuth or OpenID Connect for enhanced user security.

Performance efficiency

Performance efficiency ensures that the system meets the required speed and responsiveness even under varying loads. It involves optimizing resource usage and minimizing latency.

The following are some of the best practices:

- *Implement caching mechanisms* (e.g., Redis, Memcached) to reduce database calls and improve response times.

- *Optimize code for efficiency and lower resource consumption*, focusing on reducing computation time and memory usage.

- *Use performance testing tools* (e.g., JMeter, Locust, LoadRunner) to identify and resolve bottlenecks early in the development process.

- *Adopt* **content delivery networks** (**CDNs**) to distribute static content globally, reducing latency for end-users.

- *Implement asynchronous processing* for tasks that do not need immediate results, allowing systems to handle more requests concurrently.

Maintainability

Maintainability refers to the ease with which a system can be updated, modified, or extended. A maintainable architecture reduces technical debt and enables faster development cycles.

The following are some of the best practices:

- Write modular and well-documented code to ensure components are easy to understand, replace, and upgrade. Modular designs also promote reusability.

- Implement automated testing to facilitate continuous integration, including unit, integration, and regression tests to ensure new changes do not break existing functionality.

- Use version control and maintain clear deployment pipelines with tools like Git, Jenkins, or Azure DevOps, allowing for smooth rollbacks if issues arise.

- Adopt CI/CD practices to automate build, testing, and deployment, making it easier to push updates quickly and safely.

- Establish coding standards and code review processes to maintain consistency and quality across the codebase.

Adaptability

Adaptability ensures that the software can accommodate new requirements, technologies, and business models without major rewrites. This principle is vital for future-proofing applications.

The following are the best practices:

- *Adopt an API-first approach* to integrate easily with other systems, allowing different services to communicate seamlessly and be extended or replaced without impacting core functionality.

- *Use containers and microservices* to enable flexibility in deployment, ensuring that components can be updated, scaled, or replaced independently without affecting the entire system.

- *Implement feature toggles to enable/disable features without redeploying*, which allows teams to test new features in production with limited users (canary releases) and roll back quickly if needed.

- *Design for backward compatibility* so that new versions of services do not break existing integrations, enabling smoother updates and transitions.

- *Plan for technology evolution by decoupling application logic from infrastructure*, using cloud-agnostic designs where possible, to avoid vendor lock-in and enable smoother migrations to new technologies.

Understanding and implementing these design principles form the foundation of any successful application architecture. They guide developers in creating systems that can scale, endure, and evolve with the ever-changing technology landscape.

Utilizing an architecture review checklist

An architecture review checklist is a systematic approach to evaluating the robustness, security, and scalability of a software system. It ensures that all critical aspects of the design have been considered, reducing risks during deployment and operation. The checklist serves as a guide to validate alignment with business requirements, technical standards, and best practices, promoting quality and sustainability across projects.

Purpose of architecture review checklist

The primary goal of an architecture review is to validate that the design meets business, performance, and reliability requirements. It ensures consistency across projects, promotes best practices, and facilitates collaboration, leading to more robust and resilient systems.

Components of effective architecture review checklist

An effective checklist covers several key areas, providing a comprehensive assessment of the architecture, as shown in the following figure:

Fundamentals of Architecture Design Principles			
Scalability	Autoscaling	Load Balancing	Latency Monitoring
Reliability	Redundancy	Fail Over	Recover
Security	Authentication	Encryption	Audit
Maintainability	Automation	Observability	Incident Response
Cost	Automation	Monitoring	Optimization

Figure 5.1: Fundamental components of architecture review checklist

Scalability and performance

Scalability and performance are critical to delivering exceptional user experiences and ensuring efficient use of resources. This section provides a structured set of questions to evaluate if the application architecture effectively manages varying loads, maintains optimal performance, and dynamically adjusts resources based on demand, as shown:

- Are there mechanisms for autoscaling and load balancing across services to handle varying loads?

- Have specific performance metrics, such as latency, throughput, and response times, been defined and tested under different scenarios?

- Is there a capacity model to plan for expected usage patterns, including peak loads?

- Are elastic scaling policies implemented to automatically adjust resources based on real-time demand?

- Is the application designed to scale down resources during low-traffic periods to optimize costs?

- Are autoscaling features integrated with monitoring tools like Azure Monitor to adjust resources dynamically?

- Have components sensitive to network latency been properly configured for proximity to data sources and users?

- Are performance metrics (latency, response time, throughput) monitored and logged continuously, with alerts for deviations from baseline performance?

- Have load testing and performance tests been automated and integrated into the CI/CD pipeline?

- Is a CDN used to reduce latency for end-users across different regions?

Reliability and resilience

Reliability and resilience ensure continuous availability of applications, protecting your business from disruptions. This section outlines key considerations to evaluate whether the architecture effectively prevents, detects, and recovers from failures, maintaining consistent service quality under all conditions, as shown:

- Have availability targets been defined, including SLAs, SLOs, MTTR, and MTBF, to measure and monitor application health?

- Does the architecture include redundancy strategies, such as multi-region deployments, to avoid single points of failure?

- Are failover and failback processes automated, and have they been tested successfully?

- Are application components deployed across multiple Availability Zones or regions for enhanced reliability?

- Is there an automated recovery process to handle common failure scenarios, and has this been validated regularly?

- Have backup and disaster recovery strategies been aligned with **recovery time objectives (RTO)** and **recovery point objectives (RPO)**?

- Are traffic routing and load balancing configured to redirect to alternative regions in the event of a regional outage?

- Have data replication and backup processes been implemented across multiple regions to ensure consistency and minimize data loss?

- Are health probes configured for load balancers to check the health of application components and manage failover scenarios?

- Have resilience measures been tested using techniques like chaos engineering or fault injection to validate the system's robustness?

Security and compliance

Security and compliance are foundational to protecting your organization's data and ensuring regulatory adherence. This section presents essential questions to verify that robust security controls, proactive monitoring, and compliance measures are thoroughly integrated into your application's architecture and development lifecycle.

- Are robust authentication and authorization mechanisms, such as **multi-factor authentication (MFA)** and **role-based access control (RBAC)**, implemented?

- Is encryption applied for data at rest and data in transit using industry-standard algorithms (e.g., TLS 1.2/1.3)?

- Are Azure Service Endpoints or Private Links used to secure communication with Azure PaaS services?

- Have compliance requirements (e.g., HIPAA, GDPR) been mapped to specific security controls and verified through regular audits?

- Is there a clear incident response plan in place, including automated alerts and playbooks for potential security breaches?

- Are security patches applied regularly, and is there a process for emergency patch deployment?

- Are tools like Microsoft Defender for Cloud integrated to proactively monitor for anomalies and unauthorized access?

- Is a secure DevSecOps approach adopted, involving collaboration between development and security teams to maintain security through the software lifecycle?

- Are security best practices integrated into the CI/CD pipeline, including code scanning, secret management, and automated security testing?

- Have data backup and restore processes been tested to ensure data integrity in case of incidents?

Cost management

Effective cost management ensures maximum value from your cloud investments by eliminating waste and optimizing resource use. This section provides critical considerations to assess your organization's practices for tracking, controlling, and continuously improving cloud expenditures, as follows:

- Is there a cost model that accounts for all operational expenses, including cloud resources, support, and licensing fees?

- Have autoscaling and usage patterns been optimized to ensure resources are not over-provisioned, avoiding unnecessary costs?

- Are Azure Cost Management tools used to track spending and provide insights on areas where cost savings can be made?

- Have reserved instances or savings plans been leveraged for predictable workloads to benefit from cost savings?

- Is there regular monitoring of cost spikes, with alerts configured to notify stakeholders when costs exceed predefined thresholds?

- Have all environments (e.g., development, staging, production) been appropriately tagged to track cost per environment or project?

- Are unused resources, such as orphaned disks or public IPs, periodically cleaned up to prevent wasteful spending?

- Is there a strategy in place for multi-region cost management, especially concerning data transfer costs between regions?

- Are PaaS services utilized where possible to reduce operational overhead and optimize resource usage?

- Are regular-cost audits scheduled to identify misconfigured or underutilized resources that can be optimized?

Operational excellence

Operational excellence is critical for maintaining consistent service quality and agility. This section provides essential questions to evaluate if your architecture and operations practices enable smooth deployments, effective monitoring, and rapid issue resolution, ensuring reliability and efficiency in production environments, as follows:

- Are automated CI/CD pipelines in place to ensure reliable and repeatable deployments, including rollback and roll-forward capabilities?

- Have blue-green deployments or canary releases been configured to minimize risks during production deployments?

- Are Azure Monitor and Application Insights configured to collect logs, metrics, and telemetry data, offering real-time visibility into application health?

- Is IaC used to enable consistent and automated provisioning across all environments?

- Have monitoring tools been integrated to correlate logs, metrics, and telemetry data across all components for unified observability?

- Are there incident response plans in place, with playbooks and runbooks for handling common operational issues and failures?

- Are configuration management practices implemented to allow seamless updates to application settings without requiring redeployments?

- Have auto-scaling and load balancing been configured to automatically adjust resources based on demand, ensuring smooth operation during peak usage?

- Have periodic drills been conducted to validate disaster recovery plans, and are learnings used to improve future responses?

- Is there a continuous feedback loop from monitoring and incident management to improve development and operational processes?

Implementing the architecture review process

The architecture review process is a structured approach to ensure a thorough assessment and actionable feedback on system design. It begins with **preparation**, where the team identifies the architecture components to review and gathers all necessary documentation, including diagrams, technical specifications, performance data, and code samples. During the **review session**, the architecture design is presented, emphasizing key aspects like scalability, reliability, security, cost, and operations. The session encourages open discussions to provide feedback and identify potential risks or areas for improvement.

Post-review, the team consolidates the findings into actionable feedback by documenting issues, highlighting areas for enhancement, and assigning responsibilities for implementing changes. Once the improvements are made, a **follow-up review** is scheduled to validate the updates and ensure the architecture aligns with desired outcomes. This process is iterative and should be repeated periodically or whenever significant changes occur in the system.

Benefits of using an architecture review checklist

Using an architecture review checklist provides proactive issue identification, ensuring early detection and resolution of potential risks. It enforces consistent quality assurance, standardizing best practices across your applications. Ultimately, this leads to higher quality, improved alignment with business objectives, and compliance with key operational and regulatory requirements, as follows:

- **Proactive issue identification**: Early detection and resolution of potential issues reduce costs and prevent deployment delays.

- **Consistent quality assurance**: Standardizing the review process ensures consistent adherence to best practices across projects.

- **Collaboration and continuous improvement**: Regular reviews foster collaboration, knowledge sharing, and alignment, leading to ongoing architectural improvements.

Incorporating a robust architecture review checklist aligns with the Azure Well-Architected Framework by ensuring key factors like scalability, reliability, performance, security, and cost-efficiency are integrated into your application designs.

Implementing DevSecOps and platform engineering

The integration of DevSecOps and platform engineering practices is critical for modern application development. DevSecOps emphasizes the seamless inclusion of security into the DevOps workflow, automating security checks throughout the CI/CD pipelines. Platform engineering focuses on building scalable, efficient platforms that provide standardized tools and environments for developers, enabling them to deliver software faster and more reliably.

This section will explore how combining DevSecOps and platform engineering practices ensures that applications are secure, scalable, and maintainable from development to deployment. We will also present a phase-wise approach to increase organizational maturity in these areas and provide examples of prevalent technologies and tools.

Importance of DevSecOps

DevSecOps embeds security into every phase of the **software development lifecycle (SDLC)**. This approach ensures that security vulnerabilities are identified and mitigated early, reducing the risk of issues emerging later in production. Unlike traditional models, where security is an isolated step, DevSecOps integrates security processes within development and operations workflows, fostering collaboration between teams.

The following are the key practices:

- **Automated security testing**: Integrate tools that automatically scan code for vulnerabilities, outdated libraries, and insecure dependencies during the build process.

- **Static and dynamic analysis**: Use **Static Application Security Testing (SAST)** and **Dynamic Application Security Testing (DAST)** tools to identify vulnerabilities in both source code and running applications.

- **Secure CI/CD pipelines**: Implement security checks (e.g., code scanning, secret detection) at various stages of the CI/CD pipeline to catch potential issues before deployment.

- **Shift-left security**: Adopt a *shift-left* approach where security assessments are performed early in the development cycle, reducing remediation costs and minimizing risks. Implement code review automation, early vulnerability scanning, and secure code training for developers.

- **Monitoring and incident response**: Establish continuous monitoring of application environments for security threats, ensuring swift incident detection and response. Use automated alerts and predefined incident response playbooks.

- **Compliance best practices**: Automate compliance checks within the CI/CD pipeline to ensure adherence to standards like HIPAA, GDPR, and SOC 2. Utilize tools that provide automated audits and reporting to streamline compliance management.

The following are some of the technology and tool examples:

- **SAST and DAST tools**: SonarQube, Checkmarx, Veracode, Snyk, GitHub Advanced Security (SAST)

- **CI/CD security integrations**: GitHub Actions, GitLab CI, Azure Pipelines, Jenkins

- **Secrets management**: HashiCorp Vault, Azure Key Vault, AWS Secrets Manager

- **Monitoring and incident response**: Microsoft Defender for Cloud, Splunk, Datadog, Prometheus

Key components of platform engineering

Platform engineering is about building an internal platform that standardizes and automates development environments, tools, and workflows. This approach allows developers to focus on coding and innovation while ensuring that the infrastructure they rely on is consistent, secure, and scalable.

The following are some of the key components:

- **Infrastructure as Code (IaC)**: Define and manage infrastructure using code, ensuring that environments are consistent, reproducible, and easy to scale.

- **Containerization**: Use containers (e.g., Docker) to package applications and their dependencies, allowing them to run consistently across different environments.

- **Orchestration and automation**: Implement tools like Kubernetes to manage the deployment, scaling, and operation of containers automatically.

- **Platform abstraction**: Provide a unified platform that abstracts the complexities of the underlying infrastructure, enabling developers to deploy applications without worrying about the specifics of cloud configurations.

- **Multi-cloud and hybrid cloud management**: Platform engineering can support organizations in managing multi-cloud or hybrid cloud deployments. Use tools like Terraform and Kubernetes to ensure consistent infrastructure management across cloud providers.

- **Service meshes**: Use service meshes (e.g., Istio) to manage service-to-service communications, ensuring secure and reliable interactions between microservices.

- **Continuous improvement**: Collect feedback from developers, monitor performance, and automate updates to iteratively improve platform engineering practices.

The following are some of the technology and tool examples:

- **IaC tools**: Terraform, Ansible, **Azure Resource Manager** (**ARM**), AWS CloudFormation

- **Container and orchestration tools**: Docker, Kubernetes, OpenShift

- **Service meshes**: Istio, Linkerd, Consul Connect

- **Platform monitoring**: Grafana, Prometheus, Azure Monitor

Platform abstraction

Platform abstraction involves creating a unified, self-service platform that simplifies the deployment and management of applications by abstracting the complexities of underlying infrastructure layers. For CTOs looking to improve developer productivity and streamline operations, platform abstraction is about providing a seamless experience where developers can focus solely on writing code and delivering features without needing deep expertise in cloud configurations, networking, or infrastructure management.

This approach not only accelerates development cycles but also ensures consistency, security, and scalability across deployments, as follows:

- **Standardized development through containerization**: To achieve effective platform abstraction, the first step is to *standardize the development environment by leveraging containerization technologies*. Containers encapsulate applications and their dependencies, ensuring that they run uniformly across different environments (e.g., development, testing, production). Next, implement a container orchestration solution like Kubernetes or OpenShift to automate the deployment, scaling, and management of these containers, thus creating a managed environment that developers can use without worrying about the underlying infrastructure.

- **PaaS layer implementation**: Another essential engineering best practice is to build a **platform-as-a-service** (**PaaS**) layer that offers standardized templates, services, and APIs. This PaaS layer should include pre-configured options for commonly used services such as databases, messaging queues, and storage, allowing developers to easily integrate these components into their applications without needing to set up or manage the infrastructure manually. Moreover, the platform should provide an intuitive user interface or developer portal where teams can deploy, monitor, and manage their applications with minimal configuration. Examples of such platforms include Azure App Service, Google App Engine, and AWS Elastic Beanstalk.

- **IaC**: *Implementing IaC is critical for achieving platform abstraction.* Tools like Terraform, Pulumi, and CloudFormation allow infrastructure to be defined, managed, and deployed through code, making it possible to automate the setup of entire environments. This not only speeds up deployment but also ensures that environments are consistent and repeatable, reducing configuration errors. Additionally, IaC allows organizations to version-control their infrastructure, making it easier to track changes, roll back to previous states, and maintain compliance.

- **Integrated security practices**: *Security is another crucial aspect of platform abstraction.* By incorporating security measures into the platform itself, such as automated scanning for vulnerabilities, encryption for data in transit and at rest, and identity management using **single sign-on** (**SSO**) or OAuth, organizations can ensure that all applications deployed via the platform adhere to the same security standards. This eliminates the need for individual developers to manage security configurations, reducing the risk of security gaps. CTOs should also consider implementing service meshes like *Istio* or *Linkerd*, which handle service-to-service communications, enforce policies, and provide observability for microservices, further abstracting away complexity from developers.

Finally, *platform abstraction is about building an ecosystem that facilitates rapid development and deployment.* This involves creating a central hub for managing configurations, secrets, and access controls, allowing developers to deploy applications without having to handle these elements manually. Centralized logging, monitoring, and alerting tools should be integrated into the platform to provide real-time insights into application performance, security, and usage, enabling proactive management. Solutions like Grafana, Prometheus, Azure Monitor, and Datadog can be used to set up unified dashboards, giving CTOs a clear view of their infrastructure's health and operational status.

Multi-cloud and hybrid cloud management

In today's cloud landscape, organizations often operate in multi-cloud or hybrid cloud environments to leverage the unique benefits of different cloud providers, avoid vendor lock-in, and ensure redundancy. However, managing such diverse environments can introduce significant complexity, especially when trying to maintain consistent infrastructure and application configurations across platforms. Effective multi-cloud and hybrid cloud management requires a well-defined strategy, robust platform engineering practices, and the use of powerful tools to ensure smooth, consistent, and secure operations across cloud providers, as follows:

- **Unified infrastructure with IaC**: To achieve a seamless multi-cloud or hybrid cloud setup, the first step is to implement IaC *across all environments*. Tools like Terraform, Pulumi, and Ansible can help define infrastructure configurations in a declarative manner, making it easier to deploy, scale, and manage resources across different cloud platforms such as *AWS*, *Azure*, and *Google Cloud*. IaC ensures that the same infrastructure code can be used to deploy resources consistently, regardless of the cloud provider. This not only reduces configuration drift but also simplifies disaster recovery and scaling by allowing infrastructure to be recreated quickly and accurately in different regions or clouds. CTOs should prioritize using

IaC templates that are cloud-agnostic, enabling teams to deploy workloads on the cloud of choice with minimal changes.

- **Container orchestration with Kubernetes**: Kubernetes has emerged as a key enabler of multi-cloud and hybrid cloud strategies due to its powerful container orchestration capabilities. By deploying applications in containers, organizations can ensure that workloads are portable across environments, whether they are running on-premises or in the cloud. Kubernetes can manage the deployment, scaling, and failover of containerized applications, making it possible to shift workloads between different cloud platforms without disrupting services. Additionally, managed Kubernetes services such as **Azure Kubernetes Service (AKS)**, **Google Kubernetes Engine (GKE)**, and Amazon **Elastic Kubernetes Service (EKS)** provide the flexibility to run Kubernetes clusters on various clouds, allowing organizations to choose the most suitable cloud provider for specific workloads.

- **Standardized security and service communication**: Unified networking and security are critical for successful multi-cloud and hybrid cloud management. Using tools like service meshes (e.g., Istio, Consul, Linkerd), organizations can standardize service-to-service communication, enforce security policies, and provide observability across different environments. This is particularly useful in hybrid setups where applications may need to communicate between on-premises data centers and cloud infrastructure. Implementing *Zero Trust security principles* ensures that services are authenticated and authorized before they communicate, reducing the risk of security breaches. Moreover, **virtual private networks (VPNs)** or direct connections (e.g., Azure ExpressRoute, AWS Direct Connect) can be used to establish secure, low-latency connections between on-premises systems and cloud environments.

- **Unified monitoring and observability**: Centralized management and monitoring are also crucial for maintaining visibility and control over multi-cloud and hybrid cloud deployments. CTOs should consider implementing unified monitoring tools such as *Datadog, Prometheus, New Relic,* or *Azure Monitor* that can aggregate metrics, logs, and events from all environments into a single pane of glass. This helps operations teams monitor application performance, detect issues, and respond quickly, regardless of where the workloads are running. A consistent monitoring approach also ensures that compliance requirements are met across different jurisdictions, as organizations can track data flow and enforce security policies uniformly.

- **Automated workload placement and optimization**: Automated workload placement and scaling can further optimize multi-cloud operations. By integrating tools like *HashiCorp Nomad, Rancher,* and *Kubernetes Federation,* organizations can automate the placement of workloads based on predefined rules such as cost, latency, or resource availability. For example, a workload that needs to be closer to end-users in Europe can be automatically deployed to a European data center, while a cost-sensitive application can be routed to the most cost-efficient cloud provider. This kind of automated orchestration not only reduces manual effort but also ensures that applications are running in the most optimal locations for performance and cost-efficiency.

- **Consistent cross-cloud data management**: Consistent Data Management across clouds is another significant challenge that needs to be addressed. Multi-cloud and hybrid strategies often involve complex data management scenarios where data needs to be replicated, synchronized, or moved between different environments. CTOs should leverage cloud-native data services like Azure Arc, Google Anthos, or AWS Outposts, which extend cloud services to on-premises or other cloud providers, ensuring a consistent approach to data storage, security, and compliance. Additionally, *cross-cloud data services* such as CloudSQL or Cosmos DB can be configured to replicate data across multiple regions and clouds, ensuring data availability and resilience.

- **Unified governance and security framework:** Technologies like *Azure Arc* play a transformative role in multi-cloud and hybrid cloud management by extending Azure's capabilities to on-premises, edge, and multi-cloud environments. With Azure Arc, organizations can manage resources such as servers, Kubernetes clusters, and databases across diverse environments using a unified control plane. It enables consistent governance and security by applying Azure Policy and **role-based access controls (RBAC)** across all connected resources. Additionally, Azure Arc simplifies hybrid data management by supporting services like Azure SQL Managed Instance and PostgreSQL Hyperscale, enabling organizations to run these cloud-native data services anywhere. By leveraging Azure Arc, organizations can achieve consistency in operations, enforce compliance uniformly, and gain centralized visibility into multi-cloud and hybrid assets.

Lastly, *establishing a multi-cloud governance framework* is essential to maintaining control over disparate environments. This involves creating policies for resource management, access control, and cost management across all cloud platforms. Tools like Azure Policy, AWS Control Tower, and Google Cloud Resource Manager can help enforce these policies, ensuring that all resources comply with the organization's standards, no matter where they are deployed. This governance framework should include automated guardrails that prevent misconfigurations, detect anomalies, and ensure compliance with regulatory requirements across different regions and cloud providers.

Phase-wise approach to increase maturity

Organizations often adopt a phased approach to gradually mature their DevOps, DevSecOps, and platform engineering practices. This minimizes disruption and allows teams to build skills incrementally.

The following is a structured path for organizations to elevate their maturity cycle:

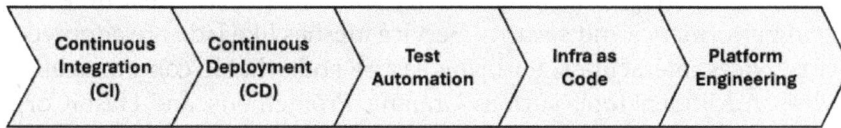

Figure 5.2: DevOps maturity phases

The following sections detail each phase, providing clear guidelines, best practices, and recommended tools to help your organization advance effectively through the maturity journey:

- **Implementing continuous integration (CI)**: In this initial phase, organizations establish foundational practices for managing and validating code changes. Version control systems like Git are implemented to track and manage code, and automated build processes ensure every code commit is compiled and tested. Unit testing is integrated early in the development cycle to maintain code quality and catch errors before they progress further in the pipeline. Tools such as GitHub, Jenkins, Azure DevOps, and CircleCI are commonly used at this stage to streamline CI practices.

- **Continuous delivery (CD)**: Building on CI, the next phase focuses on automating deployment processes to ensure consistent delivery of applications to staging environments. Automated integration tests are introduced to identify issues arising from combining new code with existing systems. Additionally, rollback mechanisms are implemented to quickly revert changes if problems are detected, reducing the risk of deployment failures. Tools like Jenkins, Azure Pipelines, GitLab CI/CD, and AWS CodePipeline support this phase.

- **Automated testing and security integration**: This phase emphasizes integrating security and advanced testing into the development process. Automated security testing, including SAST and DAST, is incorporated into CI/CD pipelines. Container scanning tools are used to identify vulnerabilities in container images, while infrastructure scanning automates the detection of misconfigurations and security risks. Tools such as SonarQube, Checkmarx, Aqua Security, and Sysdig are instrumental in implementing these practices.

- **IaC and automated scaling**: The transition to IaC ensures that infrastructure deployments are consistent and repeatable. Automated scaling policies are introduced to handle fluctuating workloads, eliminating the need for manual intervention. Orchestration tools like Kubernetes are used to manage scaling and workload distribution, while IaC tools such as Terraform and Azure Resource Manager provide robust frameworks for deploying and managing infrastructure.

- **Advanced DevSecOps and platform engineering**: In the final phase, organizations focus on creating a comprehensive platform that abstracts underlying infrastructure and accelerates application deployment. This platform integrates monitoring, logging, and observability tools to provide real-time insights into system performance and security. Service meshes like Istio are adopted to manage microservices interactions, ensuring secure and reliable communication between services. Additional tools such as Grafana, Prometheus, and HashiCorp Vault are integrated to enhance operational efficiency and security.

Let us consider some prerequisites and success criteria.

Before advancing through each phase, organizations must ensure that teams are proficient in foundational practices like version control and CI/CD. A pilot project should be identified to test new practices and tools, enabling teams to identify potential challenges and refine their processes. Rollback mechanisms and monitoring systems should be in place to ensure smooth transitions and mitigate risks during each phase.

The maturity assessment checklist for DevOps and platform engineering is as follows:

- **DevOps maturity assessment:**
  - Are there automated pipelines in place for deploying infrastructure alongside application code?
  - Is testing automated at various levels (unit, integration, system) across the pipeline?
  - Are development, operations, and security teams integrated into a unified workflow?
  - Is there a system for collecting and acting on feedback from developers about CI/CD processes?

- **DevSecOps maturity assessment:**
  - Are security tools and scans integrated at every stage of the development pipeline, from code commit to production deployment?
  - Is there a secure process for managing third-party dependencies, including regular audits?
  - Are security alerts triaged and remediated within a defined SLA?
  - Have penetration tests and security drills been conducted regularly to test the security posture of applications and infrastructure?
  - Is there an automated process to detect and manage anomalies, unauthorized access attempts, and other suspicious activities?
  - Are security best practices and coding guidelines incorporated into developer training programs?
  - Is there a process for automating compliance checks within the CI/CD pipeline to ensure adherence to industry standards?

- o Are all third-party libraries and dependencies regularly audited for vulnerabilities, and is there a process to update them?

- o Has a baseline security policy been established, and is it automatically enforced across all deployments?

- o Are there secure coding standards in place, and do they cover common vulnerabilities such as SQL injection, XSS, and CSRF?

- o Is there a training program in place to help teams adopt new tools and methodologies?

- o Are there documented strategies for integrating DevSecOps practices with legacy systems, including phased rollouts or hybrid models?

- **Platform engineering maturity assessment:**

  - o Are there monitoring tools in place to track infrastructure performance, usage, and costs in real time?

  - o Do monitoring dashboards provide a unified view of system health, security, and performance metrics?

  - o Are self-service capabilities provided to developers to manage their infrastructure without waiting for operations teams?

  - o Are there procedures for scaling platform components automatically based on usage patterns?

  - o Are platform engineering practices aligned with multi-cloud or hybrid cloud strategies, allowing seamless deployment across different environments?

  - o Is there a feedback loop in place for developers to report issues and request features for the internal platform?

  - o Are platforms regularly updated to support new development tools, frameworks, and versions?

  - o Are there processes for measuring the effectiveness of platform engineering practices, such as deployment times and developer feedback scores?

  - o Is platform security (e.g., network security, access control) integrated into the infrastructure provisioning process?

Benefits of implementing DevSecOps and platform engineering

Adopting DevSecOps and platform engineering practices can transform how organizations build, deploy, and maintain software. By integrating security into the development lifecycle and standardizing development environments, companies can enhance agility, security, and scalability across their application ecosystems. These practices streamline workflows, automate processes, and improve collaboration between development, operations, and security teams.

As businesses continue to embrace digital transformation, DevSecOps, and platform engineering are essential for maintaining competitive advantage and ensuring that technology infrastructure can keep pace with evolving business needs, as shown:

- **Developer productivity**: With a consistent and secure platform, developers can focus on building features and improving the user experience rather than dealing with infrastructure issues. Platform engineering provides standardized environments and tooling that simplify development, testing, and deployment processes. By removing the complexities of setting up environments or managing dependencies, developers spend less time on operational tasks and more time on innovation, ultimately leading to faster feature delivery and improved software quality.

- **Reduced time to market**: Automating deployment, testing, and security checks speeds up the development cycle, allowing new features and updates to be released faster. DevSecOps practices enable CI/CD, where code changes are automatically tested and deployed without manual intervention. This reduces bottlenecks, accelerates feedback loops, and ensures that teams can quickly respond to market demands. Companies that can deliver updates rapidly gain a competitive edge by being more responsive to customer needs and market trends.

- **Enhanced security**: By integrating security checks into every stage of the development process, vulnerabilities can be identified and addressed early, reducing risks. Traditional security approaches often lead to last-minute checks, which can be time-consuming and less effective. DevSecOps shifts security to the left, embedding automated security scans, code analysis, and compliance checks throughout the CI/CD pipeline. This proactive approach reduces the likelihood of security breaches, minimizes remediation costs, and ensures compliance with regulatory requirements.

- **Scalability and flexibility**: Platform engineering practices, such as container orchestration and IaC, enable applications to scale automatically in response to demand, improving resource efficiency. Organizations can ensure their applications are resilient, scalable, and highly available by deploying containers through orchestration platforms like Kubernetes. IaC tools (e.g., Terraform and Ansible) automate the provisioning of infrastructure, making it easy to replicate environments and scale resources up or down as needed. This flexibility allows organizations to handle fluctuating workloads efficiently, optimize costs, and improve overall performance.

- **Operational consistency**: Standardizing tools and environments across teams reduces the chances of configuration errors, making deployments more predictable and stable. DevSecOps and platform engineering provide consistency by enforcing standard processes and practices across development, testing, and production environments. Automated deployments eliminate manual errors, while predefined configurations ensure that all teams are working within the same framework. This simplifies troubleshooting and improves collaboration, as teams can rely on consistent environments when building, testing, and deploying software.

Common challenges and how to overcome them

Implementing DevSecOps and platform engineering practices can yield substantial benefits, but it is not without its challenges. Organizations may face resistance from teams, difficulties in integrating these practices into existing systems, or struggles to balance speed with security. However, by addressing these challenges proactively, companies can pave the way for smoother adoption and more successful outcomes.

The following are the key challenges and solutions:

- **Resistance to change**: Teams might be reluctant to adopt new security or platform engineering practices, especially if they feel it adds complexity. Resistance often stems from a lack of understanding or fear of disrupting existing workflows. Address this by providing clear training and demonstrating how these practices make their work easier and more efficient. For example, it shows how automated testing can catch errors early, reducing the workload for developers in the long run. Create champions within teams who can advocate for the benefits of DevSecOps and platform engineering, helping to build trust and drive adoption across the organization.

- **Balancing speed with security**: Development teams often prioritize speed, which can sometimes lead to security shortcuts. This is particularly problematic in fast-paced environments where teams are under pressure to release features quickly. Automate as many security checks as possible, ensuring they do not slow down the CI/CD pipeline. Use tools that integrate seamlessly into the development workflow, such as static code analysis, dynamic testing, and dependency scanning, so security checks are performed automatically with every code change. By embedding security into the pipeline, teams can maintain speed without compromising safety.

- **Handling legacy systems**: Introducing DevSecOps and platform engineering practices in environments where legacy systems are prevalent can be challenging. Legacy systems often have rigid architectures, outdated technology stacks, and manual processes that make it difficult to integrate modern practices. Start with a hybrid approach that combines new practices with existing workflows, gradually phasing out outdated processes. For instance, use containerization to encapsulate legacy applications, allowing them to run on modern platforms without significant reengineering. Additionally, prioritize automating repetitive tasks and deploying microservices alongside legacy systems to incrementally modernize the application landscape.

- **Tooling and integration challenges**: Integrating new tools and platforms into existing infrastructure can lead to compatibility issues or require significant customization. To overcome this, assess the current technology stack and choose tools that offer flexible integrations and open APIs. Adopt an API-first approach to ensure seamless communication between existing systems and new DevSecOps or platform engineering tools. Consider using orchestration platforms that can manage diverse technology stacks, reducing the effort needed to maintain consistency across various environments.

- **Skills gaps**: Moving to DevSecOps and platform engineering requires new skills and knowledge, which can lead to skills gaps within the team. Invest in training and upskilling programs that help developers, operations, and security teams understand and adopt these practices effectively. Encourage continuous learning by providing access to online courses, workshops, and certifications. Building cross-functional teams where developers, security engineers, and operations staff work closely together can also help bridge the skills gap and foster a culture of collaboration.

Implementing DevSecOps and platform engineering is about creating a holistic approach to modern software development. By embedding security into every step and providing developers with a robust, consistent platform, organizations can deliver high-quality software that is scalable, secure, and reliable.

Enhancing efficiency with continuous delivery and integration

CI and CD are foundational practices in modern software development that enable teams to build, test, and deploy applications quickly, reliably, and frequently. These practices help streamline the SDLC by automating repetitive tasks, reducing manual errors, and enabling faster delivery of features to users. For CTOs and engineering leaders, implementing CI/CD is about accelerating development cycles, maintaining high quality, and enhancing team productivity.

Role of continuous integration

CI is the practice of automatically integrating code changes from multiple developers into a shared repository several times a day. Each code commit triggers an automated build process that includes running unit tests to ensure that new changes do not break existing functionality. This approach reduces integration problems and provides teams with immediate feedback on the health of the codebase.

The following are the engineering best practices for CI:

- **Automate build processes**: Use CI tools like Jenkins, GitHub Actions, Azure DevOps, and GitLab CI to automate the build process. Every code commit should trigger a build to compile the application, run automated tests, and generate reports.

- **Enable version control with branching strategies**: Implement effective branching strategies (e.g., Gitflow, trunk-based development) to streamline code integration. This helps manage feature development, bug fixes, and releases more efficiently. Regularly merge code changes to the main branch to minimize merge conflicts.

- **Automate unit and integration testing**: Integrate automated testing frameworks (e.g., JUnit, Selenium, Mocha) to run tests as part of the CI pipeline. This ensures that each code change is validated against existing functionality, reducing the risk of defects entering production.

- **Maintain a green build**: Encourage developers to fix any issues immediately if a build fails. A green build (successful build) should be a priority, as it indicates that the software is stable and ready for deployment.

- **Feedback loop**: Create fast feedback loops by notifying developers of build failures via instant messaging tools like Slack, Microsoft Teams, or email. Quick feedback allows teams to address issues promptly and maintain a high-quality codebase.

Role of continuous delivery

Continuous delivery extends the principles of CI by automating the deployment process, ensuring that code changes can be released to production at any time. With CD, software is always in a deployable state, and deployments can be triggered at the push of a button, minimizing the risk of human error and making the release process predictable and reliable.

The following are the engineering best practices for CI:

- **Automate deployment pipelines**: Implement CD tools such as Spinnaker, Octopus Deploy, Azure Pipelines, and AWS CodePipeline to automate the process of packaging and deploying applications across environments (e.g., development, staging, production). Automated pipelines should handle tasks like environment setup, configuration management, and artifact promotion.

- **Implement continuous testing**: Beyond unit tests, integrate automated tests that cover integration, performance, security, and end-to-end scenarios. These tests should run at every stage of the pipeline to catch issues early and ensure that the software meets performance and security standards.

- **Use blue-green and canary deployments:** Reduce the risk of deployment failures by implementing deployment strategies such as blue-green and canary deployments. Blue-green deployments involve maintaining two identical environments (blue and green), where new releases are deployed to the blue environment while the green serves users. Once verified, traffic is switched to blue, minimizing downtime.

Canary deployments allow new features to be released to a subset of users, making it easier to monitor the release and rollback if issues are detected.

- **Environment parity**: Ensure that development, staging, and production environments are as similar as possible to minimize the *it works on my machine* problem. Use IaC tools like Terraform or Ansible to create consistent environments.

- **Versioning and rollback**: Properly release version applications and maintain rollback mechanisms to quickly revert to a previous version in case of unexpected issues. This reduces downtime and allows for seamless recovery.

Engineering best practices for effective CI/CD

To fully realize the benefits of CI/CD, it is essential to implement robust engineering practices that streamline workflows, enhance automation, and improve collaboration.

The following are the key best practices:

- **Create modular pipelines**: Break down pipelines into modular, reusable components to facilitate easier maintenance and updates. For example, create separate pipeline stages for building, testing, security scanning, and deployment, and reuse these modules across projects.

- **Automate security checks (DevSecOps)**: Integrate security scanning tools (e.g., Snyk, WhiteSource, Aqua Security) into the CI/CD pipeline to catch vulnerabilities early. Automating security checks ensures that code meets security standards without slowing down the release cycle.

- **Integrate IaC**: Use IaC to automate environment setup, scaling, and configuration changes. With IaC, teams can version-control infrastructure, enabling consistent deployments across environments and simplifying disaster recovery.

- **Maintain pipeline visibility and monitoring**: Implement real-time monitoring tools (e.g., Datadog, Prometheus, Azure Monitor) to track pipeline performance and detect issues early. A dashboard that visualizes key metrics (e.g., build success rate, deployment frequency) helps teams monitor and optimize the CI/CD process.

- **Build a culture of collaboration**: Foster a culture where developers, operations, and security teams work together. Adopt collaborative tools (e.g., JIRA, Confluence, Slack) to enable cross-functional teams to communicate, track progress, and resolve issues efficiently.

Measuring CI/CD efficiency

Implementing CI/CD is only the beginning. CTOs need to continuously measure the efficiency of their CI/CD practices to identify bottlenecks and opportunities for improvement.

The following are the key metrics for CI/CD efficiency:

- **Deployment frequency**: How often new code is deployed to production. Higher frequency indicates a faster and more efficient pipeline.

- **Lead time for changes**: The time it takes from code commit to successful deployment in production. Shorter lead times indicate faster feedback and quicker value delivery.

- **Change failure rate**: The percentage of deployments that result in a failure. A lower failure rate indicates higher code quality and stable processes.

- **Mean time to recovery (MTTR)**: The time it takes to restore service after a failure. Faster recovery times suggest robust rollback and monitoring mechanisms.

- **Test coverage and reliability**: Measure the extent to which automated tests cover the codebase and their success rate. High test coverage with low failure rates ensures code quality and stability.

Overcoming common challenges in CI/CD implementation

While CI/CD practices bring numerous benefits, organizations may encounter challenges in their implementation. Addressing these challenges early can help achieve a smoother transition and more effective pipeline.

The following are the challenges and solutions:

- **Resistance to automation**: Teams may resist automating manual tasks due to a lack of familiarity or fear of losing control. CTOs should advocate for automation by demonstrating its benefits (e.g., faster releases, fewer errors) and investing in training.

- **Legacy systems integration**: Integrating CI/CD with legacy systems can be complex. Gradually introduce automation by first applying CI/CD practices to new microservices or modules and incrementally integrate older systems.

- **Pipeline performance bottlenecks**: If CI/CD pipelines take too long, it can slow down development cycles. Optimize pipelines by running tasks in parallel, caching dependencies, and streamlining test suites to focus on critical cases.

- **Security concerns**: Security is often seen as a bottleneck to faster delivery. Adopting DevSecOps practices ensures that security checks are automated, shifting security left and making it a seamless part of the development process.

The following is the engineering checklist for CI/CD implementation:

- Have CI/CD pipelines been automated to handle tasks from code commit to deployment?

- Are tests (unit, integration, performance, and security) automated and integrated into the pipeline?

- Are rollback and recovery mechanisms defined and tested?

- Is there consistency between development, testing, and production environments (environment parity)?

- Have deployment strategies (e.g., blue-green, canary) been implemented to minimize deployment risks?

- Are security scans integrated into the pipeline, and do they run automatically on each build?

- Are there tools in place for real-time monitoring and logging of the CI/CD pipeline performance?

- Is pipeline performance regularly analyzed, and are optimizations implemented to reduce lead times?

Benefits of continuous integration and continuous delivery

The implementation of CI/CD brings transformative benefits to organizations by improving software quality, accelerating delivery cycles, and enhancing collaboration.

The following are the key benefits:

- **Faster time to market**: Automated testing and deployment processes enable teams to deliver new features and fixes faster, gaining a competitive edge.

- **Improved code quality**: Automated testing ensures that each code change is thoroughly tested, reducing the risk of defects reaching production.

- **Enhanced collaboration**: CI/CD fosters collaboration across development, operations, and security teams, promoting a shared responsibility for software quality.

- **Reduced deployment risks**: By automating deployments and implementing strategies like blue-green and canary releases, teams can deploy changes with minimal downtime and risk.

- **Scalability and flexibility**: CI/CD enables organizations to scale development and deployment efforts efficiently, supporting rapid growth and adaptation to market demands.

In conclusion, adopting continuous integration and continuous delivery practices is essential for modern organizations looking to enhance efficiency, improve code quality, and accelerate the software delivery pipeline. By investing in automation, optimizing pipelines, and fostering a culture of collaboration, CTOs can build resilient and scalable development processes that drive business success.

Low-code and no-code development opportunities

Low-code and no-code development platforms have emerged as game-changers in the software industry, enabling rapid application development by simplifying the process of building software. These platforms allow developers, business analysts, and even non-technical users to create applications with minimal coding effort or no coding at all. For organizations, this means faster time to market, reduced development costs, and the ability to empower a broader range of users to solve business problems through software solutions. This section will discuss how low-code and no-code platforms work, their benefits, use cases, and engineering best practices for integrating them into existing development ecosystems.

Understanding low-code and no-code platforms

Low-code platforms offer a visual development environment where users can drag and drop components, connect them with pre-built templates, and write minimal code to add custom functionality. They are designed to accelerate development for experienced developers by reducing boilerplate code, automating repetitive tasks, and simplifying integrations. Examples of low-code platforms include Microsoft Power Apps, OutSystems, Mendix, and Appian.

No-code platforms take this concept further by eliminating the need for coding altogether. They provide a set of pre-configured modules and templates that users can assemble to create full-fledged applications. No-code platforms target business users who lack technical skills but need to build apps to solve specific business needs. Examples of no-code platforms include Airtable, Zapier, Bubble, and AppSheet.

Key benefits of low-code and no-code platforms

Low-code and no-code platforms are transforming application development by enabling rapid creation, deployment, and iteration of software solutions with minimal coding expertise. These platforms bridge the gap between technical and non-technical users, empowering businesses to innovate faster and more efficiently.

- **Accelerated development**: Low-code and no-code platforms drastically reduce the time required to build applications. Pre-built components, templates, and workflows allow users to create apps quickly without starting from scratch.

- **Cost efficiency**: By reducing the need for extensive coding and specialized developers, organizations can lower development costs. This is particularly beneficial for **small and medium enterprises** (**SMEs**) that may not have large development teams.

- **Empowerment of business users**: Business analysts, marketing teams, and other non-technical users can create apps independently, freeing up IT resources for more complex tasks. This democratization of app development promotes innovation within organizations.

- **Rapid prototyping and iteration**: Teams can quickly build prototypes, test them, and iterate based on feedback. This agility enables businesses to adapt to market demands more effectively.

- **Seamless integration**: Modern low-code platforms often include pre-built integrations with various enterprise systems (e.g., Salesforce, SAP, Microsoft 365), enabling easy data exchange and workflow automation across different tools.

Engineering best practices for integrating low-code and no-code solutions

While low-code and no-code platforms offer numerous benefits, integrating them into an organization's broader development strategy requires careful planning to ensure security, scalability, and compliance.

The following are the best practices for CTOs and engineering leaders to consider:

- **Standardize governance and security:**
  - Establish governance frameworks to manage who can build, deploy, and manage applications on low-code platforms. Define **role-based access controls** (**RBAC**) to prevent unauthorized access.
  - Ensure that data handling, storage, and integration practices on these platforms comply with regulatory requirements (e.g., GDPR, HIPAA). Use built-in security features like data encryption, secure authentication, and audit trails.
  - Regularly review and audit applications created using low-code or no-code platforms to detect any potential vulnerabilities or misconfigurations.

- **Define integration strategies:**
  - Integrate low-code and no-code platforms with existing enterprise systems using APIs and connectors. Ensure these integrations are robust, scalable, and secure.
  - Leverage middleware solutions or **enterprise service buses** (**ESBs**) like MuleSoft, Azure Logic Apps, or Apache Camel to facilitate seamless data flow between the low-code apps and existing systems.
  - Adopt an API-first approach to enable low-code apps to interact efficiently with backend services, ensuring that new applications can be easily integrated into the existing architecture.

- **Enable centralized monitoring and management:**

  o Implement centralized monitoring and logging for applications built on low-code platforms using tools like Splunk, Datadog, or Microsoft Azure Monitor. This provides visibility into app performance and helps quickly identify and resolve issues.

  o Use analytics tools to track usage patterns, errors, and user feedback on low-code applications, which can help improve performance and user experience.

  o Set up dashboards that give IT teams a clear view of all low-code and no-code apps running across the organization, ensuring that compliance, security, and performance standards are consistently met.

- **Establish best practices for low-code development:**

  o Train business users and citizen developers on development best practices, including UI/UX design principles, data management, and integration methods. This ensures that the apps they build are not only functional but also user-friendly and maintainable.

  o Encourage code reviews and testing practices, even for low-code applications. Although these apps require minimal coding, it is still important to ensure code quality, especially for custom scripts or business logic.

  o Create reusable components and templates that can be shared across projects, improving consistency and reducing development time.

- **Scalability considerations:**

  o Design low-code applications with scalability in mind, especially for critical business processes. Ensure that the platform can handle spikes in traffic, data volume, and user requests without degrading performance.

  o Choose platforms that support microservices architectures and can scale horizontally, allowing the organization to increase capacity as needed without affecting the application's stability.

  o Implement load balancing and auto-scaling where possible, especially for low-code apps that need to handle a growing number of users or integrate with high-traffic backend systems.

Use cases for low-code and no-code development

Low-code and no-code platforms provide versatile solutions for a wide range of business needs, empowering organizations to build applications rapidly, streamline workflows, and reduce the dependency on IT teams. These platforms enable both technical and non-technical users to address specific challenges and innovate without the constraints of traditional development cycles.

The following are some common use cases that illustrate how businesses can leverage low-code and no-code solutions effectively:

- **Automating internal processes**: Business teams can create applications to automate routine tasks, such as employee onboarding, expense tracking, and leave management, without relying on the IT department. For example, HR teams can set up a workflow that automatically routes onboarding documents to new employees, collects necessary information, and updates internal systems, all without writing complex code. This automation reduces manual effort, minimizes errors, and speeds up routine processes across departments.

- **Customer service automation**: Low-code platforms can be used to build chatbots, automated response systems, and customer feedback tools to enhance customer service without extensive coding. Organizations can quickly develop bots that answer common customer inquiries, route complex issues to support teams, and even conduct surveys to gather customer insights. These tools help improve customer satisfaction by providing faster response times and ensuring consistent service around the clock.

- **Data collection and reporting**: Business units can build apps for collecting data, generating reports, and visualizing analytics without needing to develop complex data pipelines. For instance, marketing teams can use no-code platforms to create custom dashboards that pull data from various sources (e.g., social media, email campaigns) and present actionable insights, helping teams make informed decisions quickly. This reduces the need for manual data entry and allows teams to access real-time information without involving data engineers.

- **Rapid prototyping and MVP development**: Organizations can use low-code platforms to quickly build and deploy prototypes or **minimum viable products** (**MVPs**), validate ideas, and gather user feedback before investing in full-scale development. This approach allows companies to experiment with new concepts, assess their viability, and iterate based on feedback. By reducing the time and cost of prototyping, businesses can innovate more rapidly and bring new products to market faster.

- **Integration hubs**: Companies can create integration hubs using low-code platforms to automate data exchange between different enterprise systems, streamlining workflows and improving efficiency. For example, a sales team might use a low-code solution to integrate their CRM with marketing automation and billing systems, ensuring that customer data flows seamlessly across departments. This eliminates the need for manual data transfers, reduces errors, and ensures that all systems are updated in real time.

- **Field service management**: Low-code platforms can be used to build mobile apps that assist field service teams with tasks like scheduling, inventory management, and reporting. These apps can be quickly customized to fit specific business requirements, enabling field technicians to access job details, update service records, and process payments on the go. This improves the efficiency of field operations and enhances the customer experience by ensuring faster service delivery.

- **Regulatory compliance and auditing**: Organizations in regulated industries can leverage no-code solutions to create compliance tracking and auditing tools that ensure adherence to industry standards and internal policies. By automating compliance checks and generating audit trails, businesses can reduce the risk of non-compliance and improve transparency. For example, a financial institution can build an app that monitors transactions for compliance with **anti-money laundering (AML)** regulations, automatically flagging any suspicious activity for review.

- **Employee self-service portals**: Companies can use low-code platforms to develop self-service portals where employees can access information, submit requests, and manage tasks without needing to engage HR or IT support. For instance, an employee might use the portal to request time off, access training materials, or check the status of a submitted expense report. These portals empower employees to manage their needs independently, freeing up HR and IT teams to focus on more strategic initiatives.

- **Event management and registration systems**: Event organizers can quickly set up registration forms, attendee management systems, and event tracking apps using low-code platforms. These solutions enable users to create and manage events, send automated reminders, track attendance, and gather feedback, all without requiring a dedicated development team. This is particularly useful for organizations that regularly host webinars, conferences, or training sessions.

- **Custom CRM solutions**: **Small and medium-sized enterprises (SMEs)** can build custom **customer relationship management (CRM)** systems tailored to their specific needs using no-code tools. Unlike off-the-shelf CRM solutions, which may include unnecessary features or lack essential ones, a custom-built CRM can provide exactly what the business requires. SMEs can integrate customer data from various channels, track sales pipelines, and automate follow-ups, all within a platform that is easy to adjust as the business grows.

Engineering checklist for low-code and no-code implementation

Implementing low-code and no-code solutions requires a structured approach to ensure security, scalability, and seamless integration with existing systems.

The following engineering checklist will help you assess key considerations for selecting, managing, and optimizing low-code platforms effectively.

- **Platform selection and integration:**
  - Have you evaluated and selected a low-code or no-code platform that meets your organization's specific needs and integrates seamlessly with existing systems?
  - Are APIs and pre-built connectors available to facilitate integration with other enterprise applications?
  - Is there a centralized platform or middleware to manage data flow between low-code applications and core business systems?

- **Security and governance:**
  - Have you implemented robust security policies, including data encryption, user authentication, and role-based access controls, for all low-code and no-code apps?
  - Are compliance and data privacy standards enforced across all applications built on low-code platforms?
  - Are there guidelines in place to ensure that only authorized users can create, deploy, and manage applications?

- **Scalability and performance:**
  - Can the selected low-code platform scale to accommodate increased traffic and data volume without impacting performance?
  - Are there strategies in place for load balancing and auto-scaling for critical low-code applications?
  - Have performance benchmarks been established, and are applications monitored regularly to ensure optimal performance?

- **Monitoring and maintenance:**
  - Are monitoring tools integrated to track the performance, usage, and security of low-code applications?
  - Are IT teams able to centrally manage, monitor, and update applications built by different teams across the organization?
  - Is there a process for regularly auditing and updating low-code and no-code apps to address new business requirements or fix issues?

- **Training and best practices:**
  - Are business users trained on how to use low-code platforms effectively, including understanding data flows, UI/UX design, and integration techniques?

o Are there established best practices for maintaining code quality, even for minimal coding tasks, to ensure maintainability and scalability?

o Have reusable components, templates, and guidelines been created to help teams build consistent and standardized applications?

Low-code/no-code vs. pro code development

One of the most critical decisions CTOs face today is determining when to leverage **low-code/no-code** (**LCNC**) platforms and when to opt for traditional pro code development. The line between these approaches can often seem blurred, making it challenging to decide which is best suited for a given scenario. This decision-making framework provides a structured approach for evaluating and selecting the appropriate development methodology by considering multiple factors, including complexity, technical fit, **total cost of ownership** (**TCO**), effort, talent availability, and more. It also introduces a scoring mechanism to help CTOs arrive at a data-driven decision to use LCNC, pro code, or a combination of both (fusion development).

The following are some of the key factors for decision-making:

- **Application complexity:**

  o **LCNC**: Best suited for simple to moderately complex applications that require minimal custom functionality. Examples include internal tools, dashboards, forms, and data-driven applications.

  o **Pro code**: Ideal for complex, highly customized applications that involve intricate business logic, extensive integrations, or unique security requirements.

- **Technical fitment and integration:**

  o **LCNC**: Suitable when integrating with common enterprise systems or cloud services that have pre-built connectors on the platform. It is effective for standardized integrations that do not need extensive customization.

  o **Pro code**: Necessary when deep, complex integrations are required or when working with legacy systems that may not be supported by LCNC platforms. Custom APIs and microservices are often developed for this purpose.

- **Total cost of ownership (TCO):**

  o **LCNC**: Generally, it has a lower TCO for short-term projects or applications with a limited lifespan due to reduced development time and smaller teams. However, licensing fees and scaling costs must be considered.

  o **Pro code**: While the upfront development cost may be higher, it can result in lower TCO over the long term if the application is core to the business and requires continuous updates, scalability, and maintenance.

- **Development effort and time to market:**

  - **LCNC**: Reduces development effort by leveraging drag-and-drop tools, templates, and pre-built modules, leading to faster prototyping and deployment. Ideal for MVPs, quick proofs of concept, and applications that need to be launched rapidly.

  - **Pro code**: More effort-intensive but allows for complete control over the development process. Necessary when time to market is less of a concern, and focus is on building a robust, scalable solution.

- **Talent availability and skillsets:**

  - **LCNC**: Enables business users or citizen developers to participate in the development process, reducing dependency on specialized development talent. Useful in scenarios where IT resources are limited.

  - **Pro code**: Requires skilled developers with expertise in programming languages, frameworks, and cloud architectures. Suitable when the organization has access to a strong pool of development talent.

- **Flexibility and customization:**

  - **LCNC**: Offers limited customization, which may suffice for applications with straightforward requirements. Ideal when the focus is on creating functional, standardized solutions.

  - **Pro code**: Provides maximum flexibility, enabling the development of highly customized applications. Necessary when the business needs bespoke solutions tailored to specific processes or use cases.

- **Long-term maintenance and change management:**

  - **LCNC**: Simpler for maintaining applications that are not expected to undergo frequent or significant changes. However, reliance on platform vendors can lead to challenges if the platform's roadmap changes.

  - **Pro code**: Easier to maintain and update in the long term, especially when there are ongoing requirements for new features or integrations. Offers greater control over versioning, updates, and dependency management.

- **Internal vs. external facing applications:**

  - **LCNC**: Effective for internal-facing applications that automate processes, improve productivity, and require quick deployment with basic UI/UX requirements.

  - **Pro code**: Preferred for customer-facing applications where user experience, performance, and reliability are paramount. Allows for complete customization to meet user expectations.

- **Scalability and performance:**
  - ○ **LCNC**: Can handle small to medium-scale applications effectively. However, scalability limitations may arise as the application grows in complexity or user base.
  - ○ **Pro code**: Designed to scale seamlessly, especially for enterprise-grade applications that need to handle large volumes of data, traffic, or transactions.
- **Innovation and competitive differentiation:**
  - ○ **LCNC**: Facilitates rapid experimentation, allowing organizations to test ideas quickly and iterate based on feedback. Suitable for projects where speed and agility are essential.
  - ○ **Pro code**: Enables deep technical innovation and the creation of unique features that can provide a competitive edge. Necessary when differentiating based on technological capabilities is critical.

Choosing LCNC, pro code, or fusion development

Use the following scoring mechanism to evaluate each factor on a scale of 1-5, where 1 indicates low priority/fit for the factor, and 5 indicates high priority/fit. Calculate the total score for each approach (LCNC, pro code, fusion) and use the results to guide your decision, as follows:

Factor	LCNC score	Pro code score	Fusion Score
Application complexity			
Technical fitment and integration			
Total cost of ownership (TCO)			
Development effort & time to market			
Talent availability & skillsets			
Flexibility & customization			
Long-term maintenance			
Internal vs. external facing			
Scalability & performance			
Innovation & competitive edge			
Total score			

Table 5.1: Low-code vs. pro code decision making scoring sheet

The following is the decision guide:

- **LCNC total score | Pro code total score**: Opt for LCNC if rapid development, lower costs, and ease of use outweigh the need for customization and scalability.

- **Pro code total score | LCNC total score**: Choose pro code when flexibility, scalability, and technical depth are essential, even if it requires higher development effort.

- **Fusion development (Scores are close across categories)**: Consider a combined approach where core, critical components are developed using pro code, while non-critical features (e.g., forms, dashboards) are built using LCNC to accelerate delivery.

Engineering best practices for fusion development

Fusion development combines the strengths of both LCNC and pro code, enabling teams to develop more efficiently by utilizing LCNC for quick, iterative development while relying on pro code for complex, critical components.

The following are some of the best practices:

- **Modular architecture design:**
  - Structure your applications to allow seamless integration between LCNC and pro code components. Use microservices or a modular architecture to keep different parts of the system loosely coupled.

  - Ensure that core functionalities requiring high customization or performance are developed as standalone services using pro code, while non-critical interfaces, workflows, or automation scripts can be handled by LCNC.

- **Standardized APIs for integration:**
  - Develop well-documented, standardized APIs to facilitate communication between LCNC apps and pro code services. This ensures that data and processes flow smoothly between the two environments.

  - Use API gateways (e.g., Azure API Management, AWS API Gateway) to manage and secure interactions between different components, simplifying integration and scalability.

- **Unified security and governance:**
  - Establish consistent security protocols across both LCNC and pro code solutions. This includes unified identity management, encryption, and compliance policies.

  - Implement governance frameworks to monitor and control who can create, deploy, and manage apps in LCNC environments to avoid shadow IT problems.

- **Shared data and service layers:**
  - o Utilize a shared data layer (e.g., cloud databases, storage) accessible to both LCNC and pro code components to avoid data silos. Ensure that the data structure is designed to support both approaches seamlessly.
  - o Centralize common services (e.g., authentication, logging, notifications) that can be reused across different applications, enabling faster integration and consistency.

- **Version control and change management:**
  - o Integrate LCNC platforms with version control systems (e.g., GitHub, Azure Repos) to track changes, manage releases, and implement rollback mechanisms if needed.
  - o Ensure that both LCNC and pro code teams adhere to change management processes, including code reviews, automated testing, and CI/CD pipelines.

- **Training and collaboration:**
  - o Encourage collaboration between IT and business users to build cohesive fusion development teams. Train non-technical users on LCNC platforms and educate pro code developers on how to extend LCNC capabilities.
  - o Create joint sprints where business and technical teams work together, using LCNC to quickly prototype solutions and pro code to refine and scale those solutions.

Selecting between LCNC, pro code, or a fusion approach is not a one-size-fits-all decision. By carefully evaluating factors like complexity, time to market, and technical requirements, CTOs can determine the most appropriate development approach for their projects. The decision-making framework and scoring mechanism outlined here provide a structured way to make these decisions, ensuring that businesses leverage the right mix of speed, flexibility, and innovation. Fusion development offers the best of both worlds by integrating the agility of LCNC with the robustness of pro code, empowering teams to build efficient, scalable, and innovative applications.

Future of low-code and no-code development

The future of low-code and no-code platforms looks promising, with advancements in **artificial intelligence (AI)**, **machine learning (ML)**, and **natural language processing (NLP)** further enhancing their capabilities. As these platforms integrate AI/ML models, users will be able to build smarter applications that can analyze data, automate decision-making, and improve user experiences. Additionally, the rise of hyper-automation will see low-code platforms playing a pivotal role in connecting disparate systems, automating end-to-end workflows, and facilitating the digital transformation of businesses.

Low-code and no-code platforms offer immense opportunities for organizations to innovate quickly, reduce development costs, and empower a wider range of users to participate in the app development process. As more organizations adopt low-code and no-code platforms, CTOs will need to ensure these solutions are integrated seamlessly with existing development workflows, secure, and scalable. By following best practices, implementing proper governance, and fostering collaboration between IT and business teams, companies can unlock the true potential of these platforms, accelerating innovation and achieving greater business agility.

Conclusion

By the end of this chapter, we covered the essential elements of modern application development, focusing on strategies and practices that enhance efficiency, scalability, and security. We began by discussing the *fundamentals of architecture design principles* and the role of a comprehensive *architecture review checklist* to ensure robust and scalable system designs. We then examined the integration of *DevSecOps and platform engineering*, highlighting how embedding security throughout the development lifecycle and building standardized platforms can improve software delivery and reliability.

Our discussion on *enhancing efficiency with continuous delivery and integration* emphasized the value of automating build, test, and deployment processes to accelerate time to market, improve code quality, and minimize risks. We also explored *low-code and no-code development* Opportunities, providing insights into how these platforms can speed up application development, empower non-technical users, and lower costs. Furthermore, we offered a detailed decision-making framework for CTOs to determine when to leverage **low-code/no-code** (**LCNC**) *vs. pro code or a fusion development approach*, along with best practices to integrate these methods into a unified strategy.

Throughout the chapter, we provided actionable engineering best practices, checklists, and scoring mechanisms to help technology leaders make informed decisions, streamline development processes, and build robust, adaptable systems that align with evolving business needs.

In the next chapter, we will shift our focus to *data management in modern architectures*. We will explore critical components, including how to choose the right **Online Transaction Processing** (**OLTP**) and **Online Analytical Processing** (**OLAP**) systems based on specific business requirements and data workflows. We will also discuss *distributed data processing* methods to improve performance and fault tolerance across multiple nodes, examine *real-time data processing* techniques for handling instantaneous data streams, and cover *cloud data warehousing* solutions that offer scalable, cost-effective storage with fast access and analysis capabilities.

Key terms

- **Architecture design principles**: Fundamental guidelines that inform the planning and construction of software systems, ensuring they are robust, scalable, and maintainable.

- **DevSecOps**: A development approach that integrates security practices into DevOps workflows, embedding security checks throughout the software development lifecycle.

- **Platform engineering**: The discipline of designing and building scalable, secure platforms that standardize development environments, tools, and workflows for efficient software delivery.

- **CI**: The practice of automating the integration of code changes from multiple developers, frequently merging code to a shared repository to detect and resolve issues early.

- **CD**: Extends CI by automating the deployment process, ensuring software is always in a deployable state, and enabling faster, reliable releases.

- **Low-code development**: A visual development approach that minimizes hand-coding by using drag-and-drop components and pre-built templates, enabling faster application building.

- **No-code development**: A development method that allows non-technical users to create applications using visual tools without writing any code, relying entirely on pre-configured modules.

- **Fusion development**: A hybrid approach that combines **low-code or no-code** (**LCNC**) and pro code, leveraging the strengths of both to speed up development while retaining flexibility for complex features.

- **IaC**: The practice of managing and provisioning infrastructure using code, enabling consistent, repeatable, and automated environment setups.

- **Blue-green deployment**: A deployment strategy that reduces downtime by running two identical environments (blue and green), switching traffic to the new environment only after verification.

- **Canary deployment**: A gradual deployment strategy where new software updates are released to a small subset of users first, allowing teams to monitor and roll back changes if issues arise.

- **Microservices architecture**: A software architecture style where applications are composed of loosely coupled, independently deployable services, promoting scalability and agility.

- **API-first approach**: Designing software interfaces (APIs) before building the application, ensuring seamless integration, and facilitating collaboration across teams and platforms.

Join our book's Discord space

Join the book's Discord Workspace for Latest updates, Offers, Tech happenings around the world, New Release and Sessions with the Authors:

https://discord.bpbonline.com

CHAPTER 6

Data Architecture and Processing

Introduction

In this chapter, we will discuss the critical components of data management that form the foundation of modern application development, focusing on architectural decisions and processing techniques that ensure scalability, robustness, and efficiency. We will begin by understanding the modern database landscape and examine how relational, NoSQL and in-memory databases cater to distinct organizational needs. Criteria for selecting the right **Online Transaction Processing (OLTP)** and **Online Analytical Processing (OLAP)** systems are discussed, emphasizing the importance of aligning these systems with specific business requirements to effectively handle transactional and analytical workloads.

Moreover, we will discuss distributed data processing methods, highlighting strategies for enhancing performance and fault tolerance through data management across multiple computing nodes. Real-time data processing techniques and tools are explored, underscoring their importance for applications requiring immediate insights and actions. Additionally, we will cover cloud data warehousing, presenting it as a scalable, cost-effective solution for storing vast amounts of data while enabling rapid access and robust analytical capabilities.

Structure

In this chapter, we will cover the following topics:

- Modern database landscape
- Criteria for selecting OLTP and OLAP systems
- Techniques for distributed data processing
- Implementing real-time data processing
- Best practices for cloud data warehousing

Objectives

By the end of this chapter, we will be equipped with a comprehensive understanding of the modern database landscape and its evolution from traditional relational databases to cutting-edge, cloud-native solutions. We will gain insights into the strengths and weaknesses of various database types and their alignment with specific business requirements, including NoSQL, NewSQL, in-memory, and AI-oriented databases. With real-world examples and use cases, you will learn how to deploy these technologies effectively within OLTP and OLAP systems. We will discuss a structured framework for selecting the right database systems, emphasizing factors like scalability, data consistency, query performance, and security. You will also explore core techniques for distributed data processing, such as partitioning, replication, stream processing, and federated processing, to design reliable and efficient large-scale systems. Additionally, we will discuss real-time data processing and mastering the implementation of low-latency, scalable, and fault-tolerant pipelines with stream processing frameworks and analytics. Moreover, we will cover the best practices for cloud data warehousing, including storage optimization, automated scaling, data security, and the integration of ETL/ELT processes, while highlighting emerging trends like data lakehouses and multi-cloud architectures. Furthermore, you will explore the integration of transformative technologies like serverless databases, edge computing, vector databases, and AI/ML-embedded data systems, ensuring you stay ahead of industry innovations. Finally, the chapter equips you with tools and frameworks to develop a comprehensive data strategy aligned with your business goals, enabling you to build a scalable, secure, and efficient data infrastructure that delivers high performance, real-time insights, and solutions tailored to your organization's unique needs.

Evolution of the database landscape

The database landscape has seen significant evolution over the past few decades, driven by the growing needs of businesses to store, process, and analyze vast amounts of data efficiently. In the early days, **relational databases (RDBMS)** dominated the market, with systems like *IBM DB2, Oracle Database, Microsoft SQL Server*, and *MySQL* setting the standard for structured data management. These systems relied on structured schemas, tables, and the SQL language to manage data, providing strong consistency and transaction integrity, which were critical for business applications like financial systems, ERP, and CRM. The adoption of relational databases grew rapidly in the 1980s and 1990s as businesses sought to standardize data management across various departments and processes.

By the late 1990s and early 2000s, as the internet boom led to an explosion of unstructured data, traditional RDBMS systems struggled to keep up with new demands for scalability and flexibility. This gave rise to NoSQL databases, such as MongoDB, Cassandra, and Redis, which offered schema-less structures, horizontal scalability, and faster read/write performance. NoSQL databases allowed organizations to manage unstructured and semi-structured data, making them ideal for web applications, real-time analytics, and scenarios where flexibility was crucial. This marked a shift from the rigid schemas of RDBMS to more flexible data models that could adapt to diverse data formats like JSON, XML, and key-value pairs.

The need for handling large-scale data processing led to the development of distributed data systems and NewSQL databases in the 2010s. NewSQL systems like Google Spanner, CockroachDB, and YugabyteDB aimed to combine the scalability of NoSQL databases with the **atomicity, consistency, isolation, and durability (ACID)** properties of traditional RDBMS, ensuring consistency while supporting high transaction rates. At the same time, distributed computing frameworks like *Apache Hadoop* and *Apache Spark* emerged to facilitate big data processing, enabling businesses to process massive datasets across clusters of machines, paving the way for advanced analytics and machine learning applications.

The last few years have brought a wave of innovation in the database landscape, primarily focused on addressing the modern challenges of scalability, real-time data processing, and integration with advanced technologies like AI and ML. One of the most significant developments is the rise of cloud-native databases. Platforms like Amazon Aurora, Google BigQuery, Azure Cosmos DB, and Snowflake have transformed data management by offering **databases as a service (DBaaS)**, which eliminates the need for infrastructure management. These cloud-native solutions provide on-demand scalability, high availability, and pay-as-you-go pricing models, making it easier for organizations to scale their data operations without the complexities of on-premises systems.

Another important trend is the advent of data lakehouses, a concept popularized by Databricks. Data lakehouses combine the scalability and flexibility of data lakes (which store raw, unstructured data) with the structure and performance of data warehouses, enabling businesses to handle both batch and real-time analytics in a single platform. This hybrid approach addresses the challenges of data silos and allows organizations to analyze all their data in one place, leading to more comprehensive insights. Microsoft Fabric has also embraced this trend by integrating data engineering, data science, and real-time analytics capabilities into a cohesive, unified platform.

Integrating AI and ML within databases is another groundbreaking innovation. Modern databases are increasingly incorporating ML capabilities to automate tasks like indexing, query optimization, and anomaly detection. Platforms such as Google BigQuery ML and Amazon Redshift ML allow users to build, train, and deploy ML models directly within the database, eliminating the need for complex data pipelines and reducing time to insight. This trend aligns with the growing need for real-time decision-making, where predictive analytics and automated recommendations can be executed as part of the data workflow.

As businesses continue to expand their digital footprint, the database landscape is evolving towards more intelligent, integrated, and distributed systems. One of the key directions is the growth of multi-model databases like *Couchbase* and *ArangoDB*, which can support multiple data models (e.g., document, graph, key-value) within a single database engine. This flexibility allows organizations to simplify their data architecture, reducing the need to deploy and manage multiple specialized databases for different use cases.

The rise of edge computing is also influencing database technology. Edge databases such as *Couchbase Lite* and *SQLite* enable data processing to occur closer to where data is generated, reducing latency and bandwidth usage. This is particularly useful for IoT applications, autonomous vehicles, and industrial automation, where real-time data processing at the edge is critical.

Serverless databases like *Azure Cosmos DB* and *Amazon Aurora Serverless* are becoming more prevalent, offering auto-scaling capabilities that allow businesses to handle unpredictable workloads without manual intervention. This means that organizations can focus on building applications rather than managing infrastructure, improving agility and time-to-market.

Vector databases are emerging as a key technology for AI and ML applications. Solutions like *Pinecone*, *Weaviate*, and *Milvus* are designed to store and search high-dimensional vector data, which is essential for tasks like semantic search, recommendation systems, and natural language processing. As AI models generate embeddings that capture the semantic meaning of data, vector databases enable faster and more accurate retrieval of information, opening up new possibilities for intelligent, context-aware applications.

The future of databases is moving towards distributed, cloud-native, and AI-augmented systems that can seamlessly handle diverse data types and workloads, whether on the cloud, at the edge, or on-premises. With the convergence of database technologies and advanced analytics, organizations will be able to unlock more value from their data, driving innovation, operational efficiency, and competitive advantage.

Modern database landscape

In the evolving digital ecosystem, businesses must manage a wide variety of data, ranging from transactional records to complex analytical datasets. To effectively handle this diversity, organizations rely on different database technologies that address specific use cases. The modern database landscape can be broadly categorized into OLTP and OLAP systems. Each of these categories serves distinct purposes and employs various database technologies optimized for specific workloads, as shown:

OLTP Databases		OLAP Databases	Data Processing Tech
RDBMS		Data Warehouse	Data Partitioning
No SQL		Data Lake	Data Replication
AI Oriented Databases		HTAP	Map Reduce
In-Memory		Lakehouse	Stream Processing
New SQL		Data Mesh	Data Pipeline / ETL / ELT
Distributed SQL		Data Fabric	Federated Data Processing
Blockchain		Data Virtualization	Confidential Computing
Time Series		File Storage	DataOps and MLOps
Edge	Graph		Data Classification
Federated			Data Masking / Encryption
Serverless			

Figure 6.1: Modern database landscape

Online transaction processing systems

OLTP systems are designed to handle real-time, transactional workloads where data consistency, speed, and reliability are paramount. They are typically used for applications requiring a high volume of short, atomic transactions.

The following are some of the key types of databases under OLTP:

Relational databases

RDBMS uses a structured, schema-based approach to store and manage data, adhering to ACID properties to ensure data reliability and integrity. They are best suited for scenarios where data consistency is critical, such as financial systems, ERP applications, and e-commerce platforms. Popular examples of RDBMS include MySQL, PostgreSQL, Microsoft SQL Server, and Oracle.

NoSQL databases

NoSQL databases offer flexible storage solutions for various data types. *Key-value stores* are simple and efficient, storing data as key-value pairs, which makes them ideal for use cases requiring high-speed retrieval, such as caching and session management. Popular examples include Redis and Amazon DynamoDB. *Document databases* handle semi-structured data, such as JSON documents, making them perfect for content management systems that need flexible data structures. Examples are MongoDB and Couchbase. *Column-family stores* store data in columns rather than rows, which optimizes them for read-heavy operations and analytics; Apache Cassandra and HBase are notable examples. *Graph databases* focus on relationships between entities, making them well-suited for applications like social networks, fraud detection, and recommendation engines. Examples include Neo4j and Amazon Neptune.

Emerging AI-oriented databases

With the rise of artificial intelligence, new databases have emerged to handle AI-specific workloads. *Vector databases* are specialized in storing and querying high-dimensional vector data, which is crucial for applications like semantic search, recommendation systems, and anomaly detection that rely on AI embeddings. Examples of vector databases include Pinecone, Weaviate, and Milvus. *AI-optimized databases* integrate machine learning capabilities directly within the database engine, enabling advanced analytics, pattern recognition, and predictive modeling without the need for separate data pipelines. Examples of such databases are Google BigQuery ML and Amazon Redshift ML.

NewSQL databases

NewSQL databases combine the scalability and flexibility of NoSQL systems with the ACID compliance of traditional relational databases, providing high transaction rates alongside data consistency. They are ideal for scenarios where both high scalability and data integrity are necessary, such as financial services and online gaming platforms. Examples of NewSQL databases include CockroachDB and Google Spanner.

In-memory databases

In-memory databases store data directly in RAM rather than on disk, which significantly enhances read and write speeds. They are highly useful for applications requiring low-latency access, such as real-time analytics and caching. Examples of in-memory databases include SAP HANA, Memcached, and Redis.

Distributed SQL databases

Distributed SQL databases are designed to spread data across multiple nodes, ensuring availability, scalability, and fault tolerance. This architecture is particularly beneficial for global applications that require high availability and consistency, such as SaaS platforms. Examples of distributed SQL databases are YugabyteDB, CockroachDB and TiDB.

Blockchain databases

Blockchain databases provide immutable, distributed ledger systems that guarantee data integrity and security. They are well-suited for use cases that require secure and transparent transactions, such as supply chain management, financial services, and **decentralized applications (DApps)**. Examples include Hyperledger Fabric and Ethereum.

Time-series databases

Time-series databases are optimized for handling time-stamped data, enabling efficient storage, querying, and analysis of time-based data streams. They are ideal for scenarios like IoT data collection, financial tickers, and system monitoring. Popular examples are InfluxDB and TimescaleDB.

Edge databases

Edge databases are deployed closer to where data is generated, minimizing latency and enabling faster processing at the network's edge. This makes them highly suitable for IoT devices, autonomous vehicles, and industrial automation, where quick data processing is critical. Examples of edge databases include SQLite and Couchbase Lite.

Federated databases

Federated databases allow querying across multiple, diverse databases as if they were a single unified system. This capability facilitates data integration and analysis, enabling organizations to aggregate data from different sources across departments or subsidiaries. Examples include MySQL FEDERATED and Presto.

Serverless databases

Serverless databases automatically scale based on demand, removing the need for manual capacity planning and infrastructure management. This approach is particularly beneficial for applications with variable workloads, as it reduces overheads and improves efficiency. Examples of serverless databases are Amazon Aurora Serverless and Azure Cosmos DB.

Online analytical processing systems

OLAP systems focus on analyzing large volumes of data and enabling complex queries and aggregations. These databases are optimized for read-heavy operations, data modeling, and historical data analysis.

The key types are as follows:

Data warehouses

Data warehouses consolidate structured data from various sources into a centralized repository optimized for complex querying and reporting. They are designed to support extensive data analysis by providing a reliable, structured environment that allows businesses to perform detailed business intelligence, financial analysis, and operational reporting. Commonly used data warehouse solutions include Amazon Redshift, Google BigQuery, and Snowflake.

Data lakes

Data lakes are designed to store vast amounts of raw, unstructured, and semi-structured data, making them an ideal foundation for advanced analytics and machine learning. Unlike data warehouses, data lakes can handle a wider variety of data formats, enabling organizations to store data as-is without requiring an initial transformation. This flexibility makes them suitable for big data analytics, data science projects, and machine learning pipelines. Examples of data lakes include Azure Data Lake and Hadoop HDFS.

Hybrid transactional or analytical processing

Hybrid transactional/analytical processing (**HTAP**) systems combine the functionalities of OLTP and OLAP, enabling real-time analytics on transactional data. This dual capability allows organizations to perform immediate analysis on live data, which is particularly useful for scenarios such as real-time fraud detection, customer experience personalization, and financial analysis. Examples of HTAP systems include SingleStore and MariaDB Xpand.

Emerging architectures

New architectural approaches are transforming how organizations manage and analyze data as follows:

- **Data lakehouse**: This architecture merges the flexibility of data lakes with the structured data management of data warehouses, supporting both batch processing and real-time analytics. It allows businesses to store all their data in a single repository while also providing the data structure and governance needed for analytical workloads. Examples include Databricks Lakehouse and Delta Lake.

- **Data mesh**: Data mesh decentralizes data ownership, enabling domain-driven data management. This approach promotes a more agile, scalable infrastructure by distributing the responsibility of data across various teams, encouraging data-as-a-product thinking. An example of this architecture is Starburst Data Mesh.

- **Data fabric**: Unlike data mesh, data fabric focuses on providing a unified, integrated architecture that simplifies access to data spread across multiple locations. It provides automation for data integration, governance, and security, making it easier to manage data across cloud and on-premise environments.

- **Data virtualization**: Data virtualization provides real-time access to data across diverse systems without the need to physically move the data. This allows for seamless integration and faster data processing, facilitating real-time analytics and reporting. Examples include Denodo and Dremio.

Emerging data privacy and security technologies

Traditional security measures are no longer enough, emerging technologies are redefining how we safeguard data, even while it is being processed. From confidential computing to zero-knowledge proofs and privacy-preserving computation, these advancements are setting new standards for data security in an increasingly interconnected world, as follows:

- **Confidential computing**: Ensuring data privacy is critical, especially when dealing with sensitive information. Confidential computing enables the processing of encrypted data without exposing it, offering a new level of data security. Solutions include Microsoft Azure Confidential Computing and Intel SGX.

- **Zero-knowledge proofs**: For applications where data needs to be verified without being fully exposed (like blockchain or secure transactions), **zero-knowledge proofs (ZKPs)** are emerging as a crucial technology. They allow for the validation of data integrity and authenticity without revealing the data itself.

- **Privacy-preserving computation**: Techniques like homomorphic encryption and differential privacy enable computations on encrypted data without decrypting it, ensuring confidentiality and integrity, which is especially important for sensitive sectors like healthcare and finance.

Enhanced data integration solutions

Data integration and pipeline management are vital to handling data from different sources as follows:

- **Data pipelines**: Tools like *Apache Airflow, Azure Data Factory*, and *AWS Glue* help automate, schedule, and monitor data pipelines, ensuring smooth data flow and transformation.

- **DataOps and MLOps**: Combining data management with machine learning, DataOps, and MLOps streamline the process of preparing data, training models, and deploying them into production. Platforms like Databricks, Kubeflow, and MLflow are leading this integration.

File storage systems

The following file storage systems play critical roles in data management, especially for handling unstructured data:

- **Object storage**: Scalable and cost-effective, object storage is ideal for managing large volumes of unstructured data, such as images, videos, and backups. Popular examples are Amazon S3 and Azure Blob Storage.

- **Distributed file systems**: These systems manage large datasets across multiple machines, providing high throughput and fault tolerance, which makes them suitable for big data and AI workloads. Examples include Ceph and HDFS.

- **AI-optimized file systems**: Designed to support fast data access and input/ output operations, AI-optimized file systems are essential for efficiently training AI models. Examples of such systems include Alluxio and Delta Lake.

The modern database landscape is evolving rapidly, driven by the need for scalability, real-time insights, and new technologies like generative AI. Understanding these various database technologies and their use cases enables organizations to make informed decisions on their data architecture, ensuring they remain competitive and capable of meeting their business goals. For CTOs, recognizing emerging trends such as vector databases, data lakehouses, and data mesh can pave the way for more agile, scalable, and efficient data solutions, keeping their businesses at the forefront of innovation.

Criteria for selecting OLTP and OLAP systems

Selecting the right database system is critical for ensuring the efficiency, scalability, and performance of modern applications. Organizations need to evaluate their specific business needs and technical requirements before deciding on an appropriate OLTP or OLAP system. The following criteria can guide decision-making when choosing between these two types of systems:

Criteria for selecting OLTP systems

OLTP systems are designed for real-time, high-volume transactional workloads. When choosing an OLTP database, consider the following factors:

Consistency and ACID compliance

For applications where data integrity is crucial, such as financial systems, ERP solutions, and e-commerce platforms, it is essential that the database adheres to ACID properties. This ensures that transactions are processed reliably, preventing data corruption even during system failures or unexpected crashes. When evaluating OLTP systems, assess if strict consistency is a requirement for your application or if eventual consistency (as seen in some NoSQL databases) could suffice. Relational databases like MySQL and PostgreSQL provide strong ACID compliance, while some NoSQL solutions trade strict consistency for higher availability and scalability.

Scalability

The ability to handle increasing volumes of transactions as the business grows is a critical factor. OLTP systems must efficiently scale to accommodate surges in transaction loads without compromising performance. Scalability can be achieved vertically (by adding more resources to a single server) or horizontally (by adding more servers to a distributed system). Traditional RDBMS like Oracle or Microsoft SQL Server often scale vertically, while NoSQL databases like MongoDB and Apache Cassandra offer horizontal scalability, making them suitable for handling distributed, large-scale applications.

Performance and latency

Applications with high transaction rates demand low-latency responses to ensure smooth user experiences. OLTP systems should be optimized to handle thousands or even millions of transactions per second without delays. Factors such as indexing, query optimization, and in-memory processing can significantly improve performance. For example, in-memory databases like *SAP HANA* and *Redis* are designed to provide rapid data access, making them ideal for applications that require sub-millisecond response times, such as real-time bidding platforms and financial trading systems.

High availability and disaster recovery

For mission-critical applications, **high availability (HA)** and **disaster recovery (DR)** capabilities are non-negotiable. OLTP systems must be resilient, with built-in mechanisms for failover, replication, and automated backups. This ensures minimal downtime during system failures and enables quick recovery from data loss events. When selecting an OLTP system, assess the database's native support for replication, clustering, and automated failover features. Solutions like Amazon Aurora and PostgreSQL with multi-node replication provide robust HA and DR configurations, making them suitable for continuous operations.

Flexibility and data model support

In some scenarios, especially when dealing with dynamic or unstructured data, flexibility in data modeling becomes important. Traditional RDBMS systems require a fixed schema, which can be restrictive when the data model changes frequently. In contrast, NoSQL databases like MongoDB and Couchbase offer schema flexibility, allowing developers to store different types of data in the same database. This is beneficial for applications that need to adapt quickly to changing requirements or handle diverse datasets, such as content management systems and IoT data platforms.

Security and compliance

Data security and regulatory compliance are critical for OLTP systems handling sensitive information. The database should offer robust security features, including encryption (both at rest and in transit), role-based access controls, and audit logging to monitor and track data access. Additionally, compliance with industry regulations like GDPR, HIPAA, and PCI-DSS is essential, especially for businesses operating in healthcare, finance, and e-commerce. Evaluate if the OLTP system provides native encryption, comprehensive security policies, and audit trails. For instance, Oracle Database and Microsoft SQL Server come with built-in security features to safeguard data, while cloud databases like Azure SQL Database offer compliance certifications.

Criteria for selecting OLAP systems

OLAP systems are optimized for data analysis, complex queries, and reporting. When choosing an OLAP system, consider the following factors:

Scalability for large data volumes

OLAP systems are designed to handle large datasets, often aggregating data from multiple sources. Scalability is critical as data volumes grow, and the system must be able to process large-scale datasets efficiently. OLAP systems should support horizontal scaling, where additional resources can be added to accommodate increasing data loads. Distributed systems like Google BigQuery and Snowflake leverage cloud infrastructure to enable massive parallel processing, which allows them to handle terabytes or even petabytes of data efficiently.

Query performance and analytical capabilities

Analytical workloads often involve complex queries, aggregations, and joins across large datasets. The performance of an OLAP system depends on its ability to execute these queries quickly and provide insights without delays. Modern OLAP systems use optimizations like columnar storage, indexing, and materialized views to speed up query execution. For instance, columnar databases such as Amazon Redshift and Apache Druid store data in columns rather than rows, making read-heavy analytical queries significantly faster. Assess whether the system supports features that improve analytical performance, such as pre-aggregated data cubes or partitioning.

Integration with data processing and visualization tools

Seamless integration with **extract, transform, load** (**ETL**) tools, data processing frameworks, and visualization platforms is essential for OLAP systems. This ensures that data can be easily ingested, transformed, and analyzed. Evaluate whether the OLAP system can integrate with popular ETL tools like Apache NiFi, Talend, or Azure Data Factory, as well as **business intelligence** (**BI**) tools like Tableau, Power BI, and Looker. Compatibility with data lakes, machine learning frameworks, and cloud storage can further extend the system's analytical capabilities.

Data freshness and real-time analytics

In today's fast-paced business environment, the ability to process and analyze data in real-time has become increasingly important. Traditional OLAP systems often rely on batch processing, which may not meet the needs of applications requiring up-to-the-minute insights. Modern data warehouses and hybrid systems support streaming data ingestion, allowing real-time data processing and analytics. For example, Google BigQuery can ingest streaming data, while SingleStore combines OLTP and OLAP capabilities for real-time analytics on live data. Assess your need for real-time versus batch analytics when selecting an OLAP system.

Data storage efficiency

Efficient storage management is a vital consideration for OLAP systems, especially when dealing with large-scale datasets. Effective compression techniques, columnar storage formats, and data deduplication can significantly reduce storage costs and improve performance. Systems like Snowflake use micro-partitioning to organize data efficiently, while formats like Apache Parquet and ORC provide effective compression and fast query performance. Ensure that the OLAP system you choose has capabilities to optimize storage and manage data effectively across different formats.

Data governance and security

Governance and security are crucial for OLAP systems, particularly when they aggregate sensitive data from multiple sources. The system should offer robust access controls to ensure that only authorized users can access specific datasets, as well as encryption to protect data at rest and in transit. Compliance features are also important, especially for businesses in regulated industries. Tools like Azure Synapse Analytics and IBM Db2 Warehouse come with built-in governance features, including role-based access controls, encryption, and comprehensive audit trails. When selecting an OLAP system, consider its ability to provide strong data governance frameworks that align with your organization's compliance requirements.

Additional considerations

The following are some additional considerations when choosing an OLAP system:

Multi-cloud and hybrid cloud deployments

As more businesses adopt multi-cloud and hybrid cloud strategies, the ability to deploy OLTP and OLAP systems across different environments becomes essential. Systems that support seamless data integration and management across on-premises, public cloud, and private cloud environments offer more flexibility and reduce the risk of vendor lock-in. For example, solutions like Google BigQuery Omni and Azure Arc enable organizations to manage their data assets consistently across different platforms.

Total cost of ownership

While performance and scalability are critical, organizations must also consider the total cost of ownership. This includes not only the licensing and infrastructure costs, but also operational expenses related to maintenance, backups, and scaling. Cloud-native databases often offer pay-as-you-go pricing models, which can provide cost efficiency, but it is important to analyze long-term costs, especially for systems that need to handle large data volumes.

Decision-making framework for selecting OLTP and OLAP databases

In a crowded database market, choosing the right portfolio of OLTP and OLAP systems for your business can be a complex task. CTOs and technical leaders can benefit from a structured framework that considers multiple factors to align database capabilities with business requirements.

The following is a step-by-step framework to guide the decision-making process:

1. **Define business objectives and use cases**: The first step in selecting a database system is to clearly understand the business objectives and specific use cases. CTOs should work closely with stakeholders across different departments to identify the primary goals. Answering these questions can help clarify needs:

   The following are some of the questions to consider:

   a. What primary business processes will the database support (e.g., online transactions, customer data management, real-time monitoring)?

   b. Are the use cases primarily transactional (OLTP) or analytical (OLAP), or do they require a hybrid approach?

   c. What specific features or capabilities are critical for success (e.g., real-time data processing, complex query handling, high availability)?

   d. How will the database contribute to achieving broader business objectives (e.g., improved customer experience, operational efficiency, data-driven decision-making)?

   e. Are there any existing systems or tools that the database needs to integrate with, and what are the key dependencies?

2. **Assess data volume, velocity, and variety**: A clear understanding of the 3Vs, volume, velocity, and variety of data helps determine the scalability and performance requirements of the database systems.

   Answer the following questions to assess data characteristics:

   a. How much data will the system need to handle on a daily, weekly, and monthly basis? What are the anticipated data growth rates over time?

   b. How quickly does data need to be ingested, processed, and queried? Will the system need to support real-time or near-real-time data processing?

   c. What types of data will the system manage (structured, semi-structured, unstructured)? Are there specific data formats (e.g., JSON, XML, multimedia) that need to be supported?

d. How much data will be read vs. written? Are there specific patterns of data access (e.g., burst traffic, batch processing)?

e. Will the database need to handle time-series data, geospatial data, or other specialized data types?

3. **Evaluate scalability and performance requirements**: Assess your scalability and performance needs. Determine whether vertical or horizontal scaling will be more effective for your use cases and consider the expected load on the system during peak times.

The following are questions to help with the evaluation:

a. Will the system need to scale up (vertical) or out (horizontal) as the data volume or transaction count increases? Which approach aligns best with your architecture?

b. What are the peak performance requirements (e.g., transactions per second, query response times)? Can the system handle expected spikes in traffic?

c. Are there requirements for sub-millisecond or low-latency responses, especially for real-time applications?

d. How important is consistent performance across distributed environments, and does the system offer built-in mechanisms for load balancing and sharding?

e. What mechanisms does the database provide for performance optimization (e.g., indexing, caching, in-memory processing)?

4. **Consider data governance, security, and compliance**: Data security, privacy, and regulatory compliance should be core considerations in the selection process. Some industries have stringent compliance requirements, so ask the following questions:

a. What level of data security is required (e.g., encryption at rest, encryption in transit, access control mechanisms)?

b. Does the database support compliance with specific regulations (e.g., GDPR, HIPAA, PCI-DSS)? Are there certifications that ensure compliance?

c. How are data privacy and integrity maintained, especially when dealing with sensitive information?

d. Does the system provide fine-grained access controls to limit who can view, edit, or query specific datasets?

e. Are there audit logging features to track data access, changes, and actions? How is data protection managed in case of unauthorized access?

5. **Integration capabilities with existing ecosystem**: Evaluate how well a database integrates with existing tools and systems in your technology ecosystem. Seamless integration can streamline data operations.

   Consider the following questions:

   a. Does the database have pre-built connectors for existing ETL tools (e.g., Apache NiFi, Talend, Azure Data Factory) and data processing frameworks (e.g., Apache Spark)?

   b. Can the system easily integrate with cloud services (AWS, Azure, Google Cloud) or on-premises infrastructure?

   c. Does the database support APIs, SDKs, or other integration tools to connect with custom applications or third-party software?

   d. How well does the system integrate with business intelligence (BI) tools (e.g., Tableau, Power BI, Looker) for data visualization and reporting?

   e. What level of effort and expertise is required to set up and maintain integrations?

6. **Analyze total cost of ownership**: Cost is a critical factor, but it is important to analyze the **total cost of ownership (TCO)** rather than just the initial cost. Answer these questions to get a complete financial picture:

   a. What is the cost model (e.g., pay-as-you-go, subscription-based, perpetual licensing)? Does it align with your budget and financial planning?

   b. Are there hidden costs associated with data transfers, scaling, maintenance, or additional features (e.g., backups, security enhancements)?

   c. What is the expected cost over a 1-year, 3-year, and 5-year period, considering both infrastructure and operational expenses?

   d. Can the database system run on existing infrastructure, or will it require significant hardware upgrades or cloud resources?

   e. What are the potential costs related to disaster recovery, high availability, and data migration?

7. **Establish evaluation and benchmarking criteria**: After narrowing down your options, set clear benchmarks and performance metrics to evaluate potential database systems.

   Use the following questions to guide your evaluation:

   a. What are the **key performance indicators (KPIs)** that will determine the success of the database (e.g., transactions per second, query latency, throughput)?

    b. Can industry-standard benchmarks (e.g., TPC-C for OLTP, TPC-H for OLAP) be used to compare performance?

    c. Can the database support the required workload under simulated real-world conditions during a **proof-of-concept (PoC)** test?

    d. What is the failover and recovery time in case of a system failure or disaster?

    e. How does the database perform under heavy read/write loads, and are there bottlenecks that need to be addressed?

8. **Develop a multi-database strategy**: In many cases, a single database solution may not be sufficient. A multi-database strategy allows businesses to leverage the strengths of different systems for specific use cases. Here is how to plan effectively:

    a. Are there specific applications or use cases that would benefit from using multiple types of databases (e.g., NoSQL for unstructured data, relational databases for structured data)?

    b. How will the databases interact, and is there a need for seamless data exchange between them (e.g., using a data fabric or data mesh architecture)?

    c. Is there a mechanism to ensure data consistency and integrity when multiple databases are used in conjunction?

    d. How will data synchronization, replication, or migration be managed across multiple systems?

    e. Are there performance trade-offs to consider when deploying a multi-database environment, and what steps can be taken to optimize it?

The database landscape is vast and rapidly evolving, with new technologies emerging to address specific business challenges. By following a structured decision-making framework and answering these detailed questions, CTOs, technical leaders, and application/data teams can navigate the complexities of selecting the right OLTP and OLAP systems. This approach ensures that business requirements, data characteristics, and operational considerations are all factored into the final decision, enabling organizations to build efficient, scalable, and cost-effective data solutions.

Scoring criteria for selecting OLTP and OLAP databases

Given the crowded database landscape, CTOs and technical leaders need a structured approach to evaluate and choose the right database systems. Using a scoring mechanism allows for objective assessment based on predefined criteria, ensuring the selected technologies align with strategic business needs. Below are detailed criteria and a scoring mechanism for OLTP and OLAP systems.

The current weightages have been estimated based on typical industry requirements. For instance, criteria like data consistency and high availability receive higher weights in

OLTP systems because reliable transaction processing and uptime are essential for real-time applications. Similarly, scalability and query performance are weighted highly for OLAP systems, as they need to handle large datasets and complex queries efficiently.

While these weightages serve as a general guideline, it is essential for readers to adjust them based on their unique business priorities. For example, if an organization is operating in a highly regulated industry, security and compliance may warrant a higher weight, while a startup focusing on rapid deployment might prioritize ease of integration or cost efficiency more heavily. Tailoring the weights ensures that the evaluation process aligns with specific business goals and operational needs.

Following are the scoring criteria for OLTP systems:

- **Data consistency and ACID compliance (Weight: 10)**: Ensuring data integrity through adherence to ACID properties, Atomicity, Consistency, Isolation, and Durability, is crucial for OLTP databases. This guarantees reliable transaction processing, even during system failures, which is vital for applications like financial systems and e-commerce platforms. Maintaining strict data consistency is often non-negotiable, making this the top priority.

- **High availability and disaster recovery (Weight: 10)**: For mission-critical OLTP systems, ensuring HA and robust **disaster recovery (DR)** capabilities is essential. The database must be resilient, with features like replication, failover, and automated backups to minimize downtime and enable quick recovery from data loss. Continuous availability is crucial for uninterrupted operations, particularly in industries like finance and healthcare.

- **Transaction throughput (Weight: 9)**: The ability of a database to handle high transaction volumes efficiently is critical for OLTP systems. High throughput, measured in **transactions per second (TPS)**, ensures that the database can support real-time data processing, which is vital for environments handling large-scale transactions or rapidly changing data.

- **Scalability (Weight: 9)**: Scalability is a key consideration for OLTP systems that need to accommodate growing transaction volumes over time. Vertical scalability (adding resources to a single server) and horizontal scalability (distributing data across multiple servers) allow businesses to manage increased workloads without performance degradation. This capability is essential for growing businesses that anticipate future scaling needs.

- **Low latency (Weight: 8)**: OLTP applications often require low-latency responses to provide smooth user experiences. The database must be optimized for fast query execution to minimize delays, ensuring rapid processing of transactions. This is particularly important for real-time applications where even slight delays can disrupt the user experience.

- **Security and compliance (Weight: 8)**: Data security is paramount, especially when handling sensitive information. OLTP systems should offer robust security features, including encryption, access controls, and compliance with industry standards such as GDPR, PCI-DSS, and HIPAA. Ensuring data privacy and integrity protects businesses from potential breaches and regulatory penalties.

- **Cost efficiency (Weight: 7)**: Analyzing the **total cost of ownership (TCO)**, which includes initial setup, maintenance, and scalability costs, is essential for selecting the right OLTP database. Cost-efficiency means balancing the expenses against the performance benefits. Cloud-native databases can provide flexible, pay-as-you-go models to manage expenses effectively, but long-term costs should always be considered.

- **Ease of integration (Weight: 7)**: For seamless data flow and operational efficiency, OLTP databases must easily integrate with existing systems, middleware, and APIs. Strong integration capabilities reduce complexity and improve productivity, enabling businesses to connect their databases with various other tools and platforms effortlessly.

- **Data model flexibility (Weight: 6)**: In dynamic environments, flexibility in handling different types of data (structured, semi-structured, unstructured) is advantageous. Databases that can adapt to changing data schemas are more efficient for applications managing diverse and evolving datasets. While this is less critical than consistency and availability, it remains important for rapidly evolving businesses.

- **Vendor support and community (Weight: 6)**: Strong vendor support and an active user community can significantly ease the process of deploying, optimizing, and troubleshooting OLTP systems. Access to comprehensive documentation, technical support, and a vibrant community helps businesses resolve issues quickly and implement best practices.

Following are the scoring criteria for OLAP systems:

- **Scalability for large datasets (Weight: 10)**: OLAP systems must efficiently handle and scale with growing data volumes. Scalability ensures that as data expands, the system can still process and analyze large datasets without compromising performance. This is particularly important for big data analytics and data warehousing solutions, which often manage terabytes or petabytes of data.

- **Query performance (Weight: 9)**: Analytical workloads involve executing complex queries, aggregations, and joins across large datasets. An OLAP database must be optimized to handle these tasks efficiently, delivering fast query responses even when processing extensive data. Superior query performance is critical for providing timely insights to support data-driven decision-making.

- **Data governance and security (Weight: 9)**: Strong data governance ensures data integrity, security, and compliance across all analytical processes. OLAP systems should provide robust features for data encryption, role-based access control, and audit logging to maintain data security and support compliance with regulatory requirements, particularly in industries like finance and healthcare.

- **Integration with BI and analytics tools (Weight: 8)**: Seamless compatibility with **business intelligence** (**BI**) tools such as Tableau and Power BI and data processing frameworks like Apache Spark is essential for OLAP systems. Strong integration capabilities allow organizations to streamline data preparation, analysis, and visualization, which is crucial for developing effective analytics workflows.

- **Data storage efficiency (Weight: 8)**: Efficient data storage is vital for OLAP systems, as it reduces costs and enhances performance. Techniques like data compression, columnar storage, and partitioning help optimize storage, enabling faster query processing and cost-effective management of large datasets, especially in data warehousing contexts.

- **Support for real-time analytics (Weight: 7)**: Modern OLAP systems increasingly need to process and provide insights on real-time or near-real-time data. The ability to handle streaming data and offer real-time analysis is valuable for businesses that require live dashboards and monitoring capabilities to make immediate business decisions based on fresh data.

- **Ease of management (Weight: 7)**: Simplified setup, configuration, and maintenance are important for reducing the complexity of deploying and running OLAP systems. Features such as automated backups, monitoring, and performance tuning can enhance manageability, making the system easier to operate and maintain over time.

- **Cost efficiency (Weight: 7)**: Considering the total cost of ownership, including licensing, infrastructure, and operational expenses, is critical when selecting an OLAP system. The ideal solution should balance costs with performance and storage efficiency, ensuring that the system delivers high value without excessive financial burden.

- **Compatibility with ETL pipelines (Weight: 6)**: Compatibility with ETL tools is crucial for efficient data ingestion, processing, and movement. An OLAP system must work seamlessly with ETL processes, facilitating smooth data integration from various sources and enabling effective data transformation to support complex analytics.

- **Vendor support and community (Weight: 6)**: Effective vendor support and an active community are vital for troubleshooting, implementing new features, and sharing knowledge. Access to detailed documentation, technical assistance, and a user community helps ensure smooth deployment and continuous improvement of the OLAP system.

Analyse results and make a decision

Based on the total scores, determine which technology or architecture pattern best meets the organization's needs. While the highest score indicates the best fit, CTOs should also consider any trade-offs and strategic priorities that might affect the final decision.

The following are some of the key considerations:

- **Adjust weights based on business priorities**: The suggested weights are general; modify them to reflect the strategic importance of each criterion for your specific use case.

- **Use sensitivity analysis**: Experiment by changing weights and scores to see how results shift. This can help you understand which criteria have the most significant impact on the decision. Sensitivity analysis can help understand how changes in weights or scores might affect the final decision. For instance, if *cost efficiency* becomes a higher priority, adjust its weight and see how it impacts the overall scores. This approach ensures that the decision is robust and considers multiple scenarios.

- **Conduct multiple rounds of scoring**: Consider running the scoring exercise multiple times with different teams or stakeholders to gain diverse perspectives and ensure a well-rounded evaluation.

The following are some of the additional considerations:

- Are there specific features or criteria where a lower-scoring technology might have a strategic advantage?

- Do the results align with your initial business objectives and future growth plans?

- Are there any risks associated with the highest-scoring option (e.g., vendor lock-in, limited scalability) that need to be mitigated?

Choosing the right OLTP or OLAP system is critical for building robust, scalable, and efficient applications. While OLTP systems prioritize transaction speed, data integrity, and real-time performance, OLAP systems focus on handling large data volumes, complex analytical queries, and seamless integration with data processing tools. By understanding these criteria and additional considerations, CTOs, chief data officers, and early-career engineers can make informed decisions to align their database strategy with their business goals.

Techniques for distributed data processing

As data volumes continue to grow exponentially, organizations must adopt distributed data processing techniques to handle large-scale datasets efficiently. Distributed data processing involves breaking down massive data workloads into smaller tasks that can be executed concurrently across multiple computing nodes. This approach enhances performance, scalability, and fault tolerance, making it essential for modern data-driven enterprises.

The following are some of the key techniques for distributed data processing:

Data partitioning

Data partitioning is the process of dividing a dataset into smaller, manageable chunks (partitions) that can be processed independently across different nodes. Effective partitioning is crucial for achieving load balancing and ensuring that each node can handle its share of the workload without becoming a bottleneck.

There are several methods of data partitioning:

- **Horizontal partitioning**: Also known as sharding, this technique involves splitting data rows across multiple nodes, ensuring that each shard can be processed separately. Commonly used in databases like MongoDB and Apache Cassandra, horizontal partitioning is ideal for scaling out and managing large datasets across distributed environments.

- **Vertical partitioning**: In this method, different columns or attributes of the dataset are stored on separate nodes. This approach can be beneficial when different parts of the data are accessed by distinct applications or processes.

The following are the use cases:

Imagine an e-commerce platform handling millions of transactions daily, and dealing with customer orders, product searches, and inventory updates all happening at once. To keep things running smoothly, the company uses *data partitioning*. They *horizontally partition* (or shard) their transaction database by user ID, so no single database node gets overwhelmed. At the same time, they *vertically partition* their product catalog, keeping frequently accessed details like product names and prices separate from less frequently used metadata like supplier info. This way, searches stay fast, transactions stay smooth, and the system scales effortlessly even during peak sales events like *Black Friday*.

Data replication

Replication involves creating multiple copies of data and storing them across different nodes or data centers. This technique enhances data availability and fault tolerance by ensuring that if one node fails, data can still be accessed from another replica.

The following are the two main types of data replication:

- **Synchronous replication**: Data is replicated to multiple nodes simultaneously. While this ensures data consistency across nodes, it may add latency to the process.

- **Asynchronous replication**: Data is replicated after the initial write operation completes. This reduces latency but may lead to eventual consistency, where replicas may be temporarily out of sync.

The following are the use cases:

Data replication is particularly useful in scenarios that require high availability, such as financial transactions, **content delivery networks (CDNs)**, and distributed databases.

MapReduce

MapReduce is a programming model that simplifies processing large datasets across distributed systems by breaking down tasks into two main functions, *Map* and *Reduce*. The Map function processes and transforms data into key-value pairs, while the Reduce function aggregates the results, producing a summarized output. Popularized by Apache Hadoop, MapReduce can handle petabytes of data by distributing the workload across multiple nodes, thus speeding up data processing.

The following are the use cases:

MapReduce is effective for batch processing tasks like log analysis, web indexing, and large-scale ETL operations.

Stream processing

Unlike batch processing, which processes data in chunks, stream processing deals with real-time data streams as they arrive. Stream processing frameworks, such as Apache Kafka Streams, Apache Flink, and Apache Storm, enable real-time data analytics by processing continuous data streams in parallel across multiple nodes. This technique is ideal for scenarios where immediate insights are critical, such as fraud detection, social media monitoring, and IoT applications.

The following are the use cases:

Stream processing is used in environments that require real-time insights, including financial trading, live event monitoring, and predictive maintenance in industrial automation.

Distributed file systems

Distributed file systems, such as the **Hadoop Distributed File System (HDFS)** and Ceph, are designed to store and manage large datasets across multiple machines. They allow for high throughput and fault tolerance by distributing data blocks across various nodes and replicating them to ensure data redundancy. This makes it possible to scale storage and processing capacity seamlessly, providing a backbone for other distributed processing techniques.

The following are the use cases:

Distributed file systems are often the foundation for big data frameworks, supporting data lakes, cloud storage, and analytics platforms like Apache Hadoop and Apache Spark.

Data pipelines and workflow orchestration

Data pipelines are automated workflows that move data between systems, perform transformations, and prepare it for analysis. Workflow orchestration tools, such as Apache Airflow, Luigi, and AWS Step Functions, enable the scheduling and management of these pipelines, ensuring that data is processed efficiently and reliably across distributed environments. These tools also help in handling dependencies between tasks, retrying failed operations, and scaling workflows based on the load.

The following are the use cases:

Data pipelines and orchestration are essential for ETL processes, ML pipelines, and complex data integration tasks that involve multiple data sources and transformation steps.

In-memory distributed processing

In-memory distributed processing involves storing data in RAM across multiple nodes, significantly speeding up data processing tasks by reducing the need for disk I/O. Frameworks like Apache Spark and Apache Ignite support this technique, allowing for faster computation by keeping frequently accessed data in memory. In-memory processing is particularly useful for iterative algorithms, such as those used in machine learning, where data needs to be accessed multiple times.

The following are the use cases:

In-memory processing is ideal for real-time data analytics, ML model training, and applications that require rapid data processing, such as recommendation engines and fraud detection.

Federated data processing

Federated data processing involves processing data that is distributed across different locations or systems without requiring centralized storage. This technique is increasingly important in scenarios where data privacy and sovereignty are critical, such as healthcare and finance, where data cannot be moved freely due to regulatory constraints. Federated processing frameworks allow for decentralized data analytics, enabling insights to be derived without transferring sensitive data.

The following are the use cases:

Federated data processing is used in privacy-sensitive environments like healthcare, where patient data needs to be analyzed without violating data privacy regulations, and in collaborative ML (federated learning).

Implementing real-time data processing

In today's digital economy, the ability to process and analyze data in real-time has become a crucial competitive advantage. Real-time data processing involves continuously ingesting, processing, and analyzing data as soon as it is generated, enabling organizations to react instantly to changing conditions. Unlike batch processing, where data is collected over time and processed in bulk, real-time data processing handles data streams, providing immediate insights that support faster decision-making. This is particularly important for use cases like fraud detection, predictive maintenance, financial trading, and real-time customer personalization. Below, we explore key aspects of implementing real-time data processing.

Data ingestion and stream processing

The first step in real-time data processing is efficient data ingestion, where data is captured and processed as soon as it is generated. Stream processing frameworks, such as Apache Kafka, Apache Flink, and Apache Storm, are designed to handle high-velocity data streams, allowing organizations to ingest, buffer, and process data with minimal latency. These frameworks ensure that data flows seamlessly from sources (e.g., IoT devices, social media feeds, sensors) into the processing pipeline without delay.

The following are the key practices:

- **Scalable data ingestion**: Use scalable data ingestion platforms like Apache Kafka to handle high volumes of incoming data. Kafka's distributed architecture can support millions of events per second, making it ideal for applications that need to process large data streams.

- **Data buffers**: Implement buffers to temporarily store incoming data and prevent data loss if there are downstream processing delays. Tools like Kafka, RabbitMQ, and AWS Kinesis Streams can act as buffers, allowing for smooth data ingestion.

Stream processing frameworks

Stream processing frameworks are essential for analyzing data in motion, enabling real-time transformation, aggregation, filtering, and joining of data streams. Technologies such as Apache Flink, Apache Storm, and Kafka Streams allow developers to write applications that process data in real-time, executing operations as soon as data events are received. These frameworks can be deployed across distributed clusters, ensuring scalability and fault tolerance.

The following are the key practices:

- **Event-driven architecture**: Use event-driven programming models to design real-time processing systems where each event triggers a specific action or operation. This is effective for monitoring changes and responding instantly.

- **Windowing techniques**: Apply windowing functions to group data over time intervals, enabling operations such as calculating running averages or counts. This is useful for generating metrics on time-based data, such as website activity over the last 5 minutes.

- **Stateful stream processing**: Leverage stateful stream processing to maintain context between events. For example, in fraud detection, keeping track of the past transactions of a customer can help in identifying suspicious activity.

Real-time analytics and dashboards

A key benefit of real-time data processing is the ability to generate live analytics and visualize insights through real-time dashboards. Dashboards can be used to monitor key metrics, detect anomalies, and track performance indicators, providing instant feedback to decision-makers. Tools like Grafana, Kibana, and Power BI enable the creation of interactive dashboards that can display real-time data, allowing businesses to act on insights as soon as they are available.

The following are the key practices:

- **Low latency data visualization**: Ensure that dashboards update with minimal latency to reflect the most current data. This can be achieved by integrating with real-time data processing frameworks and minimizing data transfer times.

- **Customizable alerts**: Implement customizable alerts that trigger notifications when specific conditions are met (e.g., unusual spikes in traffic, system failures, security breaches). This allows for immediate action without needing to monitor dashboards continuously.

Real-time data storage

For many real-time applications, processed data must be stored for further analysis or historical reference. Real-time data storage solutions must be able to write data quickly, maintain high availability, and scale efficiently. Databases like Apache Cassandra, Amazon DynamoDB, and Redis are optimized for real-time data storage, supporting high-speed reads and writes.

The following are the key practices:

- **Distributed NoSQL databases**: Use distributed NoSQL databases that can handle rapid read/write operations and support horizontal scaling. These databases can store data across multiple nodes, ensuring performance and availability even under heavy loads.

- **Time-series databases**: For applications that rely on time-stamped data, time-series databases like InfluxDB and TimescaleDB are particularly effective. They are designed to efficiently handle sequential data, making them suitable for monitoring and IoT applications.

- **In-memory databases**: Consider in-memory databases like Redis and Memcached for storing frequently accessed data. In-memory storage significantly reduces access time, making it ideal for caching data and supporting low-latency applications.

Challenges in real-time data processing

Implementing real-time data processing systems comes with its own set of challenges. Ensuring low latency while maintaining data accuracy and consistency can be difficult, especially as the data volume scales. Additionally, real-time systems must be able to handle data bursts without degrading performance, which requires scalable architectures and robust fault-tolerance mechanisms.

The following are the key practices:

- **Data consistency**: Maintaining consistency across distributed systems can be challenging in real-time environments, especially when dealing with asynchronous processing and eventual consistency.

- **Scalability**: As data volumes increase, real-time systems must scale without compromising performance. Using distributed frameworks and cloud-native architectures can help manage this scalability.

- **Fault tolerance**: Real-time systems must be designed to recover quickly from failures, with mechanisms like data replication and checkpointing to prevent data loss and maintain continuous operation.

- **Latency optimization**: Reducing latency is crucial for real-time processing. This can involve optimizing data pipelines, minimizing the number of hops between services, and using in-memory processing for faster data access.

Real-time processing use cases

Real-time data processing has a wide range of applications across industries.

Some common use cases include:

- **Fraud detection**: Financial institutions use real-time processing to monitor transactions and detect fraudulent activities instantly, reducing the risk of unauthorized transactions.

- **Predictive maintenance**: Manufacturers deploy sensors on equipment to track performance metrics and predict potential failures before they occur, minimizing downtime.

- **Real-time customer personalization**: E-commerce platforms analyze customer behavior in real time to offer personalized recommendations and promotions, enhancing the shopping experience.

- **IoT monitoring**: IoT systems rely on real-time data processing to monitor devices, track performance, and take automated actions based on the data collected (e.g., controlling smart home devices or managing industrial equipment).

Best practices for cloud data warehousing

Cloud data warehousing has transformed how organizations store, manage, and analyze data, offering scalable, flexible, and cost-effective solutions compared to traditional on-premises systems. Platforms like Amazon Redshift, Google BigQuery, Azure Synapse Analytics, Snowflake, and Databricks provide high-performance data warehousing capabilities that can handle massive volumes of structured and semi-structured data. These solutions allow organizations to scale their data infrastructure seamlessly, access advanced analytics, and enable real-time data processing, all without the need for extensive hardware investments.

Evolution of data warehousing

The concept of data warehousing emerged in the 1980s as businesses recognized the need to aggregate data from multiple sources into a single repository for reporting and analysis. Early data warehouses were built on dedicated, on-premises hardware, with solutions like IBM DB2, Oracle Exadata, Teradata, Microsoft SQL Server, and Netezza leading the market. Netezza, known for its data warehouse appliances, brought a new level of simplicity and speed to data warehousing by integrating storage, processing, and analytics in a single, easy-to-deploy box. While these systems were powerful, they were also costly and required significant resources for maintenance, scaling, and upgrades. Over the years, the introduction of more efficient ETL processes, facilitated by tools like Informatica, IBM DataStage, and Microsoft SSIS, along with advancements in data storage technologies and faster processing capabilities, helped to expand the adoption of data warehousing across industries. Despite the challenges of managing on-premises infrastructure, these solutions became the backbone of enterprise data management throughout the 1990s and early 2000s, setting the stage for the shift to more flexible, cloud-based data warehousing.

The shift to cloud computing in the mid-2000s marked a significant turning point. Cloud data warehouses like Amazon Redshift emerged, providing scalable, on-demand storage and compute resources, making data warehousing more accessible to businesses of all sizes. Google BigQuery introduced serverless architecture, enabling organizations to run queries without worrying about infrastructure management. More recently, platforms like Azure Synapse and Microsoft Fabric have further advanced cloud data warehousing. Azure Synapse integrates data warehousing with big data analytics, offering a unified environment that supports both structured data and large-scale analytics across data lakes. Microsoft Fabric extends this vision by combining data warehousing, data engineering, data integration, and real-time analytics into a single platform, promoting seamless data operations across various workloads.

Snowflake and Databricks have also pushed the boundaries by offering multi-cloud flexibility and combining data warehousing with data lakes for greater versatility. This approach allows businesses to store all their data in one place while still being able to run both batch and real-time analytics.

The need for speed, scalability, and real-time insights shapes the latest trends in cloud data warehousing. Data lakehouses, a term popularized by Databricks, represent a significant trend, merging the benefits of data lakes (which store raw, unstructured data) and data warehouses (which handle structured data and analytics). This approach allows businesses to store all their data in one place while still being able to run both batch and real-time analytics. Another trend is the integration of ML and AI capabilities directly within data warehouses, enabling advanced data processing and predictive analytics without moving data between platforms. Additionally, serverless data warehousing has gained popularity, allowing organizations to pay for only the resources they use, improving cost efficiency and simplifying scalability.

Cloud data warehousing is expected to become even more integrated with other cloud services, supporting multi-cloud and hybrid cloud architectures. These integrations will allow organizations to run analytics across diverse environments, manage data across multiple cloud platforms, and ensure compliance with regional data sovereignty laws. As the need for real-time data processing continues to grow, future developments will focus on enabling faster and more efficient data pipelines, combining real-time data ingestion, processing, and storage into a seamless workflow.

The following are the key strategies to consider when implementing a cloud data warehouse, ensuring efficiency, cost-effectiveness, and scalability:

Define clear data governance policies

Effective data governance is essential for managing data integrity, quality, and security in cloud data warehouses. It involves setting rules and guidelines for how data is collected, stored, accessed, and shared within the organization. A comprehensive data governance policy ensures that sensitive data is protected and that users have access to the data they need without compromising security or compliance.

The following are the key practices:

- **Data classification and access control**: Use data classification to tag sensitive information and enforce access control policies based on user roles. For example, Azure Synapse integrates with **Azure Active Directory** (**AAD**) to provide granular, **role-based access control** (**RBAC**).

- **Data lineage and auditing**: Implement tools to track data lineage and auditing. Solutions like Google Cloud Data Catalog help monitor where data originates, how it is transformed, and who accesses it, ensuring transparency and accountability.

Optimize data storage and partitioning

Efficient data storage and partitioning are critical for performance and cost management. Partitioning divides large datasets into smaller, more manageable segments, which can significantly speed up query performance by reducing the amount of data scanned. Most cloud data warehouses, including Amazon Redshift and Google BigQuery, support partitioning and clustering to optimize data retrieval.

The following are the key practices:

- **Choose appropriate partition keys**: Select partition keys based on how frequently specific data columns are queried. For instance, time-based partitions are effective for time-series data, while customer ID or geographic region partitions might be beneficial for user data.

- **Data compression**: Utilize built-in data compression features to minimize storage costs. Platforms like Snowflake automatically compress data, reducing storage requirements and improving query performance.

Implement ETL/ELT best practices

Data warehouses rely heavily on **extract, transform, load (ETL)** or **extract, load, transform (ELT)** processes to integrate data from various sources. Properly designing these processes ensures that data is clean, consistent, and ready for analysis. Modern cloud data warehousing solutions, such as Azure Data Factory and AWS Glue, streamline ETL/ELT operations, making data integration more efficient.

The following are the key practices:

- **Incremental data loading**: Instead of performing full data loads, use incremental data loading (also known as **change data capture (CDC)**) to update only the changes since the last load. This reduces processing time and minimizes the load on the data warehouse.

- **Data transformation in the warehouse**: Where possible, offload data transformation tasks to the cloud data warehouse. Tools like Google BigQuery and Snowflake support SQL-based transformations, enabling faster processing directly within the warehouse environment.

Monitor performance and optimize queries

Monitoring performance is essential for maintaining an efficient cloud data warehouse. Regularly analyzing query patterns, data usage, and system health can help identify performance bottlenecks and optimize query execution. Cloud platforms often provide monitoring tools to help teams track key performance metrics.

The following are the key practices:

- **Use query caching**: Many cloud data warehouses, such as Google BigQuery and Snowflake, support query caching, which stores the results of frequently run queries. This allows subsequent executions of the same query to return results quickly without scanning the data again.

- **Leverage performance monitoring tools**: Utilize built-in tools like Amazon Redshift Advisor or Google BigQuery's Query Insights to analyze query performance, identify long-running queries, and suggest optimization techniques.

- **Indexing and materialized views**: Implement indexing or materialized views to pre-aggregate data, reducing query time. For instance, Azure Synapse offers materialized views that speed up query performance by storing precomputed results.

Automate scaling and resource management

One of the key benefits of cloud data warehousing is the ability to scale resources up or down based on demand. Unlike traditional on-premises systems, cloud platforms can automatically adjust compute resources, ensuring consistent performance during peak times and cost savings during off-peak periods.

The following are the key practices:

- **Auto-scaling**: Enable auto-scaling features where possible. For example, Amazon Redshift and Azure Synapse Analytics can automatically scale compute resources to handle high query loads, ensuring that performance is maintained without manual intervention.

- **Pause and resume services**: Some platforms, like Snowflake, allow you to pause and resume compute services, so you only pay for what you use. This is particularly useful for environments with sporadic workloads, as it can lead to significant cost savings.

- **Workload management**: Use **workload management** (**WLM**) features to allocate resources effectively. Platforms like Amazon Redshift allow users to set resource queues, ensuring critical queries receive the necessary resources even during peak times.

Ensure data security and compliance

Cloud data warehouses store critical business information, making data security a top priority. Organizations must ensure that their data warehouses comply with data protection regulations (e.g., GDPR, HIPAA) and employ security best practices to protect sensitive information.

The following are the key practices:

- **Encryption**: Use encryption for data at rest and in transit to safeguard data from unauthorized access. Most cloud providers, including Azure Synapse, Amazon Redshift, and Google BigQuery, offer encryption by default.

- **Role-based access control (RBAC)**: Implement RBAC to control who can access or modify specific data. Snowflake integrates with identity management systems to enforce fine-grained access controls.

- **Data masking**: Use data masking features to anonymize sensitive information, ensuring that data analysts can work with real data without exposing sensitive details. This is particularly useful for compliance with privacy laws.

Adopting hybrid data strategy where needed

Many organizations operate in hybrid environments, where data is spread across on-premises systems and cloud platforms. A hybrid data warehousing strategy allows companies to integrate data from multiple sources seamlessly, providing a unified view for analysis.

The following are the key practices:

- **Seamless data integration**: Use tools like Azure Arc and Google Anthos to integrate data across on-premises and cloud systems. This enables businesses to keep certain datasets on-premises for compliance while leveraging cloud scalability for broader analytics.

- **Federated queries**: Some cloud data warehouses, such as Google BigQuery and Azure Synapse, support federated queries that allow users to query data across different storage systems (e.g., cloud and on-premises) without moving it. This helps maintain data locality while enabling comprehensive analytics

Conclusion

By the end of this chapter, we covered the evolution and modern landscape of databases, exploring how the database ecosystem has shifted from traditional relational systems to a diverse array of solutions designed to handle various data types and workloads. We examined key categories such as OLTP and OLAP systems, highlighting the technologies best suited for transactional and analytical tasks, respectively. Additionally, we provided a decision-making framework and scoring criteria to help in selecting the right database systems based on specific business needs.

We discussed the techniques for distributed data processing, including data partitioning, replication, and stream processing, which are essential for managing large-scale datasets efficiently. We further explored real-time data processing strategies, emphasizing the importance of low-latency systems and continuous analytics for modern applications. Finally, we shared best practices for cloud data warehousing, outlining how to leverage scalable, cost-effective platforms to store, manage, and analyze data seamlessly across hybrid and multi-cloud environments.

In the next chapter, we will establish robust frameworks for managing and securing enterprise data. *Chapter 7, Data Strategy and Governance*, will introduce the fundamentals of data engineering, guiding you through the design and implementation of effective data systems. We will also explore innovative architectures, such as data mesh and data fabric, which support decentralized data management while ensuring a unified, integrated approach across diverse environments. The chapter will provide strategies for maintaining data integrity, usability, and compliance, along with best practices for safeguarding data against breaches and unauthorized access.

Key terms

- **Online Transaction Processing (OLTP)**: A system designed to handle real-time, high-volume transactional workloads. OLTP databases ensure fast, consistent processing of short, atomic transactions, making them suitable for applications such as banking systems, e-commerce, and order management.

- **Online Analytical Processing (OLAP)**: A system optimized for analyzing large datasets and complex queries. OLAP databases are used for data modeling, reporting, and aggregating historical data, supporting tasks like business intelligence, data mining, and financial analysis.

- **NoSQL database**: A category of databases that provide flexibility in data storage by supporting schema-less data models. Types of NoSQL databases include key-value stores, document databases, column-family stores, and graph databases. Examples are MongoDB, Redis, and Cassandra.

- **NewSQL database**: A modern database system that combines the scalability of NoSQL with the ACID compliance of traditional RDBMSs. NewSQL databases are designed to support high transaction rates while maintaining data consistency. Examples include Google Spanner and CockroachDB.

- **Data lakehouse**: An architectural concept that combines the storage flexibility of data lakes with the structured data management capabilities of data warehouses. It allows businesses to store both raw and structured data, enabling batch and real-time analytics in a unified environment. Databricks Lakehouse and Delta Lake are notable implementations.

- **Data mesh:** A decentralized data architecture that distributes data ownership across domain teams, enabling them to manage data as a product. Data mesh encourages a scalable, domain-driven approach to data management. Starburst is an example of a platform supporting data mesh principles.

- **Data fabric**: An integrated data management approach that creates a unified, automated architecture across diverse data environments. Data fabric facilitates seamless data access, integration, and governance across on-premises and cloud systems.

- **Vector database**: A specialized database designed to store and query high-dimensional vector data, often used in AI applications for tasks like semantic search and recommendation systems. Examples include Pinecone, Weaviate, and Milvus.

- **Data partitioning**: The process of dividing a dataset into smaller, manageable segments or partitions, which can be processed independently across multiple nodes. This is essential for load balancing and efficient distributed data processing.

- **Data governance**: The set of policies, processes, and standards that ensure data is properly managed, secure, and compliant throughout its lifecycle. Effective data governance improves data quality, security, and usability across an organization.

- **ETL**: A data integration process that involves extracting data from various sources, transforming it into a consistent format, and loading it into a data warehouse or other storage systems. ETL is essential for preparing data for analysis.

- **In-memory database**: A database system that stores data directly in RAM instead of on disk, significantly speeding up data access and processing. Examples include SAP HANA and Redis.

- **Stream processing**: A technique for processing continuous data streams in real time, enabling immediate insights. Apache Flink and Kafka Streams are popular stream processing frameworks used for real-time analytics.

- **Data replication**: The process of copying data from one location to multiple nodes or systems, ensuring data availability, fault tolerance, and faster access. Replication can be synchronous (real-time) or asynchronous (delayed).

Join our book's Discord space

Join the book's Discord Workspace for Latest updates, Offers, Tech happenings around the world, New Release and Sessions with the Authors:

https://discord.bpbonline.com

CHAPTER 7

Data Strategy and Governance

Introduction

In this chapter, we will cover establishing robust frameworks for managing and securing enterprise data. It begins with an introduction to the fundamentals of data engineering, providing a foundation for readers to design and implement efficient data systems. The chapter will then explore innovative data architectures, such as data mesh and data fabric, emphasizing their role in decentralized data management and integration across multiple environments. It will also address strategies for effective data governance and quality assurance, focusing on ensuring data integrity, usability, and regulatory compliance. Lastly, readers will be guided through best practices for data security and compliance, helping to safeguard enterprise data against breaches and unauthorized access.

Structure

This chapter covers the following topics:

- Introduction to data engineering fundamentals
- Data mesh and data fabric architectures
- Developing effective data governance and quality assurance programs
- Ensuring data security and compliance

Objectives

By the end of this chapter, we will have a comprehensive understanding of how to establish robust frameworks for data security and compliance by integrating best practices across data governance, security protocols, and compliance strategies. We will gain insights into modern techniques such as Zero Trust security, end-to-end encryption, and continuous monitoring. Additionally, we will acquire practical knowledge on implementing automated compliance management, data masking, and tokenization to protect sensitive information and streamline regulatory adherence. The chapter will also equip us with the skills to develop a proactive data breach response plan and ensure business continuity through effective data backup and resilience strategies. Furthermore, we will understand how to use a detailed development review checklist to assess and enhance your organization's data security and compliance posture, addressing emerging risks and meeting evolving regulatory requirements.

Introduction to data engineering fundamentals

In today's data-driven world, the ability to efficiently collect, process, and analyze data is critical for businesses striving to remain competitive. Data engineering is the foundation that enables organizations to harness the power of their data by creating robust, scalable, and maintainable systems that can handle vast volumes of information. It is essential to understand that data engineering goes beyond the simple collection of data; it involves designing and building infrastructure that can process, store, and make data accessible for various use cases, including real-time analytics, machine learning, and business intelligence. Effective data engineering ensures that data flows smoothly from its sources to where it is needed, supporting quick decision-making and fostering innovation.

The following are the key concepts of data engineering:

- **Data pipelines**: Data pipelines are the backbone of data engineering. They enable the seamless movement of data from source systems (e.g., databases, IoT devices, cloud storage) to destinations such as data lakes, data warehouses, or analytical tools. An efficient data pipeline should be scalable, fault-tolerant, and capable of handling both batch and real-time data processing. CTOs must consider leveraging modern tools and platforms that support orchestration, data integration, and workflow management to optimize data pipelines.

- **Scalability and performance**: As enterprises grow, their data volumes increase exponentially. Data engineering systems must be scalable to handle this growth without sacrificing performance. This involves choosing the right data storage solutions (e.g., distributed databases, cloud-based storage) and ensuring that data pipelines can process large datasets quickly and efficiently. CTOs should focus on designing systems that can scale horizontally, adding more resources as needed rather than overhauling the architecture.

- **Data storage and processing systems**: Choosing the right data storage and processing systems is fundamental for efficient data engineering. There are two primary types:

  o **Online Transaction Processing (OLTP)**: Optimized for transactional workloads that require fast read and write operations, such as customer databases.

  o **Online Analytical Processing (OLAP)**: Designed for complex queries and data analysis, OLAP systems are ideal for generating insights from large datasets. CTOs must carefully evaluate the data needs of their organization to select the appropriate mix of OLTP and OLAP systems. Cloud-based data warehousing solutions, like Azure Synapse Analytics, can offer the flexibility to scale and integrate with other services seamlessly.

The key components of data engineering and governance work together to enable efficient data processing, integration, and security while ensuring compliance and reliability.

The following figure provides a structured view of these components, highlighting how core engineering principles such as automation, scalability, and monitoring align with governance frameworks that enforce policies, security, and quality control:

Data Engineering Components	Data Governance Components
OLTP / OLAP - Storage Systems	Data Policies & Standards
Data Pipeline	Data Stewardship
Transformation & Cleaning	Security & Privacy Controls
Automation & Orchestration	Data Lineage and Metadata
Observability & Monitoring	Data Quality Monitoring
Scalability & Performance	Compliance Monitoring
Data Integration / Cost Management — Data Mesh & Fabric	
Data Catalogue & Metadata	
Data Security	
Data Ops	

Figure 7.1: Key components of data engineering

- **Data transformation and cleaning**: Raw data often comes in various formats and may contain inconsistencies, errors, or missing values. Data transformation involves cleaning, normalizing, and converting data into a consistent, usable format for analysis. Efficient data transformation is critical for accurate analytics and reporting. CTOs should invest in automated data transformation solutions to reduce manual efforts, speed up the ETL process, and ensure data integrity.

- **Data automation and orchestration**: With the increase in data sources and the complexity of workflows, automation and orchestration play a vital role in managing data engineering tasks. Tools such as Apache Airflow, Azure Data Factory, and others can automate the movement, transformation, and integration of data, reducing the need for manual intervention. Automation not only improves efficiency but also ensures that data is processed in a consistent and repeatable manner.

- **Data integration and interoperability**: Enterprises often need to integrate data from a variety of systems, including legacy databases, SaaS platforms, IoT devices, and external APIs. Ensuring seamless data integration can be complex but is crucial for building a unified data strategy. CTOs should focus on using modern integration platforms and data connectors that allow for smooth interoperability across different systems, enabling the continuous flow of data between them.

- **Data observability and monitoring**: Effective data engineering is not just about building data pipelines but also monitoring them for potential issues. Data observability tools provide insights into the health, performance, and lineage of data pipelines, ensuring data quality and consistency. By proactively identifying issues, businesses can prevent disruptions, reduce downtime, and maintain reliable data services.

- **Advanced data processing techniques**: For businesses dealing with large-scale data, distributed data processing frameworks like Hadoop and Apache Spark can help in handling massive datasets efficiently. Additionally, real-time processing frameworks such as Apache Kafka and Azure Stream Analytics can support instant data analysis, enabling quick decision-making. CTOs should evaluate batch processing and real-time streaming based on their business needs, as each approach offers different benefits.

- **Cost management and optimization**: Especially relevant for startups, optimizing the costs of data storage, processing, and cloud infrastructure can be a competitive advantage. Techniques such as data tiering, where less frequently accessed data is stored in more cost-effective solutions, can significantly reduce costs. Additionally, leveraging cloud services with pay-as-you-go models can provide flexibility in scaling without incurring unnecessary expenses.

- **Data cataloging and metadata management**: In complex data ecosystems, maintaining a data catalog can enhance data discovery, accessibility, and usability. Automated metadata management helps organizations understand data lineage, transformations, and the overall context of data, which is essential for maintaining data quality and complying with regulatory requirements. Implementing data cataloging tools can streamline the documentation and management of enterprise data assets.

- **Data as a Service**: For businesses looking to monetize their data, the **Data as a Service (DaaS)** model offers new opportunities. Organizations can package and offer their data for external consumption, enabling other businesses to access valuable insights. This requires a solid understanding of data packaging, security, and distribution strategies to ensure that data services are reliable, secure, and easy to use.

- **Data mesh and fabric**: Data mesh and data fabric are modern architectures designed to improve data accessibility, scalability, and governance in distributed environments. Data mesh decentralizes data ownership by giving domain-specific teams control over their data as a product while enforcing shared governance and interoperability. Data fabric, on the other hand, creates an intelligent, unified layer that automates data integration, discovery, and management across multiple sources. Both approaches help organizations overcome data silos, ensuring seamless data access and improved collaboration across different teams and systems.

Insights for data governance

The following are some of the strategic insights for data governance:

- **Invest in a future-proof data architecture**: Think long-term when it comes to data architecture. Building a flexible, modular, and scalable architecture can help businesses adapt quickly to new data sources, regulatory requirements, or technological advancements. Implementing a hybrid or multi-cloud approach may also provide better resilience and agility, allowing enterprises to distribute workloads across multiple platforms.

- **Embrace DataOps for continuous improvement**: DataOps is a methodology that applies agile and DevOps principles to data engineering, focusing on collaboration, automation, and continuous improvement. By adopting DataOps, you can streamline data pipeline development, reduce errors, and improve the speed at which data insights can be delivered. This approach also supports version control, monitoring, and testing of data workflows, ensuring data quality at every stage of the pipeline.

- **Prioritize data security and governance**: Building a robust data engineering framework requires incorporating security and governance from the outset. You must ensure that data pipelines adhere to security best practices, such as encryption, access control, and regular audits. Additionally, establishing data governance policies will help maintain data quality, ensure compliance with regulations, and provide transparency in data usage across the organization.

- **Focus on skill development and talent acquisition**: The success of data engineering initiatives often hinges on the skills and expertise of the team. You should invest in continuous learning and development programs to enhance the skill sets of their data engineering teams. Furthermore, attracting and retaining talent with expertise in data engineering, cloud technologies, and automation can help the organization stay ahead of the curve.

- **Implement compliance monitoring**: Compliance monitoring ensures that an organization's data practices align with regulatory standards such as GDPR, HIPAA, and CCPA. It involves continuous tracking of data usage, access, and security controls to detect and prevent policy violations. Automated compliance tools help enforce rules, generate audit reports, and provide real-time alerts on non-compliance risks. By implementing robust compliance monitoring, organizations can mitigate legal and financial risks while maintaining transparency and trust in their data operations.

- **Implement security and privacy controls**: These controls include data encryption, access management, data masking, and tokenization to prevent unauthorized access or data breaches. **Role-based access control** (**RBAC**) and Zero Trust security models ensure that only authorized users can access specific datasets. Privacy controls, such as data anonymization and consent management, help organizations comply with privacy regulations like GDPR and CCPA. Additionally, automated security policies and real-time monitoring tools enable proactive threat detection and enforcement of governance rules, ensuring that data remains secure throughout its lifecycle.

Data mesh and data fabric architectures

In the ever-evolving landscape of data engineering, two innovative approaches, data mesh, and data fabric, have emerged to address the complexities of managing and integrating data across diverse and distributed environments. Both architectures aim to solve the challenges posed by traditional, monolithic data management systems, but they do so through fundamentally different strategies. Understanding these approaches can help CTOs design modern data infrastructures that are scalable, flexible, and aligned with business needs.

Data mesh

Data mesh is a decentralized data management architecture that treats data as a product and assigns ownership of data to individual business domains. Unlike traditional approaches, where a central IT team manages all data, data mesh promotes a domain-oriented approach. This means that each business unit (e.g., finance, marketing, sales) is responsible for managing, processing, and ensuring the quality of its data, making it easier to scale and adapt to changing requirements.

The following are the core principles of data mesh:

- **Domain-driven ownership**: Each business domain becomes responsible for its data, treating it as a product. This promotes accountability, enabling teams to manage their data more effectively, as they have a deeper understanding of its context and usage.

- **Data as a product**: Data is not just a byproduct but a valuable asset that must be curated, maintained, and made accessible to other teams within the organization. This requires a product mindset where data teams focus on user experience, data quality, and ease of access.

- **Self-serve data infrastructure**: To enable domains to manage their data independently, organizations must provide a self-service platform that allows teams to build, deploy, and scale their data products without relying on centralized IT resources. This infrastructure includes tools for data integration, processing, storage, and analytics.

- **Federated governance**: While data ownership is decentralized, governance needs to be consistent across domains. Federated governance ensures compliance, security, and data quality standards are upheld without hindering the agility and autonomy of individual teams.

The following are the benefits of data mesh:

- **Scalability**: Decentralized ownership allows organizations to scale their data architecture without creating bottlenecks.

- **Agility**: Teams can quickly adapt and iterate on data products without waiting for centralized teams to make changes.

- **Improved data quality**: Domain experts managing data are more likely to ensure its accuracy and relevance, as they understand the context and business implications.

The following are the challenges and considerations for CTOs:

- **Cultural shift**: Moving to a data mesh architecture requires a shift in mindset, where different business units take on more responsibility for data management.

- **Infrastructure investment**: Organizations must invest in self-serve infrastructure and automation to support independent data management.

- **Consistent governance**: Implementing federated governance can be complex, requiring robust policies and frameworks to ensure compliance without stifling innovation.

Data fabric

Data fabric is an architecture designed to seamlessly integrate data across disparate environments, including on-premises systems, cloud platforms, and edge devices. It enables organizations to access, process, and analyze data regardless of where it resides by creating a unified layer of connectivity, metadata management, and data integration. Unlike data mesh, which decentralizes data ownership, data fabric emphasizes connectivity and integration, ensuring data is easily discoverable and usable across the enterprise.

The following are the core components of the data fabric:

- **Unified data integration**: Data fabric provides a layer that seamlessly integrates data from multiple sources, including structured, semi-structured, and unstructured data. This integration allows businesses to work with diverse data without needing to move or replicate it.

- **Metadata management**: Effective data fabric architectures include robust metadata management, which provides insights into data lineage, quality, and usage. Metadata helps in automating data discovery, governance, and integration processes, making data more accessible.

- **Data virtualization**: Data virtualization allows organizations to access data across various systems as if it were stored in a single repository, without the need for physical data consolidation. This helps in reducing the time and cost associated with data movement.

- **Intelligent automation**: Data fabric leverages AI and ML to automate data integration tasks, data quality checks, and governance processes. This reduces manual effort and ensures consistency across the data landscape.

The following are the benefits of data fabric:

- **Unified data view**: Provides a consistent view of data across multiple environments, making it easier to access and analyze.

- **Improved data governance**: With centralized metadata management, organizations can maintain better control over data security, quality, and compliance.

- **Cost efficiency**: Reduces the need for extensive data movement and duplication, cutting down storage and integration costs.

The following are the challenges and considerations for CTOs:

- **Integration complexity**: Building a data fabric requires the ability to integrate with a wide range of data sources, which can be challenging.

- **Scalability**: Ensuring that the data fabric can scale efficiently as data volumes and sources grow is critical for long-term success.

- **Security management**: Since data fabric connects multiple environments, robust security protocols must be in place to prevent unauthorized access and breaches.

Strategic approaches to data mesh and fabric

Choosing between data mesh and data fabric requires a strategic approach to align with an organization's data needs, scalability goals, and governance requirements.

The following key strategies help CTOs implement these architectures effectively:

- **Assess business requirements**: Before deciding between data mesh or data fabric, CTOs must evaluate the specific needs of their organization. Data mesh is ideal for enterprises with complex, domain-specific data needs, while data fabric suits businesses looking for a unified view across diverse environments.

- **Build a modular and scalable infrastructure**: Whether implementing a data mesh or data fabric, it is crucial to build a flexible and modular infrastructure that can scale as the business grows. Cloud platforms like Azure provide services that can facilitate these architectures, enabling easier deployment and management.

- **Invest in automation and self-serve capabilities**: Both architectures benefit from automation, whether automating data integration tasks in a data fabric or providing self-serve tools for domain teams in a data mesh. Automation reduces manual work, speeds up data processing, and ensures consistency.

- **Develop a comprehensive governance framework**: For data mesh, federated governance allows decentralized teams to maintain data quality without losing control. In a data fabric, centralized governance ensures consistent data security, compliance, and metadata management. CTOs must develop governance strategies that match the architecture they choose.

Data mesh and data fabric represent two innovative approaches to modern data architecture, each with its unique advantages and challenges. By understanding their core principles, benefits, and implementation strategies, CTOs can design data systems that are flexible, scalable, and aligned with their organization's long-term goals. In the next section, we will explore how effective data governance and quality assurance programs can further enhance data management across the enterprise.

Developing data governance and quality assurance programs

As organizations scale their data infrastructure, robust data governance and quality assurance programs become critical. Data governance involves establishing policies, procedures, and frameworks that ensure data is managed effectively, securely, and in compliance with regulations. Quality assurance, on the other hand, focuses on maintaining data's accuracy, consistency, and reliability throughout its lifecycle. Together, these programs enable businesses to maximize the value of their data assets while minimizing risks associated with poor data quality, non-compliance, and data breaches.

For CTOs, developing and implementing effective data governance and quality assurance programs is not just about compliance; it is a strategic imperative that drives better decision-making, enhances operational efficiency, and fosters innovation.

The following are the key components of data governance:

- **Data policies and standards**: A strong data governance framework begins with defining clear policies and standards that dictate how data should be managed, accessed, and used within the organization. These policies cover aspects like data security, privacy, quality, retention, and usage, ensuring consistent practices across all business units. CTOs should collaborate with legal, compliance, and business teams to develop these policies, aligning them with industry standards and regulations (e.g., GDPR, HIPAA).

- **Data stewardship and ownership**: Effective governance requires clear ownership of data assets. Data stewards are responsible for managing the quality, integrity, and security of data within their domain. By assigning data stewardship roles, organizations can ensure accountability and maintain high standards of data management. CTOs should establish a system that defines roles, responsibilities, and data ownership across various teams, promoting collaboration and accountability.

- **Data security and privacy controls**: Protecting sensitive information is key to data governance. Implementing robust security controls, such as encryption, access management, and regular audits, helps safeguard data from unauthorized access and breaches. Privacy controls ensure that data usage complies with relevant privacy laws, protecting the rights of individuals. CTOs must adopt a proactive approach to data security, continuously monitoring and updating security measures to address evolving threats.

- **Data lineage and metadata management**: Understanding the journey of data from its source to its final destination (data lineage) is essential for maintaining transparency and accountability. Metadata management enables organizations to document data assets, track changes, and provide context to users, making it easier to locate, understand, and utilize data. This is particularly useful for compliance reporting and audits, ensuring that data provenance is well-documented.

- **Regulatory compliance**: In highly regulated industries like healthcare, finance, and pharmaceuticals, compliance is a significant concern. Data governance frameworks must include mechanisms to ensure regulation adherence, such as automated monitoring of compliance rules and regular reporting. CTOs should work closely with compliance officers to integrate compliance requirements into the data management processes, reducing the risk of legal penalties.

Establishing data quality assurance programs

The following are some of the data quality assurance programs:

- **Data quality metrics**: The first step in establishing a quality assurance program is defining metrics that assess data quality. These metrics typically include accuracy, completeness, consistency, timeliness, and validity. By setting benchmarks for these metrics, organizations can evaluate their data's health and identify areas that require improvement. CTOs must ensure that these metrics are aligned with business needs and regularly updated to reflect changing requirements.

- **Data quality monitoring and automation**: Continuous monitoring of data quality is essential for identifying and resolving issues before they impact business operations. Automated tools can help in detecting anomalies, validating data, and flagging inconsistencies, reducing the need for manual intervention. Tools such as Azure Purview, Informatica, and Talend offer features for monitoring data quality, data lineage, and governance, making it easier for businesses to maintain high standards.

- **Data cleaning and enrichment**: Even with the best governance practices, raw data can still contain errors, inconsistencies, or missing values. Data cleaning involves correcting these issues, while data enrichment adds context and value to the data, making it more useful for analysis. Automated data cleaning and enrichment tools can streamline this process, ensuring data is accurate and consistent across various systems.

- **Root cause analysis and issue resolution**: When data quality issues are identified, it is crucial to conduct a root cause analysis to understand why they occurred and how they can be prevented in the future. This involves tracing back through the data pipeline to find the source of the problem, whether it is an incorrect data entry, a faulty integration, or an inconsistent data transformation process. CTOs should implement feedback loops that allow teams to learn from issues and continuously improve data processes.

Tools for data governance and quality assurance

Implementing effective data governance and quality assurance programs requires the right set of tools and technologies. These tools help automate processes, enhance data visibility, and ensure consistency across different systems.

The following are some of the key technologies that can support data governance and quality initiatives:

- **Data catalogs and metadata management tools**: Azure Purview, Alation, Collibra are tools that provide comprehensive metadata management capabilities, including automated data discovery, data lineage tracking, metadata enrichment, and search and filtering options. They help organizations catalog, classify, and track data assets across the enterprise, allowing for the creation of a data catalog that serves as a central repository for data definitions, lineage, and metadata. This enables users to discover and understand data more easily, enhancing transparency and facilitating better data governance.

- **Data quality management tools**: Informatica Data Quality, Talend, IBM InfoSphere QualityStage are platforms that offer features for data profiling, rule-based data cleansing, deduplication, validation, enrichment, and data quality monitoring. They help ensure data quality by detecting errors, anomalies, and inconsistencies and enabling automated data cleansing, validation, and standardization. These tools allow organizations to set data quality rules and enforce them to meet required benchmarks, providing ongoing monitoring to maintain data integrity.

- **Data governance platforms**: Microsoft Purview, Alation, Collibra, Informatica Axon, SAP Data Intelligence are comprehensive data governance platforms that support policy management, data stewardship workflows, compliance monitoring, role-based access control, and data privacy management. They enable organizations to define governance policies, establish data stewardship roles, and manage data governance rules. These platforms help enforce data governance frameworks that address data security, privacy, and data access, ensuring consistent practices across the enterprise.

- **Data integration and ETL tools**: Apache NiFi, Microsoft Azure Data Factory, and Apache Airflow are data integration tools that facilitate the ETL of data from various sources, ensuring it remains clean and consistent as it moves through pipelines. They offer features like workflow orchestration, data transformation, scheduling, data mapping, and error handling. These tools are crucial for automating and managing the flow of data across different systems, improving operational efficiency and enabling data to be processed and analyzed in a timely manner.

- **Data security and access management tools**: Azure Active Directory, Okta, AWS **Identity and Access Management** (**IAM**) are essential tools for securing data by managing user access permissions, authentication, and encryption. They support features such as user authentication, role-based access control, **single sign-on** (**SSO**), **multi-factor authentication** (**MFA**), and data encryption. By enforcing security protocols and managing user identities, these tools help ensure that only authorized users can access sensitive data. Integrating these access management tools with data governance platforms can further enhance security by tracking user activity and preventing unauthorized access.

- **Data lineage and monitoring tools**: Manta, Datadog, DataKitchen are data lineage tools that provide detailed tracking of data's journey from its source to its final destination, illustrating how data is transformed along the way. This helps with transparency, compliance, and troubleshooting, making it easier to understand data flows and identify any issues. Monitoring tools like Datadog and DataKitchen provide insights into the health and performance of data pipelines, alerting teams to anomalies, performance issues, or potential failures in real time. These tools help maintain the reliability and integrity of data processes.

- **Data observability platforms**: Monte Carlo, Bigeye, Metaplane are platforms enable organizations to monitor the health and performance of data pipelines, ensuring data quality, consistency, and reliability. Data observability platforms go beyond traditional monitoring by providing end-to-end visibility into data workflows. They automatically detect anomalies, track data lineage, and identify root causes of data issues, helping teams resolve problems before they impact downstream systems. Key features include automated data quality checks, pipeline health monitoring, and advanced anomaly detection.

Developing robust data governance and quality assurance programs is essential for organizations that want to maximize the value of their data while minimizing risks. Having the right tools and technologies is essential for developing robust data governance and quality assurance programs.

Ensuring data security and compliance

Developing robust data governance and quality assurance programs is essential for organizations that want to maximize the value of their data while minimizing risks. Having the right tools and technologies is essential for developing robust data governance and quality assurance programs.

Implementing data security and compliance effectively requires following best practices that have proven successful across modern enterprises. This section merges a description of each best practice with a checklist of questions that help organizations review their data security and compliance during development.

Adopt a Zero Trust security model

A Zero Trust security model operates on the principle of *never trust, always verify*, assuming that all users, devices, and applications are untrusted until proven otherwise. Unlike traditional perimeter-based security models, Zero Trust treats every access request as a potential threat, regardless of its origin. This approach is essential for minimizing the risk of internal and external threats by enforcing strict authentication and authorization at every stage.

The following checklist helps assess whether your organization has enforced key Zero Trust principles to protect against evolving security threats:

- Have **multi-factor authentication** (**MFA**) and least-privilege access controls been implemented for all users?

- Are there conditional access policies in place to adapt based on user behavior and risk level?

- Does the system continuously verify the identity of users and devices trying to access data?

- Are internal and external network segments properly isolated (micro-segmentation)?

- Are all devices, including personal and mobile devices, subject to the same Zero Trust policies as enterprise devices?

- Is there a process to continuously assess and update Zero Trust configurations based on new vulnerabilities or threat intelligence?

Integrating security into data governance

Integrating security into data governance ensures that data protection measures are embedded within the organization's data management framework from the outset. This integration aligns security policies with compliance requirements, providing consistency across data storage, processing, and usage. It prevents security from being treated as an afterthought, which can lead to vulnerabilities and non-compliance.

The following checklist helps evaluate whether security policies, compliance requirements, and governance frameworks are seamlessly integrated to safeguard data at every stage:

- Is data security integrated into the data governance framework across all departments?

- Are clear data security policies aligning with regulatory requirements and internal governance standards?

- Have security policies been automated for consistent enforcement across the organization?

- Are data lineage and metadata management tools used to track how data is processed and where it flows?

- Are there mechanisms to audit how data security policies are enforced across different departments?

- Is there a regular review of data governance frameworks to ensure they evolve with new security and compliance challenges?

Implement end-to end encryption

Encryption is a critical component of data security that converts data into an unreadable format, which can only be deciphered by authorized users. End-to-end encryption ensures that data is protected during storage (at rest) and transmission (in transit), making it difficult for unauthorized parties to access sensitive information even if they intercept it. Regularly updating encryption protocols and managing encryption keys securely is essential for robust protection.

The following checklist helps assess whether encryption best practices are consistently applied to enhance data security and compliance:

- Is data encrypted both at rest and in transit using strong encryption protocols (e.g., AES-256, TLS 1.3)?

- Are encryption keys securely managed and rotated periodically?

- Have encryption practices been applied consistently across all data storage and transmission channels?

- Is there a **key management service** (**KMS**) in place to handle encryption keys securely?

- Are encryption protocols reviewed regularly to ensure they meet current industry standards and best practices?

- Are there fail-safe mechanisms to automatically revoke encryption keys in the event of unauthorized access or suspicious activity?

Continuous monitoring and threat detection

Continuous monitoring involves real-time tracking of data activities and network behavior to identify and respond to security threats promptly. Unlike periodic audits, continuous monitoring provides immediate visibility into anomalies, unauthorized access attempts, and other suspicious activities. This proactive approach helps organizations mitigate potential risks before they escalate into significant issues.

The following checklist ensures that monitoring systems, anomaly detection, and automated response mechanisms are effectively implemented to enhance security resilience:

- Are monitoring systems in place to provide real-time visibility into data usage and network activity?

- Are there systems in place to automatically detect and alert for suspicious activity or potential breaches?

- Are ML algorithms used to identify anomalies that may indicate a security threat?

- Is there a plan for responding to detected threats quickly, including isolating affected systems?

- Are logs from all critical systems centralized and analyzed to detect patterns that might indicate a coordinated attack?

- Is there a mechanism to automate the blocking of IPs or accounts after suspicious activity is detected?

Regular security audits and penetration testing

Regular security audits and penetration testing (pen-testing) help identify vulnerabilities that might be missed during routine operations. Audits assess how well security measures adhere to policies and compliance standards, while pen-testing simulates real-world attacks to uncover potential weaknesses. This combination ensures a comprehensive assessment of the organization's security posture.

The following checklist ensures that security assessments, compliance reviews, and remediation processes are systematically implemented to minimize risks:

- Are regular security audits conducted to assess the effectiveness of existing security measures?

- Is penetration testing performed periodically to identify vulnerabilities?

- Are findings from audits and penetration tests documented, and is there a process for resolving identified issues?

- Are third-party security assessments conducted to ensure comprehensive evaluation?

- Are audit trails maintained securely and reviewed to track any unauthorized attempts to alter or delete security logs?

- Is there a plan to perform targeted audits for high-risk systems or newly implemented features to ensure no vulnerabilities are introduced?

Data masking and tokenization for privacy protection

Data masking and tokenization techniques help protect sensitive information by replacing real data with fictitious equivalents or non-sensitive placeholders. This ensures that even if unauthorized users access data, they cannot view sensitive details. These methods are especially important for non-production environments where real data may be exposed during testing or development processes.

The following checklist ensures that these techniques are effectively applied to enhance privacy protection and compliance:

- Is sensitive data anonymized or masked when used in non-production environments (e.g., testing or development)?

- Are data masking and tokenization implemented to protect PII and other sensitive information?

- Have tools been implemented to automate data masking and tokenization processes?

- Is there a process to periodically review and update data masking rules to adapt to new privacy regulations?

- Are there policies in place to periodically review the effectiveness of data masking and tokenization strategies?

- Is there a system to monitor for any unauthorized attempts to reverse data masking or tokenization processes?

Automate compliance management

Managing compliance manually can be challenging, especially when dealing with multiple regulations across different regions. Compliance automation tools streamline processes by automatically enforcing data security policies, generating compliance reports, and maintaining audit trails. Automation helps reduce errors, ensure consistent adherence to regulations, and free up resources for strategic initiatives.

The following checklist helps assess whether compliance processes are efficiently automated to enhance security, reporting, and policy enforcement:

- Are compliance automation tools deployed to monitor data practices and enforce policies?

- Do automated systems generate regular compliance reports that include audit trails?

- Are data retention, data deletion, and access control rules automatically enforced?

- Is there a process for keeping compliance rules up-to-date with changing regulations (e.g., GDPR, HIPAA, CCPA)?

- Do automated compliance tools have a dashboard that provides real-time insights into compliance status across different departments?

- Is there a fail-safe mechanism to automatically alert compliance officers of deviations or non-compliance incidents?

Developing a data breach response plan

Even with the best security measures in place, data breaches can still occur. Having a well-defined, comprehensive data breach response plan ensures that organizations can act quickly to contain and mitigate the impact of a breach. It outlines clear steps, roles, and responsibilities for addressing security incidents, minimizing potential damage, and restoring normal operations.

The following checklist ensures that response protocols, roles, and communication strategies are clearly defined, regularly tested, and continuously improved to minimize damage and restore operations efficiently:

- Is there a documented data breach response plan that outlines steps for identifying, containing, and mitigating breaches?

- Have roles and responsibilities for response teams been clearly defined and communicated?

- Are there regular training sessions to prepare response teams for potential breach scenarios?

- Is the response plan tested periodically through simulated breach scenarios to ensure effectiveness?

- Is there a communication plan in place to notify stakeholders, including customers and regulatory bodies, in the event of a data breach?

- Are third-party service providers included in the breach response plan, especially if they handle sensitive data on behalf of the organization?

Data backup and resilience planning

Data backups and disaster recovery plans are critical for maintaining business continuity. Regularly backing up data and storing it securely in multiple locations ensures that enterprises can recover quickly from data loss due to cyberattacks, hardware failures, or natural disasters. Encrypted backups also protect against unauthorized access during the backup process.

The following checklist helps assess whether backup processes, disaster recovery plans, and security measures are effectively implemented to safeguard critical data:

- Are data backups regularly scheduled, and are backup copies stored in secure, geographically dispersed locations?

- Are backups encrypted to ensure security, even during the backup process?

- Is there a disaster recovery plan ensuring quick restoration of critical data and systems?

- Has the disaster recovery plan been tested recently to verify that it can effectively execute under different failure scenarios?

- Are backup copies tested periodically to verify the integrity of the data and ensure they can be restored without issues?

- Is there a defined procedure for prioritizing which systems or data are restored first during a major outage?

Conclusion

By the end of this chapter, we covered the essential practices for ensuring data security and compliance in modern enterprises. We explored the importance of adopting a Zero Trust security model, integrating security measures within data governance frameworks, and implementing end-to-end encryption to protect sensitive information. The chapter also highlighted the need for continuous monitoring, regular security audits, and data masking to safeguard data against unauthorized access. Additionally, we discussed strategies for automating compliance management and developing comprehensive data breach response plans, ensuring your organization remains prepared and resilient against potential threats.

In the next chapter, we will understand how to harness the power of data for deeper insights and enhanced decision-making capabilities. We will begin by discussing advanced data analytics and intelligence techniques, detailing how these methodologies can be applied to derive actionable insights from complex datasets. The chapter will also introduce augmented analytics, an emerging field that leverages ML and AI to enhance data processing and business intelligence. Finally, we will cover the essentials of ML and data visualization services, providing tools and techniques for effectively presenting data in a way that is both insightful and accessible to stakeholders.

Key terms

- **Zero Trust security model**: A security approach that requires strict verification of all users, devices, and applications before granting access, regardless of their location within or outside the network perimeter.

- **Data governance**: The set of policies, processes, and frameworks that ensure data is managed securely, consistently, and in compliance with regulatory standards throughout its lifecycle.

- **Data masking**: The process of obscuring specific data within a database to prevent exposure of sensitive information while retaining its usability for testing and analysis.

- **Tokenization**: A data protection method that replaces sensitive information with a non-sensitive equivalent, called a token, which can be securely stored without compromising the original data.

- **Multi-factor authentication (MFA)**: An authentication method that requires users to provide multiple verification forms (e.g., passwords, biometric data, or security tokens) to access systems or data.

- **Compliance Automation**: The use of software tools to streamline and automate the enforcement of data security policies, reporting, and monitoring to ensure consistent adherence to regulatory requirements.

- **Data breach response plan**: A documented strategy that outlines the steps to be taken when a data breach occurs, including containment, mitigation, notification, and recovery processes.

- **Data resilience**: The ability of a system to withstand and recover from data loss, corruption, or cyberattacks, ensuring continuity of operations and data availability.

- **Penetration testing (Pen testing)**: A security testing method that simulates cyberattacks to identify vulnerabilities in systems, applications, and networks, allowing organizations to address weaknesses before they can be exploited.

Join our book's Discord space

Join the book's Discord Workspace for Latest updates, Offers, Tech happenings around the world, New Release and Sessions with the Authors:

https://discord.bpbonline.com

CHAPTER 8
Advanced Analytics

Introduction

The field of data analytics has undergone a profound transformation over the past few decades. Initially, data analysis was primarily descriptive, relying on basic statistical methods to summarize past trends and behaviors. Organizations were limited to tools like *Excel* and *SQL databases*, which made it challenging to handle large datasets or extract deeper insights. However, as data volumes grew, so did the need for more sophisticated analytical techniques. This led to the development of **business intelligence (BI)** tools like *Tableau* and *Power BI*, which enabled users to analyze structured data and create visual reports that facilitated better decision-making.

The early 2000s marked a turning point with the advent of big data. Technologies such as *Apache Hadoop* provide the infrastructure to process and analyze massive datasets from diverse sources, including social media, IoT devices, and online transactions. This was further enhanced by frameworks like *Apache Spark*, which introduced fast, in-memory data processing, making advanced data analytics more efficient and scalable.

Today, we are witnessing the rise of augmented analytics, where ML and AI are integrated into traditional analytics processes. Platforms such as *Azure Machine Learning, Google Cloud AI Platform*, and *DataRobot* are leading this evolution, offering tools that automate data preparation, insight generation, and even predictive analysis. With these technologies, data-driven insights have become more precise, dynamic, and accessible, enabling organizations to make faster, more informed decisions.

Looking ahead, the future of advanced analytics is promising. Emerging trends include real-time data processing, supported by technologies like *Apache Kafka* and *Amazon Kinesis*, which enable insights to be derived almost instantaneously. *Edge computing solutions* (e.g., *Azure IoT Edge, AWS IoT Greengrass*) are pushing data processing closer to the source, allowing for real-time analytics and decision-making at the edge. Additionally, *NLP-powered tools* such as *OpenAI's ChatGPT* and *IBM Watson Assistant* are enabling users to interact with data systems through conversational interfaces, making data insights more accessible to non-technical users.

This chapter equips readers with the skills to navigate this evolving landscape of advanced analytics. We begin by exploring various techniques in data analytics and intelligence, including tools and methodologies to derive actionable insights from complex datasets. We then introduce augmented analytics, demonstrating how platforms like *Salesforce Einstein* and *H2O.ai* leverage machine learning and AI to enhance traditional business intelligence practices. The chapter further discusses ML in data analysis, showing how frameworks like *Scikit-learn, TensorFlow,* and *PyTorch* can uncover patterns and trends within data. Lastly, we cover best practices for data visualization, focusing on tools like *Power BI, Tableau,* and *D3.js* to ensure that insights are effectively communicated to stakeholders.

By the end of this chapter, readers will have a comprehensive understanding of how to harness data analytics, augmented intelligence, and visualization tools to transform raw data into valuable insights that drive business success.

Structure

The chapter covers the following topics:

- Evolution in analytics
- Implementing augmented analytics for enhanced insights
- Utilizing machine learning in data analysis
- Best practices for data visualization services

Objectives

By the end of this chapter, you will gain a comprehensive understanding of advanced analytics and how to harness its potential to drive business success. You will learn to apply key techniques in data analytics, from descriptive and diagnostic methods to predictive and prescriptive strategies, enabling actionable insights from complex datasets. The chapter will equip you with the skills to leverage augmented analytics, integrating AI and machine learning for automated data processing and dynamic decision-making. Additionally, you will explore the role of ML in uncovering patterns and trends alongside best practices for data visualization, ensuring insights are effectively communicated to stakeholders. These capabilities will empower you to transform raw data into meaningful intelligence, fostering informed, data-driven decision-making within modern organizations.

Evolution in analytics

Let us look at the evolution of analytics in each era as follows:

- **1980s: Era of manual data analysis**: In the 1980s, data analysis was a manual, spreadsheet-driven exercise primarily focused on historical trends. Organizations relied heavily on tools like *Lotus 1-2-3* and later *Microsoft Excel*, which became the dominant data manipulation tool. At this stage, analytics was descriptive, meaning it summarized past events, such as sales performance or inventory levels. Data was small, structured, and stored in relational databases like *Oracle DB* and *SQL Server*. Analysts manually queried these databases using SQL, translating raw numbers into basic reports.

  Key characteristics of this era:

  - Limited computing power restricted analytics to small datasets.

  - Manual processes meant data extraction and reporting were slow.

  - No advanced insights. Analytics focused only on past trends without predictive capabilities.

- **1990s: Business intelligence (BI) and data warehousing**: The 1990s saw the rise of BI tools, which transformed static reporting into interactive dashboards. Platforms like *Cognos* and *MicroStrategy* allowed organizations to visualize complex datasets, making it easier for business leaders to interpret data. This era also introduced **extract, transform, load** (ETL) pipelines, enabling organizations to consolidate data from multiple sources into centralized data warehouses such as *Teradata* and *Informatica*.

  Key advancements in this era:

  - Structured data analysis became more efficient with centralized data warehouses.

  - BI tools enabled dashboards for better decision-making.

  - Descriptive and diagnostic analytics helped organizations understand what happened and why; however, the analysis was still static and limited to historical data.

- **2000s: Rise of big data and predictive analytics**: With the explosion of internet usage, social media, and IoT devices, traditional data systems struggled to keep up. The early 2000s saw the emergence of *big data technologies*, which enabled businesses to process vast amounts of unstructured and semi-structured data. *Apache Hadoop* and *MapReduce* allowed distributed computing, while NoSQL databases like *MongoDB* and *Cassandra* could handle large-scale, diverse datasets.

  This period also saw a shift towards predictive analytics, where businesses began using statistical models to forecast trends and outcomes. Industries quickly adopted these techniques:

- o **Finance**: Credit scoring to assess loan risks.

- o **Retail**: Demand forecasting for better inventory management.

- o **Healthcare**: Patient risk analysis for preventive care.

- **2010s: Real-time analytics, AI, and ML**: By the 2010s, analytics moved beyond batch processing to real-time analysis, thanks to technologies like *Apache Spark* and *Kafka*. This enabled applications such as fraud detection, dynamic pricing, and real-time recommendation engines. At the same time, ML and AI became integral to analytics workflows.

  Key transformations:

  - o AI-powered analytics democratized access to advanced insights.

  - o BI tools evolved, with Tableau and Power BI embedding interactive and predictive capabilities.

  - o Cloud-based ML platforms like AWS SageMaker, Azure ML, and Google Cloud AI provided scalable ML infrastructure.

- **2020s: Augmented analytics and conversational AI**: We now stand at the brink of an augmented analytics revolution, where AI and ML automate data preparation, generate insights dynamically, and simplify decision-making. Tools like *Azure Synapse Analytics* and *Salesforce Einstein* allow even non-technical users to analyze complex datasets. Additionally, conversational analytics, powered by **natural language processing** (**NLP**), has changed how users interact with data, enabling insights without writing a single line of code.

  Emerging trends:

  - o Natural language analytics (e.g., ChatGPT, Google Bard) makes data more accessible.

  - o Multi-modal analytics processes text, images, audio, and video in unified workflows.

  - o Edge computing (e.g., Azure IoT Edge) enables real-time analytics at the data source.

- **The future: Generative AI and intelligent agents**: Generative AI and intelligent agents are set to transform the analytics landscape. Tools like *Excel's Copilot*, now with Python integration, allow users to conduct sophisticated data analyses through natural language commands, eliminating the need for coding expertise. Additionally, Microsoft Fabric's Copilot is automating complex data workflows, streamlining data manipulation and visualization.

  What is next:

  - o AI-driven insights will become core to business intelligence.

o   Democratization of analytics will empower business users, not just data scientists.

o   Self-service analytics platforms will make data-driven decision-making more intuitive.

Organizations need advanced analytics techniques and foundational maturity blocks to build a strong analytics ecosystem.

The following figure highlights key techniques, from descriptive and diagnostic analytics to augmented and Gen AI-supported analytics. It also outlines essential maturity components like strategy, AI and ML, modern infrastructure, and self-service tools:

Analytics Techniques		Analytics Maturity Blocks	
Descriptive	Prescriptive	Strategy	AI & ML
Diagnostic	Real-Time	Modern Infra	Data Pipeline
Predictive	Augmented	Data Collection & Prep	
Gen AI and Copilot supported		Self Service Tools	

Figure 8.1: Advanced analytics techniques and maturity building blocks

Techniques in advanced data analytics and intelligence

In the modern enterprise, data analytics and **business intelligence** (**BI**) have become indispensable for driving informed decision-making. This section explores the most relevant analytics and BI techniques currently in use, ordered by their utility and prevalence in enterprise settings. Each technique is accompanied by examples of top tools and technologies that enable organizations to leverage these capabilities effectively.

Descriptive analytics

Descriptive analytics is akin to looking in the rearview mirror, it summarizes what has already occurred, providing a retrospective view of trends and patterns. Despite being foundational, its utility is immense, especially in generating operational dashboards and executive-level reports.

Technically, descriptive analytics relies on structured data warehouses or data lakes. For example, tools like Power BI and Tableau connect to a wide range of data sources, from SQL Server to Snowflake, and use query engines like *Presto* or *Dremio* to perform aggregation-heavy tasks. Modern implementations often use a star or snowflake schema in their data warehouses, ensuring optimized queries for dashboarding.

Take, for instance, an e-commerce company analyzing seasonal sales trends. This process might involve *ETL pipelines* (using tools like *Azure Data Factory*) to aggregate transactional data from multiple systems into a consolidated warehouse. The aggregated data is then visualized with filters and calculated fields to provide actionable insights. *Columnar storage formats* such as *Parquet or ORC* are often used to improve read performance.

Diagnostic analytics

While descriptive analytics tells you *what happened*, diagnostic analytics answers *why it happened*, it digs deeper into the data, employing techniques like regression analysis, clustering, and anomaly detection.

The technical backbone here often involves tools capable of handling vast datasets and running complex queries. *Apache Spark* or *Databricks* are popular for such tasks, leveraging distributed computing to analyze petabytes of data. For example, a telecom provider might analyze customer churn by integrating call records, support logs, and demographic data into a data lake. Tools like *Looker* or *Google BigQuery* can then uncover correlations, such as customers with frequent service outages being more likely to churn.

Advanced implementations might involve *causal inference models* to differentiate correlation from causation. Techniques like propensity score matching or difference-in-differences analysis can help refine these insights, ensuring business actions target root causes rather than symptoms.

Predictive analytics

Predictive analytics takes historical data and uses it to forecast future trends. Here, the synergy between statistical models, machine learning, and data engineering is most apparent.

Consider a financial institution building a predictive model for credit risk assessment. This process typically starts with feature engineering, where data attributes such as income, debt-to-income ratio, and past repayment behavior are transformed into meaningful features. Tools like Scikit-learn, TensorFlow, or Azure ML facilitate the creation of models ranging from simple regressions to complex neural networks.

Modern predictive analytics architectures often involve *pipelines* built with tools like *MLflow* or *Kubeflow,* where models are trained, validated, and deployed at scale. For time-series predictions, advanced techniques such as **Long Short-Term Memory networks (LSTMs)** or *Prophet* are used to account for sequential dependencies in data. To operationalize these models, platforms like *Azure Databricks* offer seamless integration with data pipelines, ensuring predictions are delivered in near real-time.

Prescriptive analytics

Prescriptive analytics does not just predict the future; it recommends actionable strategies to optimize outcomes. This involves integrating optimization algorithms with predictive models.

Take the example of a logistics company optimizing delivery routes. A typical pipeline here might include real-time traffic data ingested through APIs (e.g., Google Maps) and predictive models that forecast delivery delays. Prescriptive analytics then applies *integer linear programming* or *genetic algorithms* to identify the best routes.

Architecturally, this process might run on a *microservices-based system* where services like **Azure Kubernetes Service** (**AKS**) host the optimization engine. Inputs from IoT devices (e.g., GPS trackers on trucks) are processed in real-time, while the optimization logic runs in containerized environments. Tools like *Gurobi* or *IBM CPLEX* handle the heavy computational lifting required for these calculations.

Real-time analytics

Real-time analytics thrives on the speed of data processing. It transforms raw, streaming data into insights almost instantaneously, enabling immediate responses.

Key technical enablers include *streaming platforms* such as *Apache Kafka, Azure Event Hubs*, or *Amazon Kinesis*. These systems ingest and process data at low latency, using frameworks like *Apache Flink* or *Azure Stream Analytics* for real-time computation.

For example, an e-commerce website might track user behavior, like clicks, cart additions, and purchases, in real-time. This data is processed to detect fraud or recommend products instantly. The architecture here often involves *stateful stream processing*, where session information is maintained across events. To scale, *event-driven architectures* with *serverless components* like Azure Functions are deployed.

Augmented analytics

Augmented analytics integrates AI into traditional workflows, automating tasks such as data preparation, anomaly detection, and even natural language querying.

At its core, augmented analytics leverages **natural language processing** (**NLP**) to democratize data analysis. Tools like *Salesforce Einstein* or *Azure Synapse Analytics* enable business users to ask queries in plain language, for instance, *What were the top-selling products last quarter?*

Under the hood, technologies like *knowledge graphs* and *embedding models* power these insights. For example, when analyzing healthcare data, a system might automatically identify outliers in patient vitals using *unsupervised learning* techniques like *autoencoders or isolation forests*. These insights are then presented in an intuitive interface, often enriched with conversational AI capabilities using tools like *Azure Bot Framework*.

Other analytics trends

Beyond the widely adopted analytics techniques, several specialized approaches are transforming the way businesses extract insights from their data. *Cognitive analytics*, for instance, mimics human reasoning by combining AI and NLP to process unstructured data like text, images, or videos, as seen in tools like IBM Watson or Azure Cognitive Services. Meanwhile, *spatial analytics* brings a geographic dimension to decision-making, helping industries like retail and urban planning leverage geospatial tools such as ArcGIS and Azure Maps to analyze location-based data and identify patterns using spatial ML techniques.

In the realm of unstructured data, *text analytics* extracts insights through NLP techniques like sentiment analysis and named entity recognition, often powered by advanced models like BERT or GPT. Similarly, *network analytics* delves into connected systems like social networks or fraud detection graphs, utilizing graph databases like Neo4j and algorithms such as PageRank to uncover hidden patterns. Tools like Tableau and Power BI are democratizing data access with *self-service analytics*, empowering business users to explore data intuitively, while *behavioral analytics* tracks user interactions to optimize customer journeys using tools like Mixpanel or Amplitude.

Emerging fields like *quantum analytics* are pushing boundaries with quantum-inspired algorithms solving combinatorial challenges in supply chain or portfolio optimization. As AI adoption grows, *explainable analytics* ensures transparency by integrating frameworks like SHAP or LIME into MLOps pipelines, enabling organizations to demystify complex models. Together, these cutting-edge techniques are expanding the horizons of data analytics, blending deep technical sophistication with practical applications across industries.

Implementing augmented analytics for enhanced insights

Augmented analytics represents the next evolution in data analysis, combining traditional analytics with advanced AI and ML capabilities. The core idea is to automate data processing and insight generation, enabling organizations to uncover trends, patterns, and correlations that might not be immediately apparent. This technology leverages AI to assist users in preparing data, generating insights, and making data-driven decisions faster and more accurately. By simplifying complex tasks, augmented analytics democratizes data analysis, making it accessible even to business users who do not have technical expertise.

At its core, augmented analytics automates the following key aspects:

- **Data preparation**: Automated data cleansing, transformation, and enrichment to prepare datasets for analysis, significantly reducing the time spent on manual tasks.

- **Insight generation**: AI and ML algorithms analyze the data to generate insights, uncover hidden patterns, and suggest correlations, making the analysis more robust.

- **NLP**: Integrates conversational interfaces that allow users to query data and receive insights using natural language, enhancing accessibility.

Approach to achieving high maturity in analytics

For organizations aiming to leverage augmented analytics effectively, it is crucial to adopt a phased, strategic approach to reach high maturity in analytics:

- **Assessment and strategy development**: Begin with an assessment of the current analytics capabilities. Understand the maturity level, identify gaps, and define key objectives. CTOs should establish a clear strategy that aligns with business goals, detailing how augmented analytics can address current challenges and drive value.

- **Data infrastructure modernization**: Invest in scalable, cloud-based data infrastructure to support data processing and analytics. Migrating to platforms such as *Azure Synapse Analytics* or *Google BigQuery* can enable efficient storage, processing, and analysis of large datasets. This foundational step ensures that data can be integrated from multiple sources and processed at scale.

- **Building AI and ML capabilities**: Integrate machine learning models into the analytics pipeline. This involves training models to detect patterns and predict outcomes based on historical data. Platforms like *Azure Machine Learning*, *AWS SageMaker*, and *Google Cloud AI Platform* can accelerate this process by providing pre-built models and tools for custom development.

- **Automating data pipelines**: Automate data workflows to streamline the process from data ingestion to insight generation. Technologies like *Azure Data Factory* and *AWS Glue* can help automate data movement, transformation, and integration, ensuring a smooth and efficient analytics workflow.

- **Empower business users with self-service tools**: Augmented analytics is most effective when it empowers business users. Providing tools such as *Power BI* with AI insights or *Google Data Studio* integrated with ML models can allow non-technical users to explore data and generate insights independently. This reduces the reliance on data scientists for day-to-day analysis.

- **Continuous improvement and skill development**: Establish a culture of continuous improvement by regularly revisiting the analytics strategy. Encourage skill development within teams to keep up with evolving technologies and methodologies, ensuring that the organization remains agile and innovative in its use of data.

Technologies and tools in augmented analytics

Several cloud platforms and tools have emerged as leaders in enabling augmented analytics. Highlighting solutions from major hyperscalers can guide organizations in selecting the right technology as follows:

- **Azure synapse analytics**: An integrated analytics service that combines data warehousing and big data analytics, providing a unified platform for data engineers and data scientists. It integrates seamlessly with *Azure Machine Learning* to add AI capabilities directly into the analytics pipeline.

- **Power BI with AI insights**: Enables users to leverage built-in AI models, such as key influencers and anomaly detection, to gain insights directly within reports and dashboards.

- **AWS SageMaker**: A comprehensive service that allows users to build, train, and deploy machine learning models. It also integrates with **Amazon QuickSight** for visualizing insights derived from AI models.

- **Google Cloud AI platform and BigQuery ML**: Offers powerful ML integration with data analytics, enabling organizations to build and deploy ML models directly within the data warehouse environment.

- **Salesforce Einstein analytics**: Provides AI-powered analytics embedded directly into the Salesforce ecosystem, offering predictive insights and recommendations that can be acted on immediately.

Utilizing machine learning in data analysis

ML has revolutionized the way organizations analyze data by enabling systems to learn from data patterns and make predictions or decisions without explicit programming. In the context of data analysis, ML algorithms can uncover complex patterns, trends, and correlations that traditional analytics methods might miss. By training models on historical data, organizations can predict future outcomes, classify information, and automate decision-making processes, leading to more accurate and timely insights.

Key applications of ML in data analysis include:

- **Predictive modeling**: Creating models that forecast future events, such as sales trends, equipment failures, or customer churn.

- **Classification and clustering**: Grouping data into categories (classification) or identifying natural clusters within datasets, useful for segmenting customers or detecting anomalies.

- **Anomaly detection**: Identifying unusual patterns that could indicate fraud, system failures, or security breaches.

- **Recommendation systems**: Analyzing user behavior to suggest products, services, or content, enhancing customer experience and engagement.

Approach to leverage machine learning in data analysis

Implementing machine learning in data analysis requires a structured approach that aligns technology with business goals.

Organizations can effectively integrate ML into their analytics workflows as follows:

- **Identify business use cases**: Begin by defining clear use cases where machine learning can add value, such as demand forecasting, predictive maintenance, or customer segmentation. This ensures that efforts are aligned with business objectives.

- **Data collection and preparation**: ML models are only as good as the data they are trained on. Collect relevant, high-quality data from various sources, and use data preprocessing tools to clean and prepare the datasets. Solutions like *Azure Data Factory* and *AWS Glue* can help automate this process.

- **Choose the right ML algorithms**: It is critical to the appropriate algorithm. Options include regression, decision trees, neural networks, and ensemble methods. Tools like *Scikit-learn* and *TensorFlow* offer a range of algorithms that can be tailored to specific tasks.

- **Build, train, and evaluate models**: Use platforms such as *Azure Machine Learning*, *AWS SageMaker*, or *Google Cloud AI Platform* to build and train models. Continuous evaluation and tuning are essential to improve accuracy and ensure the models meet business requirements.

- **Operationalize ML models**: Once trained, deploy the models into production systems where they can be used for real-time data analysis. **Machine learning operations** (**MLOps**) practices ensure smooth integration and continuous monitoring, enabling models to evolve as new data becomes available.

- **Monitor and update**: Regularly monitor the performance of deployed models and update them as necessary to ensure they adapt to changes in data patterns or business conditions. This can be achieved using tools like *Azure Monitor* or *Google Cloud AI*.

Technologies and tools for ML in data analysis

Several technologies across cloud platforms support the implementation of ML in data analysis:

- **Azure ML**: A comprehensive platform for building, training, and deploying machine learning models integrated with tools like *Azure Databricks* for scalable data processing.

- **AWS SageMaker**: An end-to-end ML service that simplifies the process of preparing data, building models, training, and deployment.

- **Google Cloud AI platform**: A robust platform that offers tools for custom model development as well as pre-trained models for faster deployment.

- **TensorFlow and PyTorch**: Open-source frameworks that provide powerful libraries for developing deep learning models, widely adopted for complex data analysis tasks.

- **Scikit-learn**: A popular ML library in Python known for its simplicity and efficiency in implementing basic ML algorithms.

Best practices for data visualization services

Data visualization is a critical component of data analysis, transforming complex datasets into visual representations that are easy to understand and interpret. Effective visualizations can communicate insights clearly, highlight key trends, and support data-driven decision-making by making complex information accessible to a wider audience. The goal is to present data in a way that tells a story, guides decision-makers, and prompts action.

To achieve this, it is important to follow best practices that ensure visualizations are not only aesthetically pleasing but also functional and meaningful.

- **Know your audience**: Understand who will be viewing the data and what insights they are seeking. Tailor visualizations to the audience's level of expertise and focus on the metrics that matter most to them. For example, executives might prefer high-level summaries, while analysts may need detailed data breakdowns.

- **Choose the right visualization type**: Selecting the appropriate chart or graph is essential for effectively conveying information. Use bar charts for comparisons, line charts for trends over time, scatter plots for relationships between variables, and heatmaps for displaying data density. Tools like *Power BI, Tableau,* and *Google Data Studio* offer a variety of visualization options to suit different needs.

- **Simplify and focus**: Keep visualizations simple and uncluttered. Avoid overloading charts with too much information, which can distract or confuse the audience. Highlight key data points and remove any unnecessary elements to ensure the focus remains on the most important insights.

- **Use color strategically**: Color can be a powerful tool in data visualization, but it should be used thoughtfully. Choose colors that enhance readability and draw attention to key data points. Be mindful of colorblind accessibility by selecting palettes that can be easily distinguished by all viewers. Many platforms, such as *Tableau* and *Qlik*, provide color themes and guidelines to help with this.

- **Ensure data accuracy and integrity**: Accurate data is the foundation of trustworthy visualizations. Verify that the data sources are reliable and ensure that the visualizations accurately represent the underlying data. Misleading or incorrect visualizations can lead to poor decision-making and a loss of trust.

- **Provide context**: Visualizations should not be viewed in isolation. Always provide context to help the audience understand the significance of the data. This can include adding titles, labels, legends, and brief explanations that guide viewers through the insights. Annotations can also be used to highlight key findings or anomalies.

- **Leverage interactive elements**: Interactive dashboards allow users to explore data at their own pace, drill down into specific details, and customize their view. This increases engagement and provides a deeper understanding of the data. Tools like *Power BI, Tableau,* and *Google Data Studio* enable the creation of interactive visualizations that enhance user experience.

- **Test and iterate**: The best visualizations are often the result of multiple iterations. Seek feedback from stakeholders, test different formats, and refine visualizations based on input. This process ensures that the final product effectively communicates the desired message.

Technologies and tools for data visualization services

Several tools dominate the market, providing robust capabilities for creating effective data visualizations, these include:

- **Power BI**: Microsoft's business analytics service, known for its integration with other Microsoft tools, easy-to-use interface, and powerful data visualization features. It supports interactive dashboards, AI-driven insights, and seamless integration with Azure services.

- **Tableau**: A leading data visualization tool that offers extensive options for creating interactive and dynamic visualizations. Its ability to connect with various data sources and its drag-and-drop functionality makes it a popular choice among analysts.

- **Google Data Studio**: A free tool that enables users to create shareable and customizable dashboards. It integrates well with Google's ecosystem, including *BigQuery* and *Google Analytics*, making it a preferred choice for those already using Google products.

- **Qlik Sense**: A platform that combines data visualization with robust data integration and analytics features. It excels in handling large datasets and provides sophisticated tools for creating customized visual representations.

- **D3.js**: A JavaScript library that enables the creation of highly customizable, web-based data visualizations. It is suitable for developers who need full control over their visualizations and want to build complex, interactive graphics.

Expanding the horizons of advanced analytics

To truly appreciate the transformative potential of advanced analytics, it is essential to delve into its evolving landscape and emerging applications. This section explores several critical areas that deepen the technical and practical understanding of advanced analytics for developers and data scientists. This chapter positions advanced analytics as a cornerstone of modern enterprise decision-making by connecting tools, techniques, and practices with real-world scenarios.

Evolving analytical techniques and tools

The progression of analytics has extended beyond descriptive and diagnostic methods, introducing predictive and prescriptive techniques that leverage ML and AI. For example, predictive analytics uses models trained on historical data to forecast future trends, providing actionable insights that guide strategic decisions. Platforms such as Azure Machine Learning and TensorFlow have become invaluable for creating these predictive models. Prescriptive analytics builds on these predictions by recommending optimal courses of action. For instance, a logistics company may use optimization algorithms to reduce delivery times, factoring in real-time traffic data and historical delivery performance. Tools like Scikit-learn and PyTorch simplify these workflows, enabling developers to craft custom algorithms tailored to specific business needs.

The field has also embraced augmented analytics, where AI and ML automate data preparation, insight generation, and natural language queries. Developers can leverage tools like *Azure Synapse Analytics* and *Salesforce Einstein* to integrate these capabilities seamlessly into enterprise systems. The technical depth required for successful implementation includes understanding preprocessing workflows, such as data cleaning and transformation, and deploying these enhanced analytics models in scalable environments.

Scaling analytics for modern enterprises

Scalability is a core challenge in advanced analytics, particularly for organizations handling massive datasets. Distributed computing frameworks like Apache Spark and cloud-based solutions such as Azure Data Lake have revolutionized how organizations process and analyze data. These technologies allow developers to partition data across multiple nodes, enabling parallel processing that accelerates data analysis while ensuring fault tolerance.

Container orchestration platforms like Kubernetes further enable scalable analytics pipelines. By deploying containerized applications, organizations can handle fluctuating workloads and ensure high availability across multiple environments. For real-time analytics, tools like Apache Kafka or Azure Stream Analytics enable instantaneous processing, making them critical for use cases such as fraud detection or monitoring IoT devices. Combining these with observability platforms, such as Grafana or Azure Monitor, ensures that performance metrics are captured and monitored, allowing teams to optimize pipelines continuously.

Security, compliance, and ethical considerations

As organizations handle increasing amounts of sensitive data, security, and compliance have become integral to advanced analytics. Developers must implement robust encryption protocols for both data at rest and data in transit, ensuring adherence to regulations such as GDPR and HIPAA. Cloud-native tools like Azure Policy and AWS **Identity and Access Management (IAM)** provide governance frameworks that enforce these security measures consistently across environments.

Ethical considerations are equally critical in analytics. Bias in machine learning models can lead to unfair outcomes, particularly in sensitive areas like hiring or lending. Techniques such as fairness-aware learning and **explainable AI (XAI)** help mitigate these biases. By incorporating transparency into the analytics workflow, organizations not only ensure ethical outcomes but also build trust with stakeholders. The adoption of responsible AI practices, including continuous auditing and feedback mechanisms, is essential to navigating these challenges effectively.

Future directions in advanced analytics

The future of advanced analytics lies in its integration with cutting-edge technologies, pushing boundaries to enable smarter and more intuitive systems. Quantum computing, for instance, has the potential to solve complex optimization problems at speeds unattainable by classical systems. Multi-modal AI, combining data sources like text, images, and audio, is making analytics more comprehensive, while data-centric AI shifts focus from model development to improving data quality and preparation.

Edge analytics is also reshaping how organizations process data. Solutions like Azure IoT Edge bring computation closer to the data source, enabling real-time decisions without reliance on centralized systems. Similarly, conversational AI tools such as OpenAI's ChatGPT are making analytics more accessible by allowing users to query datasets through natural language interfaces, democratizing data insights for non-technical stakeholders.

As these advancements evolve, the role of the developer and data scientist will expand from simply building models to orchestrating end-to-end workflows that integrate diverse data streams, ensure compliance, and drive ethical outcomes. Staying ahead in this field requires not only mastering the current state of analytics but also embracing its future possibilities with curiosity and adaptability.

Conclusion

In this chapter, we covered the essential techniques and strategies for utilizing data analytics, augmented intelligence, and visualization tools to extract meaningful insights from complex datasets. We began by exploring various advanced analytics methods, such as descriptive, diagnostic, predictive, and prescriptive analytics, demonstrating how they help organizations understand trends, uncover root causes, forecast outcomes, and optimize decision-making. We then discussed the world of augmented analytics, discussing how AI and machine learning can automate data processing and make analytics more accessible to business users. Finally, we outlined best practices for creating effective data visualizations, ensuring that insights are communicated clearly and compellingly to stakeholders.

In the next chapter, we will discuss the architecture and operational practices that drive advancements in AI. It will open with a thorough analysis of generative AI architectures, including **large language models (LLM)**, **small language models (SLM)**, **retrieval-augmented generation (RAG)**, Lang Chain, Semantic Kernels, function calls, prompt flows, and the deployment of GPU clusters for AI training and inferencing. The chapter will also introduce emerging concepts like Agentic AI and AutoGen, which reflect the trend toward autonomous systems capable of managing tasks, decisions, and interactions without continuous human intervention. Additionally, we will examine a selection of prominent open-source LLMs, such as Llama 2 and Mistral, to showcase their role in driving innovation. The discussion on MLOps will cover strategies for development, deployment, monitoring, and maintenance across the AI model lifecycle. Furthermore, the chapter will explore the practicalities of AI model operationalization using tools like Azure ML Studio, Azure Cognitive Services, and newer frameworks that integrate AI seamlessly into business applications.

Key terms

- **Descriptive analytics**: The process of analyzing historical data to summarize past events and trends. It focuses on understanding what happened by using visualizations, reports, and dashboards. Tools like Power BI and Tableau are often used for this type of analysis.

- **Diagnostic analytics**: A deeper exploration of data that aims to determine why certain events occurred. It involves identifying correlations and causal relationships to uncover the root causes behind patterns and anomalies.

- **Predictive analytics**: The use of statistical models, machine learning, and AI algorithms to forecast future outcomes based on historical data. Examples include demand forecasting, risk assessment, and predicting customer behavior.

- **Prescriptive analytics**: An advanced form of analytics that suggests actions to optimize future outcomes. It combines predictive models with optimization techniques to guide decision-makers on the best course of action.

- **Augmented analytics**: A method that integrates AI and ML into traditional analytics workflows, automating data processing and insight generation. This approach democratizes analytics by making data insights accessible to business users without technical expertise.

CHAPTER 9

Generative AI and Machine Learning

Introduction

This chapter of the book will cover the architecture and operational practices driving advancements in AI. It begins with an analysis of generative AI architectures, exploring core concepts such as **large language models (LLM)**, **small language models (SLM)**, **retrieval-augmented generation (RAG)**, LangChain, Semantic Kernels, function calls, and prompt flows, alongside the deployment of GPU clusters for efficient AI training and inferencing. Emerging trends like agentic AI and AutoGen are also highlighted, showcasing how these innovations enable systems to autonomously manage tasks, decisions, and interactions without continuous human intervention. The chapter further examines prominent open-source LLMs, including Llama 2, offering insights into their role in shaping the future of AI. It also delves into MLOps, providing comprehensive strategies for the entire model lifecycle, from development to deployment, monitoring, and maintenance. By the end, readers will gain a clear understanding of the architecture and practices that enable scalable, efficient, and autonomous AI systems.

Structure

The chapter covers the following topics:

- Evolution of AI and trends
- In-depth analysis of generative AI architectures

- Exploring emerging trends in generative AI
- Overview of open-source large language models
- Introduction and best practices in MLOps
- Practical guide to AI model operationalization
- Generative AI application architecture patterns
- Agentic AI development trends
- Emerging developments in agentic AI
- Responsible AI

Objectives

By the end of this chapter, you will gain a comprehensive understanding of the architectures behind modern generative AI systems, including LLMs, SLMs, and advanced frameworks such as *LangChain* and *Semantic Kernel*. You will explore emerging trends like *agentic AI, AutoGen, and multimodal systems* that are reshaping the AI landscape. The chapter will equip you with practical strategies for operationalizing AI models in enterprise environments, covering best practices for deployment, scaling, and integration. You will also develop the skills needed to implement effective *MLOps pipelines*, ensuring continuous monitoring and improvement of your AI systems. Emphasis will be placed on *responsible AI practices*, highlighting principles and tools for fairness, transparency, security, and governance. Additionally, you will learn advanced techniques in *prompt engineering, including function calling and multimodal prompts*, to enhance model interactivity and utility. Finally, you will gain awareness of the tools and methods required for monitoring, securing, and governing AI applications, enabling you to build scalable, robust, and ethical AI solutions aligned with enterprise-grade standards.

Evolution of AI and trends

The field of AI has evolved dramatically over the past few decades, transforming from a niche area of academic research into a fundamental driver of digital innovation. Early AI systems were rule-based, relying on predefined algorithms to perform specific tasks. These systems, though limited, paved the way for the development of more sophisticated ML techniques, which enabled computers to learn from data patterns and improve their performance over time. The 2000s marked a significant shift with the rise of big data and cloud computing, providing the infrastructure to store and process vast amounts of information. This led to the development of deep learning, a subset of ML that achieved breakthroughs in areas such as image recognition, NLP, and more.

Today, AI is characterized by the use of generative AI technologies, which have gained prominence for their ability to create new content, from text to images, music, and even code. The advent of LLM like *OpenAI's GPT-4* and *Llama 3* has revolutionized how machines understand and generate human-like text, leading to widespread applications across industries. Technologies such as RAG, LangChain, and Semantic Kernels have further enhanced AI systems, allowing them to integrate and retrieve information seamlessly. The evolution of **multimodal AI** has also been a key development, enabling systems to process and understand multiple types of data, including text, images, and audio, leading to richer and more versatile interactions.

The current landscape of AI extends beyond digital environments into the physical world, often referred to as **physical AI**. This includes the integration of AI in robotics, autonomous vehicles, drones, and smart manufacturing systems. **Industrial AI** is a significant part of this evolution, where AI is used to automate, optimize, and enhance processes in industries such as manufacturing, logistics, and energy. By deploying AI in areas like predictive maintenance, quality control, and supply chain optimization, businesses can achieve higher efficiency, reduced downtime, and improved safety.

Another key area is **AI at the edge**, where AI models are deployed directly on devices and sensors, enabling real-time data processing and decision-making. Edge AI solutions bring AI capabilities closer to where data is generated, reducing latency and improving efficiency for applications in sectors such as healthcare, retail, and industrial automation.

The future of AI is moving towards even greater autonomy, adaptability, and versatility. Emerging concepts such as *agentic AI* and *AutoGen* are set to redefine how AI systems operate, enabling them to autonomously manage tasks, make decisions, and interact without constant human intervention. In parallel, advancements in **MLOps** are ensuring that AI models can be reliably deployed, monitored, and maintained, bridging the gap between AI research and real-world applications.

As AI continues to evolve, its integration into everyday tools and systems is poised to redefine industries, streamline processes, and create new opportunities. This chapter will explore the architecture and operational practices that make these advancements possible, providing insights into how businesses can harness both digital and physical AI to stay ahead in a rapidly changing technological landscape. From in-depth analyses of generative AI architectures and emerging trends to best practices in MLOps, edge AI, and Industrial AI operationalization, this chapter will offer a comprehensive view of the current and future state of AI.

In-depth analysis of generative AI architectures

Generative AI refers to a class of ML models designed to generate new content, such as text, images, music, or code, by learning patterns from existing datasets. Unlike traditional AI models that classify or predict, generative models create outputs that mimic the structure and characteristics of the data they were trained on. At the core of generative AI are neural networks, particularly deep learning architectures such as **generative adversarial networks (GANs)**, **variational autoencoders (VAEs)**, and **Transformer models**.

To truly harness the power of generative AI, it is important to understand the landscape from the foundational models to the emerging patterns and the infrastructure that supports it all. The following visual distills the key building blocks of the GenAI ecosystem, offering a simplified yet comprehensive view of how modern AI solutions are structured and deployed:

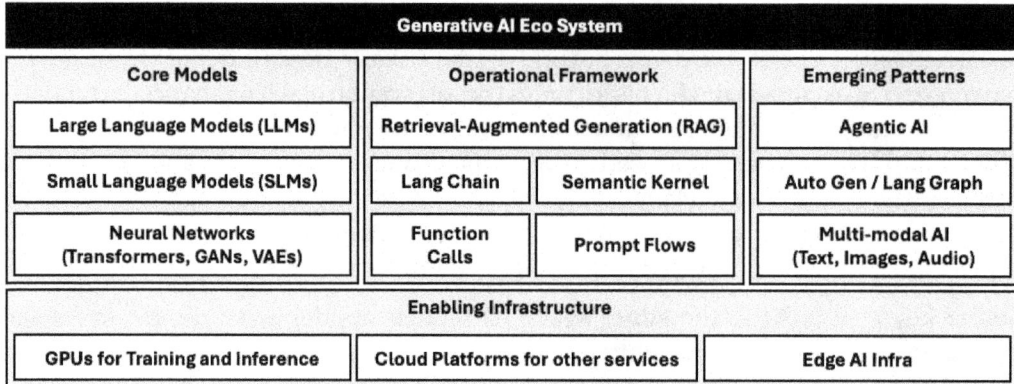

Generative AI Eco System		
Core Models	**Operational Framework**	**Emerging Patterns**
Large Language Models (LLMs)	Retrieval-Augmented Generation (RAG)	Agentic AI
Small Language Models (SLMs)	Lang Chain / Semantic Kernel	Auto Gen / Lang Graph
Neural Networks (Transformers, GANs, VAEs)	Function Calls / Prompt Flows	Multi-modal AI (Text, Images, Audio)
Enabling Infrastructure		
GPUs for Training and Inference	Cloud Platforms for other services	Edge AI Infra

Figure 9.1: Gen AI ecosystem

The *Transformer architecture*, popularized by models like *OpenAI's GPT-4* and *Llama 2*, is the backbone of most modern generative AI systems. Transformers leverage attention mechanisms, which allow the model to focus on different parts of the input data, understanding context more effectively. This makes them particularly powerful for tasks like NLP, where understanding the sequence of words and their relationships is crucial.

The key elements of a Transformer-based generative AI system include:

- **Input embeddings**: Raw data (text, image, etc.) is converted into numerical representations, called embeddings, which capture the semantic meaning of the input.

- **Attention mechanisms**: Self-attention layers analyze the input embeddings, identifying which parts of the data are most relevant to generating the output. This allows the model to understand context and dependencies across different elements of the input.

- **Multi-head attention**: Enables the model to process information from multiple perspectives simultaneously, enhancing its ability to generate coherent and context-aware outputs.

- **Feedforward neural networks**: After attention mechanisms process the input, the data is passed through feedforward layers to refine and produce the final output.

- **Decoder**: For generative tasks, a decoder takes the processed data and generates new content, such as text or images, based on the learned patterns.

Generative AI models are computationally intensive, requiring significant processing power for both training and inference. **Graphics processing units (GPUs)** play a critical role in accelerating these tasks due to their ability to handle parallel computations efficiently. Unlike traditional CPUs, which process tasks sequentially, GPUs can process thousands of operations simultaneously, making them ideal for deep learning models that require massive matrix calculations.

This demand for high-performance computing translates into three critical infrastructure considerations for generative AI, training, inference, and scalability, as follows:

- **Training**: Training generative models involves processing vast amounts of data to adjust the model's weights and biases over multiple iterations. This can take days or even weeks to complete. GPUs like *NVIDIA A100* or *H100* are often used because they offer high computational power and memory bandwidth, enabling faster training of large models.

- **Inference**: Once trained, models need to generate outputs quickly in real-world applications. GPUs are equally crucial for inference, especially when real-time responses are required. For this, smaller and more efficient GPUs, such as *NVIDIA T4*, may be deployed to balance performance and power consumption.

- **Scalability**: Cloud platforms, including **Azure**, **AWS**, and **Google Cloud**, offer GPU clusters that allow organizations to scale their generative AI workloads based on demand. This scalability is vital for handling variable workloads, ensuring that models can be trained and deployed efficiently.

Prompt engineering techniques

A unique aspect of working with generative AI models is the need for *prompt engineering*, which involves crafting inputs (prompts) to guide the model in generating desired outputs. Effective, prompt engineering can significantly enhance the quality, relevance, and accuracy of the model's responses, making it a crucial skill for developers and data scientists.

The following are the four key methods that form the foundation of effective prompt engineering:

- **Contextual prompts**: Generative models rely on the context provided by the input to produce coherent outputs. By crafting prompts that include relevant background information, users can guide the model to generate more accurate and informative responses. For example, a prompt like *Write a short summary about renewable energy focusing on solar power* will lead to more specific content compared to a vague prompt.

- **Parameter adjustment**: Developers can manipulate various parameters, such as temperature (which controls the randomness of the output) and max tokens (which sets the length of the generated content), to refine the model's behavior. A higher temperature setting might lead to more creative but less predictable responses, while a lower setting will produce more deterministic outputs.

- **Chaining prompts**: Complex tasks can be handled by breaking them into smaller, sequential prompts, where the output of one serves as the input for the next. This technique, often used in **LangChain** frameworks, allows developers to create multi-step workflows that can process information more effectively and generate nuanced results.

- **Function calls and APIs**: Advanced prompt engineering can involve the use of function calls, where the model can be directed to retrieve specific information from external databases or APIs during the generation process. This is particularly useful for applications requiring up-to-date information or interaction with existing enterprise systems.

Exploring emerging trends in generative AI

The field of generative AI continues to evolve rapidly, with new innovations enhancing the capabilities of AI systems and pushing the boundaries of what these models can achieve. These emerging trends are set to redefine the way enterprises leverage AI, making systems more autonomous, adaptive, and versatile.

This section explores some of the most significant advancements shaping the future of generative AI:

- **Agentic AI**: Moving towards autonomous systems:
  - o Agentic AI represents a shift from traditional AI models, which operate based on specific prompts, to systems that can autonomously manage tasks, make decisions, and interact with users or other systems without continuous human guidance. These systems are designed to perform complex tasks by understanding the broader context and goals, allowing them to adapt their behavior dynamically.
  - o For example, an agentic AI could autonomously navigate a series of customer support interactions, escalating issues when needed, gathering information from different systems, and even resolving complex queries without human intervention. This capability is being explored for applications in areas like autonomous vehicles, smart manufacturing, and even enterprise workflow automation, where AI agents can take on repetitive tasks and free up human resources for more strategic work.

- **AutoGen**: Adaptive interactions and workflow automation:
  - o AutoGen is an emerging framework that enables the creation of adaptive and dynamic interactions between AI systems and applications. Unlike

traditional models, which require specific programming for every interaction, AutoGen allows AI systems to generate responses and workflows that can change based on the situation, user inputs, or external data.

o This adaptability is particularly useful for businesses that need AI to handle unpredictable or variable tasks. For instance, AutoGen can be employed in e-commerce to generate personalized product recommendations in real time, adjusting based on user behavior as they navigate through a website. It can also enable more dynamic chatbot interactions, where the AI can pivot conversations based on user feedback, access external databases, and make decisions to provide more accurate and relevant information.

- **Multimodal AI**: Integrating multiple data types:

  o Traditional generative AI models have primarily focused on a single modality, such as text or images. However, the development of **multimodal AI** has introduced models that can process and generate content across different types of data, including text, images, audio, and even video. This integration allows for richer, more dynamic interactions, making AI applications more versatile and capable of handling complex real-world tasks.

  o For example, multimodal AI can be used in virtual assistants that not only understand and respond to voice commands but can also analyze visual inputs (e.g., photos or videos) to provide a more comprehensive response. Enterprises can leverage this to build more interactive customer experiences, such as AR/VR applications that integrate voice recognition, gesture tracking, and visual processing to deliver immersive training or support solutions.

- **Industrial AI**: Automating and optimizing physical processes:

  o While generative AI has seen widespread use in digital applications, its integration into the physical world has given rise to **industrial AI**. This trend involves using generative models to automate, optimize, and enhance industrial processes across sectors like manufacturing, logistics, and energy. Industrial AI systems can predict machine failures, optimize production schedules, and even generate new designs for products based on specific requirements.

  o By combining the power of generative AI with industrial IoT (Internet of Things) devices, companies can create smart factories where machines are not only automated but can also adapt to changes in production demand, maintenance schedules, or supply chain disruptions. Platforms like *NVIDIA's Jetson* and *Azure Percept* are leading this integration by enabling AI at the edge, where real-time data processing is critical for smooth operations.

- **AI at the edge**: Real-time processing and decision-making:

  o The traditional approach to deploying AI models involves sending data to centralized cloud servers for processing. However, this can lead to latency issues, especially for applications that require real-time responses. **AI at the edge** addresses this challenge by deploying AI models directly on devices and sensors, enabling data processing closer to the source. This reduces latency, enhances data privacy, and ensures faster, more efficient decision-making.

  o Edge AI is particularly beneficial for applications like autonomous vehicles, where real-time decision-making is critical for safety, or in industrial settings, where equipment needs to respond instantly to sensor data. By integrating edge AI, businesses can build systems that process data locally, reducing the need for constant cloud connectivity and ensuring that critical operations can continue even in environments with limited internet access.

- **Future of generative AI:**

  o The convergence of these emerging trends is leading towards more autonomous, adaptive, and integrated AI systems. From agentic AI that can manage tasks independently to multimodal models capable of interacting across different types of data, the future of generative AI promises to be more versatile and capable than ever. As businesses continue to adopt and refine these technologies, they will be able to create smarter, more efficient systems that drive innovation across every sector.

  o These advancements highlight the dynamic and evolving nature of generative AI, offering new possibilities for enterprises to innovate and adapt in a rapidly changing technological landscape. By staying ahead of these trends, organizations can harness the full potential of AI, transforming the way they operate and engage with their customers.

Shift to mixture of experts (MoE) and sparse models

Modern LLMs are increasingly moving away from **dense transformer architectures** to **MoE** and **sparse activation strategies**. Models like *GPT-4o (OpenAI)*, *Mixtral (Mistral. ai)*, and *Gemini 1.5 (Google)* exemplify this shift by selectively activating portions of the model during inference, leading to dramatic efficiency gains. MoE models enable greater specialization for specific tasks, more cost-effective inference, and support for extended context lengths. This architectural direction is shaping the next generation of scalable and sustainable LLMs for both cloud and edge deployment.

GPT-4o and the rise of native multimodal models

The release of GPT-4o in March 2024 marked a leap forward in truly multimodal AI. Unlike previous models that combined separate vision and text components, GPT-4o is natively multimodal, trained from scratch on image, audio, and text in a shared embedding space. This architectural approach allows seamless reasoning across modalities.

Larger context Windows and implications for RAG

Models like *Gemini 1.5 (1M tokens)*, *Claude 2.1 (200K)*, and *GPT-4o (128K+)* now support massive context windows, changing the game for RAG. Traditional RAG approaches emphasized chunking, summarization, and embedding-based search. With extended context windows, models can ingest entire documents or codebases directly, reducing the need for external retrieval.

Function calling to agentic workflows

The evolution from simple *function calling to agentic frameworks* has accelerated. Early function calling enabled LLMs to trigger API calls. **Toolformer** extended this by dynamically choosing tools during inference. Today, platforms like *AutoGen*, *LangGraph*, *Functionary*, and *CrewAI* orchestrate entire agent workflows with planning, execution, and error recovery.

Shift from chat-based agents to state-aware agents

Enterprises are moving from **stateless chatbots** to agents with **persistent memory and state-awareness**. Frameworks like *LangGraph* and *Functionary* now allow developers to build graph-based, observable workflows where agents manage history, context, and coordination. These stateful agents represent the next phase in enterprise AI maturity, capable of handling multi-step tasks, error correction, and complex decision chains across time.

AI and API integration patterns for enterprises

In enterprise settings, the most valuable GenAI systems combine LLMs with internal APIs, tools, and databases. Common patterns include agentic loops with fallback strategies, tool chaining for complex tasks, and guardrails for safety. Frameworks like *LangChain, Semantic Kernel, LangGraph, Azure AI Studio*, and the *OpenAI Assistants API* have matured to support these patterns at scale.

Enterprises moving from chatbots to Gen AI workflows

Enterprises are moving beyond generic AI chatbots toward embedded Gen AI workflows that solve real business problems. The new wave focuses on verticalized solutions that integrate deeply with existing tools and processes. These AI-powered apps deliver contextual, domain-aware value, far beyond a chat window. This evolution highlights the **Copilot pattern** as the dominant design principle in enterprise AI strategy.

AI evaluation and observability

LLMOps has evolved with a growing focus on evaluating model quality, safety, and cost-efficiency. Human-in-the-loop evals, structured A/B testing, and Eval-as-a-Service are now standard. Platforms like *TruLens*, *PromptLayer*, *HumanLoop*, and OpenAI's evals framework allow enterprises to monitor drift, hallucinations, and response fidelity at scale.

Overview of open-source large language models

LLMs have become a cornerstone of generative AI, enabling machines to understand and generate human-like text. While large tech companies develop many leading LLMs and remain proprietary, the rise of **open-source LLMs** has democratized access to advanced AI capabilities.

These open-source models provide developers, researchers, and enterprises with the flexibility to customize and deploy LLMs without the restrictions of proprietary systems, driving innovation across various sectors:

Llama

Meta's Llama 3 is the latest release in one of the most widely adopted families of open-source LLMs. Announced in April 2024, Llama 3 models deliver significantly improved performance across **language understanding, reasoning,** and **instruction-following tasks**. The release includes Llama 3-8B and Llama 3-70B models, trained on a high-quality, diverse dataset with over 15 trillion tokens. These models are widely used for general-purpose text generation, enterprise NLP applications, and chat agents. Meta is expected to release multimodal and longer context Llama 3 variants in mid-2025. For resource-constrained environments, the earlier Llama 2-7B and 13B models remain popular, especially in mobile and on-prem deployments.

DeepSeek

DeepSeek AI, a fast-growing AI lab from China, has gained rapid recognition with its DeepSeek-VL, DeepSeek-Coder, and DeepSeek-LLM model families. The latest DeepSeek-LLM models, available in 7B and 67B sizes and trained on 2 trillion high-quality tokens, offer a strong balance between performance, cost efficiency, and speed. What sets DeepSeek apart is its focus on training innovations. It uses **token-level curriculum learning** that enables the model to progress from simple to complex data. It also applies **layer-wise**

quantization to reduce model size while keeping accuracy intact. **Hybrid attention windows** further enhance the model's ability to handle long context efficiently while lowering compute requirements. These techniques allow DeepSeek models to compete with or outperform larger models in benchmarks while *keeping training and inference costs lower*. The DeepSeek Coder models, available in 1.3B, 6.7B, and 33B sizes, are among the most capable open-source models for code generation.

Mistral

Mistral.ai has quickly become a standout contributor in the OSS LLM space with *highly optimized and permissively licensed models*. Its latest offering, Mixtral 8x22B, is a MoE model featuring 12.9B active parameters per forward pass. It delivers top-tier performance in reasoning and multilingual tasks while being more cost-efficient than monolithic models of similar size. Mistral also maintains Mistral 7B, a dense, decoder-only model *optimized for speed and open-source flexibility*, ideal for finetuning and edge inference. Many developers use Mixtral for sophisticated chatbot agents and RAG pipelines, while Mistral 7B remains the go-to base model for rapid experimentation and domain adaptation. Mistral's models are among the most permissively licensed, making them popular in commercial deployments.

Gemma

Google's Gemma 2 models, launched in early 2025, are part of its growing open-source commitment to responsible and efficient LLM development. Gemma 2 builds on the strengths of its predecessor (Gemma 1) with improvements in safety, alignment, and performance, especially for developers looking to embed AI into production-grade systems. The family includes Gemma 2-2B and Gemma 2-7B, both decoder-only transformer models trained with reinforcement learning and curated datasets aligned to Google's safety principles. Lightweight, transparent, and designed for fine-tuning, Gemma models are ideal for building assistants, question-answering systems, and domain-specific agents. Google also offers quantized and TPU-optimized versions, making Gemma attractive for performance-sensitive cloud and edge use cases.

Phi-3.5 series

In August 2024, Microsoft introduced the Phi-3.5 series of *small language models*, comprising three distinct models tailored for diverse applications:

- **Phi-3.5-mini-instruct**: With 3.82 billion parameters, this model is optimized for efficient reasoning tasks in environments with limited computational resources. It excels in code generation, mathematical problem-solving, and logic-based reasoning, outperforming larger models like *Meta's Llama-3.1-8B-instruct* and *Mistral-7B-instruct* on benchmarks such as *RepoQA*, which assesses long-context code understanding.

- **Phi-3.5-MoE-instruct**: Featuring a MoEs architecture with 41.9 billion parameters, this model adeptly handles complex reasoning tasks by dynamically activating different parameters based on input. It surpasses larger counterparts, including Google's Gemini 1.5 Flash, in various benchmarks, making it suitable for applications requiring deep, context-aware understanding and decision-making.

- **Phi-3.5-vision-instruct**: This 4.15 billion-parameter model integrates text and image processing capabilities, enabling tasks such as image understanding, optical character recognition, and video summarization. Its multimodal approach and support for a 128K token context length make it particularly effective in handling complex, multi-frame visual tasks.

The following are some of the other popular open-source and multi-modal models:

Several open-source models continue to gain traction beyond the core families like Llama, DeepSeek, Gemma, and Mistral.

- **CSM-1B (Sesame/Maya)**: Developed by Sesame Labs, CSM-1B is a lightweight, billion-parameter language model that has captured attention for powering *Maya*, a viral AI personal assistant gaining traction across GitHub and social platforms like X (formerly Twitter). Designed for speed, interactivity, and low compute usage, CSM-1B delivers impressive conversational capabilities while maintaining a minimal footprint. Its success underscores the rising importance of small, efficient LLMs in real-world deployments where latency and cost matter. As more developers explore AI assistants tailored for mobile and embedded systems, CSM-1B has emerged as a compelling benchmark for what is possible with compact models.

- **OpenChat**: OpenChat is a family of open-source LLMs fine-tuned specifically for conversational quality, using **reinforcement learning from human feedback (RLHF)** techniques. Built on top of strong base models like Mistral, OpenChat consistently ranks among the best in alignment, reasoning, and multi-turn dialogue on Hugging Face's Open LLM Leaderboard. What sets OpenChat apart is its balance between raw performance and human-like response quality, making it a favorite in open chatbot deployments and experimentation. It exemplifies how open models, when aligned well, can rival or exceed proprietary chatbots in naturalness and contextual relevance.

- **Stable diffusion (by stability AI)**: The dominant open-source model for text-to-image generation. With ongoing upgrades in fidelity and control (e.g., SDXL), it is widely used across design, media, and marketing workflows. Its flexible fine-tuning support has led to a massive ecosystem of custom models and extensions.

- **StarCoder2 (by BigCode)**: A leading open-source code model trained on permissively licensed datasets. It supports over 80 programming languages and outperforms many proprietary code models, making it the top open alternative for software development use cases.

- **TinyLlama**: TinyLlama is a 1.1 billion parameter model that has been fine-tuned to support long-context tasks, making it a strong contender for edge and mobile deployments where memory and compute are constrained. Despite its compact size, TinyLlama demonstrates impressive performance on reasoning and language understanding benchmarks, showing how smaller models can still deliver meaningful capability when trained with optimized data and architecture tweaks. Its open release has sparked interest among developers working on on-device AI applications, chatbots, and low-latency use cases, reinforcing the trend toward highly efficient, portable LLMs.

- **AudioCraft (by Meta)**: One of the most promising open-source text-to-audio and music generation frameworks. It is gaining traction for applications in gaming, sound design, and content creation.

- **ModelScope (by Alibaba)**: A rising multi-modal framework with open-source support for text-to-video generation. While early-stage, it is one of the few open models pushing boundaries in video synthesis from prompts.

Hugging Face

An important player in the open-source AI ecosystem is **Hugging Face**, a platform that has made accessing, deploying, and fine-tuning LLMs significantly easier. Hugging Face provides a comprehensive library called **Transformers**, which hosts thousands of pre-trained models, including popular LLMs like *Llama 2*, *GPT-NeoX*, and *BLOOM*. This platform has become a hub for developers, researchers, and enterprises to explore, share, and contribute to AI models.

Hugging Face's platform offers several advantages:

- **Ease of integration**: The Hugging Face Transformers library makes it straightforward to integrate LLMs into applications. With user-friendly APIs and extensive documentation, developers can deploy and customize models without needing deep technical expertise.

- **Community and collaboration**: Hugging Face fosters a collaborative community where users can share their fine-tuned models, code snippets, and tutorials. This spirit of open collaboration accelerates innovation, as users can build on each other's work.

- **Fine-tuning and model hub**: Hugging Face allows enterprises to fine-tune existing models on their own datasets, which helps customize models for specific tasks. The **model hub** features pre-trained models that can be quickly adapted, reducing the time and resources needed to develop AI solutions from scratch.

- **Hugging Face's integration with robotics projects**: The open-source community is working on integrating LLMs with robotics platforms, enabling machines to perform tasks based on natural language instructions. This is part of a broader effort to make **language-driven robotics**, where generative models like *GPT-4* can control robotic arms or drones by interpreting commands that were once only possible through specific programming languages. Open-source projects are making strides in providing SDKs and modules that combine NLP capabilities with robotics, creating more adaptable systems for industrial use.

Hugging Face has thus become a key enabler for enterprises looking to leverage open-source LLMs, providing tools that simplify the deployment and scaling of these models across diverse use cases. Several noteworthy community-driven projects and techniques have emerged that are shaping the future of AI development and deployment, as shown:

- **BigScience and BLOOM's Collaborative Framework**: BigScience's project that developed BLOOM is an excellent example of a decentralized, collaborative approach to building LLMs. The community-driven effort pulled together resources and expertise from researchers around the world to create a multilingual model. This project has opened the door for more initiatives where decentralized contributions lead to the development of shared, open-source AI resources.

- **Federated learning for privacy-preserving AI**: Federated learning is gaining traction as a method for training models without centralizing data, which is crucial for privacy. Open-source projects are experimenting with federated learning to train generative models across distributed networks, ensuring that sensitive data (such as medical or financial information) remains on local devices while still contributing to a global AI model. This is particularly promising for sectors with stringent data privacy regulations.

- **AutoGen and BabyAGI**: Projects like **AutoGPT** have inspired a wave of innovation in the open-source community. AutoGPT extends the capabilities of traditional LLMs by enabling models to chain tasks together, make decisions, and execute complex workflows autonomously. Developers have built upon this concept to create more advanced **AI agents** that can handle multiple interrelated tasks, from data collection and analysis to content generation and scheduling.

- **LangChain**: Another key project that has emerged is **LangChain**, which provides frameworks for connecting language models to various APIs, enabling them to perform more practical, task-oriented activities. Open-source contributors have been actively expanding their libraries, making it easier to integrate LLMs with databases, web scraping tools, and even IoT devices, further extending the utility of generative AI in real-world applications.

- **CodeGen and StarCoder**: Building on the success of models like OpenAI's Codex, the open-source community has been creating models like *CodeGen* and *StarCoder* to assist with software development. These models can help write, debug, and optimize code, enabling developers to streamline their workflows. Recent efforts focus on making these models more language-agnostic, capable of understanding and generating code across multiple programming languages.

- **Hugging Face's BigCode project**: This is an initiative focused on developing an open-source generative model specifically for code. It aims to support developers by offering suggestions, identifying bugs, and even generating new code from scratch. The community-driven nature of this project allows for continuous improvements and updates, making it a valuable tool for developers worldwide.

- **Parameter-efficient fine-tuning (PEFT)**: Open-source projects are exploring ways to make training LLMs more efficient, particularly through PEFT methods. This approach allows models to be fine-tuned with fewer parameters, reducing the computational resources required and making it easier for smaller organizations to deploy sophisticated models.

- **Low-rank adaptation (LoRA)**: Another technique gaining popularity in the open-source community is LoRA, which aims to enable models to adapt to new tasks without retraining from scratch. This significantly lowers the cost and energy requirements for training, making it possible to deploy and scale models faster.

Key advantages of open-source LLMs

Open-source LLMs represent a significant step forward in making advanced AI technologies more accessible and customizable.

Here are some of the advantages:

- **Customization**: Organizations can fine-tune open-source models on their own datasets, making them more accurate for specific tasks, industries, or languages. This adaptability is crucial for enterprises looking to deploy AI solutions tailored to their unique needs.

- **Cost efficiency**: While proprietary models may require licensing fees or subscription costs, open-source models eliminate these expenses, reducing the overall cost of AI adoption. This makes it easier for smaller companies and startups to integrate advanced AI.

- **Transparency and trust**: Open-source models allow developers to inspect the underlying code and model architecture, providing insights into how the models work. This transparency fosters trust and accountability, especially in applications where understanding the decision-making process is critical.

Challenges and risks in using open-source LLMs

While open-source LLMs offer flexibility and cost benefits, enterprises must also be aware of the challenges and risks associated with their use.

Here are some key considerations:

- **Data security and privacy**: Open-source models often require fine-tuning on proprietary datasets, raising concerns about data security and privacy. Enterprises need to ensure that data is anonymized and encrypted during the training process and that any sensitive information is adequately protected.

- **Model reliability and bias**: Open-source LLMs are trained on vast amounts of data sourced from the internet, which can include biased, inaccurate, or inappropriate content. This can lead to models generating outputs that reflect those biases or inaccuracies, posing risks in sensitive applications such as healthcare, legal services, or customer support. Enterprises need to conduct rigorous testing and apply bias-mitigation strategies before deploying these models.

- **Legal and compliance risks**: The use of open-source software comes with legal implications, particularly regarding licensing. Enterprises must ensure they comply with the licenses under which the models are distributed, avoiding any legal disputes related to intellectual property. Additionally, using AI models that produce outputs based on external datasets can lead to compliance issues, especially in regulated industries.

- **Maintenance and updates**: Unlike proprietary models, where the provider handles updates and maintenance, enterprises using open-source LLMs need to take responsibility for maintaining and updating the models. This can be resource-intensive, requiring a dedicated team to monitor performance, apply patches, and update models as needed to keep them current and effective.

- **Scalability and performance**: Deploying open-source LLMs at scale can be challenging, particularly for organizations that lack robust IT infrastructure. High computational demands during training and inference may necessitate significant investments in hardware or cloud services. Companies need to carefully assess the costs and benefits of scaling these models to ensure they can meet their performance requirements.

- **Newer architectures like DeepSeek's MoE also introduce operational complexity** in routing mechanisms and inference optimization. While these models reduce cost, they may require fine-tuning infrastructure and inference engines tailored to MoE workloads.

The open-source community's contributions to generative AI are diverse and rapidly evolving. From innovations in multi-modal systems and federated learning to the development of more efficient training techniques, these projects are democratizing access to advanced AI technologies and fostering a collaborative environment for innovation. As these projects continue to mature, they are likely to lead to more robust, adaptable, and ethically grounded AI systems that can be used across a wide range of industries.

Introduction and best practices in MLOps

MLOps is a set of practices that combines ML with DevOps principles to streamline the development, deployment, and monitoring of machine learning models. Just as DevOps brought efficiency and automation to software development, MLOps aims to standardize and automate the lifecycle of ML models, ensuring that they can be integrated into production systems reliably and at scale.

The following figure provides a structured overview of the key components that make up a comprehensive MLOps workflow tailored for generative AI:

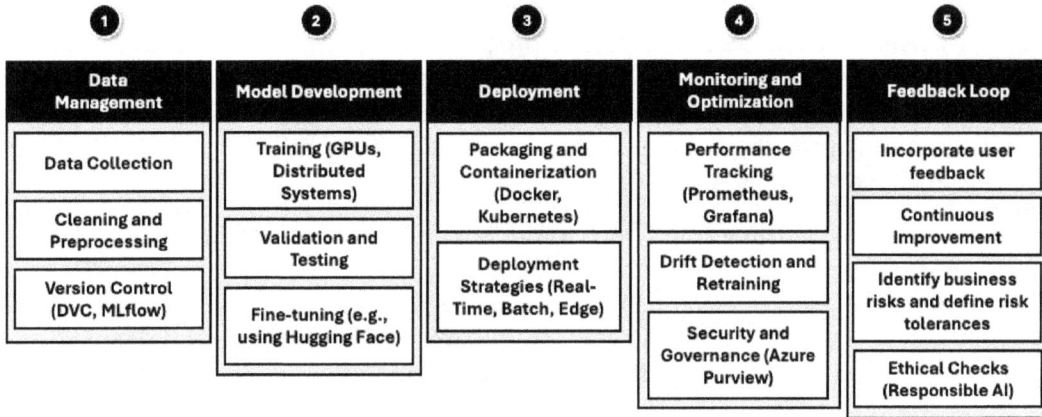

Figure 9.2: MLOps lifecycle for generative AI

The adoption of MLOps has become essential as organizations move from experimental AI projects to deploying AI-driven solutions across the enterprise. Without effective MLOps practices, companies often face challenges such as longer development cycles, unreliable deployments, and difficulties in maintaining and updating models. MLOps addresses these issues by providing a framework that covers the entire model lifecycle, from data preparation and model training to deployment, monitoring, and maintenance.

The key components of MLOps are as follows:

- **Data management**: The foundation of any successful ML project lies in effective data management. MLOps practices emphasize the automation of data ingestion, cleaning, and transformation to ensure that models are trained on high-quality, consistent data. Tools like *Azure Data Factory*, *Apache Airflow*, and *AWS Glue* can help manage complex data pipelines, facilitating smooth data flow from multiple sources.

- **Version control for code and models**: Just as DevOps uses **version control systems** (**VCS**) like **Git** for code, MLOps extends this practice to include datasets and models. Versioning ensures that every change is tracked, making it easier to reproduce results, roll back to previous versions, and audit the model development process. Platforms like *data version control (DVC)* and *MLflow* provide integrated solutions for managing model versions alongside code.

- **Automated testing**: Before deploying a model, it is essential to ensure that it performs as expected across different datasets and scenarios. MLOps encourages the use of automated testing frameworks to validate models, check for biases, and identify edge cases. This includes testing not just the model's accuracy but also its scalability, robustness, and security. Automated testing can catch potential issues early, reducing the risk of deploying faulty models.

- **Continuous integration and continuous deployment (CI/CD)**: CI/CD pipelines are integral to MLOps, enabling rapid and reliable deployment of models. Automated pipelines streamline the process of integrating new model versions into production environments, reducing manual intervention and ensuring consistent performance. Tools like *Jenkins, GitHub Actions*, and *Azure Pipelines* facilitate CI/CD for ML projects, making it easier to deploy updated models without disrupting ongoing operations.

- **Monitoring and logging**: Once a model is deployed, continuous monitoring is essential to track its performance, detect anomalies, and identify potential drifts (i.e., when a model's predictions become less accurate over time due to changes in the data distribution). Monitoring tools like *Prometheus, Grafana*, and *Azure Monitor* can be used to log **key performance indicators** (**KPIs**), alert on any unexpected behaviors, and automate the retraining process if needed.

- **Scalability and resource management**: MLOps involves ensuring that models can handle varying workloads efficiently. This requires scalable infrastructure that can automatically adjust resources based on demand. Solutions like *Kubernetes, Docker*, and *Azure Kubernetes Service (AKS)* are widely used to containerize ML models, making them portable and scalable across different environments. Cloud platforms also offer **auto-scaling features**, ensuring that resources are allocated dynamically, which is particularly useful for handling spikes in traffic.

The best practices in MLOps are as follows:

- **Establish clear governance and compliance standards**: With the increasing scrutiny of AI ethics, privacy, and data security, it is vital to establish robust governance practices that ensure compliance with regulations and industry standards. This includes maintaining transparency around data sources, model decision-making, and how AI systems are used. Governance frameworks should also address data privacy concerns, especially when dealing with sensitive information.

- **Adopt a modular approach**: Building modular pipelines enables teams to work on different parts of the ML workflow independently, such as data processing, feature engineering, model training, and deployment. This modularity promotes reusability, simplifies debugging, and accelerates the development process. For example, a team can update the data processing module without affecting the rest of the workflow.

- **Implement feedback loops**: Continuous feedback is essential for improving models and maintaining their relevance. MLOps practices should include mechanisms to collect feedback from end-users, monitor real-world performance, and use this information to refine models. Feedback loops are particularly useful for applications that need to adapt to changing user behaviors or external conditions.

- **Emphasize collaboration between data scientists and engineers**: One of the goals of MLOps is to bridge the gap between data science and engineering teams. By fostering collaboration, companies can ensure that models developed in the lab can be seamlessly deployed in production. This requires integrating tools and platforms that support both data science and software development workflows, facilitating communication and reducing friction.

- **Ensure model explainability and interpretability**: In many industries, especially those dealing with regulatory compliance, it is important to understand how a model arrives at its decisions. MLOps practices should include tools and techniques for enhancing model explainability, ensuring that stakeholders can trust the AI's outputs. Solutions like *SHapley Additive exPlanations (SHAP)* and *Local Interpretable Model-agnostic Explanations (LIME)* help in making models more transparent by highlighting which features influenced specific predictions.

Challenges in MLOps

While MLOps provides a structured approach to deploying and managing machine learning models, organizations often face several challenges when implementing these practices. Addressing these challenges is crucial for ensuring successful AI deployment:

- **Data quality and management**: One of the most significant hurdles in MLOps is maintaining high-quality, consistent data across different stages of the ML lifecycle. Inconsistent, biased, or outdated data can lead to inaccurate models. Organizations often struggle with data silos, where data is stored in multiple, disconnected systems, making it difficult to access, integrate, and preprocess effectively.

- **Model drift and performance degradation**: After deployment, models may encounter scenarios where their predictions become less accurate over time due to changes in the data distribution (model drift). Detecting and responding to model drift requires continuous monitoring, which can be resource-intensive without proper automation.

- **Infrastructure complexity**: Managing the infrastructure needed for model training, deployment, and scaling can be complex, especially for large-scale applications. Organizations need to balance resource allocation, cost management, and performance, which often requires sophisticated orchestration tools and cloud services.

- **Lack of standardization**: Many companies lack standardized processes for deploying and maintaining ML models, leading to inconsistencies and inefficiencies. Without clear guidelines, teams may use different tools and approaches, making it harder to collaborate and scale solutions effectively.

- **Integration with existing systems**: Deploying machine learning models requires seamless integration with existing IT systems, databases, and software. This can be challenging, especially when legacy systems are involved. Ensuring compatibility and interoperability across different platforms often necessitates additional development work.

- **Collaboration between data science and engineering teams**: Bridging the gap between data scientists, who build models, and engineers, who deploy and maintain them, is often a challenge. Differences in workflows, tools, and priorities can lead to miscommunication and delays, affecting the overall productivity of ML projects.

- **Governance, security, and compliance**: Ensuring that AI models adhere to data privacy regulations and security standards is a complex yet essential aspect of MLOps. Organizations need to implement robust governance frameworks to track data usage, model decisions, and compliance requirements, which can be time-consuming and difficult to manage across multiple teams and projects.

Checklist to ensure MLOps maturity

Achieving MLOps maturity involves more than just implementing basic ML workflows; it requires a comprehensive approach that integrates automation, scalability, security, and collaboration across the entire model lifecycle. For organizations aiming to streamline their AI deployments and maximize the benefits of ML, it is crucial to regularly assess their MLOps practices against established benchmarks.

The following checklist provides a structured way to evaluate and enhance MLOps processes, ensuring that models are developed, deployed, and maintained with reliability, efficiency, and compliance:

- Are data pipelines automated for seamless data ingestion, cleaning, and preprocessing?

- Is data versioning implemented to track changes and maintain consistency?

- Are there mechanisms to handle data anomalies, biases, and missing values?

- Are code, datasets, and models version-controlled to ensure reproducibility and auditability?

- Can models be rolled back to previous versions if needed?

- Are CI/CD pipelines established for automating the testing, integration, and deployment of models?

- Is there an automated process to deploy new models or updates without disrupting ongoing services?

- Are models continuously monitored for performance metrics such as accuracy, latency, and throughput?

- Are there alerts set up for detecting anomalies, model drift, or performance degradation?

- Is there a feedback loop to retrain models when performance drops below a defined threshold?

- Is the infrastructure scalable, with capabilities for auto-scaling to manage varying workloads?

- Are containerization tools (e.g., Docker, Kubernetes) used to simplify deployment and scaling?

- Are there standardized workflows that promote collaboration between data scientists and engineers?

- Are tools integrated to ensure smooth handoffs between development and deployment teams?

- Are there clear governance policies for data security, privacy, and model transparency?

- Are compliance requirements integrated into the MLOps workflow, including data anonymization, encryption, and regular audits?

- Are models designed with mechanisms to explain their predictions, making it easier to understand how decisions are made?

- Are there tools in place to interpret model outcomes, especially for applications in regulated industries?

- Are cost-efficient cloud services used to optimize resources during training and deployment?

- Is there a balance between on-premises and cloud infrastructure to manage workloads efficiently?

- Are team members regularly trained on the latest MLOps tools and best practices?

- Is there a culture of continuous improvement, with regular reviews of the MLOps process?

Practical guide to AI model operationalization

AI model operationalization, often referred to as model deployment, is the process of taking trained machine learning models and integrating them into production environments where they can deliver real-world value. While building and training a model is a significant part of AI development, operationalizing these models effectively ensures they are scalable, reliable, and continuously delivering insights. Without a robust operationalization strategy, even the most advanced models can fail to make an impact due to performance issues, integration challenges, or maintenance difficulties.

The key steps for seamless AI model operationalization are as follows:

- **Model packaging and containerization**: Packaging models in a standardized format makes it easier to deploy them across different environments. Containerization tools like *Docker* allow models to be encapsulated with all their dependencies, ensuring consistency and eliminating conflicts during deployment. Containers can be run on various platforms, making the model portable and reducing the complexities involved in moving from development to production.

- **Small language models (SLMs)**: While LLMs have garnered much attention, SLMs are gaining traction for their efficiency and suitability in edge or resource-constrained environments. SLMs can be fine-tuned for specific tasks without requiring extensive computational resources, making them ideal for applications that need quick, on-device processing. Operationalizing SLMs involves optimizing their deployment to ensure minimal latency and efficient performance, especially in mobile or embedded systems.

- **Deployment strategies**: Choosing the right deployment strategy is critical for model performance and scalability. Common deployment approaches include:

  - **Real-time inference**: Suitable for applications that require instant predictions, such as chatbots or recommendation engines. Models deployed for real-time inference need to be optimized for low-latency and high-throughput environments.

  - **Batch processing**: Ideal for scenarios where predictions can be made on bulk data at scheduled intervals, such as analyzing sales data or processing large datasets overnight.

  - **Edge deployment**: Deploying models on edge devices (e.g., IoT sensors, mobile phones) enables real-time processing without relying on continuous cloud connectivity. This is particularly useful in applications like autonomous vehicles or industrial monitoring systems.

- **Leveraging SDKs and tools:** Integrating AI models into applications often requires robust **software development kits** (**SDKs**) and frameworks that simplify communication between the model and the application. Some of the key tools include:

  - **Semantic Kernel**: A lightweight SDK designed to enable seamless interaction with LLMs and SLMs. It facilitates the integration of generative AI capabilities into enterprise applications, making it easier to build systems that leverage advanced language understanding.

○ **LangChain**: A framework that connects language models to external APIs, databases, and services. It allows developers to create workflows where models can interact with real-world data, providing richer, context-aware outputs.

○ **Prompt flow**: A tool that helps manage and optimize prompt engineering, enabling developers to craft effective prompts that guide the model's behavior. It is essential for applications that need consistent and reliable outputs from generative AI.

○ **AutoGen**: A platform that facilitates the creation of autonomous agents capable of executing tasks independently based on high-level instructions. AutoGen is useful for building systems where AI models need to perform multi-step operations without manual intervention.

- **Agentic AI development:** One of the emerging trends in operationalizing AI is the development of agentic AI systems, which can autonomously manage tasks, make decisions, and interact without human intervention. These systems can assess different situations, adapt their behavior dynamically, and take actions based on pre-defined rules or learned patterns. Agentic AI is particularly valuable in use cases like automated customer support, process optimization, and real-time data analysis. Operationalizing agentic AI requires robust frameworks that can integrate with multiple data sources, monitor performance, and ensure fail-safe mechanisms for critical decisions.

Generative AI application architecture patterns

Generative AI application development is anchored in a layered architecture that brings together core models, orchestration frameworks, memory handling, and integration mechanisms. At the heart of this approach is the *Copilot Development Stack*, which organizes the technical components required to build intelligent, context-aware, and secure AI-powered applications. From foundational models and prompt management to workflow automation and compliance controls, each layer plays a distinct role in shaping how generative AI delivers value across use cases.

Copilot Development Stack

The Copilot Development Stack is a multi-layered framework designed to help developers build and integrate generative AI capabilities into applications. This stack facilitates the seamless integration of AI models, enabling contextual, interactive, and autonomous functionalities. Each layer of the stack addresses a specific aspect of development, from core AI models to integration and automation.

Here is an overview of each layer of the Copilot Development Stack:

- **Foundation models layer:**

  - This is the base layer where LLMs and SLMs reside. These models, such as *GPT-4*, *Codex*, and other generative AI systems, form the core intelligence of the Copilot Stack.

  - The models are pre-trained on vast datasets and can be fine-tuned for specific tasks, such as generating text, writing code, or creating summaries. They provide the generative capabilities that underpin all Copilot features.

- **AI orchestration layer:**

  - This layer manages how AI models are utilized, including **prompt engineering** and **task orchestration**. It ensures that the models generate accurate, contextually relevant responses based on user inputs.

  - **Semantic Kernel** plays a key role in this layer. It is a lightweight SDK that helps developers build pipelines for AI models, enabling them to create modular AI-driven functions. For example, Semantic Kernel can handle prompt templates, chaining of multiple tasks, and memory storage, allowing AI to maintain context across interactions.

  - This layer also includes tools for managing and optimizing prompts, ensuring that the interaction with the models is efficient and produces reliable outcomes. **Prompt flow** is an example of a tool that aids in this by refining how prompts are structured and processed, improving the quality of responses from the AI.

- **Skills and function layer:**

  - At this layer, the focus is on **skills** and **functions** that leverage AI capabilities to perform specific tasks. Skills are pre-configured sets of actions that AI can execute, like summarizing text, generating code snippets, or parsing data.

  - Developers can use **LangChain** to create workflows that integrate various functions, enabling AI to interact with external data sources or APIs. LangChain facilitates building complex, multi-step processes where the AI can retrieve information, process it, and deliver it as part of a broader operation.

  - This modularity allows businesses to create customized skills tailored to specific use cases, enhancing the utility of Copilot for different applications, from customer service to software development.

- **Integration layer:**

  - The integration layer connects the AI models and functions to external systems, services, and applications. This is where the development stack integrates with cloud services, databases, APIs, and other enterprise tools.

- o For example, through **Azure Cognitive Services** and **APIs**, developers can enable Copilot to pull data from CRM systems, respond to emails, interact with IoT devices, or even control aspects of software platforms. Integration tools make it possible to embed AI-driven capabilities directly into existing software ecosystems, streamlining workflows and enhancing productivity.

- o **AutoGen** can also be part of this layer, where it helps create autonomous AI agents capable of performing multi-step tasks by interacting with various systems without manual intervention.

- **Memory and context management layer:**

  - o Effective AI applications require the ability to maintain **context** and **memory** across multiple interactions. This layer handles how information is stored, retrieved, and used over time, ensuring that AI can provide consistent and coherent responses.

  - o For instance, in a conversation, the AI needs to remember previous queries to respond appropriately. The **Semantic Kernel** provides the capability to store this contextual information, which can be accessed and reused as needed. This makes interactions more natural and relevant, especially in applications like chatbots or personal assistants.

  - o Context management also involves defining how long-term and short-term memories are processed, ensuring that the AI does not lose track of important details during complex operations.

- **Automation and workflow layer:**

  - o The automation and workflow layer is where AI-driven processes are set up to run automatically, reducing the need for manual intervention. This includes automating repetitive tasks, setting up triggers based on specific conditions, and creating workflows that integrate various AI capabilities.

  - o Azure Logic Apps and Power Automate can be used to build these automated workflows, allowing developers to connect AI services with other software systems. For instance, a workflow can be created to automatically generate reports by combining data analysis skills with document generation capabilities.

  - o Agentic AI capabilities are implemented at this layer, enabling the creation of autonomous systems that can adapt to new tasks, make decisions, and perform actions independently. This is especially useful for applications that need to handle complex, multi-step tasks autonomously, such as processing customer orders or conducting routine system maintenance.

- **Security, governance, and compliance layer:**

  o The top layer of the Copilot Development Stack addresses security, governance, and compliance, ensuring that AI models are deployed safely, ethically, and in accordance with regulatory standards.

  o This involves implementing strict access controls, data encryption, and audit logs to protect sensitive information and maintain data integrity. Governance frameworks also ensure that the AI's actions are traceable and that its use aligns with legal and ethical guidelines.

  o Tools like *Azure Active Directory* and *Microsoft Purview* offer integrated solutions for managing permissions, securing data, and enforcing compliance across AI deployments. This ensures that businesses can confidently use Copilot functionalities without risking data breaches or non-compliance issues.

Successful integration of generative AI models into enterprise applications often requires adopting specific architectural patterns that ensure reliability, performance, and scalability:

- **Microservices architecture**: Deploying AI models as microservices allows them to be independently managed, scaled, and updated. This approach promotes modularity, making it easier to integrate models into existing systems without major disruptions.

- **Event-driven architecture**: Generative AI models can be integrated into applications using event-driven patterns, where models respond to specific triggers or events. For instance, a chatbot might generate a response every time a user sends a query, or an AI-based content generator could create marketing copy based on a new product launch event.

- **Serverless computing**: Serverless platforms, such as *Azure Functions* or *AWS Lambda*, can host generative AI models, enabling them to run on-demand without the need to manage servers. This architecture is cost-effective for applications that need to scale dynamically and handle intermittent workloads.

Prompt manipulation techniques

Prompt manipulation techniques are essential strategies for optimizing how generative AI models interpret and respond to inputs. These techniques help refine the quality of the output, improve the relevance of responses, and enhance the efficiency of AI models, especially when dealing with complex or varied tasks. Here are some key techniques, including embedding, chunking, and grounding, along with other methods that are commonly used:

- **Embedding:**

  o **Embeddings** are numerical representations of words, phrases, or entire documents that capture the semantic meaning of the text. In prompt manipulation, embeddings are used to ensure that the AI model can understand and generate responses based on contextual similarities rather than just the literal meaning of words.

o By converting text into embeddings, models can process information in a way that recognizes relationships, nuances, and patterns, improving accuracy and relevance. Embeddings are also useful for RAG, where the model retrieves related information based on semantic similarity to refine responses.

- **Chunking:**

  o Chunking involves breaking down large pieces of text into smaller, manageable segments (or chunks) before processing. This technique is particularly useful for handling long documents, where feeding the entire content at once might exceed the model's token limit.

  o By dividing the text into coherent chunks, the model can generate responses for each segment and then combine them to produce a comprehensive output. This approach ensures that important information is not lost and allows the model to handle more extensive datasets without compromising performance.

- **Grounding:**

  o Grounding is the process of anchoring AI responses to specific, factual information. This technique is often used to ensure that the AI provides accurate and contextually relevant outputs by linking the response generation to a verified source or dataset.

  o Grounding can involve feeding the AI model-specific pieces of reference data (e.g., documents, databases, APIs) and instructing it to base its responses on this information. For example, a chatbot grounded in a company's knowledge base can provide precise answers based on internal documentation, improving reliability and reducing the risk of misinformation.

- **Contextual expansion:**

  o Contextual expansion involves providing the AI model with additional context or background information as part of the prompt. This helps the model understand the broader scenario, reducing ambiguities and ensuring that it generates responses that align with the intended use case.

  o For instance, if an AI is asked to draft an email, providing context such as the recipient's role, the relationship to the sender, and the purpose of the email can help the model craft a more suitable and tailored message.

- **Prompt chaining:**

  o Prompt chaining is a technique where multiple prompts are used sequentially to guide the AI through a complex task. The output of one prompt serves as the input for the next, allowing the model to handle tasks that require multiple steps or layers of processing.

- o This method is especially useful for tasks like *multi-turn conversations*, *data analysis*, and *complex decision-making workflows*, where a single prompt might not be sufficient to cover all aspects of the process.

- **Controlled language generation:**

  - o Controlled language generation allows developers to guide the model's output by specifying rules or constraints within the prompt. This can include setting tone, style, formality, and other parameters to ensure that the generated content matches the desired output format.

  - o For example, a prompt might instruct the AI to write a summary in a formal tone, limit the response length, or generate outputs that emphasize specific keywords or phrases. This helps in maintaining consistency across generated content, especially in applications like marketing or technical writing.

- **Temperature adjustment:**

  - o Temperature adjustment is a technique that controls the randomness of the model's outputs. Setting a higher temperature value makes the model more creative and diverse in its responses, while a lower temperature produces more deterministic and repetitive outputs.

  - o Adjusting the temperature helps fine-tune how the model responds, balancing between creativity and precision. For example, a higher temperature might be used for creative writing tasks, while a lower temperature is better for tasks requiring accurate, fact-based answers.

- **Few-shot and zero-shot learning:**

  - o Few-shot learning involves providing the model with a few examples within the prompt to help it understand the desired output format. This technique helps in guiding the model to follow a particular style or approach by showing it a couple of instances.

  - o Zero-shot learning, on the other hand, expects the model to understand and perform the task based solely on the prompt without any examples. Both methods are essential for cases where training the model on specific data might not be feasible, allowing the model to adapt quickly to new tasks based on how the prompts are designed.

- **In-context learning (ICL):**

  - o In-context learning is a method where the model is prompted to generate responses by providing it with examples of inputs and outputs during the interaction. Unlike traditional training, this technique teaches the model to perform specific tasks on-the-fly, using the context provided within the prompt.

- o This is useful when working with dynamic tasks where training might not cover all variations. For example, providing a few pairs of questions and answers within the prompt can teach the model to respond accurately to similar questions during the same interaction.

- **Repetition penalty and stop phrases:**

  - o Repetition penalty is used to discourage the model from repeating phrases or words excessively. This is important when generating longer outputs, as it ensures that the content remains engaging and coherent without unnecessary repetition.

  - o Stop phrases are predefined phrases that instruct the model where to stop generating. For example, if the desired output should end after a specific point, including a stop phrase prevents the model from continuing beyond that limit. This is particularly useful when generating content that requires a precise length, such as tweets or short answers.

- **Function calls and API integration:**

  - o Advanced prompt manipulation can involve function calls, where the AI is directed to perform specific actions based on external functions or APIs. This technique enables the AI to interact with real-world data and systems, retrieve information, and produce outputs that are up-to-date and contextually enriched.

  - o For instance, prompting the AI to check the latest weather forecast can involve an API call to retrieve current data, allowing the model to provide accurate, real-time information. Integrating function calls enhances the interactivity of AI systems, especially in complex applications like chatbots or autonomous agents.

- **Dynamic prompting with templates:**

  - o Dynamic prompting uses templates that can adjust the prompt based on specific inputs or conditions. This allows the AI model to handle a variety of scenarios without manually reconfiguring the prompts for each case.

  - o Templates might include placeholders for user inputs, which get dynamically filled during interaction. For example, `Generate a summary for [Document Title]` can be adjusted to handle multiple documents by simply replacing the placeholder, making the prompting process more efficient and scalable.

Multimodal prompt techniques

Multimodal AI involves processing and generating responses based on multiple types of data, such as text, images, audio, and video. When handling multimodal prompts, the following techniques are used to ensure the AI can effectively understand and respond:

- **Cross-modal embeddings:**

  - Cross-modal embeddings allow AI to create a unified representation of different data types. For example, combining text and image embeddings helps the model understand the relationship between a caption and an image. This technique ensures that the AI can generate relevant text descriptions based on visual inputs or interpret images based on accompanying text.

  - These embeddings help in tasks like image captioning, **visual question answering (VQA)**, and audio-visual synchronization, where understanding and correlating different modalities is essential.

- **Data fusion and alignment:**

  - Data fusion involves integrating multiple types of data into a single prompt, allowing the AI to analyze and respond using insights derived from various sources. For instance, combining textual data with audio inputs can help the model provide more accurate transcriptions or language translations.

  - Alignment techniques ensure that data from different modalities are synchronized correctly. For example, in a video, the audio and visual streams need to be aligned so the AI can understand and describe events accurately, maintaining the temporal coherence between sound and visuals.

- **Visual prompting:**

  - Visual prompting uses images or video frames as part of the prompt to guide the AI in generating responses. For example, providing an image and asking the AI to describe its content, identify objects, or explain the visual context. This is common in use cases like image recognition, object detection, and scene understanding.

  - This technique can also work in reverse, where a text prompt guides the generation of visual outputs, such as creating images based on descriptions, useful in design, content creation, and creative industries.

- **Temporal context management:**

  - When dealing with audio or video data, managing temporal context is essential. Temporal prompts help the AI understand sequences over time, such as identifying actions in a video or processing continuous speech.

  - This technique is crucial for applications like *video summarization, speech-to-text transcription,* and *behavioral analysis,* where understanding the sequence of events is necessary to generate accurate and coherent responses.

Function calling in AI

Function calling is a technique that allows AI models to interact with external systems, perform specific tasks, and retrieve real-time data. This enables more dynamic and contextually enriched outputs by making the AI capable of actions beyond just text generation. Here is how function calling is integrated into AI workflows:

- **How function calling works:**
  - Function calling involves embedding specific commands or function triggers within the prompt, instructing the AI to perform tasks that require external data or services. For example, an AI can be prompted to `fetch the current weather`, which would trigger a function that retrieves weather data from an external API.
  - This technique extends the capabilities of generative AI by enabling **real-time interactions**. It is particularly useful in scenarios where up-to-date information is essential, such as **financial reporting, weather forecasting, database queries**, and **IoT control**.

- **Use cases for function calling:**
  - **Dynamic data retrieval**: AI systems can call functions to gather data from APIs, databases, or other services, enabling it to provide updated and accurate information. For instance, an AI assistant could retrieve the latest stock prices or query a CRM system to check client details.
  - **Task automation**: Function calling allows AI to execute specific actions, such as scheduling appointments, sending emails, or updating records. This is achieved by linking the AI to backend services that handle these tasks, making the system more interactive and practical.
  - **Enhanced multi-step workflows**: By integrating function calls, AI can manage multi-step processes autonomously. For example, in a customer support scenario, the AI can identify an issue, look up solutions in a database, and execute a script to resolve the problem without human intervention.

- **Challenges and considerations:**
  - While function calling enhances the interactivity of AI systems, it requires robust security measures to prevent unauthorized access or data breaches. Ensuring that APIs and external services are securely integrated is critical.
  - Error handling is also essential, as functions might fail due to connectivity issues, service outages, or unexpected inputs. Effective function design includes contingency plans to handle such scenarios gracefully, ensuring a seamless user experience.

Agentic AI Development Stack

The Agentic AI Development Stack builds upon the foundational elements of the Copilot Development Stack but introduces additional layers and functionalities to enable autonomous, decision-making capabilities. Unlike traditional generative AI models that respond to specific prompts, agentic AI systems are designed to autonomously manage tasks, make decisions, and adapt their behavior based on context and environmental changes. Here is a detailed breakdown of the layers in the Agentic AI Stack:

- **Core intelligence layer (foundation models):**

  o Similar to the Copilot Stack, the Agentic AI Stack starts with LLMs and SLMs. These models provide the core generative capabilities, but agentic AI requires more sophisticated, context-aware models that can interpret and act on nuanced inputs.

  o The models are often fine-tuned to not only generate responses but also to understand broader contexts, scenarios, and multi-modal inputs (e.g., combining text, images, and data streams).

- **Dynamic task management layer:**

  o One of the key differentiators in agentic AI is the ability to autonomously manage and prioritize tasks. This layer enables the AI to understand and sequence tasks dynamically, adjusting priorities based on real-time inputs and contextual cues.

  o Unlike standard task orchestration, which is pre-defined, dynamic task management allows agentic AI systems to adapt workflows as situations change. For example, an autonomous customer service agent could escalate issues, redirect queries, or switch tasks based on the urgency and complexity of the interaction.

- **Decision-making and planning layer:**

  o This is a crucial addition to the Agentic AI Stack. While Copilot systems execute tasks based on user prompts, agentic AI models can make decisions and plan sequences of actions autonomously.

  o The decision-making layer integrates reinforcement learning and scenario planning techniques, enabling the AI to evaluate multiple options and select the most effective course of action. This allows the system to learn from past interactions, adapt strategies, and handle complex workflows independently.

  o Tools like *AutoGen* play a critical role here by enabling the creation of autonomous agents that can interpret high-level instructions, break them down into smaller tasks, and execute them step-by-step.

- **Multi-modal processing layer:**

  - While the Copilot Stack primarily focuses on text-based interactions, agentic AI extends this capability to multi-modal processing. This layer allows the AI to handle and integrate different types of data inputs, such as text, images, audio, and video.

  - By processing multi-modal inputs, agentic AI systems can make more informed decisions. For example, an autonomous inspection drone could analyze visual data from a camera feed, interpret signals, and decide to take action if it detects an anomaly. This capability is essential for applications in healthcare, security, and manufacturing, where diverse data types are crucial for accurate decision-making.

- **Contextual memory and adaptation layer:**

  - While Copilot systems have a memory for handling context within a session, agentic AI requires longer-term memory and the ability to adapt over extended interactions. This layer ensures that the AI retains relevant information across multiple sessions, allowing it to learn user preferences, recall previous conversations, and adapt its behavior accordingly.

  - This adaptive memory helps the AI refine its responses over time and improve its decision-making by leveraging past data. Tools like *Semantic Kernel* are critical here, as they enable the creation of memory modules that can store and retrieve information efficiently, maintaining coherence and context across different tasks and sessions.

- **Autonomous workflow and interaction layer:**

  - This layer is where agentic AI truly stands out from traditional Copilot systems. The AI is equipped to autonomously manage complex workflows that involve multiple, interdependent tasks. It can seamlessly switch between tasks, handle interruptions, and even initiate actions without explicit prompts.

  - Agentic capabilities are facilitated by platforms like *LangChain*, which allow the AI to interact with external systems, databases, and APIs autonomously. This enables agentic AI to create self-directed workflows, such as processing customer orders, generating reports, or monitoring systems for anomalies, without the need for continuous user input.

  - AutoGen further extends this by enabling the AI to set up new tasks, integrate with various services, and even create sub-agents to handle specific components of a larger operation.

- **Contextual monitoring and feedback loop layer:**

  - For agentic AI to operate effectively, it needs continuous monitoring of its actions and performance, with the ability to self-correct when necessary. This layer involves real-time feedback mechanisms that enable the AI to learn from outcomes and improve its strategies autonomously.

  - The system can assess its actions, understand where it deviated from expected results, and adjust its approach to future tasks. For instance, in a sales automation scenario, the AI could analyze its own interactions, identify where it failed to convert leads and adapt its engagement strategies for better outcomes.

- **Security, governance, and ethical decision-making layer:**

  - Security and governance are critical in both the Copilot and Agentic AI Stacks, but the Agentic AI Stack includes enhanced capabilities for ethical decision-making. This ensures that autonomous actions are performed within predefined ethical guidelines, legal frameworks, and compliance standards.

  - The AI is equipped with mechanisms to evaluate the ethical implications of its actions, making it suitable for sensitive applications like healthcare, finance, and legal services. Compliance tools, such as *Azure Security Center* and *Microsoft Purview*, provide robust frameworks for managing data privacy, user consent, and regulatory compliance, ensuring that the AI behaves responsibly and transparently.

Additional elements in the industrial AI Development Stack are listed as follows:

- **Edge computing integration:**

  - Unlike traditional AI systems that primarily operate on cloud-based infrastructure, **industrial AI** often relies heavily on **edge computing**. This allows AI models to process data directly on devices like sensors, machines, and IoT devices, rather than sending data to a central server.

  - Edge computing is crucial in scenarios where real-time processing and low-latency responses are necessary, such as predictive maintenance, quality inspection, and automated control systems. Platforms like **Azure IoT Edge** and **NVIDIA Jetson** are commonly used to deploy AI models at the edge, enabling real-time decision-making close to where the data is generated.

- **Sensor data integration and multi-modal inputs:**

  - Industrial AI systems typically need to handle and integrate data from various sensors and multi-modal inputs, such as visual, thermal, audio, and environmental data. This requires robust frameworks to process diverse data types and fuse them into coherent, actionable insights.

- o Effective **data fusion** is critical for applications like robotics, where multiple sensor types work together to help machines navigate environments or perform complex tasks autonomously. Industrial AI stacks often include specialized **sensor fusion software** that allows AI models to process and analyze these inputs in real-time.

- **Real-time monitoring and predictive maintenance:**

  - o One of the core applications of Industrial AI is **predictive maintenance**, which involves monitoring equipment health, detecting anomalies, and predicting failures before they occur. This requires continuous data collection, real-time processing, and advanced analytics.

  - o Industrial AI stacks often integrate with **Supervisory Control and Data Acquisition (SCADA)** systems to pull data from industrial machinery and sensors. AI models use this data to analyze patterns, forecast potential issues, and alert operators to take preventive actions. Tools like *Azure Machine Learning* can be combined with *Azure IoT Hub* for seamless integration between cloud and edge AI components.

- **Digital twins and simulation:**

  - o **Digital twins** are virtual replicas of physical assets, systems, or processes. They allow Industrial AI to simulate and analyze real-world scenarios, providing insights without disrupting actual operations. This is especially useful for testing AI-driven optimizations or conducting what-if analyses.

  - o Industrial AI stacks often include **simulation platforms** that can create digital twins of machinery, production lines, or even entire factories. These platforms enable companies to test AI algorithms in a virtual environment before deploying them on the physical equipment, reducing risks and enhancing the efficiency of AI integration.

- **Operational safety and compliance:**

  - o Safety is a paramount concern in industrial environments, and any AI deployment must adhere to strict **safety protocols**. Industrial AI systems need to incorporate layers that ensure safety in operations, such as automatically shutting down machines when anomalies are detected or controlling robotic systems to avoid collisions.

  - o Additionally, industrial AI must comply with **regulatory standards** specific to industries like manufacturing, energy, or transportation. Compliance frameworks ensure that AI solutions adhere to safety regulations, environmental standards, and industry-specific certifications, such as **ISO 13849** for machinery safety or **IEC 61508** for safety-critical systems.

- **Resilient and fault-tolerant systems:**

    o Industrial environments are prone to harsh conditions, equipment wear, and unexpected failures. Therefore, industrial AI systems must be designed to be **resilient and fault-tolerant**, ensuring they continue operating smoothly even under adverse conditions.

    o This involves incorporating **redundant systems** and failover mechanisms that can take over if the primary system fails. The AI stack may include features for self-healing, where systems can automatically restart or reroute processes if an issue is detected, minimizing downtime and maintaining operational continuity.

- **Scalability and distributed systems:**

    o Industrial AI often requires deployment across multiple locations, facilities, or even countries. Therefore, the AI development stack must be **scalable** and capable of supporting distributed systems. This means that the AI models need to be deployable across various devices, machines, and geographic locations while still functioning as a cohesive system.

    o **Edge-cloud hybrid architectures** are commonly used, where AI models can operate independently at the edge but also synchronize with centralized cloud systems for more extensive data processing and long-term analysis. This hybrid approach ensures scalability and flexibility, allowing companies to adjust their AI deployments based on specific operational needs.

- **Specialized AI models for industrial applications:**

    o Unlike general-purpose AI models, industrial AI requires specialized models that can handle specific tasks such as **predictive analytics**, **anomaly detection**, **image recognition** for quality inspection, and **control optimization**for robotics.

    o These models must be trained on domain-specific data, and they often use specialized architectures designed to handle time-series data, equipment logs, sensor readings, and other industrial data types. The development stack must accommodate these specialized models, providing the necessary tools and frameworks to build, train, and deploy them effectively.

- **Enhanced security and industrial IoT (IIoT) governance:**

    o Security is a significant concern for industrial AI, particularly because it involves connecting various devices and sensors to broader networks, increasing the potential for cyberattacks. **Enhanced security protocols** are essential to protect sensitive operational data and ensure the integrity of industrial processes.

- o **IIoT governance** plays a crucial role in managing these connected systems, ensuring that all devices comply with organizational security standards and industry regulations. Solutions like *Azure Sphere* provide security at the hardware, software, and network levels, ensuring that AI models deployed across IIoT networks remain secure and reliable.

- **Integration with existing industrial systems and processes:**

  - o Finally, industrial AI must seamlessly integrate with existing **industrial control systems (ICS)**, **Enterprise Resource Planning (ERP)** software, **Manufacturing Execution Systems (MES)**, and other business-critical systems.

  - o The AI stack must include robust APIs and middleware that allow AI models to interface with these legacy systems, ensuring smooth data exchange and coordination between new AI-driven insights and traditional operational processes. This integration layer ensures that industrial AI solutions can work alongside existing workflows without causing disruptions or requiring extensive overhauls.

Agentic AI development trends

Agentic AI is redefining the boundaries of automation, enabling systems to not only execute predefined tasks but also adapt dynamically, make informed decisions, and collaborate with other agents or systems. Imagine a fleet of drones coordinating in real-time to deliver packages efficiently or a virtual customer support agent resolving issues autonomously by integrating insights from diverse data streams. These systems showcase the transformative power of agentic AI, an AI paradigm where agents can perceive their environment, make decisions, and take actions autonomously while learning from their experiences.

Core components of multi-agent system development

Building agentic AI requires orchestrating several foundational components to create systems that are both intelligent and reliable.

The following elements are essential building blocks for designing robust agentic AI architectures:

- **Agent perception and context awareness**: Agents must continuously gather and interpret data from their environment. This involves integrating sensors, APIs, or real-time data feeds to maintain situational awareness. For instance, a warehouse robot might use computer vision models powered by frameworks like *YOLO* or *OpenCV* to detect obstacles, while simultaneously querying inventory databases for task prioritization. Context awareness can also involve **knowledge graphs** that help agents understand relationships between entities, ensuring decisions align with broader system goals.

- **Decision-making frameworks**: Decision-making in agentic AI systems typically employs techniques like rule-based reasoning, **reinforcement learning (RL)**, or Bayesian networks, depending on the complexity of the environment. For example, RL enables agents to learn optimal actions through trial and error in dynamic environments, as seen in tools like *OpenAI Gym* or *RLlib*. However, in critical domains such as healthcare or finance, hybrid approaches combining rule-based logic with machine learning are preferred to ensure transparency and compliance.

- **Action and execution layer**: Agents translate decisions into actions using a modular action-execution framework. This layer interacts with external systems or physical components, often via API calls, actuator interfaces, or low-latency message buses. For instance, a logistics agent optimizing delivery routes might leverage Google Maps APIs for routing and trigger notifications through Twilio.

- **Communication and collaboration**: Multi-agent systems thrive on collaboration, which necessitates robust communication protocols. Technologies like **message brokers** (e.g., RabbitMQ or Kafka) and **agent communication languages** (e.g., KQML or FIPA-ACL) facilitate information sharing. A swarm of drones might exchange positional data via **peer-to-peer protocols** to avoid collisions and optimize coverage dynamically.

- **Monitoring and governance**: Ensuring reliability and accountability in agentic AI systems requires real-time monitoring and governance mechanisms. Platforms like *Azure Monitor* or *Prometheus* enable tracking of performance metrics, while governance frameworks enforce fail-safe mechanisms such as rolling back decisions if anomalies are detected. This is especially critical in high-stakes domains where incorrect decisions can have significant consequences.

Key design patterns for agent decision-making

Agentic AI systems often rely on well-defined patterns to manage conversations and decision-making effectively:

- **Goal-oriented dialogue**: In this pattern, agents focus on achieving specific goals during interactions. For example, a customer support chatbot may navigate a conversation to resolve an issue, transitioning between intent identification, solution proposal, and user confirmation. Underlying this process are **state machines** that guide agents through conversation flows and **natural language understanding (NLU)** models that interpret user input.

- **Consensus-based decision-making**: When multiple agents need to agree on a course of action, consensus algorithms like **leader election**, **voting-based systems**, or **blockchain-inspired protocols** ensure consistency. For instance, a fleet of autonomous vehicles might use consensus to decide which vehicle will take on a high-priority delivery, balancing factors like proximity, load, and energy levels.

- **Blackboard architecture**: This collaborative pattern involves a shared blackboard where agents contribute partial solutions or knowledge. Common in problem-solving scenarios, the blackboard acts as a shared memory, facilitating coordination among agents. An example is a disaster response system where agents representing resources (e.g., ambulances, fire trucks) post their status and receive assignments dynamically.

- **Bidding and auction mechanisms**: Inspired by economic models, this pattern enables agents to compete or cooperate based on resource availability. A cloud computing system, for instance, might use a **contract-net protocol** to allocate tasks dynamically across available nodes, ensuring optimal utilization.

- **Hierarchical control**: In systems with varying levels of autonomy, a hierarchical design ensures that lower-level agents handle routine tasks while higher-level agents oversee strategy. For example, in a factory automation setup, local agents might control individual machines while a supervisory agent optimizes overall production flow.

Ensuring scalability and robustness

Agentic AI systems operate in dynamic, often unpredictable environments, making scalability and robustness critical. Techniques like **containerization** (using Docker or Kubernetes) enable horizontal scaling of agent instances, while **distributed computing frameworks** like *Ray* or *Apache Flink* handle data-intensive tasks. Fail-safe designs include fallback mechanisms where agents revert to predefined safe states in case of errors or network failures.

Additionally, incorporating **simulation environments** during development ensures agents are tested extensively under diverse conditions. Platforms like *Unity ML-Agents* or *MATLAB Simulink* allow developers to simulate real-world scenarios, refining decision-making algorithms before deployment.

Reinforcement learning and reward functions

Reinforcement learning (RL) is at the heart of enabling intelligent agents to make decisions and learn autonomously through trial and error. Unlike supervised learning, which relies on labeled data, RL focuses on learning optimal actions in dynamic environments by interacting with them and receiving feedback in the form of rewards or penalties. For agentic AI development, RL offers a powerful framework to design agents capable of adapting to complex, unpredictable scenarios.

The core aspects of RL in agent AI are as follows:

- **Agent-environment interaction**: At its core, RL involves continuous interaction between an agent and its environment, which is modeled as a **Markov decision process** (**MDP**). The MDP is defined by states, actions, rewards, and transitions:

    o **State (S)**: Represents the current context or environment perceived by the agent.

    o **Action (A)**: The possible decisions the agent can take in the given state.

    o **Reward (R)**: Feedback the agent receives after taking an action.

    o **Transition (T)**: Probability of moving from one state to another after an action.

    For example, in a warehouse management system, the agent (a robotic picker) perceives its state (current location and inventory map), takes an action (moving to a shelf), and receives a reward (efficiently picking the correct item).

- **Policy learning**: The agent learns a **policy** (π), which maps states to actions. The goal is to find an optimal policy that maximizes the cumulative reward over time. Policies can be deterministic (specific action for a state) or stochastic (probability distribution over actions).

- **Value functions**: RL often involves learning value functions, which estimate the expected cumulative reward:

    o **State value function (V)**: The value of being in a state and following the policy thereafter.

    o **Action value function (Q)**: The value of taking a specific action in a state and following the policy thereafter. Algorithms like **Q-learning** focus on learning these values iteratively.

- **Exploration vs. exploitation**: Agents face the dilemma of exploring new actions to discover potentially higher rewards (exploration) versus exploiting known actions to maximize immediate rewards. Strategies like *epsilon-greedy* balance this trade-off.

- **Deep reinforcement learning**: When the state or action space is large, traditional RL struggles. **Deep RL** integrates neural networks to approximate policies and value functions. For example, **Deep Q-Networks** (**DQN**) uses convolutional layers to process visual inputs in tasks like autonomous driving.

Designing effective reward functions

The reward function is the most critical component in RL, as it directly drives the agent's learning behavior and decision-making process. Designing an effective reward function requires careful consideration to ensure the agent achieves the desired outcomes without unintended behaviors.

The following principles are essential for designing effective reward functions that align agent behavior with intended objectives and outcomes:

- **Alignment with objectives**: Rewards should align with the overarching goals of the system. For instance, in a customer service chatbot, the reward could be tied to metrics like user satisfaction, query resolution time, and accuracy of responses.

- **Immediate vs. delayed rewards**: RL requires balancing immediate rewards (e.g., picking the closest item) with long-term rewards (e.g., completing all orders efficiently). Temporal discounting factors (γ) are used to prioritize immediate vs. future rewards:

  - A high γ (close to 1) values future rewards more heavily.

  - A low γ emphasizes immediate rewards.

- **Shaping rewards**: Reward shaping involves providing intermediate rewards to guide the agent toward the goal. For example, in a maze-solving agent, partial rewards for moving closer to the exit help accelerate learning.

- **Avoiding perverse incentives**: Poorly designed rewards can lead to unintended behaviors. For example, a delivery robot incentivized solely to minimize travel time might ignore traffic laws. Penalizing undesirable actions (e.g., traffic violations) alongside rewarding desirable ones ensures ethical and practical behavior.

- **Sparse vs. dense rewards**:

  - **Sparse rewards**: Provide feedback only when specific goals are achieved. These can be challenging for agents to learn but encourage strategic behavior.

  - **Dense rewards**: Offer frequent feedback for incremental progress. While easier for agents to learn, they risk overfitting to suboptimal behaviors.

- **Multi-objective reward functions**: In complex systems, agents often need to optimize multiple objectives. For instance, in energy grid management, rewards might balance cost reduction, energy efficiency, and grid stability. Techniques like Pareto optimization or weighted reward functions help agents manage trade-offs.

The key challenges and solutions in RL for agent AI are as follows:

- **Sample efficiency**: RL often requires a large number of interactions to learn effectively. Techniques like experience replay (storing and reusing past experiences) and off-policy algorithms (learning from actions not taken by the current policy) improve sample efficiency.

- **Stochastic environments**: In real-world environments with uncertainties, agents must handle stochasticity. Probabilistic models or Bayesian RL help agents make robust decisions under uncertainty.

- **Scalability**: Multi-agent systems where multiple RL agents interact require additional mechanisms like cooperative learning or competitive learning, depending on the desired behavior. For example, multi-agent **Deep Deterministic Policy Gradient** (DDPG) trains agents in cooperative environments like team-based robotics.

Practical applications and architectures

Reinforcement learning is being deployed in various domains with agentic AI:

- **Autonomous vehicles**: RL enables dynamic decision-making for navigation, obstacle avoidance, and traffic compliance.

- **Energy optimization**: Smart grid systems use RL to optimize energy distribution and consumption based on real-time demands.

- **Healthcare**: AI agents learn treatment policies personalized to patient data, optimizing outcomes in dynamic clinical environments.

From a development perspective, frameworks like *Ray RLlib, TensorFlow Agents,* and *Stable Baselines* offer modular architectures for scaling RL algorithms. Training environments like *OpenAI Gym* or custom simulators ensure agents are tested rigorously before real-world deployment.

Emerging developments in agentic AI

As agentic systems mature, two architectural innovations, the **Model Context Protocol (MCP)** and **Agent Development Kits (ADKs),** are rapidly shaping how developers build, orchestrate, and scale intelligent agents. These developments offer foundational abstractions and tooling that reduce complexity, increase interoperability, and accelerate adoption across domains such as enterprise systems, cloud optimization, and architecture.

Model Context Protocol

The **Model Context Protocol (MCP)** is a groundbreaking framework designed to standardize communication between AI agents, models, external tools, and data sources. Much like HTTP enabled the interoperability of the web, MCP offers a structured protocol to integrate intelligent agents into diverse environments without requiring custom bridges for every system.

The following are the key capabilities of MCP include:

- **Standardized communication layer**: MCP allows agents to interface with APIs, tools, and other models using a consistent protocol, reducing coupling and increasing reusability.

- **Dynamic context awareness**: Agents receive live updates from external environments, allowing them to adjust plans and priorities based on real-time metrics or situational data. For example, a construction site monitoring agent might adapt its actions based on sensor readings or project timeline changes.

- **Scalable and secure orchestration**: By acting as a centralized hub, MCP servers support distributed multi-agent systems while maintaining secure, auditable channels for agent interactions.

- **Cross-agent collaboration**: MCP enables agents to coordinate and share context, making it ideal for applications involving swarms or inter-agent workflows.

Recent open-source specifications and SDKs for MCP are expanding its adoption, offering out-of-the-box support for integration with document management systems, simulation engines, and version control tools.

Agent Development Kits

The **Agent Development Kit (ADK)** is a modular development environment purpose-built for creating, deploying, and scaling intelligent agents. Similar to SDKs in traditional software development, ADKs package critical agent infrastructure, such as memory models, decision engines, tool interfaces, and lifecycle management, into reusable components.

The following are the key features commonly offered by ADKs:

- **Pre-built agent templates**: ADKs provide modular blueprints for perception, planning, reasoning, and action execution.

- **Tool and API integration frameworks**: Seamlessly plug agents into databases, APIs, simulation environments, or third-party software (e.g., CAD tools or energy models).

- **Multi-agent orchestration**: Define workflows between agents with support for asynchronous communication, parallel execution, and conditional task routing.

- **Memory and state management**: Support for both short-term and long-term memory enables context-aware and stateful agents.

- **Simulation and evaluation environments**: Test agents under controlled scenarios to evaluate reliability, scalability, and adaptability before production deployment.

Notable ADKs include:

- **AutoGen (Microsoft)**: A Python-based framework for orchestrating collaborative multi-agent conversations and toolchains.

- **LangChain Agents** and **CrewAI**: Open-source ADKs supporting dynamic tool calling, task planning, and memory chaining.

- **Semantic Kernel**: Microsoft's SDK to build AI copilots with reusable functions, vector memory, and planner-executor loops.

- **Google ADK:** A modular framework integrated with Gemini and Vertex AI, enabling multi-agent workflows, tool integration, and responsible AI development at scale.

These ADKs reduce development friction and enable rapid experimentation, making agent development accessible to teams across industries.

Responsible AI

As AI technologies continue to advance and integrate into various aspects of business and society, the importance of **responsible AI** has become more critical than ever. Responsible AI refers to the development and deployment of AI systems in a way that ensures fairness, transparency, accountability, and ethical alignment. It involves not only adhering to regulatory standards but also implementing best practices that ensure AI systems operate safely, securely, and without unintended biases.

Companies need to be mindful of the ethical implications of their AI solutions, ensuring that they do not reinforce harmful stereotypes, infringe on privacy, or lead to unfair treatment. This requires a holistic approach that spans from the design and development of AI models to their deployment and ongoing monitoring.

The key principles of responsible AI are as follows:

- **Fairness and bias mitigation:**
  - One of the most significant challenges in AI is ensuring **fairness**. AI models, trained on large datasets, can inadvertently learn and perpetuate biases present in the data. These biases may lead to unfair or discriminatory outcomes, especially in sensitive applications like hiring, lending, or law enforcement.
  - Responsible AI practices include **bias detection** and **mitigation techniques**, such as ensuring diverse and representative training datasets, applying bias correction algorithms, and regularly auditing models to identify and address potential biases. Organizations should conduct **impact assessments** to understand how their AI systems affect different user groups, ensuring equitable treatment across demographics.

- **Transparency and explainability:**
  - Transparency involves making the workings of AI systems understandable to users, stakeholders, and regulators. **Explainability** is the ability of an AI system to provide clear, understandable insights into how decisions are made, especially in complex models like neural networks.
  - **Explainable AI (XAI)** techniques, such as **SHapley Additive exPlanations (SHAP)** and **Local Interpretable Model-Agnostic Explanations (LIME)**, help users understand the reasoning behind the AI's outputs. This

transparency is crucial in building trust, as it allows stakeholders to see how and why decisions are made, making the AI system more accountable.

- **Accountability and governance:**

  o AI systems should have mechanisms to ensure accountability, meaning that there is a clear framework for assigning responsibility if something goes wrong. Organizations need to establish governance structures that define roles and responsibilities, outlining who is accountable for different aspects of AI development and deployment.

  o Governance frameworks include guidelines for model auditing, performance monitoring, and regular reviews to ensure compliance with ethical standards and legal requirements. This structured approach ensures that AI systems are used responsibly and that any issues can be traced and addressed promptly.

- **Privacy and data security:**

  o AI systems often require access to vast amounts of data, which raises concerns about privacy and data security. Responsible AI involves implementing practices that protect user data, ensuring it is collected, processed, and stored securely, with consent from the individuals involved.

  o Data anonymization, encryption, and access controls are essential techniques for safeguarding privacy. Additionally, organizations should follow data minimization principles, collecting only the data necessary for the AI to function effectively and ensuring compliance with regulations such as *GDPR* and *CCPA*.

- **Ethical use and social impact:**

  o The ethical use of AI goes beyond technical considerations, involving questions about how AI impacts society. Organizations must evaluate the social implications of their AI systems, ensuring that they do not cause harm, perpetuate inequality, or erode trust.

  o Ethical AI frameworks encourage developers to consider the long-term consequences of AI deployments. This involves stakeholder engagement, where developers, policymakers, and end-users collaborate to set guidelines that reflect societal values and ethical norms. Companies like *Microsoft* and *Google* have developed ethical AI guidelines to help steer their AI projects in a direction that aligns with their corporate values and broader societal goals.

The best practices for implementing responsible AI are as follows:

- **Inclusive development teams:**

  o Diverse teams lead to more inclusive AI systems. By involving people from various backgrounds, disciplines, and perspectives, organizations can better identify and address biases and other issues that might not be apparent to a homogenous team.

- o Companies should foster cross-functional collaboration among data scientists, ethicists, legal experts, and domain specialists to build AI systems that reflect a wide range of viewpoints and expertise.

- **Regular audits and monitoring:**
  - o AI systems should undergo regular audits to ensure they are functioning as intended and to identify any unintended consequences. Monitoring should cover model performance, data integrity, and compliance with ethical guidelines.
  - o Third-party audits can provide an unbiased assessment, helping organizations identify and address issues that internal teams might overlook. Continuous monitoring also ensures that any shifts in data patterns or model performance are detected early, enabling prompt action.

- **Clear documentation and communication:**
  - o Responsible AI development includes maintaining clear and comprehensive documentation throughout the AI lifecycle. This documentation should cover how the model was developed, what data was used, and how decisions are made, ensuring that there is a record for accountability and future reference.
  - o Organizations should communicate transparently with users about how AI systems function, what data is being used, and the limitations of AI. This transparency helps manage expectations, and fosters trust.

- **Frameworks and standards for ethical AI:**
  - o Several frameworks and standards guide the implementation of responsible AI. For example, the AI ethics guidelines from the European Commission, ISO standards for AI, and NIST's AI Risk Management Framework provide comprehensive guidelines for ethical AI development.
  - o These frameworks help organizations create consistent, reliable, and ethical AI solutions by providing structured guidelines on data governance, transparency, and accountability. Adopting these standards ensures that AI systems are built on a solid ethical foundation.

Tools and technologies supporting responsible AI

Several tools and platforms support the implementation of responsible AI by providing built-in features for bias detection, transparency, and data security, as follows:

- **Azure responsible AI dashboard**: An integrated tool that helps developers identify and mitigate bias, improve explainability, and monitor AI models in real-time.

- **IBM Watson OpenScale**: A platform that tracks and measures AI outcomes to ensure transparency and fairness, offering bias detection, explainability, and governance features.

- **Fairlearn**: An open-source Python toolkit that helps developers assess and mitigate fairness issues in AI models, providing visualizations and metrics to evaluate model fairness.

Monitoring, security, and governance

Beyond technical deployment, ensuring continuous monitoring, strong security, and governance is critical. AI models must be monitored for performance issues such as drift, latency, or unexpected behavior. Additionally, robust security practices must be in place to prevent unauthorized access and data breaches. Governance is essential for maintaining the integrity and ethical use of AI systems. It involves setting up policies and frameworks that define how AI models are developed, deployed, and managed, ensuring compliance with industry standards and regulations. Effective governance also includes monitoring for biases, ensuring transparency, and maintaining accountability throughout the AI lifecycle.

The best practices for effective monitoring, security, and governance are as follows:

- **Implement continuous monitoring and alerts**: Set up real-time monitoring systems that can detect anomalies, latency issues, and performance degradation. Automated alerts ensure that issues are addressed quickly, minimizing the impact on business operations.

- **Adopt a multi-layered security approach**: Combine encryption, access controls, and regular security audits to protect data at all stages. Ensure that AI systems are compliant with data privacy regulations like *GDPR* and *CCPA*, and adopt Zero Trust security models where possible.

- **Establish clear governance policies**: Develop a framework that outlines the ethical use of AI, compliance requirements, and accountability structures. Regularly audit AI models to ensure they are free from biases and that their decisions are transparent and explainable.

- **Maintain comprehensive documentation**: Proper documentation is vital for governance. Maintain records of how models were developed, the data they were trained on, and their decision-making processes. This documentation helps in auditing, troubleshooting, and ensuring transparency in AI operations.

- **Ensure explainability and accountability**: Incorporate explainability tools that allow stakeholders to understand how AI models make decisions. This not only builds trust but also ensures that models can be held accountable, especially in scenarios where automated decisions impact users directly.

Conclusion

In this chapter, we covered the critical architecture and operational practices that drive advancements in AI. We began by exploring generative AI architectures, discussing foundational concepts like LLMs, SLMs, and frameworks such as LangChain and Semantic Kernel. We also examined emerging trends including agentic AI and AutoGen, highlighting how these innovations enable more autonomous, interactive, and scalable AI systems.

The chapter provided a practical guide to AI model operationalization, focusing on strategies for seamless deployment, scalability, and integration. We discussed the importance of leveraging SDKs, implementing MLOps best practices, and using tools like Azure ML Studio and Kubernetes to ensure efficient and robust AI deployment. Additionally, we explored advanced prompt manipulation techniques, including embedding, grounding, and function calls, which enhance the interactivity and efficiency of AI models.

We also emphasized the principles of responsible AI, covering essential aspects such as fairness, transparency, security, and ethical governance. Practical insights and tools were shared to ensure compliance and ethical use of AI systems, along with robust practices for monitoring, security, and governance to maintain performance, integrity, and trust in AI deployments.

In the next chapter, we will shift focus to strategies and tools for automating infrastructure management, exploring how automation enhances system reliability and operational efficiency. We will begin with a deep dive into IaC, explaining how to manage and provision infrastructure through code to increase deployment speed and reduce human error. The chapter will also cover tools like Helm and Crossplane for defining and developing applications within Kubernetes environments, along with practices in observability and monitoring to maintain system health. Finally, we will introduce **site reliability engineering** (**SRE**), outlining methods to improve system reliability through automated operations and consistent service delivery.

Key terms

- **LLM**: AI models that are trained on vast datasets of text to understand and generate human-like language. They can be used for tasks such as translation, summarization, and conversation.

- **SLM**: More compact versions of language models that are optimized for specific tasks or environments, often used where computational resources are limited, such as edge devices.

- **RAG**: A technique that combines traditional language models with retrieval systems to fetch relevant data, ensuring more accurate and contextually relevant outputs.

- **Semantic Kernel**: A lightweight SDK that allows developers to build workflows with generative AI, enabling seamless integration of language models into applications.

- **LangChain**: A framework that helps AI models interact with external data sources and APIs, creating workflows that enrich responses with real-world data.

- **Agentic AI**: AI systems that can autonomously manage tasks, make decisions, and interact without continuous human intervention, capable of adapting to new scenarios dynamically.

- **AutoGen**: A tool that facilitates the creation of autonomous AI agents that can carry out multi-step operations independently, enhancing automation capabilities.

- **MLOps**: Practices that combine machine learning with DevOps principles, ensuring efficient development, deployment, monitoring, and maintenance of AI models.

- **Prompt engineering**: The process of designing inputs (prompts) to guide AI models in generating accurate and relevant outputs. Techniques include contextual expansion, embedding, and chunking.

- **Function calling**: A method that allows AI models to trigger specific actions or retrieve data from external systems through API calls, enabling real-time interactions and automation.

- **Responsible AI**: The development and deployment of AI systems that are ethical, transparent, fair, and accountable, ensuring compliance with legal and social standards.

- **Bias mitigation**: Techniques and processes aimed at identifying and reducing biases in AI models to ensure fair and equitable outcomes across diverse user groups.

- **Explainable AI (XAI)**: Tools and techniques that make AI models' decision-making processes transparent and understandable, fostering trust and accountability.

- **Data drift**: Changes in the underlying data distribution can lead to a decline in model performance over time, making continuous monitoring essential.

Join our book's Discord space

Join the book's Discord Workspace for Latest updates, Offers, Tech happenings around the world, New Release and Sessions with the Authors:

https://discord.bpbonline.com

CHAPTER 10

Automation and Infra Management

Introduction

This chapter will cover the strategies, principles, and tools necessary to achieve efficient automation and effective infrastructure management in modern IT environments. Automation is the cornerstone of scalable, reliable, and high-performing systems, reducing human error and accelerating deployment cycles. By adopting IaC, leveraging advanced application definition tools, and implementing robust observability and monitoring practices, organizations can ensure their systems remain resilient and adaptable to ever-evolving demands. Additionally, the chapter introduces key **site reliability engineering (SRE)** principles that integrate automation into operations to maintain and improve infrastructure reliability.

Structure

This chapter covers the following topics:

- Evolution of infrastructure automation
- Infrastructure as code key practices
- Application definition and development tools
- Techniques for enhancing observability and monitoring
- Site reliability engineering

Objectives

By the end of this chapter, you will have a comprehensive understanding of IaC principles and tools, such as **Azure Resource Manager** (ARM) templates, Bicep, and Terraform, enabling you to effectively automate infrastructure provisioning and management. You will gain knowledge of application definition and development tools like Helm, Crossplane, and **Azure Kubernetes Service** (AKS) application configurations, empowering you to streamline the management of applications and their resources within Kubernetes environments. Additionally, you will acquire practical techniques to enhance observability and monitoring using tools like Azure Monitor, Log Analytics, and Application Insights, ensuring visibility into system performance and health. Finally, you will develop a solid grasp of SRE practices, with a focus on Azure-native capabilities such as Azure Automation and Azure Policy, equipping you with actionable strategies to improve infrastructure reliability and achieve operational excellence.

Evolution of infrastructure automation

The story of infrastructure automation spans decades of innovation, with each era marked by technological breakthroughs and paradigm shifts that transformed how IT systems are managed. From manual processes to intelligent orchestration, the journey reflects a relentless pursuit of scalability, reliability, and efficiency. The next section will highlight the evolution, era by era.

Era of shell scripts (1980s–1990s)

In the early days of IT, infrastructure management relied heavily on manual processes. System administrators configured hardware, networks, and software by physically interacting with servers. Automation was rudimentary at best, relying on **shell scripts** written in **Bash**, **Perl**, or **Batch** to streamline repetitive tasks like backups, user account creation, and log rotation. These scripts, while helpful, were fragile and lacked standardization. Without version control systems or centralized management, they often became *snowflake configurations*, unique and prone to failure during updates or system changes.

This era revealed the inefficiencies and risks associated with manual management, sparking interest in creating more scalable and structured approaches. While the tools were limited, the foundational idea of automation began to take root, setting the stage for future advancements.

Rise of configuration management (1990s–2000s)

As enterprise IT systems grew in complexity, manual methods could no longer keep up with the demands of scalability and consistency. This led to the emergence of **configuration management tools** like *Puppet, Chef,* and *CFEngine,* which revolutionized infrastructure management by introducing **declarative configurations**. Instead of manually scripting actions, administrators defined the desired state of their systems, and these tools enforced compliance automatically.

This era marked the beginning of IaC, where infrastructure configurations were treated as software code. By storing these configurations in version-controlled repositories like *Git*, teams could collaborate more effectively and track changes with precision. Concepts like **idempotency**, ensuring repeated application of configurations yielded the same results, brought reliability and predictability to deployments. This shift allowed IT teams to manage hundreds or even thousands of servers with unprecedented uniformity and efficiency.

Virtualization and the cloud revolution (2000s–2010s)

The advent of **virtualization** and **cloud computing** brought about one of the most transformative eras in IT. Virtualization technologies like *VMware, Xen,* and *Hyper-V* enabled organizations to run multiple **virtual machines** (**VMs**) on a single physical server, vastly improving resource utilization. At the same time, cloud providers like *AWS, Azure,* and *Google Cloud* introduced on-demand infrastructure, making it possible to provision and scale resources programmatically.

Tools like *AWS CloudFormation* and *Azure Resource Manager (ARM)* extended the principles of IaC to the cloud, allowing developers to define infrastructure in code and deploy it across data centers worldwide. This era popularized the concept of treating infrastructure as *cattle* instead of *pets*, emphasizing standardization and disposability. If a VM failed, it could simply be replaced by redeploying its template. The rise of **DevOps** practices during this time further strengthened automation by fostering collaboration between development and operations teams, integrating infrastructure changes directly into application delivery pipelines.

Era of containers and microservices (2010s–2020s)

The rise of **containers**, led by **Docker**, marked a major leap forward in infrastructure automation. Containers provided lightweight, portable environments for running applications, solving the *works on my machine* problem by ensuring consistency across development, testing, and production. However, managing large-scale containerized applications required orchestration platforms like *Kubernetes*, which became the de facto standard for deploying, scaling, and maintaining container workloads.

Tools like *Helm* simplified Kubernetes deployments by packaging configurations into reusable charts, while **Terraform** enabled multi-cloud IaC, allowing organizations to manage hybrid environments with a unified approach. Automation extended beyond infrastructure to application lifecycle management, with practices like *GitOps* advocating for version-controlled repositories as the single source of truth for both infrastructure and application definitions. This era underscored the importance of convergence, where infrastructure and application automation merged into cohesive workflows.

Age of serverless and declaratives (2020s–present)

In the modern era, **serverless computing** and *declarative infrastructure management* have pushed automation to new heights. Platforms like **AWS Lambda**, **Azure Functions**, and **Google Cloud Run** abstract away the underlying infrastructure, allowing developers to focus entirely on business logic and code. IaC has evolved with tools like *Pulumi*, which uses general-purpose programming languages, and Crossplane, which extends Kubernetes to manage cloud resources alongside containers.

AI-driven automation has begun to play a significant role, with systems leveraging machine learning to optimize provisioning, scaling, and performance in real-time. Observability has become a critical component of modern automation, with tools like *OpenTelemetry* ensuring visibility into metrics, logs, and traces across highly automated workflows. This era reflects a shift toward complete abstraction and self-management, where infrastructure adapts autonomously to workload demands while maintaining transparency and control.

The following framework illustrates the foundational principles, core practices, and resulting benefits that form the backbone of modern infrastructure automation:

Automation Principles	Core Practices	Outcomes & Benefits
Infrastructure as Code (IaC)	Provisioning and Scaling	Scalability and Elasticity
Declarative Configurations	Configuration Management	Consistency and Repeatability
Idempotency	Monitoring and Observability	Reduced Downtime
Version Control	CI/CD	Turn Around Time / Resiliency

Figure 10.1: Key building blocks of infrastructure automation

Infrastructure as code key practices

IaC has revolutionized how modern IT infrastructures are provisioned and managed. By defining infrastructure through code, organizations achieve unprecedented levels of consistency, scalability, and efficiency. IaC replaces manual configurations with automated, repeatable processes, reducing human error and accelerating deployment cycles. For architects and chief technology officers, adopting IaC is not just a technical shift but a strategic enabler for digital transformation, DevOps, and multi-cloud strategies.

Principles of IaC

At its core, IaC operates on a few fundamental principles that guide its implementation and ensure its effectiveness:

- **Declarative vs. imperative models**: Declarative IaC focuses on defining the desired state of infrastructure, leaving the implementation details to the tool being used. For instance, ARM templates and Terraform allow users to specify infrastructure configurations such as virtual networks, databases, or Kubernetes clusters. In contrast, the imperative approach involves step-by-step instructions to achieve a particular configuration. While declarative methods are more common in IaC, understanding both models helps architects choose the right approach based on project requirements.

- **Idempotency**: A critical aspect of IaC is ensuring that running a script multiple times yields the same result. Idempotency eliminates risks of unintended changes during redeployments, fostering reliability and predictability.

- **Version control and collaboration**: IaC scripts are treated as source code and should be maintained in repositories like *GitHub* or *Azure DevOps*. This not only allows for collaboration and peer reviews but also introduces versioning, enabling rollbacks to previous configurations when necessary.

- **Policy enforcement**: For enterprise-grade architectures, governance is essential. Tools like Azure Policy ensure that IaC adheres to organizational standards, preventing the deployment of non-compliant resources.

Best practices for IaC implementation

Architects and CTOs must align their IaC strategies with industry best practices to ensure successful implementation:

- **Modular code design**: Break down complex IaC scripts into smaller, reusable modules. For instance, separate modules can define network configurations, compute resources, and storage setups. This modularity simplifies updates and promotes reusability across projects.

- **Parameterization for flexibility**: Introduce parameters to adapt IaC scripts for different environments, such as development, testing, and production. Azure Bicep, for example, supports parameter files that allow configurations to be customized without modifying the core script.

- **Automated testing and validation**: Implementing unit tests for IaC is as vital as it is for application code. Tools like *Azure DevTest Labs* or *Terratest* can validate configurations, ensuring that changes do not break existing setups.

- **Continuous integration and delivery**: Integrate IaC into CI/CD pipelines to automate testing and deployment. For example, using Azure Pipelines, you can automate the deployment of IaC scripts across environments, enabling rapid and reliable infrastructure changes.

IaC tools are central to its adoption, and selecting the right tool depends on an organization's architecture, cloud strategy, and operational needs.

The following are some of the most prominent IaC tools:

- **Azure resource manager templates**: ARM templates are a declarative framework for provisioning Azure resources. They integrate natively with the Azure ecosystem, enabling seamless deployments directly from the Azure portal or CI/CD pipelines.

- **Bicep**: A more human-readable evolution of ARM templates, Bicep simplifies complex configurations while maintaining Azure-native functionality. For architects, Bicep reduces the learning curve and accelerates deployments without sacrificing control.

- **Terraform**: As a multi-cloud tool, Terraform is indispensable for organizations operating across Azure, AWS, or GCP. Its provider ecosystem allows for managing not just infrastructure but also services like *DNS*, monitoring, and Kubernetes clusters.

- **Pulumi**: Pulumi enables IaC using familiar programming languages like *Python*, *TypeScript*, and *Go*. This bridges the gap between developers and operations teams, fostering collaboration while providing powerful scripting capabilities.

Real-world applications of IaC

The impact of IaC is best understood through its applications in real-world scenarios:

- **Multi-region deployments**: Large enterprises often require resilient, globally distributed systems. Using Terraform, for instance, architects can define multi-region setups, ensuring failover and high availability.

- **Disaster recovery**: IaC scripts can codify disaster recovery strategies, automating the provisioning of backup environments in alternate regions. Azure's geo-redundant storage and paired regions make this particularly seamless.

- **DevTest environments**: For organizations with extensive development pipelines, IaC automates the provisioning and teardown of DevTest environments, optimizing resource utilization and reducing costs.

Application definition and development tools

Applications today are no longer monolithic; they are composed of microservices running across distributed systems. Each microservice often has its own dependencies, networking requirements, and scaling rules. Manually managing these configurations is error-prone and infeasible at scale.

Application definition tools provide a declarative approach to specify as follows:

- The application's configuration, including services, volumes, and ingress rules.

- Resource dependencies, such as databases, caches, and storage.
- Scaling and fault-tolerance policies for high availability.

These tools are indispensable for technical leaders in bridging the gap between development and operations, ensuring consistency across environments. Defining and managing applications, along with their associated resources, is a foundational aspect of modern infrastructure management. With the rise of container orchestration platforms like Kubernetes, the process of application definition has evolved to handle complex, distributed systems at scale. This subsection explores the tools and practices that simplify application definition and management, focusing on technologies like *Helm, Crossplane,* and Azure-native solutions such as *AKS*. These tools enable seamless integration between application logic and infrastructure resources, offering architects and CTOs robust mechanisms to automate deployments, enforce governance, and optimize operations.

Tools for application definition and development

- **Helm (The Kubernetes package manager)**: Helm is a powerful tool for defining, installing, and managing Kubernetes applications. It uses *charts*, which are pre-configured application templates, to simplify deployment. For architects managing large-scale Kubernetes environments, Helm provides:

  o **Parameterized deployments**: Use values files to customize deployments for different environments (e.g., dev, test, production).

  o **Versioning and rollbacks**: Helm tracks deployment histories, allowing seamless rollbacks in case of failures.

  o **Extensibility**: Helm charts can be tailored to include dependencies, enabling applications to bundle their required infrastructure.

  For example, deploying a web application with an associated Redis cache becomes as simple as executing a single Helm command, drastically reducing deployment complexity.

- **Crossplane (IaC for Kubernetes)**: Crossplane elevates Kubernetes to a universal control plane by extending its API to manage not just containerized workloads but also external infrastructure resources. This allows architects to define both applications and their dependencies in a unified manner. Key features include:

  o **Declarative resource management**: Define infrastructure components such as databases, storage, and DNS alongside application manifests.

  o **Multi-cloud support**: Crossplane abstracts cloud provider APIs, enabling consistent application definitions across Azure, AWS, and GCP.

  o **Composability:** Using **custom resource definitions (CRDs)**, architects can create reusable infrastructure templates tailored to organizational needs.

For example, Crossplane can define an AKS cluster, a managed PostgreSQL instance, and a Redis cache as part of the same application manifest, ensuring end-to-end consistency.

- **Azure Kubernetes Service and native tooling**: AKS integrates deeply with Azure's ecosystem, offering a managed Kubernetes environment with built-in support for application definition tools. AKS benefits architects by:

  o **Seamless integration with Azure services**: Use Azure Service Operator to provision Azure resources like SQL databases or Cosmos DB alongside Kubernetes workloads.

  o **Built-in CI/CD support**: Integrate AKS with Azure DevOps or GitHub Actions to automate application deployments.

  o **Scaling and governance**: Leverage Azure-native tools like *Azure Policy* and *Azure Monitor* to enforce governance and track the health of applications.

By combining AKS with Helm or Crossplane, architects can build a unified, scalable framework for managing applications and their resources.

The following are some of the best practices for application definition:

- **Adopt a declarative approach**: Define both application and infrastructure as code to ensure consistency across environments. Use YAML manifests, Helm charts, or Crossplane CRDs to codify configurations.

- **Parameterize configurations**: Enable reusability and adaptability by using parameterized templates for different environments and workloads.

- **Implement governance**: Use tools like *Azure Policy* to enforce naming conventions, resource tagging, and compliance standards within Kubernetes environments.

- **Focus on observability**: Integrate monitoring tools like *Azure Monitor*, *Prometheus*, and *Grafana* into application definitions to ensure end-to-end visibility.

The following are some of the real-world applications:

- **Multi-tier application deployment**: Use Helm to deploy a microservices-based e-commerce platform with pre-configured services, load balancers, and database connections.

- **Hybrid cloud management**: Leverage Crossplane to define applications that span on-premises Kubernetes clusters and Azure resources, ensuring a consistent configuration across hybrid environments.

- **Event-driven architectures**: Combine AKS with Azure Event Grid or Kafka to define and deploy event-driven systems where application logic and event sources are tightly integrated.

Emerging tools in application definition and management

Kustomize offers a template-free way to customize Kubernetes configurations. Unlike Helm, which uses templating, Kustomize allows for overlaying modifications on existing manifests without altering the original files. This approach is beneficial for managing configurations across multiple environments, such as development, staging, and production, by applying environment-specific customizations cleanly and maintainably.

Argo CD is a declarative GitOps continuous delivery tool for Kubernetes. It automates the deployment of applications by monitoring Git repositories and applying the desired state to the Kubernetes cluster. This ensures that the cluster's state is always in sync with the repository, providing a single source of truth and facilitating rollback capabilities.

The *Operator Framework* is an open-source toolkit designed to manage Kubernetes-native applications, known as **Operators**, in an effective, automated, and scalable manner. Operators extend Kubernetes' capabilities by encapsulating operational knowledge into code, enabling complex applications to be managed declaratively. This is particularly useful for stateful applications that require intricate management.

Recent trends in application development

GitOps is gaining traction as a methodology where Git repositories serve as the single source of truth for declarative infrastructure and applications. By leveraging tools like *Argo CD*, organizations can implement continuous deployment pipelines that are auditable, version-controlled, and easily reproducible. This approach enhances collaboration between development and operations teams and accelerates deployment cycles, as follows:

- **AI-augmented development**: The integration of AI into development workflows is transforming application development. AI-powered tools assist in code generation, error detection, and performance optimization, thereby increasing developer productivity and code quality. For instance, AI-based code assistants have evolved from early adoption to becoming standardized tools in the development process, offering both positive and negative impacts.

- **Low-code and no-code platforms**: The rise of low-code and no-code platforms is democratizing application development by enabling users with minimal coding experience to build applications. These platforms provide drag-and-drop interfaces and pre-built components, accelerating development timelines and reducing costs. For example, FlutterFlow web app development is a prime example of a low-code platform that falls into popular application development trends.

- **Service meshes like Istio and Linkerd** are becoming integral in managing microservices architectures. They provide functionalities such as traffic management, service discovery, load balancing, and security, all abstracted from the application code. This abstraction simplifies the development process and enhances the observability and resilience of applications.

As organizations scale, *platform engineering* is emerging as a discipline focused on building self-service platforms that streamline infrastructure provisioning, deployment, and observability for developers.

Techniques for enhancing observability and monitoring

In an era where distributed systems and microservices architectures dominate, observability and monitoring have become essential components of reliable and performant infrastructures. While monitoring traditionally focuses on tracking metrics and alerts, observability extends this concept to provide deep insights into system behavior, enabling architects and CTOs to troubleshoot issues and optimize performance proactively. Modern tools and techniques for observability and monitoring empower organizations to ensure seamless operations, minimize downtime, and enhance the end-user experience.

Evolution from monitoring to observability

Monitoring has historically been about collecting predefined metrics, such as CPU usage or memory consumption, and triggering alerts when thresholds are breached. Observability, on the other hand, encompasses not just metrics but also logs and traces, offering a holistic view of the system's state and behavior. The key difference lies in the ability to answer unexpected questions: observability enables you to explore and diagnose issues that haven't been explicitly predefined.

Observability relies on three primary pillars:

- **Metrics**: Quantifiable measurements (e.g., latency, throughput, error rates) that provide high-level insights into system performance.

- **Logs**: Detailed, time-stamped records of events that capture what happened within a system.

- **Traces**: End-to-end representations of requests as they traverse a system, highlighting bottlenecks and latencies.

Enhancing observability and monitoring

The following are some of the key techniques for observability and monitoring:

- **Instrumenting applications for visibility**: Implement instrumentation in your code to generate meaningful telemetry data. This can include using SDKs like *OpenTelemetry*, which standardizes the collection of metrics, logs, and traces. Adopt distributed tracing tools such as Jaeger or Azure Monitor Application Insights to visualize the flow of requests through microservices.

- **Establishing monitoring pipelines**: Create robust pipelines for collecting, processing, and visualizing monitoring data. Tools like *Azure Monitor* and *Prometheus* can aggregate metrics, while Grafana or Azure Dashboards present data in actionable formats. Use alerting systems integrated with tools like *Azure Monitor Alerts* or *PagerDuty* to notify teams proactively when anomalies occur.

- **Real-time observability with AIOps**: Leverage AI-driven observability solutions that detect patterns and predict failures before they impact users. Azure Monitor's smart alerts or Dynatrace's AI engine provide anomaly detection and root cause analysis at scale.

- **Centralizing logs for unified insights**: Consolidate logs from multiple services and platforms using tools like *Azure Log Analytics* or *Elasticsearch*. Centralized logging enables faster correlation of events across distributed systems. Use structured logging formats like JSON to make logs easier to parse and analyze programmatically.

- **Establishing service-level objectives (SLOs)**: Define clear SLOs based on KPIs such as response time or availability. Observability tools can track adherence to these SLOs, providing actionable insights for maintaining service reliability.

The following are some of the best practices for enhancing observability:

- **Automate observability**: Integrate observability practices into CI/CD pipelines to ensure all new features and updates are automatically instrumented.

- **Contextualize alerts**: Reduce alert fatigue by designing alerts that provide sufficient context, including affected systems and potential causes.

- **Enable correlation across systems**: Use tools like *Azure Monitor Workbooks* to correlate metrics, logs, and traces across applications, infrastructure, and network layers.

- **Implement sampling strategies**: Avoid data overload by employing smart sampling techniques for traces and logs, focusing on high-value information.

- **Drift detection**: Integrate drift detection tools like Terraform drift detection or Azure's Blueprint to continuously reconcile infrastructure state against source-of-truth definitions.

The following are some of the tools for observability and monitoring:

- **Azure Monitor**: Offers end-to-end observability across Azure and hybrid environments, integrating metrics, logs, and traces for holistic insights.

- **Prometheus**: A widely used open-source tool for metrics collection and alerting, often paired with Grafana for visualization.

- **OpenTelemetry**: A vendor-neutral framework for collecting observability data, providing seamless integrations with popular monitoring backends.

- **Elastic Stack (ELK)**: A comprehensive solution for log aggregation, search, and analytics using Elasticsearch, Logstash, and Kibana.

The following are some of the emerging trends in observability:

- **Shift-left observability**: Incorporating observability during the development phase by instrumenting applications as they are built rather than retrofitting them later.

- **Multi-cloud observability**: Tools like Datadog and Azure Arc enable organizations to monitor and observe systems spread across multiple cloud providers, ensuring consistent visibility.

- **Contextual observability for edge computing**: With the rise of edge computing, tools are evolving to provide insights into geographically distributed nodes and devices.

The following are some of the real-world applications:

- **Improving microservices performance**: Distributed tracing in a microservices architecture helps pinpoint performance bottlenecks and optimize inter-service communication.

- **Proactive incident management**: AI-driven observability tools predict failures in an e-commerce platform, allowing preemptive action to prevent customer impact.

- **Ensuring compliance**: Centralized logging enables organizations to meet audit requirements by providing a clear and searchable history of system events.

Site reliability engineering

Site reliability engineering bridges the gap between development and operations, focusing on automating operational tasks and ensuring systems are highly reliable, scalable, and efficient. Originating at Google, SRE has become a cornerstone for modern IT operations, emphasizing the use of engineering practices to meet SLOs and maintain operational excellence. For architects and CTOs, SRE is not merely a methodology but a strategic framework for achieving system reliability while enabling rapid innovation.

Core principles of SRE

SRE is built on several foundational principles that guide its implementation:

- **Error budgets**: SRE operates on the concept that perfect reliability is neither achievable nor desirable. Error budgets define the acceptable level of downtime or errors, balancing system reliability with development velocity. For example, if a service has an availability SLO of 99.9%, the remaining 0.1% constitutes the error budget. Teams can use this margin to deploy changes without over-investing in unnecessary reliability.

- **Toil reduction**: Toil refers to repetitive, manual operational tasks that are automatable. SRE aims to minimize toil by automating these tasks, freeing engineers to focus on strategic initiatives. Examples include automating incident response, scaling infrastructure, and creating self-healing systems.

- **Service-level indicators (SLIs) and objectives (SLOs)**: SLIs are measurable metrics that reflect the health of a system, such as latency, throughput, or error rates. SLOs are targets set for these metrics, defining acceptable performance levels. These metrics and objectives provide a shared understanding between teams and ensure alignment with business goals.

- **Blameless postmortems**: After incidents, SRE promotes conducting blameless postmortems to understand root causes without attributing individual faults. This fosters a culture of learning and continuous improvement.

The following are some of the best practices in SRE:

- **Automating operations**: Automation is at the heart of SRE. Tasks such as deployments, scaling, and incident resolution are automated to reduce human error and accelerate response times. Tools like Azure Automation and Terraform scripts enable organizations to automate routine processes, while workflows in Azure Logic Apps can orchestrate complex incident responses.

- **Defining and managing SLOs**: SLOs are not arbitrary; they are derived from user expectations and business requirements. Teams must:

  o Identify critical SLIs, such as latency for a web service or availability for a database.

  o Define achievable SLOs based on historical performance and organizational goals.

  Azure-native tools like Application Insights and Azure Monitor help track these metrics and evaluate compliance with SLOs.

- **Proactive incident management**: SRE shifts incident management from reactive to proactive. This includes implementing automated monitoring and alerting systems that detect anomalies before they escalate and using chaos engineering techniques, such as Azure Chaos Studio, to simulate failures and test system resilience.

- **Error budget policies**: Teams should use error budgets to balance reliability and innovation. If a service exceeds its error budget, new feature releases may be paused in favor of improving stability. For example, if an e-commerce platform experiences frequent outages, development efforts may shift toward optimizing caching layers or database performance.

- **Capacity planning and scalability**: SRE ensures systems are prepared to handle current and future demands. This involves regular capacity analysis using tools like Azure Advisor, which provides recommendations for scaling resources and implementing autoscaling mechanisms in AKS or virtual machine scale sets.

- **Building self-healing systems**: SRE emphasizes creating systems that detect and resolve issues autonomously. Techniques include:

  o Auto-restart mechanisms for failed services.

  o Health probes in Kubernetes that trigger automated rescheduling of pods in AKS.

  o Implementing circuit breakers and retries in application code.

The following are some of the best practices for successful SRE implementation:

- **Foster collaboration between Dev and Ops**: Break down silos between development and operations teams by aligning their goals and incentivizing shared success metrics.

- **Invest in tooling**: Equip teams with robust tools for monitoring, automation, and incident response. Azure-native solutions like *Azure Monitor, Log Analytics*, and *Azure Sentinel* are key enablers.

- **Create feedback loops**: Use postmortems, real-time monitoring dashboards, and periodic reviews to continuously refine processes and improve system reliability.

The following are some of the emerging trends in SRE:

- **AI-driven reliability**: Leveraging AI for predictive analytics and anomaly detection is becoming a cornerstone of modern SRE practices. Tools like *Azure Machine Learning* integrate AI-driven insights into operational workflows.

- **Multi-cloud and hybrid observability**: As enterprises adopt multi-cloud strategies, SRE practices are evolving to manage reliability across diverse environments. Solutions like *Azure Arc* extend monitoring and governance capabilities to hybrid and multi-cloud setups.

- **Infrastructure as code for operations**: SRE teams are increasingly using IaC tools to codify operational practices, ensuring consistent deployments and reducing manual interventions.

The following are some of the real-world applications of SRE:

- **Global e-commerce platform**: A multinational e-commerce provider uses SRE practices to manage traffic spikes during sales events. Automation scripts provision additional capacity, while chaos engineering ensures the platform remains resilient under high loads.

- **Financial services application**: A banking application employs SLO-based monitoring to track transaction latency and availability. When performance dips, automated alerting systems trigger a rollback of the latest release.

- **Video streaming service**: A streaming service uses error budgets to balance feature rollouts with reliability. New features are only released if the system maintains a 99.95% uptime SLO.

Conclusion

In this chapter, we covered the foundational strategies and tools essential for automating infrastructure management and ensuring system reliability. We began by exploring the principles and practices of IaC, detailing its role in automating resource provisioning and the use of tools like ARM templates, Bicep, and Terraform. We then delved into application definition and development tools such as Helm, Crossplane, and AKS, highlighting their ability to streamline application and resource management. The chapter also examined techniques for enhancing observability and monitoring, emphasizing metrics, logs, and traces, along with tools like Azure Monitor and OpenTelemetry. Finally, we discussed the key practices of SRE, including error budgets, proactive incident management, and automation, demonstrating how SRE ensures scalability and operational excellence. Together, these practices equip architects and CTOs with the insights and tools necessary to design and operate robust, efficient, and scalable systems in modern IT environments.

In the next chapter, we will discuss essential principles and practices of FinOps, which focus on strategically managing cloud spending and optimization. We will guide readers through methodologies to align financial and cloud operational goals effectively, ensuring cost efficiency while maintaining scalability and agility in cloud investments. It will explore models for understanding and predicting cloud costs, implementing budget controls, and optimizing spending through continuous monitoring and refinement. Furthermore, the chapter will emphasize fostering collaboration between finance and tech teams to enable more informed and impactful decision-making processes.

Key terms

- **IaC**: A method of managing and provisioning infrastructure using machine-readable code to automate deployments, reduce errors, and increase scalability.

- **Declarative configuration**: A model where the desired state of the system is specified, and the tool ensures the system matches that state, used in IaC tools like Terraform and Bicep.

- **SLOs**: Defined targets for service performance metrics, such as uptime or response time, that align with user expectations and business goals.

- **Distributed tracing**: A technique for tracking requests as they traverse through microservices, enabling root cause analysis and performance optimization.

- **Observability**: The ability to understand system behavior through metrics, logs, and traces, providing insights to diagnose and resolve issues proactively.

- **Helm**: A Kubernetes package manager that simplifies the deployment and management of applications through reusable charts.

- **Crossplane**: An open-source tool extending Kubernetes to manage infrastructure resources alongside application workloads using a unified declarative approach.

- **SRE**: A discipline that applies software engineering principles to improve the reliability, scalability, and efficiency of systems through automation and proactive practices.

- **Error budget**: The allowable margin of error for a service, balancing system reliability with development velocity.

- **Azure monitor**: A comprehensive observability tool providing metrics, logs, and alerts for monitoring applications and infrastructure in Azure environments.

- **Azure chaos studio**: A service for implementing chaos engineering to test the resilience of applications by simulating failures.

Join our book's Discord space

Join the book's Discord Workspace for Latest updates, Offers, Tech happenings around the world, New Release and Sessions with the Authors:

https://discord.bpbonline.com

CHAPTER 11

FinOps Foundations

Introduction

In this chapter, we will cover the foundational principles and practices of **financial operations (FinOps)**, a discipline dedicated to the strategic management of cloud spending. As organizations increasingly rely on cloud services to scale their operations, managing cloud costs efficiently becomes a critical competency. FinOps provides a framework to align financial accountability with technical execution, ensuring cost efficiency without compromising on scalability or agility. This chapter explores the methodologies, governance models, and collaborative approaches necessary to optimize cloud investments and foster a culture of financial accountability within tech teams.

Structure

The chapter covers the following topics:

- Introduction to FinOps basics
- Building financial accountability in tech teams
- Effective cloud cost management and forecasting
- Governance and cost control mechanisms
- Tools and strategies for continuous cost optimization

Objectives

By the end of this chapter, we will have a solid understanding of FinOps principles and their practical application in managing cloud costs effectively. We will discuss strategies to foster a culture of financial accountability within tech teams, encouraging collaboration between finance and IT. The chapter will equip us with techniques for creating accurate cloud cost models and forecasts, enabling better budget planning and resource allocation. Additionally, we will gain insights into best practices for implementing governance and cost control mechanisms to prevent overspending and ensure compliance. Finally, we will explore tools and methodologies for continuous cost optimization, ensuring that our cloud investments remain efficient, scalable, and aligned with organizational goals.

Introduction to FinOps basics

FinOps, is a discipline that bridges the gap between technology teams and financial management, providing a framework for managing cloud costs effectively in dynamic environments. As organizations increasingly adopt cloud-native architectures and scale their operations, the traditional separation between technical and financial functions becomes a bottleneck. FinOps enables a culture of collaboration, shared responsibility, and data-driven decision-making, ensuring that cloud investments align with both technical goals and business objectives.

The following figure illustrates the FinOps lifecycle framework, which outlines the key principles, lifecycle stages, and tools essential for managing cloud financial operations effectively:

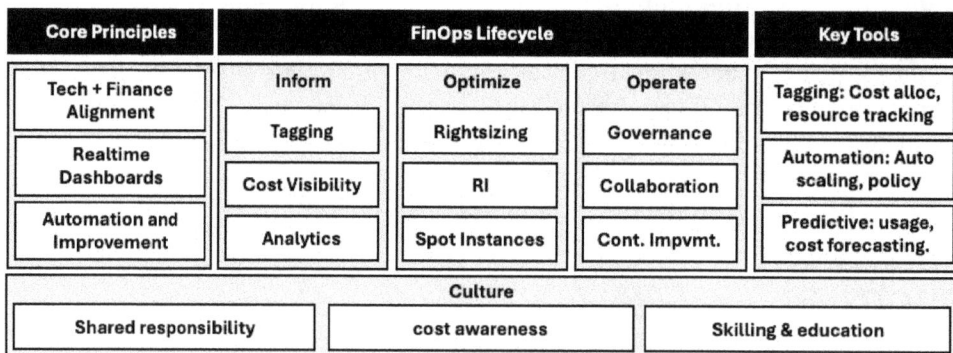

Core Principles	FinOps Lifecycle			Key Tools
Tech + Finance Alignment	**Inform**	**Optimize**	**Operate**	**Tagging: Cost alloc, resource tracking**
	Tagging	Rightsizing	Governance	
Realtime Dashboards				**Automation: Auto scaling, policy**
	Cost Visibility	RI	Collaboration	
Automation and Improvement				**Predictive: usage, cost forecasting.**
	Analytics	Spot Instances	Cont. Impvmt.	
Culture				
Shared responsibility		cost awareness		Skilling & education

Figure 11.1: FinOps lifecycle framework

Need for FinOps in modern cloud environments

The cloud has introduced unprecedented flexibility, allowing teams to provision and scale resources on-demand. However, this flexibility also brings challenges. Unlike traditional data centers with fixed costs, cloud environments operate on a pay-as-you-go model, where costs fluctuate based on usage. This can lead to inefficiencies, overspending, and budgetary surprises without proper oversight. For developers, architects, and technology officers, understanding FinOps is critical not only to optimize costs but also to make informed decisions that balance innovation with financial accountability.

FinOps addresses several key challenges in modern cloud environments, which are as follows:

- **Visibility**: Lack of clear insights into cloud spending often leads to inefficiencies and overspending.

- **Predictability**: Variable cloud costs make budget planning and forecasting complex.

- **Collaboration**: Misalignment between finance and technical teams results in delayed decision-making and missed opportunities for optimization.

Core principles of FinOps

At its core, FinOps is built on the following three guiding principles that shape its practices and methodologies:

- **Collaboration between teams**: FinOps emphasizes a shared responsibility for cloud spending across the organization. Developers, architects, and finance teams work together to align technical decisions with financial goals. This ensures that all stakeholders are informed and empowered to contribute to cost optimization.

- **Data-driven decision making**: Real-time visibility into cloud usage and costs is central to FinOps. By leveraging detailed analytics and reporting tools, organizations can identify trends, pinpoint inefficiencies, and make proactive adjustments to resource allocation.

- **Continuous optimization**: FinOps is not a one-time effort but an ongoing process. Teams continuously monitor usage, refine forecasts, and implement cost-saving measures to adapt to evolving needs and market conditions.

FinOps lifecycle

FinOps operates as a continuous lifecycle with three primary phases, outlined as follows, each addressing specific aspects of cloud cost management:

- **Inform phase**: The first step in the FinOps lifecycle is gaining visibility into cloud spending. This involves collecting and analyzing detailed cost data to understand where money is being spent, which teams or projects are driving usage, and how costs align with organizational priorities. Tools like *Azure Cost Management*, *Amazon Web Service (AWS) Cost Explorer*, or *Google Cloud Billing Reports* are invaluable during this phase.

- **Optimize phase**: Once visibility is established, the next step is to identify inefficiencies and implement optimization strategies. This may include rightsizing resources, leveraging reserved instances, or employing spot instances for non-critical workloads. The goal is to maximize value while minimizing waste.

- **Operate phase**: The final phase focuses on governance and continuous improvement. This involves setting budgetary controls, enforcing policies, and automating routine cost optimization tasks. Collaboration between teams is emphasized to ensure that optimization efforts are sustained over time.

Key concepts in FinOps

To fully grasp FinOps, it is essential to understand the following fundamental concepts:

- **Unit economics**: FinOps encourages teams to measure cloud costs in terms of business-relevant units, such as the cost per user, transaction, or API call. This helps link technical metrics to financial outcomes.

- **Shared responsibility model**: In FinOps, all teams share accountability for cloud spending. Developers are responsible for building cost-efficient applications, architects design scalable and economical systems, and finance teams provide oversight and ensure alignment with budgets.

- **Cost allocation**: Accurate cost allocation is a cornerstone of FinOps. By tagging resources and using cost allocation tools, organizations can assign expenses to specific teams, projects, or departments, fostering accountability and transparency.

Role of technology leaders in FinOps

For developers, architects, and technology officers, FinOps is more than a financial management practice; it is a strategic enabler. Developers must be mindful of the financial implications of their code, such as inefficient database queries or underutilized compute resources. Architects play a crucial role in designing systems that are both technically robust and cost-effective, leveraging best practices like autoscaling, serverless architectures, and reserved capacity. Technology officers, meanwhile, serve as enablers of collaboration, ensuring that the organization's financial and technical goals are aligned.

Building financial accountability in tech teams

Financial accountability within tech teams is the cornerstone of effective FinOps. In modern cloud environments, where spending is directly tied to resource usage, fostering a culture that prioritizes cost-conscious decision-making is as crucial as technical excellence. For developers, architects, and technology leaders, building this culture involves more than simply setting budgets; it requires embedding financial considerations into every stage of the technology lifecycle, from design to deployment and operations.

Importance of financial accountability

The dynamic nature of cloud services presents both opportunities and challenges. On one hand, developers can innovate at speed, leveraging on-demand resources to build scalable applications. On the other hand, this agility often leads to inefficiencies, provisioned resources are left unused, misaligned services generate unnecessary costs, and budget overruns impact the organization's financial health. A lack of financial accountability not only wastes resources but also hinders the trust between technical and financial teams.

For technology leaders, fostering financial accountability transforms these challenges into opportunities. When engineers understand the financial implications of their technical decisions, they become empowered to make smarter choices, aligning innovation with cost efficiency. This alignment ensures that cloud investments deliver maximum business value without sacrificing operational agility.

Building a culture of accountability

Creating a culture of financial accountability requires a deliberate, structured approach that integrates cost awareness into the technical fabric of the organization.

The following are the key strategies to achieve this transformation:

- **Make costs visible and actionable**: Transparency is the first step toward accountability. Teams cannot manage what they cannot measure. Leaders must provide engineers with real-time visibility into cloud spending through tools like Azure Cost Management, AWS Cost Explorer, or Google Cloud Billing Reports. Dashboards should break down costs by project, team, and service, enabling developers to understand where their resources are being consumed and how their decisions impact the overall budget.

- **Establish shared responsibility**: Traditional financial management often places the burden of cost control solely on finance teams. In a FinOps culture, accountability is distributed across technical teams. Developers, architects, and operations personnel share responsibility for optimizing resource usage. This shared model requires clear ownership. For instance, developers might own the costs associated with computing resources, while architects are accountable for the overall infrastructure design.

- **Embed financial metrics into development processes**: Cost awareness must be integrated into the development lifecycle. Teams should consider financial metrics alongside traditional KPIs, such as performance and scalability. For example:

  o During architecture reviews, evaluate not just the technical feasibility of a solution but also its cost implications.

    o   In CI/CD pipelines, implement automated checks to flag costly configurations or excessive resource provisioning. Use tools like Terraform Cost Estimation or Kubecost to provide cost insights directly within development workflows.

- **Train and educate teams**: Engineers often lack formal training in financial concepts, which can create a barrier to accountability. Organizations must invest in educating their teams about cloud pricing models, billing structures, and optimization techniques. Workshops, FinOps certifications, and regular knowledge-sharing sessions can equip teams with the skills to make cost-aware decisions. For instance, a workshop on *Optimizing Azure Virtual Machines* might cover choosing the right virtual machine size, leveraging reserved instances, and using autoscaling effectively.

- **Foster a feedback-driven culture**: Financial accountability thrives in an environment where teams are encouraged to experiment, learn, and improve. Leaders should establish mechanisms for continuous feedback, where engineers can review the cost impact of their deployments and identify opportunities for optimization. Post-deployment cost reviews or quarterly cost-efficiency retrospectives are excellent ways to institutionalize this feedback loop.

Overcoming resistance and challenges

Transforming organizational culture is never easy, and fostering financial accountability in technical teams is no exception. Leaders may encounter resistance from developers who perceive cost considerations as constraints on innovation or added complexity to their workflows. Addressing these challenges requires empathy, communication, and alignment with team goals.

Resistance and challenges can be overcome in the following ways:

- **Bridge the gap between finance and tech**: Create opportunities for collaboration, such as cross-functional FinOps teams, where finance professionals and engineers work together to solve cost-related challenges.

- **Align financial goals with technical outcomes**: Show how cost efficiency directly supports technical objectives. For example, optimized resource usage can reduce latency or enable the adoption of new services within budget constraints.

- **Gamify accountability**: Introducing elements of gamification, such as team leaderboards for cost savings or recognition for innovative cost optimizations, can make financial accountability engaging and rewarding.

Real-world applications

Organizations that adopt a culture of financial accountability often see transformative results. Consider the case of a SaaS company struggling with unpredictable cloud costs.

By implementing FinOps practices, they established cost visibility through detailed dashboards, trained their teams on cost-saving techniques, and embedded financial metrics into their DevOps workflows. The result was a 30% reduction in monthly cloud spending without compromising product performance or customer experience.

Another example comes from a global retail enterprise that aligned its development teams' bonuses with cost-efficiency metrics. This simple incentive led to the widespread adoption of resource optimization strategies, significantly lowering their cloud expenditure during peak shopping seasons.

Effective cloud cost management and forecasting

Effective cloud cost management and forecasting are critical for ensuring the financial sustainability of cloud operations and maintaining operational agility. For technology architects and finance controllers alike, this involves balancing technical efficiency with financial accountability. While architects focus on resource optimization and operational performance, finance controllers prioritize budget alignment, compliance, and the strategic impact of cloud investments. Combining these perspectives ensures cloud spending delivers maximum business value without compromising innovation.

Cost visibility and tagging

Visibility is foundational to both technical and financial management of cloud costs. Tagging cloud resources with metadata such as project names, departments, and environments (e.g., dev, test, production) enables detailed tracking and cost attribution. For architects, tagging simplifies operational oversight and allows better resource management. For finance controllers, it ensures costs are allocated correctly across teams and business units, fostering accountability.

For example, a healthcare organization tags resources by application type (e.g., patient portals, analytics dashboards) and department, enabling both IT and finance to evaluate costs at granular levels. Tools like Azure Cost Management and AWS Cost Explorer facilitate this level of insight, while dashboards can present the following:

- Cost breakdown by team or department.
- Trends in resource utilization by tags.
- Highlighting unallocated or orphaned resources for remediation.

Rightsizing resources

Rightsizing ensures that allocated resources align with workload demands, reducing overprovisioning and inefficiencies. Architects focus on analyzing resource utilization to adjust configurations, such as resizing virtual machines or optimizing Kubernetes clusters. Finance controllers, in turn, evaluate the cost implications of these optimizations, ensuring that savings align with budget goals.

For example, a media company discovers that certain Kubernetes nodes are underutilized during off-peak hours. By consolidating workloads and resizing the cluster, the technical team achieves significant savings, while the finance team reports a measurable reduction in computing costs.

Key metrics for dashboards include the following:

- Percentage of underutilized resources.
- Estimated savings from rightsizing actions.
- Historical trends in resource optimization.

Leveraging reserved instances and savings plans

Reserved instances (RIs) and savings plans are critical for predictable workloads. For architects, these options provide a consistent resource base for steady-state operations, while finance controllers focus on their financial impacts, such as cost savings and contract utilization.

For example, a retail enterprise running an e-commerce platform commits to one-year RIs for virtual machines used during non-peak periods, achieving a 40% cost reduction. Dashboards track the following:

- Commitment utilization rates.
- Savings achieved from RIs.
- Upcoming expiration and renewal opportunities.

Using spot instances

Spot instances offer substantial cost savings by utilizing unused cloud capacity, though they come with the risk of interruptions. Architects ensure workloads like batch processing or data analysis are optimized for spot instances, while finance teams quantify the savings and assess their risk-adjusted value.

For example, a biotech firm uses spot instances for genome sequencing jobs, achieving significant cost reductions while implementing fallback mechanisms for interruptions.

A combined dashboard could show the following metrics:

- Spot instance usage percentage.
- Savings compared to on-demand instances.
- Impact of spot terminations on workload completion.

Automating cost management

Automation reduces human error and enforces consistent cost-saving practices. Architects implement automation for tasks like shutting down unused resources, adjusting scaling rules, and applying policy-based governance. Finance controllers use these automated processes to ensure compliance and predict cost savings over time.

For example, a SaaS company automates the deactivation of development environments outside business hours using Azure Logic Apps, saving thousands of dollars monthly. Dashboards for automation might include the following:

- Savings are achieved through automated shutdowns.

- Scaling adjustments based on workload trends.

- Compliance metrics are enforced through automation.

Forecasting cloud costs with historical analysis

Forecasting relies heavily on historical data. For architects, analyzing past trends informs resource planning and scaling decisions. For finance controllers, this data forms the basis for budget forecasts and cost projections.

For example, an e-commerce retailer uses historical data to anticipate increased computing and storage needs during *Black Friday*. Azure Monitor provides insights that guide both technical planning and financial forecasting.

Key metrics for dashboards include the following:

- Historical spending trends by service.

- Predicted costs for upcoming cycles.

- Variance analysis between forecasts and actuals.

Building predictive models for cost forecasting

Predictive models enable proactive planning by combining historical data with ML. Architects can use these models to anticipate scaling needs, while finance controllers assess the impact on budgets and profitability.

For example, a gaming company launching a new title uses ML-driven predictive models to forecast server costs during the launch period. Tools like Azure Machine Learning or AWS Forecast can generate scenarios for both technical and financial decision-making.

A dashboard might include the following metrics:

- Predictive trends for resource usage.

- Forecasted costs under different scenarios.

- Impact on budgetary targets.

Scenario planning for dynamic workloads

Scenario planning is essential for preparing for varying workloads and business needs. Architects use this technique to design scalable systems, while finance controllers create multiple cost models to anticipate financial outcomes.

For example, a fintech firm models' scenarios for doubling transaction volumes during tax season, enabling proactive resource scaling and budget adjustments.

Dashboards for scenario planning could show the following metrics:

- Best-case, worst-case, and expected-case cost scenarios.

- Impact of workload changes on costs and performance.

- Recommendations for budget adjustments.

Governance metrics and compliance

Governance ensures that cloud spending aligns with organizational policies and financial controls. Architects focus on enforcing tagging, budget limits, and usage policies, while finance controllers track compliance and policy violations.

For example, a logistics company uses Azure Policy to enforce tagging compliance and prevent unauthorized provisioning of high-cost resources.

Dashboards provide insights into metrics such as the following:

- Tagging compliance rates by team.

- Violations of cost policies and associated financial impacts.

- Alerts triggered by budget overruns or anomalous spending.

Collaborative accountability

Collaboration between technical and financial teams is key to effective cost management. Architects align resource planning with financial goals, while finance controllers provide insights into cost-saving opportunities and track progress.

For example, quarterly reviews where architects present optimization actions (e.g., rightsizing or RI purchases) and finance controllers quantify their impact on budget adherence. Dashboards might display some metrics, such as the following:

- Team-specific spending reports.

- Variance analysis for budgets vs. actuals.

- Pending and implemented optimization actions.

Cloud cost management and forecasting demand a holistic approach combining technical efficiency and financial governance. Architects and finance controllers can align cloud investments with organizational goals by integrating practices like resource tagging, rightsizing, predictive modeling, and governance metrics. Dashboards tailored to both perspectives ensure actionable insights, fostering collaboration and driving accountability. These techniques enable organizations to achieve cost efficiency, operational agility, and long-term financial sustainability in their cloud strategies.

Governance and cost control mechanisms

In cloud environments, governance and cost control are essential to maintaining financial discipline and operational efficiency. The flexibility of cloud platforms, offering instant provisioning, dynamic scaling, and pay-as-you-go models, requires a robust governance framework to prevent misuse, overspending, and policy violations. For technology architects, governance focuses on enforcing standards, policies, and configurations to ensure systems run securely and efficiently. For finance controllers, cost control mechanisms translate these efforts into tangible financial outcomes by aligning resource utilization with budgetary constraints and compliance requirements. Together, these practices form a foundation for sustainable cloud operations.

Importance of governance in cloud environments

Governance in cloud environments extends beyond compliance and security; it encompasses the policies, procedures, and tools needed to control costs, manage risks, and enforce operational consistency. Without governance, organizations risk overspending due to untagged resources, underutilized commitments, or runaway provisioning. Governance frameworks ensure that cloud operations align with organizational goals, enabling architects to manage complexity while finance controllers maintain financial predictability.

The key governance outcomes are as follows:

- **Cost efficiency**: Preventing resource waste by setting limits and enforcing policies.

- **Compliance**: Ensuring adherence to industry standards, regulatory requirements, and internal policies.

- **Operational consistency**: Standardizing resource configurations to avoid variability and reduce errors.

Establishing governance policies

Governance policies are the foundation of cost control mechanisms. These policies define the rules and standards for cloud resource usage, guiding both technical teams and financial oversight.

Effective policies include the following:

- **Tagging standards**: Every cloud resource should be tagged with metadata, such as project name, department, and environment. Tags enable cost attribution, accountability, and visibility into resource usage.

  For example, a retail company requires all resources to include tags for the region, environment (e.g., production or test), and business function. This allows finance teams to generate precise cost reports and architects to identify optimization opportunities.

- **Resource quotas and budgets**: Setting quotas and budgets for specific teams or projects prevents overprovisioning and enforces spending limits.

  For example, a software development team has a monthly budget of $50,000 for computing and storage resources. Alerts are triggered when usage approaches this limit, enabling proactive adjustments.

- **Access and provisioning controls**: Governance policies should define who can provision resources and under what conditions. **Role-based access control (RBAC)** ensures that only authorized personnel can create, modify, or delete resources.

  For example, a financial institution restricts resource provisioning in production environments to senior engineers, reducing the risk of unauthorized changes.

Automating governance and cost controls

Manual enforcement of governance policies is inefficient and prone to errors. Automation ensures consistency, scalability, and real-time enforcement of governance rules.

Tools and practices for automating governance include the following:

- **Policy engines**: Tools *like Azure Policy, AWS Config,* and *Google Cloud Organization Policies* enforce rules for resource configurations, tagging compliance, and security settings. These tools automatically detect and remediate violations, ensuring that resources align with organizational policies.

  For example, a healthcare provider uses Azure Policy to enforce encryption for all storage accounts and block untagged resource creation.

- **Budget alerts**: Automated alerts notify teams when spending exceeds predefined thresholds, allowing for quick interventions. For example, Azure Cost Management can send alerts when a project's monthly costs exceed 90% of its allocated budget.

  For example, Azure Cost Management can send alerts when a project's monthly costs exceed 90% of its allocated budget. A retail company might use this to monitor and control spending during a major promotional campaign, ensuring costs do not spiral out of control and impact overall profitability.

- **Compliance monitoring**: Tools like *Azure Security Center* and *AWS Trusted Advisor* continuously monitor environments for compliance with best practices, highlighting areas for improvement.

    For instance, a financial institution can use AWS Trusted Advisor to identify and fix security gaps in its infrastructure, ensuring that sensitive customer data complies with financial regulations like GDPR and PCI-DSS.

Cost control mechanisms for financial accountability

Cost control mechanisms go hand-in-hand with governance to ensure financial accountability. These mechanisms focus on tracking, optimizing, and forecasting costs in alignment with organizational goals.

The following are key cost control mechanisms for ensuring financial accountability:

- **Regular cost reviews**: Monthly or quarterly cost reviews involve both technical and financial teams. These reviews identify areas of overspending, evaluate optimization efforts, and align budgets with business priorities.

    For example, a media company conducts quarterly reviews where architects present savings achieved through resource rightsizing while finance controllers assess the impact on the overall budget.

- **Chargeback and showback models**: Chargeback assigns costs directly to teams or departments based on their cloud usage, while showback provides visibility without direct cost allocation. Both models foster accountability and encourage cost-conscious behavior.

    For example, a global logistics company uses a chargeback model, assigning storage and compute costs to regional operations teams. This approach ensures that each region manages its resources efficiently.

- **Reserved and spot instance management**: Reserved instances and spot instances require continuous monitoring to ensure commitments are fully utilized and risks are managed effectively.

    For example, a tech startup closely monitors its usage of spot instances for batch processing jobs, ensuring they are deployed when the spot prices are low and reserving instances for critical workloads to avoid potential cost spikes.

Governance metrics for dashboards

A governance-focused dashboard provides leaders with real-time visibility into the effectiveness of governance policies and cost controls.

Key metrics include the following:

- **Tagging compliance**: The percentage of resources tagged according to organizational standards.

- **Policy violations**: The number and type of violations detected by automated tools.

- **Budget utilization**: This shows the percentage of allocated budgets used by each team or project.

- **Savings opportunities**: Identified cost-saving measures, such as unused resources or underutilized commitments.

For example, a finance controller's dashboard might show a 95% tagging compliance rate, five active policy violations, and projected savings of $20,000 from shutting down idle resources.

Governance challenges and solutions

Governance initiatives often face resistance from teams concerned about additional restrictions or complexity. The following can help in addressing these challenges:

- **Clear communication**: Explaining the value of governance in reducing risks, controlling costs, and ensuring compliance.

- **Collaboration**: Involving both technical and financial teams in policy development to ensure buy-in and practicality.

- **Phased implementation**: Rolling out governance policies incrementally, starting with critical areas like tagging and access control.

Tools and strategies for continuous cost optimization

Continuous cost optimization is a critical component of effective cloud financial management. Unlike one-time efforts, continuous optimization ensures that organizations consistently identify, address, and prevent inefficiencies in their cloud environments. For architects, this involves designing and maintaining systems that adapt to changing workloads without wasting resources. For finance controllers, it requires tracking financial outcomes and ensuring optimization aligns with broader budgetary goals. By leveraging the right tools and strategies, organizations can achieve sustainable cost efficiency without compromising performance or scalability.

Leveraging cloud-native tools for cost management

Cloud platforms provide native tools designed to simplify cost management and optimization efforts. The following tools integrate seamlessly into cloud environments, offering real-time insights and actionable recommendations:

- **Azure Cost Management and AWS Cost Explorer**: Both platforms provide comprehensive dashboards for monitoring spending patterns, forecasting costs, and identifying inefficiencies. For example, these tools can highlight underutilized virtual machines or overprovisioned storage.

- **AWS Compute Optimizer and Azure Advisor**: These tools analyze resource usage patterns and suggest optimizations, such as resizing instances, consolidating workloads, or shifting to reserved capacity. For instance, a retail company might use Azure Advisor to reduce costs by consolidating lightly used databases into fewer, larger instances.

These tools enable both technical and financial teams to make informed decisions, bridging the gap between operational needs and budgetary constraints.

Adopting automation for proactive optimization

Automation plays a key role in continuous cost optimization by minimizing manual intervention and ensuring consistent enforcement of best practices. By automating routine tasks, organizations can reduce human error, scale optimizations across environments, and react quickly to changes in workload demand in the following ways:

- **Autoscaling**: Implement autoscaling policies for compute resources to automatically adjust capacity based on demand. For example, an e-commerce platform might scale up during peak traffic periods and scale down during off-peak hours, ensuring cost efficiency without affecting performance.

- **Scheduled resource shutdowns**: Automatically shut down development or testing environments during non-business hours using tools like *Azure Automation* or AWS *Lambda*, saving costs on idle resources.

- **Policy enforcement**: Use policy engines such as *Azure Policy* or *AWS Config* to automatically enforce tagging, usage limits, and other governance measures.

These automated processes not only reduce operational overhead but also create a foundation for proactive rather than reactive cost management.

FinOps platforms for advanced optimization

Third-party FinOps platforms provide additional layers of insight and control, especially for organizations operating across multiple cloud providers or managing complex workloads. These platforms go beyond native cloud tools by offering features like unified reporting, advanced analytics, and cross-cloud recommendations:

- **CloudHealth by VMware**: This tool enables multi-cloud visibility and provides actionable insights for cost optimization, such as identifying cost-saving opportunities across **Amazon Web Service (AWS)**, Microsoft Azure, and **Google Cloud Platform (GCP)**.

- **Kubecost**: Specifically designed for Kubernetes environments, Kubecost provides granular cost tracking and optimization recommendations, helping organizations manage containerized workloads more efficiently.

- **Flexera One**: It offers comprehensive cloud cost management capabilities, including forecasting, rightsizing, and identifying shadow IT usage.

For example, a fintech company using CloudHealth identified redundant resources across AWS and Azure, consolidating workloads to save $50,000 annually.

Strategies for long-term cost efficiency

Continuous cost optimization is about reacting to immediate inefficiencies and building sustainable practices that ensure long-term efficiency.

The following strategies can help achieve long-term cost efficiency:

- **Rightsizing as an ongoing process**: Regularly review and adjust resource allocations to match workload demands. For instance, a media company might periodically resize its streaming servers based on evolving user behavior, ensuring that resources are neither underutilized nor overprovisioned.

- **Commitment to reserved and spot instances**: Continuously evaluate the suitability of reserved or spot instances for changing workloads. For example, a data analytics firm might shift batch processing jobs to spot instances during periods of low demand, significantly reducing costs.

- **Utilizing savings plans**: Explore cloud provider-specific savings plans, such as *AWS Savings Plans* or *Azure Reserved Instances*, for predictable workloads. Organizations can achieve significant discounts over on-demand pricing by committing to a consistent usage level.

Monitoring and refining optimization efforts

Optimization efforts must be monitored and refined to adapt to evolving workloads and business needs. This involves tracking the effectiveness of implemented measures and identifying new opportunities for improvement in the following ways:

- **Metrics to track**: Monitor key metrics such as cost savings achieved, utilization rates of reserved or spot instances, and the percentage of resources optimized. For example, a dashboard might show that 80% of RIs are utilized effectively, with potential savings identified for the remaining 20%.

- **Iterative reviews**: Conduct regular reviews to evaluate the impact of optimization efforts and adjust strategies as needed. A quarterly review might highlight new inefficiencies or validate the success of recent actions.

- **Forecasting future costs**: Use historical data and predictive analytics to anticipate future resource needs and costs. A gaming company might forecast increased server usage during a new game launch, enabling proactive adjustments to reserved capacity.

Emerging FinOps trends and strategies

As cloud environments evolve, so do the practices for managing and optimizing costs. In this section, we explore some of the emerging trends and strategies in FinOps that are reshaping how organizations handle cloud financial management. These topics include multi-cloud cost management, hybrid environments, AI-powered optimization, sustainability, and change management, all of which are vital for modern cloud operations.

Multi-cloud cost management

With many organizations adopting multi-cloud strategies to leverage the unique strengths of different cloud providers like *AWS*, *Azure,* and *GCP*, managing costs across these platforms has become a crucial challenge. A holistic FinOps approach must incorporate tools like *CloudHealth* and *Flexera*, which provide cross-cloud visibility and enable organizations to track, manage, and optimize costs across multiple cloud environments. These tools offer centralized reporting and cost analytics, empowering teams to make data-driven decisions that help prevent overspending while ensuring cost efficiency across all cloud platforms.

Cloud cost allocation for hybrid environments

Organizations operating in hybrid cloud environments where both on-premises infrastructure and cloud-based resources coexist, face unique challenges in allocating costs accurately. **Azure Arc** and **VMware vSphere** are tools that assist in managing costs across these hybrid setups by providing visibility into both on-premises and cloud resources. These platforms allow for seamless integration of on-premises assets with cloud resources, enabling accurate cost allocation and resource optimization across mixed environments. Effective cost allocation in hybrid environments ensures financial accountability while optimizing cloud resource usage.

AI-powered cloud optimization

AI-driven insights for cloud optimization are transforming the way organizations manage cloud costs. Tools like *Azure Cost Management*, *Azure AI Services*, and *AWS Cost*

Anomaly Detection use ML algorithms to predict cost spikes, recommend resource scaling, and identify inefficiencies in real-time. These platforms analyze historical data, forecast future usage patterns, and automatically flag anomalies, allowing teams to proactively adjust resources before issues arise. By integrating AI and machine learning into FinOps, organizations can optimize cloud spending with precision, driving greater financial and operational efficiency.

FinOps and sustainability

Sustainability has become a critical consideration in cloud operations, and FinOps practices can help organizations not only reduce costs but also minimize their environmental impact. By optimizing resource usage, reducing waste, and selecting energy-efficient cloud services, companies can align their financial strategies with their sustainability goals. Tools like *Azure Sustainability Calculator* can help track the environmental impact of cloud resources, while FinOps principles guide teams in making decisions that balance both financial efficiency and sustainability. This integration of sustainability into FinOps helps companies contribute to environmental goals while optimizing their cloud spend.

Change management in FinOps

Successfully adopting FinOps requires careful change management, as it often involves restructuring processes and workflows within organizations. Key to the success of FinOps adoption is ensuring that both technical and financial teams are aligned and committed to the shared goal of cloud cost optimization. This alignment is achieved through clear communication, training, and the establishment of cross-functional FinOps teams. Using tools like *CloudHealth* and *Flexera*, teams can easily track progress and adjust strategies in response to feedback, ensuring continuous improvement and alignment with organizational goals.

Real-world applications

Organizations across industries have demonstrated the value of continuous cost optimization through targeted strategies and tool usage. Consider the following examples:

- A SaaS company automated resource shutdowns for unused environments, saving $100,000 annually without affecting development timelines.

- An e-commerce giant used Kubecost to optimize its Kubernetes workloads, reducing its container orchestration costs by 25%.

- A financial institution leveraged CloudHealth to streamline its multi-cloud operations, identifying shadow IT usage and reallocating resources for a 15% cost reduction.

These examples highlight how combining cloud-native tools, third-party platforms, and sustainable strategies can drive significant financial and operational benefits.

Continuous cost optimization is an ongoing process that combines technical ingenuity with financial discipline. By leveraging cloud-native tools, automating routine tasks, and integrating advanced FinOps platforms, organizations can build a proactive approach to managing cloud costs. For architects, the focus is on designing adaptable systems that optimize resource usage. For finance controllers, the goal is to ensure these efforts align with budgetary goals and deliver measurable savings. Together, these tools and strategies create a resilient, efficient, and scalable cloud environment that supports both innovation and fiscal responsibility.

Conclusion

In this chapter, we covered the foundational principles and practices of FinOps to manage cloud spending effectively. We began by understanding FinOps as a framework for aligning technical and financial goals, emphasizing visibility, collaboration, and continuous optimization. Next, we discussed fostering a culture of financial accountability within technical teams by embedding cost awareness and collaboration into workflows. We covered techniques for effective cost management and forecasting, including rightsizing, leveraging RIs, and predictive modeling to plan for variable workloads. The chapter also examined implementing governance and cost control mechanisms, highlighting automated tools, tagging strategies, and access controls to prevent overspending and ensure compliance. Finally, we discussed tools and strategies for continuous cost optimization, focusing on cloud-native solutions, automation, and FinOps platforms to sustain efficiency.

In the next chapter, we will understand the intricate landscape of security, privacy, and ethics in the digital age. We will discuss critical topics such as **confidentiality, integrity, and availability (CIA)**, Zero Trust architecture, and **privacy-enhancing technologies (PETs)**, offering readers a deep understanding of cybersecurity best practices. This includes comprehensive insights into threat modeling, security assessments, and compliance frameworks. Additionally, the chapter will explore the ethical implications of AI technologies, emphasizing responsible AI development, fairness, transparency, and accountability. By addressing these crucial aspects, the chapter equips readers to navigate the complexities of securing digital systems while upholding ethical principles.

Key terms

- **FinOps**: A framework for aligning financial accountability with cloud operational goals, enabling organizations to optimize cloud spending while maintaining agility and scalability.

- **Cost visibility**: The ability to track and analyze cloud expenses in detail, often enabled by tagging resources and using cloud-native tools like Azure Cost Management and AWS Cost Explorer.

- **Rightsizing**: The process of adjusting resource allocations to match workload requirements, ensuring efficient utilization and cost reduction.

- **Reserved instances (RIs)**: A cost-saving mechanism where organizations commit to a fixed usage level for specific resources over a defined period, receiving significant discounts compared to on-demand pricing.

- **Spot instances**: Unused cloud capacity available at a reduced cost, ideal for non-critical, interruptible workloads such as batch processing and data analysis.

- **Governance policies**: Rules and standards for managing cloud resources, including tagging, access controls, and compliance measures, are enforced to ensure operational and financial discipline.

- **Automation**: The use of tools and scripts to streamline cost management tasks, such as shutting down idle resources, scaling workloads dynamically, and enforcing policies.

- **Predictive modeling**: The use of historical data and ML algorithms to forecast future cloud usage and costs, enabling proactive planning and budgeting.

- **Chargeback and showback models**: Methods for allocating cloud costs to specific teams or departments, with chargeback assigning costs directly and showback providing visibility without direct allocation.

- **Continuous cost optimization**: An ongoing process of identifying and addressing inefficiencies in cloud spending, leveraging tools, automation, and best practices to sustain financial and operational efficiency.

Join our book's Discord space

Join the book's Discord Workspace for Latest updates, Offers, Tech happenings around the world, New Release and Sessions with the Authors:

https://discord.bpbonline.com

CHAPTER 12

Security, Privacy, and Ethics

Introduction

This chapter of the book will cover the multifaceted dimensions of security, privacy, and ethics in the digital age, focusing on how modern applications and enterprises can navigate an increasingly complex threat landscape while maintaining trust and accountability. Readers will explore foundational concepts like the **confidentiality, integrity, and availability (CIA)** triad and advanced practices like zero trust architecture. The chapter also introduces emerging technologies, such as **privacy-enhancing technologies (PETs)**, essential for ensuring robust data protection. Ethical considerations surrounding AI technologies are a focal point, addressing the critical need for fairness, transparency, and responsible AI governance. By combining technical and ethical perspectives, this chapter equips readers with a holistic understanding of the challenges and strategies in securing applications and systems while upholding privacy and ethical standards.

Structure

The chapter covers the following topics:

- Concepts of cloud-native app protection platform
- Zero Trust architecture
- Privacy-enhancing technologies

- Security and compliance standards and frameworks
- AI ethics and governance principles
- Emerging trends in security, privacy, and ethics

Objectives

By the end of this chapter, you will have a comprehensive understanding of modern security practices, including the **Cloud Native App Protection Platform** (**CNAPP**) and zero trust architecture, enabling you to design and implement robust defenses for cloud-native applications and enterprise systems. You will also gain insights into advanced PETs for safeguarding sensitive data, along with key security and compliance standards to ensure regulatory adherence and operational integrity. Furthermore, this chapter will equip you with the knowledge to address ethical challenges in AI development, emphasizing fairness, transparency, accountability, and responsible governance to foster trust in digital ecosystems.

Concepts of cloud-native app protection platform

Cloud-native applications are rapidly becoming the backbone of modern digital enterprises, offering unmatched scalability and agility. However, they also bring unique security challenges due to their distributed architectures, dynamic workloads, and reliance on ephemeral resources like containers, serverless functions, and microservices. Traditional security approaches, which operate in silos, are ill-equipped to address these complexities. Enter the CNAPP, a unified and holistic solution designed to secure cloud-native applications throughout their lifecycle, from development to runtime.

About cloud-native app protection platform

At its core, CNAPP consolidates multiple security capabilities into a single platform. It integrates tools for runtime protection, vulnerability management, misconfiguration detection, compliance monitoring, IaC scanning, and behavioral analysis. By providing a unified view of an organization's security posture, CNAPP enables seamless protection across hybrid and multi-cloud environments. This approach eliminates the operational inefficiencies of managing fragmented tools while providing deeper insights into application security.

Key capabilities of cloud-native app protection platform

The following outlines the key capabilities of a CNAPP, designed to secure cloud-native applications throughout their lifecycle. These capabilities provide comprehensive protection by integrating security across development, runtime, and data management, ensuring that organizations can mitigate risks, comply with regulations, and safeguard critical application infrastructure:

- **Unified contextual security**: CNAPP offers end-to-end visibility into workloads, configurations, and identities, providing context-aware insights that help prioritize risks. Correlating vulnerabilities with runtime behavior ensures that security teams focus on issues with the highest exploitability.

- **Shift-left security**: CNAPP aligns with **DevSecOps methodologies**, embedding security checks directly into the development lifecycle. It integrates with popular CI/CD pipelines and developer tools like Jenkins, GitHub Actions, and Azure DevOps, enabling real-time feedback and automated fixes for code, container images, and IaC templates.

- **Runtime protection**: During operation, CNAPP continuously monitors applications for threats, leveraging **AI** and **ML** to detect anomalies such as privilege escalations or lateral movement attempts. This proactive approach reduces the **mean time to detect (MTTD) and respond (MTTR)** to attacks.

- **Misconfiguration management**: Misconfigurations in cloud resources remain a leading cause of breaches. CNAPP automates the detection and remediation of these misconfigurations in both live environments and IaC, ensuring compliance with best practices.

- **Cloud identity and entitlement management (CIEM)**: Identity security is a growing focus for CNAPP. By dynamically enforcing the principle of least privilege and integrating with **Zero Trust architecture**, CNAPP ensures that access permissions are minimized and contextually verified.

- **Compliance and governance**: Modern CNAPP platforms provide automated compliance assessments for standards like the **General Data Protection Regulation (GDPR), Health Insurance Portability and Accountability Act (HIPAA)**, *ISO/IEC 27001*, and **System and Organization Controls (SOC 2)**, simplifying audits and ensuring adherence to regulatory requirements.

- **API security**: APIs are the backbone of cloud-native applications but are highly vulnerable to exploitation. CNAPP includes capabilities for API discovery, runtime monitoring, and posture management, safeguarding these critical interfaces.

- **Data-centric security**: CNAPP integrates data security tools to discover, classify, and protect sensitive information stored or processed in cloud-native applications. Techniques like *encryption enforcement* and *data masking* are often employed.

Emerging trends in cloud-native app protection platform

The following are some of the key capabilities that a CNAPP offers to enhance the security, compliance, and operational efficiency of cloud-native applications across their entire lifecycle:

- **Integration of threat intelligence**: Modern CNAPP solutions leverage real-time threat intelligence feeds to identify and mitigate emerging vulnerabilities. These feeds ensure platforms remain up-to-date with the latest attack vectors.

- **Support for emerging workloads**: As enterprises adopt **serverless architectures** and **edge computing**, CNAPP platforms are evolving to secure ephemeral workloads and distributed environments.

- **Risk scoring and prioritization**: Not all vulnerabilities are equally critical. Advanced CNAPP platforms use risk-scoring mechanisms to prioritize vulnerabilities based on factors like exploitability, runtime context, and business impact.

- **Security automation and orchestration**: Automation is central to CNAPP's value proposition. Platforms automate processes like patching, remediation, and incident response, often integrating with **security orchestration, automation, and response (SOAR)** tools.

Role of CNAPP in Zero Trust security

Zero Trust architecture is a critical element in the functionality of CNAPPs, focusing on the principle that trust should never be implicitly granted, regardless of the network location. CNAPP plays a pivotal role in Zero Trust by continuously verifying the identity of users and devices, enforcing strict access controls, and ensuring that least-privilege access is maintained for all interactions. It dynamically authenticates and authorizes access based on the context, such as user role, device security posture, and real-time risk assessments, minimizing the potential for unauthorized access. CNAPP integrates with **identity and access management (IAM)** systems and Zero Trust frameworks, providing granular control over data and application access, thereby enhancing security posture and reducing attack surfaces.

Modern capabilities highlight

The following modern capabilities highlight the key features of CNAPP, designed to address the evolving security needs of cloud-native environments:

- **Behavioral analytics**: Detect anomalies in workload and user behavior.

- **Agentless and agent-based security**: Cater to diverse application architectures with flexible deployment options.

- **Multi-cloud scalability**: Provide consistent security across hybrid and multi-cloud setups.

- **Real-time compliance monitoring**: Automate compliance checks and generate audit-ready reports.

The rise of *hybrid workforces, multi-cloud strategies, and advanced threat actors* has elevated the need for an integrated approach to application security. CNAPP represents a paradigm shift in securing cloud-native applications. Its unified, intelligent, and context-aware capabilities make it a critical component of any modern security strategy, ensuring resilience in an ever-evolving threat landscape.

Zero Trust architecture

In today's digital-first landscape, where applications span hybrid and multi-cloud environments, and users connect from diverse locations and devices, traditional perimeter-based security models are no longer sufficient. **Zero Trust architecture (ZTA)** has emerged as a critical framework for modern security, designed to mitigate the risks posed by increasingly sophisticated threats and distributed systems. The Zero Trust model operates on the principles of *never trust, always verify*, and **assume breach**, focusing on continuous verification and least-privilege access to ensure robust security across applications, users, and data.

The following figure illustrates key components of the security ecosystem, focusing on **Zero Trust Architecture**, **AI Ethics & Governance**, and relevant **Security & Compliance Standards**. It outlines the guiding principles, essential tools, emerging trends, and regulatory frameworks that support modern security strategies in cloud-native environments:

Zero Trust Architecture			AI Ethics & Governance	
Principles	**Key Tools**	**Trends**	Fairness	Bias detection tools
			Transparency	Explainability
Verify explicitly	MFA, SSO, PAM	AI Driven	Accountability	Oversight, ethical reviews
Least privilege	SIEM, SOAR	IoT and Edge	Privacy	PET integration
			Sustainability	Carbon-neutral AI.
Assume breach	Segmentation	SASE	Inclusivity	Accessible AI tools

Security & Compliance Standards						
ISO 27001	NIST CSF	GDPR	PCI DSS	DPDP Act	RBI Guidelines	MEITY Critical Infrastructure

Figure 12.1: Security ecosystem components

About Zero Trust architecture

ZTA is a strategic approach to cybersecurity that eliminates implicit trust in any entity, whether inside or outside the network. Instead, it enforces *strict identity verification, granular access controls, and dynamic security policies* based on real-time context. The framework is widely adopted to safeguard modern, cloud-native applications, protect sensitive data, and meet stringent compliance requirements.

Core principles of Zero Trust architecture

The following are the core principles of Zero Trust architecture, which form the foundation of its security model. These principles ensure that access is tightly controlled, continuously verified, and proactively safeguarded against potential threats, as shown:

- **Verify explicitly**: Authentication and authorization are performed based on multiple data points, including user identity, device status, location, and behavioral analytics.

- **Use least-privilege access**: Access is restricted to the minimum level required for specific tasks, limiting the potential impact of compromised credentials or insider threats.

- **Assume breach**: Security measures are implemented with the assumption that breaches are inevitable, ensuring robust containment, monitoring, and rapid response capabilities.

Key components of Zero Trust architecture

The following key components form the backbone of Zero Trust architecture, providing a comprehensive approach to securing modern digital environments by continuously verifying and enforcing strict access controls at every level.

These components ensure that resources are protected, and that security is maintained through real-time monitoring, policy enforcement, and comprehensive data protection strategies, as shown:

- **Identity and access management**: IAM is the cornerstone of Zero Trust, ensuring secure access to resources based on verified identities and contextual information. Popular tools and frameworks include:

  - **Multi-factor authentication (MFA)**: Widely adopted in IAM solutions such as Okta, **Azure Active Directory (Azure AD)**, and Ping Identity.

  - **Single sign-on (SSO)**: Simplifies authentication for users while maintaining security.

  - **Privileged access management (PAM)**: Tools like CyberArk and Thycotic manage access to sensitive systems based on least-privilege principles.

- **Network micro-segmentation**: Zero Trust segments networks into smaller zones, minimizing the attack surface and limiting lateral movement. Technologies like **VMware NSX**, **Cisco Tetration**, and **Microsoft Azure Virtual Network** enable granular segmentation and enforcement of dynamic policies.

- **Endpoint and device security**: Endpoint security ensures devices meet compliance requirements before accessing resources. Tools include:

- o **Endpoint detection and response (EDR)**: Solutions like CrowdStrike Falcon, Microsoft Defender for Endpoint, and SentinelOne detect and mitigate endpoint threats.

- o **Mobile Device Management (MDM)**: Tools such as Microsoft Endpoint Manager (Intune) and Jamf enforce device compliance.

- **Continuous monitoring and threat detection**: Continuous monitoring tools analyze real-time telemetry from applications, users, and network traffic to detect anomalies and potential breaches. Popular options include:

  - o **Security information and event management (SIEM)**: Tools like *Splunk, Microsoft Sentinel,* and *Elastic Security* provide actionable insights.

  - o **Security orchestration, automation, and response (SOAR)**: Automates incident response using platforms like *Palo Alto Cortex XSOAR* and *ServiceNow Security Operations.*

- **Dynamic policy enforcement**: Dynamic policies adapt based on context, such as location, device status, and risk level. Examples include **Conditional Access Policies** in **Azure AD** and risk-based policies in **Okta** and **Google Workspace**.

- **Data protection and privacy**: Data-centric security ensures sensitive information is protected across its lifecycle. Popular tools include:

  - o **Data loss prevention (DLP)**: Offered by *Microsoft Purview, Symantec DLP,* and *Forcepoint DLP.*

  - o **Encryption and tokenization**: Services like **AWS Key Management Service** (**KMS**) and *Google Cloud Key Management* secure data at rest and in transit.

Implementation framework for Zero Trust

A phased approach to Zero Trust adoption ensures smooth integration and alignment with organizational goals.

Key steps include:

1. **Assess and map resources**: Identify critical assets, data flows, and access dependencies across applications and infrastructure.

2. **Strengthen identity controls**: Implement robust IAM practices like passwordless authentication, conditional access, and just-in-time privilege management.

3. **Deploy micro-segmentation**: Use software-defined networking tools to isolate workloads and enforce granular access.

4. **Adopt continuous monitoring**: Implement SIEM and SOAR solutions to monitor, detect, and respond to threats in real time.

5. **Automate security processes**: Use automation tools to streamline compliance checks, patching, and incident response.

6. **Integrate across the ecosystem**: Ensure compatibility and integration with existing tools, including CI/CD pipelines, cloud platforms, and endpoint solutions.

Emerging trends in Zero Trust

The following emerging trends in Zero Trust highlight how security strategies are evolving to address the complex challenges of modern digital environments. As organizations adapt to new technologies and shifting threats, these trends showcase how Zero Trust is being integrated into cutting-edge solutions for enhanced protection, scalability, and resilience, as shown:

- **AI-driven security**: Advanced analytics and machine learning enhance threat detection and automate policy adjustments. Tools like *Darktrace* and *Microsoft Azure Sentinel* incorporate AI for proactive security.

- **Zero trust for IoT and edge**: Solutions such as *Azure IoT Hub* and *AWS IoT Device Defender* extend Zero Trust principles to IoT and edge devices.

- **Secure Access Service Edge (SASE)**: Platforms like *Zscaler* and *Cisco Umbrella* integrate Zero Trust with network security, enabling secure access for distributed users.

- **Identity threat detection and response (ITDR)**: Tools like *Azure AD Identity Protection* and *CrowdStrike* focus on mitigating identity-based threats.

The shift to remote work, cloud adoption, and increasingly sophisticated cyberattacks have made zero trust essential for modern enterprises. By emphasizing continuous verification, granular access control, and breach containment, zero trust minimizes the risk of data breaches and ensures compliance with global security standards. **Zero Trust architecture** is the foundation of resilient security in the digital age. Its principles and practices are technology-neutral, yet it finds robust implementation in popular tools and frameworks from leading providers like Microsoft, AWS, Google, and others.

Privacy-enhancing technologies

As organizations increasingly rely on data-driven innovation, balancing the need for valuable insights with the mandate to protect privacy has become paramount. In this evolving landscape, **privacy-enhancing technologies** (PETs) have emerged as essential tools for enabling secure, compliant, and ethical data usage. PETs allow organizations to process, analyze, and share sensitive data without compromising privacy, thus meeting regulatory requirements while fostering innovation.

About privacy-enhancing technologies

PETs encompass a range of methods, tools, and frameworks designed to protect sensitive data throughout its lifecycle. PETs enable secure data handling during sharing, processing, and analysis, often by embedding privacy measures directly into systems and workflows. These technologies play a crucial role in adhering to global privacy regulations like *GDPR*, *CCPA*, and *HIPAA* while unlocking data's potential for analytics, ML, and collaboration.

Core techniques in privacy-enhancing technologies

The following core techniques in PETs demonstrate how advancements in data privacy are being applied to modern computing, ensuring security and confidentiality while enabling innovation and collaboration. These techniques are shaping the future of privacy, providing solutions to safeguard sensitive information in an increasingly interconnected world:

- **Differential privacy**: Differential privacy introduces controlled noise into datasets, ensuring individual data points remain anonymous while allowing aggregate insights. It is widely used in public data releases, customer analytics, and compliance-driven data sharing.

  For example, Microsoft Azure confidential computing integrates differential privacy into its analytics tools. **Apple** employs differential privacy in iOS to analyze usage patterns without compromising user privacy.

- **Homomorphic encryption:** Homomorphic encryption enables computations on encrypted data without requiring decryption, ensuring privacy during data processing in untrusted environments like public clouds.

  For example, Microsoft **Simple Encrypted Arithmetic Library** (**SEAL**) is a widely adopted open-source library for homomorphic encryption. **IBM Watson** uses this technique for secure healthcare analytics.

- **Federated learning**: Federated learning allows decentralized training of machine learning models across multiple datasets without sharing raw data. This approach ensures privacy while enabling collaboration.

  For example, **Google's GBoard** leverages federated learning to enhance typing predictions without sending user data to central servers. **OpenMined**, an open-source project, promotes federated learning in privacy-critical applications.

- **Secure Multi-Party Computation (SMPC)**: SMPC enables multiple parties to collaboratively compute a function over their private inputs without revealing them to one another. It is particularly valuable in inter-organizational data collaboration.

  For example, *Microsoft's Cryptography Research Group* develops SMPC protocols for secure financial and healthcare data sharing.

- **Synthetic data generation**: Synthetic data replicates the statistical properties of real-world datasets without containing actual personal information. It is used for testing, training, and sharing data safely.

  For example, *Hazy AI* and *Mostly AI* are leading providers of synthetic data solutions. **AWS Data Exchange** supports synthetic data for secure sharing in multi-party collaborations.

- **Confidential computing**: Confidential computing uses **trusted execution environments** (**TEEs**) to process sensitive data securely in isolated hardware environments. It ensures data confidentiality even during processing.

  For example, *Microsoft Azure Confidential Computing* and *Intel SGX* are pioneers in enabling secure computation environments. *Google Confidential VMs* offer similar functionality for secure cloud workloads.

- **Zero-knowledge proofs (ZKPs)**: ZKPs allow one party to prove to another that a statement is true without revealing any information beyond the statement itself. They are increasingly used in blockchain, identity verification, and secure financial transactions.

Key benefits of privacy-enhancing technologies

The following are the key benefits of **privacy-enhancing technologies** (**PETs**), highlighting how these technologies enable organizations to protect sensitive data while maximizing its utility and ensuring compliance with privacy regulations.

PETs not only enhance data security but also foster trust and facilitate collaboration, making them essential in the modern digital landscape, as follows:

- **Regulatory compliance**: PETs embed privacy directly into systems, ensuring compliance with regulations like *GDPR, HIPAA,* and *CCPA*.

- **Data utility without risk**: PETs enable organizations to derive insights from data while safeguarding sensitive information.

- **Trust and reputation**: Adopting PETs signals a commitment to privacy, strengthening customer and partner trust.

- **Collaboration enablement**: PETs facilitate secure data sharing across organizations and borders without compromising privacy.

Operationalizing privacy-enhancing technologies

Implementing PETs requires strategic planning and technical integration. Security professionals must address the following key challenges such as compatibility, scalability, and performance trade-offs:

- **Integration with existing systems:** Embed PETs into existing workflows and data pipelines using tools like **Microsoft Purview** for data governance and classification. Leverage cloud-native PET solutions offered by **Azure confidential computing**, **AWS**, and **Google Cloud**.

- **Performance optimization**: Techniques like optimized encryption algorithms and distributed processing reduce latency in PET implementations.

- **Scalability**: Use modern orchestration tools such as Kubernetes and Terraform to scale PETs across large datasets and environments.

- **Testing and validation**: Employ frameworks to validate privacy guarantees, such as epsilon values in differential privacy or leakage assessments in federated learning.

Emerging trends in privacy-enhancing technologies

The following emerging trends in PETs illustrate how these advancements are evolving to meet the increasing demands for privacy protection in a complex and interconnected digital landscape. As technology continues to progress, these trends enable organizations to enhance data privacy while maintaining functionality and adaptability in their systems, as shown:

- **AI-powered PETs**: AI-driven PETs dynamically balance privacy and utility by optimizing noise levels or encryption parameters.

- **Composable PETs**: Combining multiple PET techniques (for example, differential privacy with homomorphic encryption) addresses complex privacy scenarios.

- **Privacy for IoT and edge devices**: PETs are expanding to secure sensitive data from IoT devices using techniques like encrypted communication and federated analytics.

- **Quantum-resistant privacy**: PETs are evolving to mitigate risks posed by quantum computing, particularly in encryption.

- **Privacy by design**: Organizations are embedding PETs into system architectures from inception rather than treating them as add-ons.

In an era of heightened data privacy concerns and regulatory scrutiny, Privacy-Enhancing Technologies are indispensable for modern enterprises. Whether through homomorphic encryption for secure cloud processing, federated learning for collaborative AI, or synthetic data for safe sharing, PETs empower businesses to unlock data's potential without compromising privacy.

Security and compliance frameworks

Security and compliance standards are critical in today's digital-first world, ensuring organizations can protect sensitive data, meet regulatory obligations, and maintain customer trust. As businesses increasingly adopt cloud-native technologies and multi-cloud architectures, aligning with globally recognized standards and region-specific regulations is essential. These frameworks provide a structured approach to managing risks, implementing robust security measures, and achieving compliance in a complex and evolving threat landscape.

This chapter explores key global standards like *ISO/IEC 27001, NIST Cybersecurity Framework (CSF),* and *GDPR,* alongside regional regulations such as India's *Digital Personal Data Protection (DPDP) Act, RBI Guidelines,* and *MEITY Recommendations.* It also discusses actionable insights for applying these standards across hybrid and cloud environments, ensuring a practical approach for enterprises, developers, and cybersecurity professionals.

Key global security and compliance standards

The following are key global security and compliance standards that organizations must adhere to, in order to ensure the security, privacy, and integrity of their data and operations. These standards help businesses meet regulatory requirements and build trust with customers and partners across various industries:

- **ISO/IEC 27001 (Information security management system)**: ISO 27001 is a globally recognized standard for managing information security risks. It helps organizations establish, implement, and continually improve an ISMS by focusing on protecting confidentiality, integrity, and availability of data. It is widely adopted by cloud providers like *Microsoft Azure, AWS,* and *Google Cloud,* offering enterprises assurance that their workloads are hosted securely.

- **NIST Cybersecurity Framework (CSF)**: The NIST CSF provides a flexible framework to identify, protect, detect, respond to, and recover from cybersecurity incidents. It is widely used in sectors like healthcare, finance, and critical infrastructure. Organizations adopt this framework to align their cybersecurity practices with globally recognized standards while customizing it to their unique needs.

- **General Data Protection Regulation (GDPR)**: The GDPR governs the collection, processing, and storage of personal data in the European Union. Its emphasis on transparency, user consent, and data protection makes it a critical compliance standard for organizations worldwide. Tools like *Microsoft Purview, AWS Compliance Center,* and *Google Cloud DLP* enable businesses to comply with GDPR while maintaining operational efficiency.

- **Payment Card Industry Data Security Standard (PCI DSS)**: PCI DSS sets stringent guidelines for securing payment card data, focusing on encryption, network segmentation, and access control. It is mandatory for businesses handling payment card transactions. Cloud platforms like *Azure PCI Compliance Tools* and *AWS Artifact* offer pre-configured environments to simplify adherence to PCI DSS.

- **Service Organization Control 2 (SOC 2)**: SOC 2 compliance ensures that systems handling customer data meet high standards of security, availability, confidentiality, and privacy. This is particularly important for SaaS providers, IT services, and cloud vendors operating in global markets.

Regional and industry-specific standards

The following are key regional and industry-specific standards that guide organizations in ensuring data security, privacy, and compliance within their respective sectors. These standards address unique regulatory needs while promoting best practices for managing sensitive data and mitigating risks:

- **Digital Personal Data Protection (DPDP) Act, 2023 (India)**: The DPDP Act is a comprehensive regulation designed to protect personal data in India. It emphasizes data minimization, consent-based processing, and stringent penalties for non-compliance. Organizations can leverage PETs like homomorphic encryption and differential privacy to ensure compliance while maintaining data usability.

- **Reserve Bank of India cybersecurity guidelines**: The RBI mandates robust cybersecurity and IT risk management frameworks for financial institutions. These guidelines include regular audits, incident reporting, and secure development practices. Platforms like the *Azure Financial Services Compliance Program* enable Indian banks and fintech companies to meet these requirements effectively.

- **MEITY guidelines for critical information infrastructure**: The **Ministry of Electronics and Information Technology** (**MEITY**) in India provides security recommendations for sectors like telecom, energy, and healthcare. These guidelines focus on incident response, vulnerability management, and periodic audits to secure critical infrastructure.

- **Health Insurance Portability and Accountability Act (HIPAA)**: HIPAA sets standards for protecting healthcare data, requiring robust administrative, technical, and physical safeguards. Solutions like *Azure for Healthcare, Google Healthcare API,* and *AWS HealthLake* provide tailored support for achieving HIPAA compliance.

Application of security and compliance frameworks

Implementing security and compliance frameworks involves aligning technical practices, governance models, and automation tools to address the specific needs of modern enterprises. The following highlights key strategies for applying security and compliance frameworks, ensuring organizations meet security requirements, and automating governance in cloud-native and multi-cloud environments:

- **Conducting a gap analysis**: Organizations begin by assessing their existing security measures against relevant standards to identify gaps and prioritize improvements.

- **Automation and continuous monitoring**: Cloud-native tools like **Azure Policy**, **AWS Security Hub**, and **Google Cloud Security Command Center** enable real-time compliance checks, risk assessment, and automated remediation, ensuring adherence to standards at scale.

- **Governance across multi-cloud environments**: Managing security across hybrid and multi-cloud architectures requires unified governance solutions. Platforms like *CloudHealth* and *Google Cloud Anthos* help enterprises maintain consistent compliance and monitoring.

- **Embedding compliance into development pipelines**: Compliance-as-code integrates security controls into CI/CD workflows, ensuring that applications meet compliance requirements during development. Tools like *HashiCorp Terraform*, *Azure DevOps,* and *GitHub Advanced Security* enable developers to embed security from the ground up.

Emerging trends in security and compliance

The following emerging trends in security and compliance highlight the evolving landscape of data protection, privacy, and risk management. These trends reflect the growing need for advanced technologies and global collaboration to ensure organizations remain secure and compliant in the face of new challenges:

- **Zero Trust integration**: Security standards are increasingly adopting **Zero Trust principles**, emphasizing identity-first security, micro-segmentation, and continuous monitoring to mitigate modern threats.

- **AI-driven compliance**: AI enhances risk management by automating compliance checks, detecting anomalies, and prioritizing remediation efforts. Platforms like *Microsoft Sentinel* and *Splunk* lead in leveraging AI for compliance.

- **Cross-border data harmonization**: As regulations like GDPR, DPDP, and China's **Personal Information Protection Law** (**PIPL**) evolve, frameworks are focusing on simplifying compliance for global operations through unified standards and interoperable tools.

- **Quantum-resilient standards**: Post-quantum cryptography is becoming a focus area as organizations prepare for the potential risks posed by quantum computing. Standards like NIST's quantum-resilient cryptographic algorithms are emerging as a safeguard.

AI ethics and governance principles

As AI continues to shape industries and societies, its development and deployment bring significant ethical considerations. AI systems influence critical decisions across sectors such as healthcare, finance, education, and governance, making it essential to ensure that these systems operate responsibly. Without clear ethical guidelines and governance principles, AI risks amplifying biases, eroding privacy, and creating unintended consequences.

AI Ethics and Governance Principles provide a structured framework to align AI innovation with human values, emphasizing fairness, transparency, accountability, inclusivity, privacy, and safety. By adhering to these principles, organizations can foster trust, mitigate risks, and maximize AI's societal benefits.

Core principles of AI ethics and governance

The following core principles of AI ethics and governance are essential for ensuring responsible AI development and deployment:

- **Fairness**: AI systems should treat all individuals equitably, avoiding biases that disproportionately disadvantage specific groups. Ensuring fairness requires diverse training datasets, pre-processing techniques to remove biases, and ongoing monitoring. Tools like *Microsoft's Fairlearn, IBM's AI Fairness 360*, and *Google's What-If Tool* assist organizations in detecting and mitigating biases.

- **Transparency**: AI systems must operate transparently, providing clear explanations of how decisions are made. This includes both technical interpretability and accessible communication of AI behavior to stakeholders. Techniques such as **Local Interpretable Model-Agnostic Explanations (LIME), SHapley Additive exPlanations (SHAP)**, and **Microsoft's InterpretML** are widely used to enhance AI transparency.

- **Accountability**: Organizations are responsible for the decisions and outcomes of their AI systems. Accountability requires defining governance structures, assigning roles for oversight, and addressing failures proactively. Governance frameworks like *Microsoft's Responsible AI Standard* and *Google's AI Principles* provide actionable guidelines for organizations to uphold accountability.

- **Privacy and data protection**: AI systems must handle data securely and comply with privacy regulations like *GDPR, HIPAA*, and *India's Digital Personal Data Protection (DPDP) Act*. PETs such as homomorphic encryption, federated learning, and differential privacy ensure that AI systems can protect sensitive data while maintaining usability.

- **Safety and security**: AI systems should function reliably under varying conditions and be resilient against adversarial attacks. Robust testing, secure development practices, and tools like *Microsoft Azure Security Center for AI* and *AWS AI Security Services* are critical for ensuring safety.

- **Inclusivity**: AI must be designed to serve diverse populations, addressing varying needs and ensuring accessibility. Examples include Microsoft's **Seeing AI** for the visually impaired and **Azure Speech Services** for those with hearing impairments.

- **Sustainability**: AI systems must minimize environmental impact, especially in resource-intensive processes like training large models. Efforts to optimize energy usage and leverage carbon-neutral infrastructure are essential for sustainable AI.

AI governance frameworks

The following AI governance frameworks are key to ensuring ethical and responsible AI development and deployment:

- **Global initiatives**: Ethical AI principles are shaped by organizations like the **OECD, European Commission**, and **World Economic Forum**, which emphasize transparency, accountability, and human-centric AI. These frameworks set global benchmarks for ethical AI development.

- **Microsoft responsible AI framework**: Microsoft's Responsible AI standard is a comprehensive guide for developing and deploying ethical AI. It operationalizes principles such as fairness, transparency, and accountability through tools like the **Responsible AI Dashboard, Fairlearn**, and **InterpretML**.

- **Google AI principles**: Google's AI principles emphasize avoiding harm, upholding accountability, and prioritizing social benefit. These principles guide the development of AI across critical domains, including healthcare and finance.

- **ISO/IEC AI governance standards**: The **ISO/IEC 42001 series** provides emerging standards for AI risk management and governance, helping organizations align with international guidelines for responsible AI.

Implementing AI ethics and governance

The following are the key steps for implementing AI ethics and governance: These steps ensure that AI systems are developed, deployed, and monitored with a focus on transparency, fairness, and accountability:

- **Establishing governance structures**: Organizations must define clear governance models, including AI ethics committees and roles like *Chief AI Ethics Officer*, to oversee ethical AI practices. Regular audits and ethical reviews are essential for high-impact AI applications.

- **Operationalizing ethical principles**: Ethical principles must be integrated into workflows using tools like *Azure Responsible AI Toolkits, DataRobot AI Explainability*, and *H2O.ai*. These tools automate tasks such as fairness checks, bias detection, and explainability testing.

- **Continuous monitoring and auditing**: AI systems require ongoing evaluation to detect performance drift, bias, or unintended consequences. Tools like *IBM Watson OpenScale* and *Microsoft Sentinel* provide real-time monitoring and insights to ensure AI aligns with ethical principles.

- **Compliance with regional regulations**: Organizations must adhere to regional laws governing AI. For example, the **EU Artificial Intelligence Act** emphasizes transparency and accountability for high-risk AI applications, while India's **AI for All** initiative promotes inclusivity.

- **Stakeholder engagement**: Engaging a diverse set of stakeholders—developers, policymakers, ethicists, and affected communities ensures AI systems address societal needs and concerns effectively.

AI ethics and governance maturity

For organizations building AI-enabled products and services that are globally accessible to thousands or even millions of people, ensuring ethical AI development and governance is not just a compliance requirement but a critical responsibility. This is especially vital for companies operating in domains such as healthcare, finance, education, and public services, where AI directly impacts human lives and decision-making. For example, a healthcare platform powered by AI-driven diagnostics, a financial service offering credit-scoring algorithms, or a global tech firm releasing generative AI tools like chatbots or content creators must adopt a structured approach to AI ethics. These companies face high stakes, as ethical lapses in AI could lead to significant regulatory penalties, loss of trust, or unintended societal harm. To build trust, reduce risks, and scale responsibly, such organizations need a phased roadmap to embed ethical AI practices into their operations.

The following section is a phase-wise approach to AI ethics and governance maturity:

- **Awareness and foundation building**: The journey begins by creating organizational awareness of the importance of AI ethics and governance. Companies need to educate leadership, developers, and key stakeholders about the potential risks of unethical AI, such as biases in algorithms, privacy violations, or security vulnerabilities. This can be achieved through internal workshops, industry discussions, and case studies highlighting ethical challenges faced by peers.

  Once awareness is established, the organization should define its core ethical principles, drawing inspiration from global frameworks like *Microsoft's Responsible AI Standard* or *Google's AI Principles*. These principles, such as fairness, transparency, accountability, inclusivity, privacy, and safety, must be adapted to the organization's unique context. Establishing governance structures, such as forming an AI Ethics Committee or designating a Chief AI Ethics Officer, is a critical step in laying the foundation. The organization should also conduct an initial audit of existing AI systems to identify risks, gaps, and alignment with ethical principles. These foundational efforts ensure that ethical considerations are integrated into strategic discussions and decision-making.

- **Operationalizing ethical AI practices**: In this phase, companies move from conceptual understanding to practical implementation. Operationalizing AI ethics involves embedding ethical principles into the workflows of AI development and deployment. Developers and data scientists must integrate fairness and bias checks into their workflows using tools like *Microsoft's Fairlearn* or *SHAP*. PETs, such as differential privacy and federated learning, become essential to ensure data protection while maintaining the utility of AI models.

Automation plays a pivotal role in ensuring scalability. Organizations can use tools like Azure's Responsible AI Dashboard or IBM Watson OpenScale to automate ethical oversight, including real-time monitoring of AI bias, model performance, and compliance. This phase also requires clear communication mechanisms to enhance transparency. Creating explainability reports for AI models and developing dashboards that convey complex AI behavior in simple terms ensures stakeholders can understand how AI systems make decisions and where risks might arise.

- **Scaling governance and ensuring continuous improvement**: As organizations scale their AI operations, governance structures must evolve to manage the increased complexity. The AI ethics committee can be expanded to include external advisors, regulators, and community representatives to provide a diverse perspective on ethical challenges. Continuous monitoring becomes essential to ensure AI systems remain aligned with ethical principles even as they are updated or scaled. Tools like *Microsoft Sentinel* and *Google Cloud AI Platform Monitoring* enable real-time anomaly detection and performance tracking.

  In addition to monitoring, organizations must develop AI incident response capabilities to handle ethical breaches or failures effectively. Simulating ethical incidents and testing response frameworks can help refine protocols. Collaboration with industry groups, such as the partnership on AI or regional initiatives like India's AI for all, fosters a collective approach to addressing ethical challenges while keeping the organization aligned with global best practices.

- **Industry leadership and advanced governance**: In the final phase, organizations mature into industry leaders in AI ethics by setting benchmarks and influencing global standards. They can publish white papers, case studies, and research that share their journey and best practices, establishing thought leadership. Advocacy efforts, such as participating in shaping international standards like *ISO/IEC AI* frameworks or regional regulations like the *EU AI Act*, further enhance their credibility.

  This phase also involves adopting advanced technologies to address emerging risks. Federated governance models become critical for multinational organizations operating under diverse legal jurisdictions. Emerging technologies like *SMPC* or *Zero-Knowledge Proofs (ZKP)* can address complex ethical challenges. Sustainability becomes a key focus, with organizations optimizing the energy usage of AI systems to minimize their carbon footprint. By addressing these advanced challenges, companies are pioneers in building ethical, inclusive, and sustainable AI systems.

Emerging trends in AI ethics and governance

The following highlights key emerging trends in AI ethics and governance, showcasing how organizations are evolving their approaches to address ethical considerations, security concerns, and sustainability in AI.

These trends reflect the growing complexity of AI systems and the need for robust frameworks to ensure responsible, secure, and environmentally conscious AI development and deployment, as follows:

- **Responsible AI Operations (RAIO)**: RAIO focuses on embedding ethical principles throughout the AI lifecycle, from design to deployment, using automated tools for monitoring and governance.

- **Federated governance models**: As organizations collaborate across borders, federated governance models enable consistent ethical practices while respecting regional legal requirements.

- **Explainability for complex models**: With advancements in models like *GPT-4* and *BERT*, tools for explainability are evolving to make even black-box AI systems interpretable.

- **AI and climate ethics**: Governance frameworks are increasingly addressing the environmental impact of AI, emphasizing sustainable practices in model training and deployment.

- **Zero Trust AI security**: AI governance intersects with security frameworks, emphasizing secure model access, adversarial resilience, and robust data protection.

Lessons from Microsoft's Responsible AI principles

Microsoft's Responsible AI principles provide a robust foundation for building ethical AI systems by offering actionable insights that bridge principles with practice. A key focus of these principles is **operationalizing fairness**, ensuring AI systems avoid perpetuating bias and treat all users equitably. Tools like *Fairlearn*, integrated into Microsoft's Responsible AI ecosystem, help developers detect and mitigate biases throughout the AI lifecycle. This proactive approach ensures models remain fair and equitable, even as data evolves.

Transparency is another cornerstone of Microsoft's Responsible AI initiative. By leveraging tools such as the **Responsible AI Dashboard**, organizations can enhance model explainability, making AI systems more understandable to both technical and non-technical stakeholders. These dashboards simplify the communication of complex decision-making processes, enabling stakeholders to trust AI-driven outcomes while understanding their limitations.

Accountability is deeply embedded in Microsoft's governance framework. The organization emphasizes clear accountability structures, including **mandatory ethical reviews** for high-impact AI systems and defined roles for monitoring and oversight. These practices ensure that AI deployments align with organizational values and societal expectations, minimizing risks and promoting responsibility across teams.

Privacy is a central focus of Microsoft's Responsible AI and **Secure Future** initiatives. By embedding **PETs**, such as differential privacy, federated learning, and homomorphic encryption, Microsoft ensures that AI workflows safeguard sensitive data while complying with global regulations like **GDPR** and India's **Digital Personal Data Protection (DPDP) Act**. These technologies enable organizations to harness data for AI without compromising user confidentiality.

Inclusivity is another pillar of Microsoft's ethical AI efforts, demonstrated through applications like *Seeing AI*, which enhances accessibility for visually impaired individuals. By designing AI solutions with diverse user needs in mind, Microsoft highlights the potential of inclusive AI to create meaningful societal impact. Through its responsible AI and secure future initiatives, Microsoft sets a global standard for ethical AI, empowering organizations to innovate responsibly while aligning with regulatory and societal expectations.

Emerging trends in security, privacy, and ethics

As organizations continue to innovate and deploy advanced technologies, several emerging trends are reshaping the landscape of security, privacy, and ethics. These trends focus on bridging the gap between powerful technologies and the need for responsible governance, security, and data privacy.

The following are three key developments that demand attention in the context of modern security and ethics:

- **AI explainability and interpretability**: The demand for **explainable AI (XAI)** is growing, particularly in industries such as healthcare, finance, and law, where AI-driven decisions directly impact human lives. With AI systems becoming more complex, stakeholders, including regulators, users, and affected communities, are increasingly calling for transparency in how AI systems make decisions. Tools such as **Local Interpretable Model-agnostic Explanations (LIME)** and **SHapley Additive exPlanations (SHAP)** have emerged to help explain the inner workings of black-box AI models, ensuring that decision-making processes are understandable and justifiable. To build trust and comply with regulations like GDPR, organizations must prioritize making AI systems interpretable and provide clear, understandable explanations for automated decisions.

- **AI for cybersecurity**: As cyber threats become more sophisticated, **AI for cybersecurity** is emerging as a vital tool to enhance threat detection and response. AI-driven solutions are being leveraged to detect **advanced persistent threats**

(APT), **phishing attempts, and zero-day vulnerabilities**, all of which pose significant risks to organizational data and operations. By using machine learning algorithms to analyze vast amounts of network traffic and user behavior data, AI systems can proactively identify anomalies and alert security teams in real-time. Tools like *Microsoft Sentinel* and *Darktrace* help automate incident responses and speed up threat remediation.

- **Quantum computing and security**: The advent of quantum computing poses a new frontier in the world of encryption and data security. While quantum computing has the potential to revolutionize industries like medicine and logistics, it also threatens the existing cryptographic methods that underpin modern security protocols. Quantum computers can break widely used encryption algorithms, such as RSA and ECC, which rely on the computational difficulty of certain mathematical problems. As a result, the development of *quantum-resistant cryptography* is becoming essential for organizations to prepare for a post-quantum world. Standards such as *NIST's quantum-resistant algorithms* are already being developed to ensure the security of sensitive data against future quantum-enabled threats. Preparing for quantum computing involves both investing in quantum-safe encryption solutions and ensuring data privacy for a new generation of threats.

Conclusion

In this chapter, we explored the critical aspects of AI ethics and governance principles, emphasizing their importance in ensuring responsible AI development and deployment. From understanding core principles such as fairness, transparency, accountability, privacy, inclusivity, and safety to implementing governance frameworks like Microsoft's Responsible AI standard and global initiatives from OECD and ISO, this chapter provided a comprehensive guide for organizations navigating the ethical complexities of AI. We outlined a practical, phase-wise approach for building AI ethics maturity, incorporating foundational steps, operationalizing ethical practices, scaling governance, and addressing advanced challenges. Drawing from initiatives like Microsoft's Responsible AI and Secure Future frameworks, we demonstrated how tools, technologies, and governance models can enable organizations to align AI innovation with societal values. As AI continues to shape industries and societies, embedding ethical principles into AI systems is not just a best practice—it is an imperative for creating trusted, inclusive, and sustainable solutions that benefit humanity.

In the next chapter, we will discuss emerging trends and cutting-edge innovations that are redefining the digital landscape. *Chapter 13* takes readers on a comprehensive journey through transformative technologies such as multi-cloud and hybrid architectures, IoT, edge computing, and advanced paradigms like **high-performance computing (HPC)**, GPU-based architectures, quantum computing, blockchain, and sustainable computing. Alongside these topics, we will explore detailed reference architectures and industry-leading solutions from pioneers like Red Hat, VMware, SAP, Oracle, Citrix, NetApp, and Nutanix, offering readers actionable insights into the modernization of enterprise environments. This chapter provides a holistic understanding of how these innovations converge to drive agility, scalability, and sustainability in organizations worldwide.

Key terms

- **AI ethics**: The set of principles and practices that ensure artificial intelligence systems are designed and deployed responsibly, with fairness, transparency, accountability, and inclusivity as core pillars.

- **Governance frameworks**: Structured guidelines and mechanisms, such as Microsoft's Responsible AI Standard or ISO/IEC standards, used to oversee and ensure ethical AI practices throughout the AI lifecycle.

- **Fairness in AI**: The principle of ensuring that AI systems provide equitable outcomes, avoiding biases that could disproportionately disadvantage certain individuals or groups.

- **Transparency**: The ability to explain and communicate how AI systems make decisions, enabling trust and understanding among stakeholders through tools like dashboards and interpretable models.

- **Privacy-enhancing technologies (PETs)**: Techniques such as homomorphic encryption, differential privacy, and federated learning that enable secure data usage while safeguarding sensitive information.

- **Accountability**: The responsibility of organizations to monitor, evaluate, and address the impacts of their AI systems, including the establishment of ethical review boards and response frameworks.

- **Sustainability in AI**: Practices and technologies aimed at minimizing the environmental impact of AI systems, such as optimizing energy usage and adopting carbon-neutral infrastructure.

- **Responsible AI dashboard**: A Microsoft toolkit that provides developers with tools to monitor and mitigate issues like bias, transparency gaps, and performance drift in AI systems.

- **Zero-Trust security for AI**: A security framework that ensures AI systems are protected from unauthorized access and adversarial attacks through strict identity verification and continuous monitoring.

- **Inclusive AI**: AI solutions designed to cater to diverse user needs, ensuring accessibility and fairness for all, as demonstrated by tools like Microsoft's Seeing AI.

CHAPTER 13

Innovation and Future Technologies

Introduction

This chapter will cover the transformative technologies driving the future of enterprise IT, offering a detailed exploration of multi-cloud and hybrid architectures, IoT and edge computing, **high performance computing** (**HPC**), GPU-based architectures, quantum computing frameworks, blockchain platforms, and sustainable computing practices. These innovations are reshaping how businesses operate by enabling greater flexibility, scalability, and efficiency while addressing critical challenges in security, data processing, and environmental impact. The readers will learn how these technologies are being applied across industries, from real-time decision-making at the edge to decentralized solutions powered by blockchain. By combining practical insights with emerging trends, this chapter equips readers with the knowledge to leverage these technologies for driving modernization and innovation in the digital enterprise.

Structure

The chapter covers the following topics:

- Multi-cloud and hybrid architectures
- Internet of Things and edge computing
- High performance computing and GPU-based architectures

- Quantum computing
- Blockchain platforms and decentralized technologies
- Sustainable computing
- Bioinformatics progress with generative AI
- Robotics progress with generative AI

Objectives

By the end of this chapter, readers will have a comprehensive understanding of the transformative technologies reshaping enterprise IT. They will explore how multi-cloud and hybrid architectures provide flexibility and resilience, enabling seamless integration across diverse environments. The chapter delves into the role of IoT and edge computing in delivering real-time intelligence and smarter systems across industries, alongside the power of HPC and GPU-based architectures in accelerating complex workloads and driving breakthroughs in AI and analytics. Readers will also gain insights into the potential of quantum computing to solve previously unsolvable challenges and the evolution of blockchain platforms in creating secure, decentralized systems beyond cryptocurrencies. Furthermore, the chapter emphasizes the principles of sustainable computing, highlighting eco-friendly IT practices, energy efficiency, and technologies like digital twins and federated learning. Collectively, these topics equip readers to embrace innovation, drive modernization, and align with the transformative potential of these technologies in a rapidly evolving digital landscape.

Multi-cloud and hybrid architectures

The rise of multi-cloud and hybrid architectures marks a significant shift in enterprise IT strategy, offering organizations the flexibility to optimize their workloads across diverse environments. These architectures provide a unified approach to leveraging the strengths of multiple public cloud providers, private clouds, and on-premises infrastructure, enabling businesses to balance cost, performance, scalability, and compliance. As businesses continue to scale and innovate, multi-cloud and hybrid strategies have become foundational for addressing the complexities of modern IT landscapes.

At their core, multi-cloud architectures involve deploying applications and services across multiple public cloud providers such as AWS, Microsoft Azure, and Google Cloud. This approach minimizes dependency on a single vendor, reducing risks and allowing access to best-in-class features from each provider. For instance, a financial services firm might use AWS for scalable computing, Azure for its robust AI and data capabilities, and Google Cloud for advanced machine learning. However, managing such environments requires seamless orchestration, interoperability, and workload portability. Tools such as *Terraform*, *Kubernetes*, and *HashiCorp Consul* play a critical role in achieving consistent deployment, networking, and policy enforcement across cloud providers.

Hybrid architectures, on the other hand, integrate public and private clouds with on-premises infrastructure to create a cohesive ecosystem. This model is particularly relevant for organizations with stringent regulatory requirements, such as those in healthcare, finance, or government sectors, where sensitive data must remain on-premises while other workloads benefit from the scalability of the public cloud. Microsoft's Azure Arc and VMware's vSphere with Tanzu exemplify solutions that bridge these environments, enabling centralized management and consistent operations across hybrid setups.

A critical component of multi-cloud and hybrid environments is network connectivity, which ensures that applications can span geographically dispersed environments without performance degradation. Technologies like **software-defined wide area networking (SD-WAN)** and cloud interconnect solutions such as *AWS Direct Connect, Azure ExpressRoute,* and *Google Cloud Interconnect* are vital for maintaining low-latency, high-throughput connections between environments. Security in such setups is also paramount, with **identity and access management (IAM)** frameworks like *Azure Active Directory, Okta,* and *Ping Identity* providing centralized control over user access across multiple platforms.

Workload portability is a key enabler of flexibility in these architectures. Containers and microservices, orchestrated by tools like *Kubernetes*, allow workloads to move seamlessly between environments while maintaining performance and scalability. Managed Kubernetes services, including **Azure Kubernetes Service (AKS)**, **Amazon Elastic Kubernetes Service (EKS)**, and **Google Kubernetes Engine (GKE)**, simplify container orchestration and deployment across clouds. Emerging trends in serverless computing, such as *AWS Lambda, Azure Functions,* and *Google Cloud Functions*, are further transforming workload portability by offering lightweight, event-driven compute options that are inherently cloud-agnostic.

Managing data in multi-cloud and hybrid setups presents unique challenges, as it is often distributed across various environments. Data management solutions like *NetApp Cloud Volumes, Azure Data Share,* and *Google BigQuery Omni* enable secure and efficient data sharing while ensuring compliance with privacy regulations. Distributed databases such as *CockroachDB, Cassandra,* and *Amazon Aurora Global Database* are instrumental in maintaining consistency and high availability across geographically dispersed environments. Data synchronization, particularly in transactional systems, is critical, and advancements in event-driven architectures using tools like *Kafka* or *Azure Event Grid* are streamlining this process.

Governance and compliance are integral to the success of multi-cloud and hybrid strategies. Organizations must enforce policies across diverse environments without compromising visibility or control. Solutions like *Azure Policy, Open Policy Agent (OPA),* and *AWS Config* automate the enforcement of security, compliance, and operational standards. These policy-as-code frameworks ensure that workloads adhere to organizational and regulatory requirements, even as they scale across multiple environments.

Observability and automation are vital for managing these complex environments effectively. Observability platforms like *Datadog, Splunk,* and *Azure Monitor* provide insights into system performance, application dependencies, and potential bottlenecks. Meanwhile, infrastructure-as-code tools like *Terraform* and *Pulumi* enable automated provisioning and consistent deployment of resources across multi-cloud and hybrid setups. Combined, these capabilities help organizations manage the increasing complexity of their IT environments with agility and confidence.

An emerging trend in multi-cloud and hybrid architectures is the integration of AI and machine learning to optimize operations. AI-driven tools like *Google Cloud's AI Operations* (*AIOps*) and *Azure Machine Learning* analyze workload patterns to recommend optimal placement strategies, improve resource utilization, and reduce latency. Predictive scaling technologies are also being adopted, leveraging AI to forecast demand and scale resources dynamically. Additionally, edge computing is increasingly becoming a part of hybrid strategies, enabling localized data processing and reducing the dependency on centralized cloud infrastructure. Solutions like *AWS Outposts, Azure Stack,* and *Google Anthos* demonstrate how edge and hybrid capabilities work together to deliver real-time insights and enhanced performance.

Another critical advancement is the rise of federated learning frameworks, which allow AI models to be trained across decentralized datasets without compromising data privacy. This approach is particularly beneficial for industries like healthcare and finance, where data sensitivity is paramount. Federated learning, combined with secure multi-cloud architectures, enables organizations to harness the power of distributed data while ensuring regulatory compliance.

Finally, sustainability is gaining importance in multi-cloud and hybrid architectures. Energy-efficient designs, such as optimized data center cooling and renewable energy sources, are becoming standard in cloud operations. Cloud providers like *AWS, Azure,* and *Google Cloud* have made significant commitments to carbon-neutral or carbon-negative operations, and organizations are increasingly aligning their architectures with these sustainability goals. Technologies like **digital twins** further enhance resource optimization by creating virtual replicas of physical assets, enabling predictive maintenance and reducing waste.

Multi-cloud and hybrid architectures are foundational to modern enterprise IT, offering flexibility, scalability, and resilience. The convergence of advancements in AI, edge computing, federated learning, and sustainability further underscores the transformative potential of these strategies, positioning organizations to thrive in an increasingly interconnected and dynamic digital landscape.

Internet of Things and edge computing

The convergence of the **Internet of Things** (**IoT**) and edge computing is revolutionizing data generation, processing, and utilization, enabling real-time decision-making, localized intelligence, and enhanced operational efficiency. This transformation is evident across industries such as healthcare, manufacturing, transportation, retail, and agriculture, where smarter and more connected ecosystems are emerging.

IoT connects a diverse range of physical devices, sensors, actuators, and smart appliances that generate vast amounts of data. These devices communicate over the internet or local networks, seamlessly integrating the physical and digital worlds. However, as IoT networks expand, traditional centralized cloud architectures face challenges, including latency, bandwidth limitations, and data privacy concerns. **Edge computing** addresses these issues by processing data closer to its source, reducing reliance on centralized data centers, and enabling near-instantaneous responses. For example, autonomous vehicles utilize edge computing to process sensor data locally for real-time decision-making, while non-critical data is transmitted to the cloud for further analysis and optimization.

Recent advancements in **small language models (SLMs)**, such as *Microsoft's Phi-3*, are bringing the power of AI foundational models to edge devices. Unlike larger models that require extensive computational resources, SLMs are optimized for efficiency, allowing them to operate on resource-constrained hardware without compromising performance. This development opens new possibilities for IoT and edge systems, enabling devices to perform complex tasks like natural language understanding, anomaly detection, and decision-making directly at the edge. For instance, an industrial IoT system equipped with an SLM like *Phi-3* can process maintenance logs and sensor data locally, identifying potential failures without relying on cloud-based inference.

The deployment of advanced AI models at the edge has been further accelerated by *NVIDIA Jetson Orin Nano Super Developer Kit*, introduced in December 2024. Priced at $249, this upgraded AI computer offers significant improvements in AI processing capabilities, delivering 70% higher neural processing power at 67 TOPS and a 50% increase in memory bandwidth at 102GB/s compared to its predecessor. These enhancements make it feasible to run complex AI models, including small foundational models like *Phi-3*, on edge devices, enabling applications such as real-time object detection, predictive maintenance, and edge-based generative AI.

Connectivity remains a cornerstone of IoT and edge computing ecosystems. Technologies like *5G*, *Wi-Fi 6*, and *Low Power Wide Area Networks* (*LPWAN*), such as *LoRaWAN* and *NB-IoT*, have been instrumental in enabling high-speed, low-latency communication between devices and edge nodes. These advancements are particularly critical for applications requiring real-time responsiveness, including telemedicine, autonomous vehicles, and industrial automation. Edge-enabled IoT devices, supported by these connectivity solutions, can process data locally while ensuring seamless communication with broader networks.

Security is a critical aspect of IoT and edge computing, given the distributed nature of these systems. **Zero Trust security models** are increasingly adopted to protect IoT ecosystems, implementing stringent identity verification and encryption protocols. Solutions like *Microsoft Azure Sphere*, *AWS IoT Device Defender*, and *Google Cloud IoT Core* offer comprehensive frameworks to safeguard devices, data, and networks from cyber threats, enabling secure deployment and operation of IoT systems in industries where data sensitivity is paramount.

The integration of AI and machine learning at the edge has been transformative for IoT systems, allowing devices to perform advanced analytics and inference locally. Hardware platforms like *NVIDIA Jetson Orin Nano Super Developer Kit*, *Google Coral*, and *Intel Movidius* provide the computational power necessary for edge-based AI applications. For example, retail stores utilize edge AI to analyze customer behavior in real-time, while drones equipped with edge AI monitor agricultural fields for pests or optimize irrigation strategies.

Additionally, **digital twin technologies** are emerging as vital complements to IoT and edge computing. Digital twins create virtual replicas of physical assets or systems, enabling real-time monitoring, simulation, and predictive maintenance. Tools like *Azure Digital Twins* allow organizations to gain actionable insights into their operations, improving efficiency and reducing downtime. For instance, a smart factory can use digital twins of its machinery to simulate production scenarios, predict failures, and optimize workflows.

The environmental impact of IoT and edge computing is also being addressed through sustainable practices. Energy-efficient IoT devices powered by renewable energy sources are becoming the norm, while edge computing reduces the energy required to transmit data to centralized cloud environments. The ability to deploy AI models like *Phi-3* locally further minimizes energy consumption, as smaller models require fewer computational resources compared to traditional cloud-based systems.

WebAssembly for edge computing

As we move beyond traditional cloud-native patterns, **WebAssembly (Wasm)** is emerging as one of the most promising runtimes for the next generation of distributed applications.

Today, most modern apps run in containers, orchestrated by Kubernetes and often extended with DAPR for service discovery and communication. This is where most of us are right now, as illustrated in the middle of the cloud-native progression diagram below. But if you look further right, you will notice a shift in architecture. The application logic is compiled into bytecode, sitting above serverless containers and adaptive networking. This is where WebAssembly comes in.

In the below architecture diagram, this evolution is shown clearly from data center monoliths to virtual machines, then containers, and now bytecode-based execution with Wasm and DAPR running on serverless container fabrics across cloud and edge nodes. This marks the beginning of true compute portability, untethered from specific OSes or providers, as shown:

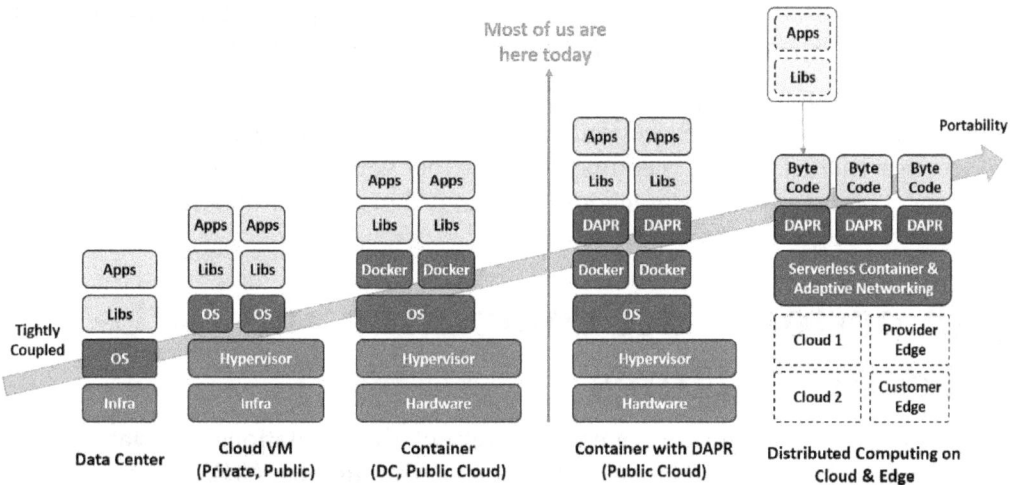

Image: Cloud Native Progression and Hypothesis of Future Architetcure| Created By: Bikramjit Debnath

Figure 13.1: *cloud-native progression and emergence of Web Assembly*

Originally built for the browser, Wasm has grown up. It now offers a lightweight, portable, and secure runtime for cloud and edge workloads. Unlike containers, which are often hundreds of megabytes in size and take seconds to start, Wasm modules are just a few megabytes and can cold-start in under 10 milliseconds. That makes them ideal for on-demand, serverless, or edge-based scenarios where speed, scale, and resource efficiency matter.

Imagine deploying logic to the edge for a payment validator or an AI model running right where the data is generated. Instead of shipping a full container image, you send a small Wasm module, already sandboxed, fast to boot, and portable across cloud and edge providers. This gives developers and architects a new level of flexibility and unlocks use cases that were previously difficult to support.

Wasm ecosystem is maturing

While Wasm is still early in its server-side journey, the ecosystem is gaining serious traction. Some important developments include:

- **WebAssembly System Interface (WASI)**: Standard APIs that allow Wasm to talk to the host system (files, network, etc.).

- **Wasmtime, Spin, wasmCloud**: Lightweight runtimes to execute Wasm outside the browser, in server-side and edge contexts.

- **Cloudflare Workers, Fermyon, Fastly Compute**: Platforms offering production-ready, low-latency Wasm hosting.

- **Krustlet**: A Kubernetes kubelet implementation that lets you run Wasm workloads natively in your cluster.

These tools form the foundation of a Wasm-native development model, enabling fast, secure, and language-agnostic deployments across cloud and edge environments.

WebAssembly would not replace containers overnight. But it is increasingly being used alongside them for plugin execution, sandboxed workloads, extensibility layers, and edge services. In the future, it is entirely possible that your core services run in containers while your customer-facing interactions, real-time AI models, or data filters run as Wasm modules at the edge.

High performance computing and GPU-based architectures

HPC and GPU-based architectures are at the forefront of computational innovation, driving advancements across scientific research, **artificial intelligence** (**AI**), and complex data analysis. Recent developments in this domain have significantly enhanced computational capabilities, enabling more efficient and powerful processing solutions.

NVIDIA's *Hopper architecture*, introduced with the H100 GPU, represents a significant leap in accelerated computing. The H100 integrates 80 billion transistors and is designed to handle demanding HPC and AI workloads. It features advancements such as the Transformer Engine, which accelerates AI model training and inference and supports the FP8 data format, enhancing performance for AI applications.

Complementing the Hopper architecture, NVIDIA's *Grace Hopper Superchip* combines the Arm-based Grace CPU with the Hopper GPU, connected via the high-speed NVLink-C2C interconnect. This integration facilitates efficient data sharing between the CPU and GPU, optimizing performance for large-scale HPC and AI applications. The Grace Hopper Superchip is being adopted in numerous AI supercomputers worldwide, collectively delivering substantial AI processing power to drive scientific innovation.

AMD has made significant strides with its *Instinct MI300 series* accelerators, designed to deliver exceptional performance for AI and HPC workloads. The *MI300A* combines *Zen 4 CPU cores* and *CDNA 3 GPU cores* into a single package, providing a unified platform for diverse computational tasks. The *MI300X*, focusing on generative AI applications, offers up to 192 GB of HBM3 memory, facilitating the training of LLMs and complex simulations. These accelerators are supported by AMD's *ROCm™ 6.3* open software platform, which includes optimized libraries and tools to enhance AI and HPC workflows.

In addition to hardware advancements, the development of AI-specific hardware within GPUs is pushing the boundaries of artificial intelligence. This trend emphasizes the integration of AI accelerators and specialized cores within GPU architectures to enhance AI processing capabilities.

The integration of quantum computing with GPUs is another emerging trend. In quantum-classical hybrid systems, GPUs can be utilized for preprocessing and postprocessing data, while **quantum processing units** (**QPUs**) execute quantum algorithms. This synergy is expected to be beneficial for tasks such as cryptography, drug discovery, and materials science, where quantum speeds can be crucial.

Energy efficiency remains a critical focus in GPU development. Manufacturers are striving to enhance performance-per-watt ratios, ensuring that increased computational power does not lead to proportional rises in energy consumption. This emphasis on energy efficiency is vital for sustainable computing practices.

The evolution of software ecosystems is also pivotal in maximizing the potential of GPU-based architectures. Comprehensive software stacks, such as *NVIDIA's HPC SDK*, provide developers with the tools necessary to create and optimize GPU-accelerated applications using standard languages and directives. This flexibility facilitates the adoption of GPU acceleration across a wide range of HPC applications.

The landscape of HPC and GPU-based architectures is rapidly evolving, with innovations that enhance computational capabilities, energy efficiency, and integration with emerging technologies like AI and quantum computing. These advancements are poised to drive the next generation of computational solutions, enabling breakthroughs across various scientific and industrial domains.

Quantum computing

Quantum computing represents a paradigm shift in computational technology, leveraging the principles of quantum mechanics to process information in fundamentally new ways. Unlike classical computers that use bits as the smallest unit of data, represented as either 0 or 1, quantum computers utilize quantum bits, or qubits, which can exist simultaneously in multiple states through a property known as superposition. This enables quantum computers to perform complex calculations more efficiently than their classical counterparts.

Classical vs. quantum computing

Classical computers process information using binary bits. All computations are ultimately built from deterministic logic gates acting on these bits in a sequential or parallel fashion. Their performance scales linearly or polynomially with the number of operations required.

Quantum computers, in contrast, use **qubits**, which can exist in a superposition of 0 and 1 states simultaneously. When combined with entanglement and quantum interference, this allows quantum systems to explore an exponentially large solution space in parallel.

For example:

- A classical computer requires 2^n operations to search an unsorted database of size n, while a quantum computer using **Grover's algorithm** can do it in $\sqrt{n}$ operations.

- Shor's algorithm allows a quantum computer to factor a 2048-bit integer, commonly used in RSA encryption, in polynomial time, which would take even the best classical supercomputers billions of years.

Computational capacity

A system with *n qubits* can theoretically represent 2^n quantum states simultaneously. For instance:

- **30 qubits** ≈ the state space of a classical computer with over 1 billion variables.

- **300 qubits** ≈ more classical states than atoms in the observable universe.

Application domains

Quantum computing is especially promising in the following domains:

- **Drug discovery and chemistry**: Simulating molecular interactions and quantum chemistry problems that are intractable for classical systems.

- **Optimization**: Solving NP-hard problems in logistics, finance, and supply chain using hybrid quantum-classical algorithms like QAOA.

- **Material science**: Discovering new materials with specific properties by simulating atomic behavior.

- **Machine learning**: Accelerating certain linear algebra subroutines, kernel methods, and probabilistic inference using quantum-enhanced techniques.

- **Cryptography**: Breaking widely used public key cryptosystems (e.g., RSA) using Shor's algorithm.

Quantum computing is not a general-purpose replacement for classical computing but a specialized tool that can outperform classical systems in problem domains with high-dimensional state spaces and complex probability distributions.

Qubit implementation and architectures

Qubits can be realized through various physical systems, each with unique advantages and challenges:

- **Superconducting qubits**: Employed by companies like *IBM* and *Google*, these qubits are fabricated using superconducting circuits that operate at cryogenic temperatures to minimize decoherence and quantum noise. Recent advancements include *Google Willow Chip*, which has demonstrated significant improvements in error correction and qubit stability, maintaining quantum states for nearly 100 microseconds.

- **Trapped ion qubits**: Utilized by organizations such as *IonQ*, this approach traps individual ions using electromagnetic fields, with quantum information encoded in their electronic states. Trapped ion systems benefit from long coherence times and high-fidelity gate operations.

- **Topological qubits**: Still largely theoretical until recently, this method aims to encode qubits in topological states of matter, potentially offering inherent protection against certain types of errors and thereby enhancing fault tolerance.

In a significant breakthrough, Microsoft announced that it has successfully achieved the first experimental evidence of Majorana zero modes, a key building block for creating stable topological qubits. Majorana-based qubits promise long coherence times and natural error resistance, potentially enabling scalable quantum computing architectures with fewer physical qubits.

Quantum gates and circuits

Quantum computations are executed through quantum gates, which manipulate qubits by altering their probability amplitudes. These gates are analogous to classical logic gates but operate on the principles of quantum mechanics, enabling operations like superposition and entanglement. A sequence of quantum gates forms a quantum circuit, capable of performing complex computations. Universal gate sets, such as the combination of single-qubit rotations and two-qubit entangling gates (e.g., CNOT gates), are sufficient to construct any quantum algorithm.

Quantum error correction

A significant challenge in quantum computing is decoherence, where qubits lose their quantum properties due to environmental interactions. To mitigate this, **quantum error correction (QEC)** schemes have been developed, encoding logical qubits into entangled states of multiple physical qubits to detect and correct errors without directly measuring the quantum information. Recent research by *Google* has demonstrated advances in QEC, showing that increasing the number of qubits can exponentially reduce error rates, a crucial step toward building scalable, fault-tolerant quantum computers.

Quantum algorithms

Quantum computers have the potential to outperform classical computers in specific tasks by utilizing algorithms that exploit quantum parallelism:

- **Shor's algorithm**: Efficiently factors large integers, posing implications for cryptographic systems that rely on the difficulty of such factorization.

- **Grover's algorithm**: Provides a quadratic speedup for unstructured search problems, offering advantages in database search applications.

- **Quantum Approximate Optimization Algorithm (QAOA)**: Designed for solving combinatorial optimization problems, with potential applications in logistics, finance, and machine learning.

Recent developments and future prospects

The field of quantum computing is rapidly evolving, with notable recent advancements:

- **Google's Willow Chip**: Achieved a benchmark computation in under five minutes that would take a current supercomputer 10 septillion years, demonstrating the potential for quantum supremacy in specific tasks.

- **Microsoft's Majorana milestone**: In a landmark achievement in 2025, Microsoft has experimentally confirmed the presence of Majorana zero modes, a foundational element for building topological qubits. This marks a key step toward developing fault-tolerant quantum computers with fewer error-correction overheads. Microsoft's long-term bet on topological qubits now appears closer to realization, potentially redefining quantum computing architecture and scalability.

- **IBM's quantum processors**: IBM has been developing quantum processors with increasing qubit counts and improved coherence times, contributing to the advancement of quantum hardware.

- **Quantum software development**: The emergence of quantum software platforms and programming languages is facilitating the development of quantum algorithms and applications, enabling researchers and developers to explore quantum solutions for complex problems.

Quantum computing is poised to revolutionize various fields by providing computational capabilities far beyond the reach of classical systems. Ongoing research and development in qubit architectures, error correction, and algorithm design continue to address existing challenges, bringing us closer to realizing the full potential of quantum technologies.

Blockchain platforms and decentralized technologies

Blockchain platforms and decentralized technologies have revolutionized the way data is managed, transactions are conducted, and trust is established in digital ecosystems. At their core, these systems eliminate the need for central authorities by distributing control across a network of participants, enhancing transparency, security, and resilience.

Blockchain architecture

A blockchain is a distributed ledger that records transactions across a network of computers, ensuring that once data is added, it becomes immutable and tamper-resistant. The primary components of blockchain architecture include:

- **Blocks**: Data structures that store a list of transactions. Each block contains a cryptographic hash of the previous block, linking them together to form a chain.

- **Nodes**: Individual computers that participate in the network, maintaining copies of the ledger and validating transactions. Nodes can be full (storing the entire blockchain) or lightweight (storing only a subset).

- **Consensus mechanisms**: Protocols that enable network participants to agree on the validity of transactions. Common mechanisms include **Proof of Work (PoW)**, **Proof of Stake (PoS)**, and **Byzantine Fault Tolerance (BFT)**.

- **Smart contracts**: Self-executing contracts with the terms directly written into code, allowing for automated and trustless transactions.

Types of blockchain networks

Blockchain networks can be categorized based on their access permissions:

- **Public blockchains**: Open to anyone; participants can read, write, and audit the blockchain. Examples include Bitcoin and Ethereum.

- **Private blockchains**: Restricted to a specific organization or group; access is controlled, and only authorized participants can interact.

- **Consortium blockchains**: Governed by a group of organizations, access and consensus processes are shared among the consortium members.

Decentralized applications

Decentralized applications (dApps) operate on blockchain networks, offering services without centralized control. The architecture of dApps typically includes:

- **Frontend interface**: User-facing component, often similar to traditional applications.

- **Smart contracts**: Backend logic running on the blockchain, handling application functionality and data management.

- **Decentralized storage**: Systems like the **InterPlanetary File System (IPFS)** are used to store application data in a distributed manner, ensuring data availability and resilience.

Design considerations for blockchain-based systems

When architecting blockchain solutions, several factors must be considered:

- **Scalability**: Ensuring the system can handle increased load. Techniques like sharding, off-chain transactions, and layer 2 solutions are employed to enhance scalability.

- **Security**: Implementing robust cryptographic methods and consensus algorithms to protect against attacks and ensure data integrity.

- **Interoperability**: Facilitating communication between different blockchain networks to enable seamless data and asset transfers.

- **Governance**: Establishing decision-making processes for protocol upgrades, dispute resolution, and policy enforcement within the network.

Emerging trends in decentralized technologies

The landscape of decentralized technologies is rapidly evolving, with several notable trends:

- **Decentralized finance (DeFi)**: Platforms offering financial services like lending, borrowing, and trading without intermediaries, built on blockchain networks.

- **Non-fungible tokens (NFTs)**: Unique digital assets representing ownership of specific items or content, enabling new models for digital ownership and monetization.

- **Decentralized autonomous organizations (DAOs)**: Organizations governed by smart contracts and community consensus, operating without centralized leadership.

- **Layer 2 solutions**: Protocols built on top of existing blockchains to improve scalability and transaction speeds, such as the *Lightning Network for Bitcoin* and *Optimistic Rollups for Ethereum*.

Challenges and future directions

Despite significant advancements, challenges remain in the adoption and implementation of blockchain and decentralized technologies:

- **Regulatory uncertainty**: Varying legal frameworks across jurisdictions can impact the deployment and operation of blockchain-based systems.

- **Energy consumption**: Some consensus mechanisms, notably Proof of Work, are energy-intensive, prompting a shift towards more sustainable alternatives like Proof of Stake.

- **User experience**: Improving the usability of decentralized applications to match the convenience of traditional centralized services is crucial for broader adoption.

Blockchain platforms and decentralized technologies offer transformative potential across various industries by enabling trustless, transparent, and efficient systems. Architecting these systems requires careful consideration of design principles, security measures, and scalability solutions to fully leverage their capabilities.

Sustainable computing

Sustainable computing focuses on designing and operating computing systems in ways that minimize environmental impact, emphasizing energy efficiency, resource conservation, and reduced carbon emissions. From an architectural and design perspective, this involves a comprehensive approach that addresses both the operational and embodied carbon footprints of computing infrastructure.

Operational carbon footprint

The operational carbon footprint pertains to the emissions resulting from the day-to-day functioning of computing systems. Key strategies to mitigate this include:

- **Energy-efficient hardware design**: Developing processors and components that deliver high performance per watt, thereby reducing energy consumption during operation. For instance, integrating low-power design techniques in multi-core architectures can significantly enhance energy efficiency.

- **Dynamic power management**: Implementing mechanisms that adjust power usage based on workload demands, such as *dynamic voltage and frequency scaling (DVFS)*, to optimize energy consumption during varying operational loads.

- **Efficient cooling solutions**: Designing advanced cooling systems, including liquid cooling and airflow optimization, to maintain optimal operating temperatures with minimal energy expenditure. Innovations like microfluidic cooling have been explored to enhance thermal management in high-performance computing systems.

Embodied carbon footprint

Embodied carbon refers to the emissions associated with the entire lifecycle of computing equipment, from manufacturing to disposal. Strategies to address this include:

- **Sustainable materials and manufacturing**: Utilizing eco-friendly materials and adopting manufacturing processes that reduce carbon emissions. This encompasses selecting materials with lower environmental impact and optimizing fabrication techniques to minimize waste.

- **Modular and upgradeable designs**: Creating systems with components that can be easily replaced or upgraded extends the lifespan of devices and reduces the need for complete replacements. Companies like *Framework* have introduced laptops with modular components, allowing users to upgrade parts such as screens, webcams, and processors, thereby promoting sustainability.

- **Recycling and end-of-life management**: Designing products with recyclability in mind and establishing programs for responsible disposal and recycling of electronic waste to reclaim valuable materials and reduce environmental harm.

Holistic design approaches

A comprehensive approach to sustainable computing involves:

- **Life cycle assessment (LCA)**: Evaluating the environmental impact of a product throughout its entire lifecycle to identify areas for improvement in sustainability. This assessment helps in understanding the cumulative environmental effects and informs better design choices.

- **Architectural carbon accounting tools**: Employing tools that model and estimate the carbon footprint of architectural decisions, enabling designers to make informed choices that balance performance with environmental impact. For example, the **Architectural Carbon Modeling Tool** (**ACT**) assists in evaluating the carbon emissions associated with different design options.

- **Design for reusability and reconfigurability**: Developing systems that can be repurposed or reconfigured for different applications reduces the need for new hardware production, thereby lowering embodied carbon. **Field Programmable Gate Arrays** (**FPGAs**) exemplify this by allowing reprogramming for various tasks, enhancing their sustainability profile.

Data center design

Data centers are significant consumers of energy; thus, sustainable design principles are crucial:

- **Energy-efficient infrastructure**: Incorporating energy-efficient servers, storage, and networking equipment to reduce power consumption. The NCAR-Wyoming Supercomputing Center, for instance, achieved a design that is 89% more efficient than typical data centers by utilizing advanced cooling and energy management systems.

- **Renewable energy integration**: Powering data centers with renewable energy sources, such as wind or solar, to decrease reliance on fossil fuels and reduce carbon emissions. This transition supports the sustainability goals of computing facilities.

- **Advanced cooling techniques**: Implementing innovative cooling methods, like free cooling and liquid immersion cooling, to maintain optimal temperatures with reduced energy usage. These techniques enhance energy efficiency and lower operational costs.

Software design considerations

Sustainable computing also encompasses software design:

- **Efficient algorithms**: Developing algorithms that require fewer computational resources to perform tasks, thereby reducing energy consumption during execution. Optimized code contributes to lower operational carbon footprints.

- **Resource management**: Designing software to utilize hardware resources judiciously, avoiding unnecessary computations and efficiently managing memory and processing power. This approach ensures that applications run effectively without overtaxing the system.

- **Sustainable software development practices**: Adopting practices that consider environmental impact, such as minimizing the use of high-energy consumption features and optimizing software for energy efficiency. Following the principles of green computing, which synthesize knowledge from climate science, software design, and hardware, can lead to the creation of environmentally friendly software.

Emerging trends

The field of sustainable computing is continually evolving, with emerging trends including:

- **Carbon-aware computing**: Designing systems that adapt their operations based on the carbon intensity of the electricity grid, performing energy-intensive tasks when renewable energy availability is high. This approach aligns computing workloads with periods of low carbon emissions, enhancing sustainability.

- **Edge computing**: Processing data closer to its source reduces the need for extensive data transmission to centralized data centers, thereby lowering energy consumption associated with data movement. Edge computing also enables real-time processing, improving efficiency.

- **Sustainable AI**: Developing artificial intelligence models and systems that are energy-efficient, considering the substantial computational resources required for training and inference in large AI models. This involves optimizing model architectures and utilizing efficient hardware to reduce the environmental impact of AI applications.

Sustainable computing requires a holistic approach that encompasses hardware design, software development, data center operations, and emerging technologies. Ongoing research and development in this field continue to uncover new strategies and technologies that contribute to a more sustainable digital future. Sustainable computing is integral to achieving **Environmental, Social, and Governance** (**ESG**) objectives, particularly in reducing the environmental impact of IT operations. In India, the regulatory landscape is evolving to emphasize ESG compliance. The **Securities and Exchange Board of India** (**SEBI**) has introduced the **Business Responsibility and Sustainability Report** (**BRSR**), mandating the top 1,000 listed companies to disclose their ESG initiatives, including efforts in sustainable computing. Additionally, the *Central Consumer Protection Authority's* recent regulations against greenwashing, effective from October 2024, underscore the importance of genuine ESG practices. These developments highlight the critical role of sustainable computing in meeting ESG goals and ensuring compliance with India's regulatory standards.

Bioinformatics progress with generative AI

In the past decade, bioinformatics has evolved from a niche field focused on analyzing genomic sequences to a cornerstone of modern science that integrates massive multi-omics dataset, genomics, proteomics, transcriptomics, and metabolomics, to decode the complexity of life. The journey has been one of growing sophistication, from using simple algorithms to detect genetic variations to deploying highly complex machine learning models capable of finding intricate patterns in multi-dimensional biological data. Enter GenAI, a transformative force that is rewriting the rules of bioinformatics.

Traditional bioinformatics relied heavily on deterministic algorithms, such as BLAST for sequence alignment and HMMER for protein structure prediction. These tools, while groundbreaking, were constrained by their static nature and inability to process the massive datasets produced by **next-generation sequencing** (**NGS**) and mass spectrometry technologies. The introduction of machine learning and deep learning in the early 2010s brought adaptability and higher prediction accuracy. Neural networks began finding patterns in data that were invisible to traditional methods, such as predicting gene-disease associations or protein-ligand interactions.

However, these models often required extensive feature engineering and worked best on specific datasets. This limitation began to change with the advent of transformer-based architectures, originally developed for NLP, that enabled the understanding of sequence and structure in biological data. GenAI, with models like *GPT-4* and *AlphaFold*'s successors, has since revolutionized bioinformatics by not just analyzing biological data but also generating hypotheses, designing proteins, and predicting biological pathways.

GenAI has made significant strides in bioinformatics by applying its generative capabilities to real-world biological problems:

- **Protein design**: Models like *OpenFold* and *RoseTTAFold*, inspired by *AlphaFold*, use GenAI to predict protein structures with atomic accuracy. These systems go a step further by designing entirely new proteins for specific functions, such as enzymes for biomanufacturing or therapeutic antibodies for disease treatment.

- **Multi-omics integration**: GenAI models trained on diverse omics datasets can correlate data layers to uncover causal mechanisms in diseases. For example, a model might link a specific genetic mutation (genomics) to an altered protein pathway (proteomics) and a dysregulated metabolic process (metabolomics), enabling a holistic view of complex conditions like cancer or neurodegenerative disorders.

- **Drug discovery**: GenAI has revolutionized the process of identifying drug candidates. Instead of manually screening millions of compounds, GenAI models can predict molecular interactions and suggest novel chemical structures tailored to a target protein.

- **Large language models for biology**: Tools like *BioGPT* and *ESMFold* interpret scientific literature, extract meaningful relationships between biological concepts, and generate plausible experimental hypotheses. These models reduce the bottleneck of literature review and accelerate research workflows.

The integration of GenAI in bioinformatics is just beginning. Future innovations include:

- **Dynamic biological simulations**: By training GenAI on time-series multi-omics data, researchers could simulate biological processes, such as tumor evolution or microbial ecosystem dynamics, in real time.

- **Personalized medicine**: GenAI could process an individual's genomic and phenotypic data to generate entirely personalized therapeutic strategies, from drug combinations to lifestyle recommendations.

- **Omics-driven generative design**: Beyond proteins, GenAI could design entire metabolic pathways to synthesize novel biomolecules for industrial, pharmaceutical, or agricultural applications.

Robotics progress with generative AI

The evolution of robotics has been a journey of groundbreaking innovation, spanning decades of progress from basic automation to intelligent, autonomous systems. The field began with mechanical systems performing repetitive, rule-based tasks, evolving through the integration of sensors and computational control, to today's robots powered by sophisticated AI capabilities. The convergence of GenAI, RL, and agentic AI has unlocked unprecedented potential, enabling robots to think, learn, and act with human-like autonomy and creativity.

In the 1960s and 1970s, robots were primarily industrial machines designed for structured environments, such as assembly lines. These early robots followed predefined rules, with limited adaptability to changing conditions. The 1980s and 1990s saw the rise of computer vision and early AI integration, allowing robots to interact with dynamic environments. However, these systems were still deterministic, relying heavily on human programming and lacking true learning capabilities.

The introduction of reinforcement learning in the late 1990s and early 2000s marked a pivotal shift. RL allowed robots to learn optimal behaviors by interacting with their environment, guided by reward functions that incentivized desirable outcomes. For example, a robotic arm could learn to stack blocks through trial and error, adjusting its actions based on feedback. While promising, these early RL applications were computationally intensive and limited to narrow tasks.

In the last decade, the rise of deep learning significantly enhanced RL, enabling robots to process vast amounts of sensory data and learn more complex behaviors. Coupled with advancements in simulation technologies, robots began to train in virtual environments, reducing reliance on costly real-world experimentation. The introduction of GenAI further revolutionized this space, providing the ability to simulate diverse scenarios, predict outcomes, and generate creative solutions, propelling robotics into the current era of autonomy and adaptability.

Reinforcement learning plays a central role in robotics, where an agent learns to achieve a goal by maximizing cumulative rewards. The reward function serves as the agent's guide, encoding the objectives of the task. Early RL applications often struggled with reward function design, making it either too simple, leading to suboptimal learning, or too complex, slowing down the training process.

GenAI addresses this challenge by enhancing the design and optimization of reward functions. By simulating task scenarios, GenAI can identify key success metrics and suggest reward structures that balance simplicity with effectiveness. For example, in robotic path planning, GenAI might simulate thousands of routes and reward the agent for minimizing both travel time and energy consumption, accelerating convergence to optimal strategies.

In tandem, RL algorithms like **proximal policy optimization (PPO)** and **soft actor-critic (SAC)** have enabled robots to handle tasks with high-dimensional state spaces, such as controlling multi-joint humanoid robots. These advancements are now amplified by GenAI, which generates synthetic training data to improve sample efficiency and robustness, reducing the reliance on physical interactions.

Agentic AI represents the next frontier in robotics, empowering machines to operate with high degrees of autonomy, self-governance, and proactive decision-making. Unlike traditional robots that execute predefined tasks or RL agents that optimize for specific goals, agentic AI enables robots to define their own sub-goals and adapt strategies dynamically based on real-time feedback.

For instance, a search-and-rescue drone equipped with agentic AI can autonomously prioritize objectives, identify areas with the highest likelihood of survivors, navigate hazardous environments, and reallocate resources based on new data. This capability arises from the integration of reinforcement learning, generative reasoning, and advanced decision-making frameworks.

Agentic AI also incorporates techniques like **hierarchical reinforcement learning (HRL)**, where complex tasks are decomposed into sub-tasks, each governed by its own reward function. This approach mirrors human problem-solving, allowing robots to tackle challenges that require multi-step planning and adaptive strategies.

The fusion of GenAI and RL is driving remarkable innovations in robotics across industries:

- **Collaborative robots (Cobots)**: Cobots are leveraging GenAI to understand natural language instructions and RL to learn collaborative behaviors. In manufacturing, these robots adapt their movements to human co-workers in real-time, improving productivity and safety.

- **Autonomous vehicles**: RL and GenAI enable self-driving cars to train in diverse simulated environments, mastering edge cases such as rare traffic scenarios or adverse weather conditions. GenAI enhances this by predicting long-term outcomes of navigation strategies, ensuring robust decision-making.

- **Surgical robotics**: Surgical robots use GenAI to model patient-specific anatomy and RL to refine their precision during minimally invasive procedures. This integration reduces recovery times and improves outcomes by personalizing surgical interventions.

- **Dynamic reward adaptation**: Modern systems employ dynamic reward functions that evolve as robots encounter new situations. For instance, a logistics robot delivering packages adjusts its reward priorities based on factors like delivery urgency and route conditions, optimizing operations.

- **Agentic AI in swarm robotics**: Swarm robotics, inspired by natural phenomena like ant colonies, benefits from agentic AI to enable autonomous coordination. In agriculture, drones equipped with agentic AI collaborate to optimize irrigation, pest control, and yield analysis, reducing resource usage and enhancing crop health.

Robotics systems powered by GenAI and RL are underpinned by a modular architecture that integrates perception, policy generation, and action execution:

- **Perception layer**: Robots gather data from sensors such as cameras, LIDAR, and tactile systems. GenAI enhances this layer by filling in gaps in sensor data and generating probabilistic predictions, enabling robots to operate in low-visibility conditions.

- **Policy layer**: RL algorithms drive the decision-making process, guided by reward functions and enhanced by GenAI simulations. Hierarchical RL structures allow robots to manage complex, multi-step tasks, while generative models predict long-term outcomes of actions.

- **Execution layer**: Robots execute learned policies in real-world settings, constantly refining their strategies through feedback loops. Agentic AI enables robots to reassess their goals and adapt policies dynamically, ensuring resilience in changing environments.

Hardware advancements, such as NVIDIA's Jetson Orin Nano and Google's TPU edge devices, provide the computational power necessary for on-device learning and inference. Frameworks like *OpenAI Gym* and *Microsoft Bonsai* enable scalable development and deployment of these intelligent systems.

The intersection of GenAI, reinforcement learning, and agentic AI paves the way for transformative advancements in robotics:

- **Autonomous exploration**: Robots could autonomously explore uncharted environments, such as deep-sea trenches or extraterrestrial terrains, generating hypotheses and adapting strategies in real-time.

- **Personalized assistance**: Robots in healthcare or home settings could adapt to individual preferences and needs, using RL to refine behaviors and GenAI to understand nuanced human instructions.

- **Human-robot collaboration**: Agentic AI could enable seamless collaboration between humans and robots, with machines acting as creative problem solvers, enhancing human productivity and innovation.

Future of humanoid robotics

Humanoid robots and AI-enabled robotics are on the brink of a transformative shift, driven by technological advancements and increasing readiness to scale production. Key players in this field are making significant strides, and the future of humanoid robotics promises practical applications across multiple industries.

Leading companies in humanoid robotics:

- **Tesla**: With its Optimus robot, Tesla is revolutionizing industries like manufacturing and logistics by automating tasks traditionally performed by humans. Designed for affordability and adaptability, Optimus is set to transform service automation as well.

- **Figure AI**: Known for its humanoid robots, Figure 01 and 02, Figure AI is enhancing human productivity with robots that perform tasks in logistics and household environments, capable of navigating complex spaces.

- **Agility Robotics**: Their bipedal robot, Digit, is leading in automating logistics and material handling, with robots designed to replicate human movement in human-centric environments.

- **Boston Dynamics**: A robotics pioneer, Boston Dynamics continues to innovate with Atlas, a humanoid robot capable of complex movements and navigating hazardous environments.

- **1X Technologies**: The NEO Gamma robot, designed for household tasks, integrates human-like movements and interactions, making it an effective autonomous home assistant.

- **Apptronik**: Apollo, Apptronik's modular humanoid robot, brings productivity enhancements across industries from warehousing to healthcare.

- **Neogamma**: An emerging player, Neogamma is working on humanoid robots for complex environments like logistics, search-and-rescue, and eldercare.

- **NVIDIA**: With the GROOT N1, NVIDIA is enhancing real-time decision-making and AI learning capabilities, improving robot performance, especially in industrial settings.

- **Kiva Systems (Amazon Robotics)**: Known for revolutionizing warehouse logistics, Kiva's AI-powered robots have significantly improved operational efficiency.

Emerging technologies and future prospects

The future of humanoid robotics is primed for significant innovation driven by cutting-edge AI models from leading tech companies. Google's DeepMind has introduced its Gemini 2.0 framework, featuring two groundbreaking AI models, *Gemini Robotics* and *Gemini Robotics-ER*. These models are designed to enhance robotic capabilities, enabling robots to interpret natural language commands and adapt to dynamic environments. This shift marks a departure from traditional AI, as these models are tailored for real-world interactions, allowing robots to execute complex tasks like folding paper or handling delicate objects in response to verbal prompts.

In addition to Google, several other prominent companies are making strides in humanoid robotics. *NVIDIA's GROOT N1* continues to set new standards in real-time learning and robot autonomy, while *Apptronik's NEO Gamma* is enhancing human-robot collaboration with AI-driven sensors. *Tesla's Optimus robot*, leveraging Tesla's AI and automation expertise, is designed to assist in logistics and household tasks, further advancing the role of robots in everyday life. Adding to this dynamic landscape is *Figure AI*, which has gained attention for its innovative humanoid robots designed for home assistance. Their upcoming model **Helix** promises advanced capabilities tailored for personal and household tasks, with plans for testing in residential settings.

As humanoid robots become increasingly integrated into daily life, we can expect significant advancements in key areas such as emotion recognition, decision-making, and collaborative capabilities. These innovations will have a profound impact across sectors, including healthcare, customer service, logistics, and manufacturing, where robots will fill vital roles.

With substantial investments and technological breakthroughs ahead, humanoid robotics is poised for a transformative year in 2025. We can expect the shift from experimental prototypes to commercially viable solutions, bringing humanoid robots into homes, workplaces, and public spaces, ultimately enhancing operational efficiency and improving quality of life. These advancements will redefine our interactions with machines and open new possibilities for their application across a wide range of industries.

Conclusion

In this chapter, we explored several advanced computing paradigms that are shaping the future of technology. We began with multi-cloud and hybrid architectures, discussing how organizations leverage multiple cloud services and integrate on-premises infrastructure to enhance flexibility, scalability, and resilience. We then delved into the *IoT* and *edge computing*, examining how the proliferation of connected devices and the shift toward processing data closer to its source are transforming industries by enabling real-time analytics and reducing latency. Our discussion on HPC and GPU-based architectures highlighted the role of specialized hardware in accelerating complex computations, particularly in fields like scientific research and artificial intelligence. We also covered quantum computing, providing insights into its foundational principles, potential applications, and the architectural challenges that must be addressed to realize its full potential. The section on blockchain platforms and decentralized technologies shed light on how distributed ledger systems are redefining trust and transparency in digital transactions. Finally, we addressed sustainable computing, emphasizing the importance of designing energy-efficient systems and adopting environmentally responsible practices to meet ESG goals and comply with evolving regulations, particularly in the Indian context. These topics collectively underscore the computing landscape's dynamic nature and the continuous innovation required to address emerging challenges and opportunities.

Key terms

- **Multi-cloud architecture**: A computing strategy that leverages multiple cloud providers to optimize workloads, enhance resilience, and avoid vendor lock-in.

- **Hybrid architecture**: The integration of on-premises infrastructure with public and private clouds to create a cohesive and flexible computing environment.

- **IoT**: A network of interconnected devices that collect, exchange, and process data to enable real-time analytics and automation.

- **Edge computing**: A distributed computing paradigm that processes data near its source, reducing latency and bandwidth usage.

- **HPC**: The use of supercomputers and parallel processing techniques to solve complex computational problems.

- **GPU-based architecture**: Systems that utilize GPUs for accelerated computing, particularly in AI and scientific research.

- **Quantum computing**: A computing approach leveraging quantum mechanics to perform computations exponentially faster for specific tasks compared to classical computing.

- **Blockchain**: A decentralized ledger technology that ensures secure, transparent, and tamper-resistant record-keeping.

- **Smart contracts**: Self-executing contracts with terms encoded into blockchain-based software, enabling automated and trustless transactions.

- **Sustainable computing**: The design and operation of computing systems with minimal environmental impact, focusing on energy efficiency and resource conservation.

- **ESG goals**: Environmental, Social, and Governance objectives that organizations aim to achieve for sustainable and ethical operations.

CHAPTER 14

CTO's Playbook for Transformation

Introduction

This chapter will cover the practical application of everything discussed so far in the book. While earlier chapters focused on what modern digital transformation requires across architecture, engineering, data, AI, security, and operations, this chapter brings it all together through a cohesive, end-to-end transformation journey. It walks through how a company navigated its evolution from legacy complexity to a modern, intelligent, and trusted digital enterprise. You will see how challenges were diagnosed, strategies were prioritized, and technology was used not just to modernize systems, but to enable business agility, resilience, and innovation. Instead of abstract theory or isolated case studies, you will follow a relatable narrative structured across 11 transformation phases that mirrors what many technology leaders face today.

Structure

This chapter covers the following topics:

- The transformation mandate
- Phase 1, understanding the problem
- Phase 2, laying the cloud foundation
- Phase 3, cloud operations and governance

- Phase 4, modernizing application architecture
- Phase 5, engineering maturity
- Phase 6, building a modern data architecture
- Phase 7, analytics, AI and insights
- Phase 8, infrastructure management
- Phase 9, cost control and business alignment
- Phase 10, security, ethics and trust
- Phase 11, future readiness

Objectives

By the end of this chapter, readers will have a practical understanding of how to lead a full-scale enterprise transformation by applying the core concepts, frameworks, and tools introduced in the previous chapters. Through the newly appointed **chief technology officer (CTO)** journey at a hypothetical company, readers will see how architecture, cloud, DevSecOps, data, AI, security, and FinOps come together to drive meaningful change. They will learn how to sequence transformation phases, align technology with business goals, and navigate both organizational resistance and technical complexity. Most importantly, readers will be able to visualize how these strategies translate into real-world outcomes and feel equipped to lead similar initiatives in their own context.

Overview

In this chapter, we will explore a fictional, yet highly relatable story of a company called *XYZ Consumer Retail Inc.* and its newly appointed CTO, *Aditya*. This narrative has been crafted purely for learning purposes, drawing inspiration from real-world challenges and industry dynamics. Any resemblance to actual persons or organizations is purely coincidental.

Through Aditya's journey, you will see how a CTO navigates complex transformation challenges by methodically applying the principles, frameworks, and strategies covered across the previous 13 chapters. This chapter is a practical synthesis to help you connect the dots and visualize how everything you have learned so far can come together to drive meaningful business impact.

Wherever technical solutions, tools, or architectures are referenced, we have used examples from Microsoft Azure to bring the story to life. However, these are illustrative only. Readers should feel free to apply the same thinking, patterns, and approaches using alternate technologies or cloud platforms that align with their own preferences or organizational standards.

Read on to witness how technology, when thoughtfully applied, becomes a powerful catalyst for change.

The transformation mandate

Aditya stepped into the role of CTO at XYZ Consumer Retail Inc.

The company, a household name in India's **fast-moving consumer goods** (**FMCG**) space, had built its empire over the last three decades by mastering brick-and-mortar distribution. With a vast product portfolio ranging from personal care items to packaged foods and home cleaning supplies, XYZ had deep roots in Tier 2 and Tier 3 cities, a robust network of distributors and Kirana stores, and strong top-line growth.

But times were rapidly changing.

Indian consumers across metros and hinterlands were no longer satisfied with browsing physical shelves. Mobile-first, convenience-hungry, and digitally savvy, new buyers expected brands like XYZ to meet them on their screens.

They wanted to:

- Discover products online through personalized digital experiences.
- Buy directly from the brand or through integrated quick-commerce platforms.
- Track deliveries in real time with predictable timelines.
- Receive discounts, bundles, and smart recommendations tailored to their region and shopping behavior.

At the same time, the supply chain had started feeling the pressure. Distribution managers were relying on spreadsheets and gut instinct to forecast demand in cities like *Guwahati, Surat*, and *Kochi*. Overstocks in one warehouse and stockouts in another were eating into profits. Competitors with smarter analytics were responding faster with localized offers and flexible pricing.

The CEO, board, and private equity investors had one message for Aditya, *We don't need another IT initiative. We need a business transformation powered by technology.*

Business expectations

Aditya's transformation chart came with six strategic imperatives that had become critical for XYZ Consumer Retail Inc. to stay competitive in a fast-evolving market:

- **Direct-to-consumer (D2C) enablement**: Launch a modern, mobile-first digital storefront to allow consumers to discover, order, and engage directly with XYZ while integrating channel partners into the fulfillment and promotions engine.

- **Demand sensing and micro-market intelligence**: Build predictive models that forecast demand down to the pin code level, factoring in festivals, local trends, pricing elasticity, and real-time inputs from stores and customers.

- **Smart inventory and logistics optimization**: Redesign the supply chain to enable just-in-time restocking, minimize inventory waste, and support last-mile delivery and quick commerce use cases with real-time coordination.

- **Data-driven decision-making**: Create a unified data layer across customers, products, operations, and finance to deliver real-time, trustworthy insights and empower faster, evidence-based decision-making across all levels.

- **Agile product launches and promotions**: Enable the business to rapidly launch new products, test promotions, and dynamically adjust offers across geographies without waiting on weeks of IT change cycles.

- **Omnichannel experience and partner integration**: Deliver a consistent and coordinated experience across XYZ's direct digital channels, marketplaces, distributors, and local retailers, ensuring that pricing, inventory, and delivery are aligned.

Reality on the ground

However, the reality was sobering.

The company's core ERP system was over 15 years old, rigid, and monolithic, incapable of supporting real-time integrations or scaling with evolving needs.

Sales and distribution data lived on isolated on-prem servers, updated manually and often delayed, making it impossible to respond to shifting demand signals from the market. Each regional office had built its own Excel-based forecasting model, relying on historical averages and gut feel rather than data science.

Technology ownership was fragmented, with most of the IT talent outsourced and internal teams lacking exposure to cloud-native development or modern data platforms. Critical customer data was scattered across distributors, retail partners, and outdated CRM systems, with no unified view of the end consumer and no personalization capability.

To complicate matters further, shadow IT had quietly mushroomed across the organization. Marketing had its own analytics tool, the supply chain used another dashboard, and finance relied on a legacy BI system, all of which contradicted each other and eroded trust in the numbers.

Compliance audits were slow, access logs were manual, and teams scrambled to patch gaps right before the auditors arrived.

Integration across systems was a nightmare. The warehouse system could not talk to the CRM, the pricing engine was not connected to promotions, and data had to be manually reconciled across platforms, resulting in operational drag and missed opportunities. Legacy vendor contracts, signed years ago, had locked the company into systems that had not evolved in a decade but continued to demand premium renewals.

New product rollouts took months, and each release was treated like a minor crisis. Teams were afraid to touch existing codebases. If it works, do not touch it was an unspoken mantra. There was no centralized monitoring or observability, so issues often surfaced only when customers complained or orders failed.

Culturally, there was resistance at every level. Aditya realized this was not going to be just a tech project. It would be a mindset shift, an architectural overhaul, a culture transformation, and a game of chess across silos, systems, and stakeholders.

But he also knew one thing for sure: The future of XYZ Consumer Retail Inc. depended on how well they could connect their physical strengths with digital agility and do it fast.

Phase 1, understanding the problem

Aditya did not rush into solutioning. In his first 45 days, he took a deliberate pause to listen, map, and make sense of the labyrinth that XYZ Consumer Retail had become. He met every business leader, from the head of sales in Mumbai to the logistics director in Bhiwandi, and even sat through ride-along with field agents in Tier 2 towns. He wanted to hear directly from the ground what was working and, more importantly, what was not.

What he discovered was not entirely surprising. Everyone was frustrated with IT, but no one had a shared definition of the real problem. The tech stack had become a convenient scapegoat, but the real issues ran deeper, structural gaps, architectural complexity, and cultural inertia. The lack of alignment across teams and systems had eroded trust, and in its place, every function had created its own way of working.

Rather than proposing fixes right away, Aditya decided to establish a foundation. He rolled out three parallel initiatives, drawing from modern solution architecture principles, to bring clarity and direction

This phase applies the learning from *Chapter 1, Introduction to Solution Architecture.*

Defining business capabilities

Aditya's first move was to shift the conversation. Instead of talking about systems or tools, he started with a business capability map, a structured way of looking at what the company needed to be good at in order to win in the market.

He asked simple but important questions:

- What are the critical capabilities that support XYZ's brand promise?
- Which ones are broken, missing, or duplicated?
- Where are the disconnects between business expectations and system support?

This led to a set of capability heatmaps that visually highlighted problem areas, like real-time inventory visibility, customer personalization, and multi-channel fulfillment coordination. It helped move discussions away from generic tool complaints and toward designing a resilient, modular architecture tied to business outcomes.

Establishing the architecture vision

Once the capability view was clear, Aditya began sketching the *Target State Architecture*. Not a 300-page blueprint, but a directional architecture, something that could guide decision-making without overwhelming teams with technical depth.

The vision centered around a few core principles:

- API-first, composable systems
- Cloud-native data backbone
- Event-driven integration
- Real-time observability
- Multi-channel orchestration
- Zero Trust security posture

He presented this vision not as a technical diagram, but as a business enabler, for instance, he said, *Our inventory APIs can reduce working capital by ₹12 crore*, or *This data lake project will give us the ability to predict demand at pin-code level*.

The architecture started gaining traction not because of its technical merit alone but because it was linked to business levers the leadership cared about.

Gap assessment and roadblock discovery

With the vision in place, the next step was to get grounded in the present. Aditya led a *Rapid Architecture Assessment* across systems, teams, and processes.

The team captured:

- A detailed system and integration inventory.
- A backlog of technical debt and outdated platforms.
- Organizational bottlenecks in decision-making and ownership.
- Gaps in data accessibility, SLAs, and security baselines.

Aditya consolidated these findings into a *Solution Maturity Heatmap*, which became a powerful tool to prioritize investments and sequence the transformation journey.

Outcome of phase 1

By the end of this phase, Aditya had done something far more valuable than launching a project. He had:

- Unified the leadership team around a capability-first view, not a tech wish list.

- Established a clear architectural vision tied to business outcomes.

- Exposed hidden challenges in integration, data, and decision-making.

- Built early momentum and trust without deploying a single line of code.

The transformation had not begun yet in execution, but it had begun in mindset. Aditya now had a goal, a shared vocabulary, and a coalition. With the vision in place and the gaps clearly surfaced, the next step was to lay the foundation of migrating from legacy systems to a cloud-ready core that could support the business ambitions ahead.

Human side of architecture

Beyond frameworks and architecture diagrams, what truly moved the needle in this phase was Aditya's ability to listen deeply, build trust, and communicate with clarity.

He did not come in swinging with jargon or a mandate. He asked thoughtful questions in town halls, paraphrased concerns in one-on-ones, and showed genuine curiosity about how people worked. His approach was to invite co-creation rather than enforce top-down mandates.

In meetings, he avoided tech-speak and instead framed architecture in terms of what it would enable for each function, like faster launches for marketing, better forecasting for sales, and more accurate financial planning for the CFO's team.

Driving a transformation of this scale also demanded a set of soft skills that are often overlooked in technical roles but are vital for success. Aditya had to navigate ambiguity, build consensus among diverse stakeholders, and lead without direct authority.

He demonstrated:

- Empathy, to understand the frustrations of frontline teams and the pressures faced by business leaders.

- Storytelling, to communicate the technical vision in a way that makes business impact tangible.

- Influence, to get buy-in across functions without relying solely on hierarchy.

- Adaptability to respond when plans met real-world friction or resistance.

- Emotional intelligence, to manage conflicts, rally people through change, and celebrate small wins.

- Patience, to let the transformation take root gradually rather than forcing rapid shifts.

For architects and CTOs leading such transformations, these human skills are just as critical as any design pattern or platform choice. Technology may build the foundation, but it is people who bring it to life.

Phase 2, laying the cloud foundation

With clarity in place and alignment secured, it was time to move from why to how. Aditya knew that before the business could launch digital storefronts or predict demand in real time, the underlying tech stack had to evolve. The current systems simply could not support the speed, flexibility, or intelligence the company needed.

The first priority was to create a modern technology foundation. That meant moving out of the aging data center, dealing with years of accumulated tech debt, and designing a cloud environment that was secure, scalable, and ready for future needs. The leadership team understood the vision, but now they were looking for visible progress and impact.

Aditya began by setting up a focused migration office within the CIO function, combining internal architects, infrastructure leads, and a few trusted partners. His first move was to split the work into three tracks, assessment, landing zone setup, and workload planning.

This phase applies the learning from *Chapter 2, Cloud Migration Essentials.*

Understanding what could move

The assessment team began mapping all core systems and infrastructure across the enterprise. They categorized every workload based on its cloud readiness. Some applications, like the customer portal and internal reporting tools, were simple enough to rehost with minimal changes. Others, like the pricing engine and demand forecasting logic, were tightly coupled with legacy platforms and would need significant rework.

They used Azure Migrate to automate parts of this discovery and dependency mapping. But the real value came from working with the people who had kept these systems running for years. By sitting down with business and operations teams, the migration office identified technical dependencies, business criticality and operational nuances of each system.

Aditya introduced a scoring model to prioritize what to move first. It considered factors like stability, scalability issues, licensing costs, integration pain points, and the strategic importance of each workload.

Designing the right cloud environment

While the assessment was underway, a parallel track focused on designing the target cloud environment. Aditya did not want a lift-and-shift setup that would replicate old problems in a new place. He worked with his team to define the cloud architecture with strong guardrails around identity, networking, cost management, and compliance.

The focus areas included:

- Identity and access management to ensure secure, role-based access using Azure Active Directory.

- Networking baselines, including firewall rules, private endpoints, and secure connectivity with on-premises systems.

- Cost controls using budgets, tags, and cost allocation structures tied to business units.

- Compliance and policy enforcement to meet regulatory requirements from day one.

To bring this vision to life, the team implemented Azure Landing Zones, which offered a modular and standardized approach to cloud environment setup. These zones provided:

- Predefined configurations for subscriptions, policies, and resource hierarchies.

- Blueprint templates to enable secure, repeatable deployments.

- Native integration with monitoring and cost governance tools.

In parallel, Aditya ensured the provisioning of multiple dedicated environments like sandbox, development, testing, and production to support safe experimentation and continuous delivery. This separation of environments encouraged agility while minimizing the risk of service disruption, especially during early migration waves.

This created confidence among developers and reduced the risk of breaking critical processes during migration.

Moving in waves, not all at once

One of the most important decisions Aditya made was to organize the migration into small, manageable waves. Each wave focused on a group of related applications and data workloads that served a common business function. The first wave included internal tools and dashboards that had low risk but high visibility. This gave the business teams a chance to see something live and work early in the program.

The second wave targeted customer-facing services that needed better performance and uptime. These systems were moved to cloud-native components like *Azure App Service* and *Azure SQL*. The process revealed several hidden dependencies, especially around APIs that connected to third-party logistics partners. These surprises slowed the team down, but Aditya used this as an opportunity to build shared learning and improve planning for future waves.

Throughout the waves, his team created runbooks, standardized rollback plans, and ran simulations. Aditya brought in cloud center-of-excellence leads from other companies to run peer reviews and validate their migration plans.

Upskilling and building confidence

Aditya realized early that successful migration was not just about tools or timelines. People needed to feel comfortable in the new environment. So, while systems were being moved, he launched an internal upskilling program. Engineers, data analysts, and IT support staff went through structured hands-on training on cloud fundamentals, security, and monitoring.

More importantly, he created a cloud champion network within each business unit. These were volunteers who were trained to explain what was changing, why it mattered, and how to work with the new systems.

This reduced resistance and helped surface operational feedback that would have otherwise been missed.

Outcome of phase 2

By the end of this phase, Aditya had established a strong and visible foundation for change. The cloud environment was in place, two successful waves of migration were complete, and internal teams were beginning to take ownership.

Key outcomes included:

- Reduced operational risk by moving away from unsupported legacy infrastructure.
- Enabled real-time data access for selected customer-facing systems.
- Created a repeatable migration playbook for future waves.
- Increased confidence among internal teams and reduced resistance to upcoming changes.

Most importantly, Aditya had started shifting the culture from seeing IT as a bottleneck to recognizing it as an enabler. The migration was not just a technical win; it had started to build momentum inside the organization.

But as the cloud footprint grew, Aditya knew the next step was critical. Without the right operational controls, cost transparency, and disaster recovery plans, the momentum could stall. It was time to focus on operational excellence, to bring in the governance, observability, and cost accountability needed to scale safely.

Phase 3, cloud operations and governance

As the initial excitement from successful migrations settled, new challenges began to surface. The move to the cloud had brought greater flexibility and speed, but it also introduced a fresh set of operational concerns.

Cloud costs were rising faster than expected. Different teams were provisioning resources without oversight. There were inconsistencies in how environments were set up. And most concerning, the organization had no clear disaster recovery plan for its cloud workloads.

Aditya knew that if left unchecked, these issues would slow down progress and erode the trust he had started to build. It was time to put in place the operational discipline required to manage cloud at scale, and create the conditions for safe, scalable innovation.

This phase applies the learning from *Chapter 3, Operational Excellence in Cloud*.

Setting up a cloud governance framework

Aditya began by establishing a cloud governance charter. The goal was to strike a balance between innovation and control. He set up a small **cloud center of excellence** (**CCoE**) within the CIO's office, composed of architects, security leads, FinOps analysts, and DevOps engineers.

This team defined a governance model that included:

- Role-based access controls and standard identity policies.
- Naming conventions and tagging requirements for all resources.
- Subscription design patterns tied to business units or cost centers.
- Guardrails around geolocation, VM sizes, and networking.
- They used Azure Policy and Blueprints to enforce these rules at scale. Any new resource deployed had to comply with these baseline policies. It was a simple, non-intrusive way to bring consistency without heavy-handed approvals.

This helped reduce shadow IT, streamline compliance, and make future audits easier.

Getting a handle on cloud costs

One of the earliest pain points was cost visibility. Business leaders were receiving monthly cloud bills with little understanding of where the money was going. Aditya wanted to bring transparency and accountability without creating friction.

He introduced Azure Cost Management + Advisor dashboards, which were customized for each department. Every leader could now see their own team's consumption broken down by service, environment, and project.

To drive better practices, the CCoE rolled out a series of cost optimization initiatives:

- Identifying and shutting down underutilized resources.
- Rightsizing compute workloads based on usage patterns.
- Reserving capacity for stable, always-on services.
- Automating the start/stop of non-production environments.
- These efforts reduced costs and made teams more thoughtful about provisioning and usage.

Building business continuity and resilience

With core systems now running in the cloud, the risk profile has changed. The legacy DR plan was outdated and did not cover cloud-native components or distributed data.

Aditya worked with the infrastructure and application teams to define **recovery time objective** (**RTO**) and **recovery point objective** (**RPO**) targets for each critical system. They then mapped these to cloud capabilities like *Azure Site Recovery*, zone redundancy, and geo-replication. He also introduced simulated failure drills and recovery testing. These exercises helped surface hidden gaps and created a stronger incident response culture across IT and operations.

Improving visibility and monitoring

As more services moved to the cloud, observability became a top priority. Issues were sometimes going unnoticed until users reported them. Aditya wanted to shift from reactive to proactive operations.

His team standardized on Azure Monitor and Log Analytics for telemetry, alerting, and diagnostics. Dashboards were created for different roles, infra teams tracked performance metrics, application owners monitored error rates, and security teams watched access logs.

For critical business flows like order processing and inventory sync, they set up end-to-end transaction monitoring. This gave teams early warning signals when something started to degrade.

Embedding operational ownership in teams

Aditya did not want operations to be seen as a central IT responsibility. He encouraged product and app teams to take ownership of their environments. They were given access to their own dashboards, cost views, and policy exceptions (with approval gates).

The CCoE served as an enabler, offering templates, best practices, and hands-on help when needed. This shift in mindset empowered teams to move faster while staying within guardrails.

Improving incident response and change management

As the number of cloud workloads increased, so did the complexity of incident handling. Aditya's team introduced a standardized incident response framework. Every major incident was tracked through a shared system, with clear escalation paths, impact assessments, and time-stamped resolution logs.

They also implemented structured change management workflows, requiring automated validations and peer approvals for production changes. High-risk changes were gated behind change windows, with rollback plans tested in staging environments. This reduced deployment failures and gave stakeholders greater confidence during peak business periods.

Communication during incidents was streamlined through Microsoft Teams channels, integrating alerts from Azure Monitor and change logs from GitHub Actions. This ensured faster coordination and visibility for all involved teams.

Outcome of phase 3

By the end of this phase, Aditya had created a stable, transparent, and well-governed cloud environment that business teams could trust.

Key outcomes included:

- Policy-driven governance across environments without slowing delivery.
- Cost transparency at the department level with actionable insights.
- DR and failover plans aligned to business continuity needs.
- Real-time visibility into system health and application performance.
- Teams taking greater operational ownership, supported by a strong CCoE.
- With these foundations in place, the organization could now accelerate application modernization and product innovation with far less risk.

The stage was now set for engineering teams to build faster, scale better, and deliver more responsive user experiences. With the cloud foundation in place, the next challenge was to modernize how applications were designed and delivered. The next phase would focus on reimagining the architecture, moving toward modular, event-driven, and scalable services that could power the digital storefront, personalized offers, and demand forecasting models the business needed.

Phase 4, modernizing application architecture

With the cloud foundation now in place and two successful migration waves behind them, Aditya's focus shifted to the next challenge, reimagining how applications were built, scaled, and evolved.

The initial cloud migrations delivered quick wins, better availability, lower infrastructure risk, and some early performance gains. However, as the team looked deeper, they realized many of the migrated workloads were still bound by outdated assumptions. Business logic was tightly coupled, change cycles were slow, and new features often required complex coordination across teams.

If XYZ Consumer Retail wanted to launch digital storefronts, deliver promotions in real time, and respond to customer demand with agility, they needed a fundamentally different application architecture that was modular, loosely coupled, and responsive by design.

Aditya and his team began a transformation journey that touched not just code and infrastructure but also product thinking, team structures, and ways of working.

But Aditya did not treat this as a top-down mandate. He worked closely with product managers, business stakeholders, and engineering leads to co-create the new application vision. Every decision was anchored in a business outcome, whether it was reducing the time to launch a campaign, increasing accuracy in order fulfillment, or improving the availability of product catalogs across multiple storefronts.

This phase applies the learning from *Chapter 4, Modern Application Architecture.*

Shifting from monoliths to modular services

The first step was identifying applications that were tightly coupled and brittle. Several core systems like pricing, promotion, and inventory workflows had grown large and inflexible. Even small changes often required coordination across multiple teams; code freezes, and long testing cycles.

Aditya introduced the concept of bounded contexts, inspired by domain-driven design. This helped his team separate the business into logical domains, such as catalog management, customer orders, inventory visibility, and last-mile tracking. Each domain became a candidate for its own set of APIs and services.

Instead of rewriting everything from scratch, the team began strangling the monoliths, carving out small, independently deployable services for well-defined functionalities. For example, the legacy promotion engine was gradually replaced by a new microservice that could be updated without impacting the rest of the order workflow.

This shift improved delivery speed reduced the blast radius of changes, and gave product teams more control over their own release cycles.

Building event-driven workflows

As the architecture matured, Aditya introduced event-driven design to handle scenarios where responsiveness and scale mattered.

Previously, the system operated on scheduled batch jobs. Promotions went live after midnight syncs. Inventory updates happened every few hours. The new design allowed the system to react in near real-time to business events.

They implemented Azure Event Grid and Service Bus to handle business events like order placed, inventory updated, or payment failed. Each microservice could subscribe to the events it cared about and act without waiting for upstream systems to complete their work.

This significantly improved responsiveness. When a customer places an order, confirmation and fulfillment can begin within seconds. Local inventory levels were updated in near real time, enabling better demand planning and fewer stockouts.

Integrating APIs and third-party systems

Modernization also meant connecting more seamlessly with external partners. Retailers, logistics providers, and payment gateways all needed to be part of a well-orchestrated ecosystem.

Aditya's team invested in an API gateway and built a catalog of well-documented APIs. These APIs were secured with role-based access, monitored for usage, and versioned to avoid breaking downstream consumers.

This effort made it easier for partners to integrate with XYZ systems. Distributors could pull stock availability on demand. Quick-commerce platforms could place bulk orders using real-time pricing. It unlocked new possibilities for channel collaboration and operational automation.

Laying the groundwork for serverless and containers

As some services stabilized, Aditya began experimenting with serverless functions for lightweight, event-triggered logic. For example, when a new product was added to the catalog, a serverless function automatically triggered image optimization and pushed the updated SKU to all relevant storefronts.

For event-driven workloads that did not require persistent computing or complex orchestration, Aditya introduced Azure Functions. These serverless components offered a cost-effective and scalable way to respond to specific triggers without managing infrastructure. This reduced complexity for developers and allowed rapid deployment of small units of logic. Examples of serverless use cases include:

- **Catalog updates**: When a new product was onboarded, a serverless function triggered automatic image optimization and metadata tagging before pushing it to all storefronts.

- **Notifications**: Functions were used to send low-latency alerts to supply chain systems when stock dipped below threshold levels.

- **Scheduled maintenance tasks**: Lightweight scripts such as data syncs or stale cache purges were moved from cron jobs to Azure Functions for better observability and control.

For more complex business services that needed full control over scaling, availability, and lifecycle management, Aditya's team standardized on **Azure Kubernetes Service (AKS)**. Containers offered consistency across dev, test, and prod and enabled better resource isolation, especially for services with variable load profiles. AKS was used to host:

- Core microservices such as pricing engines, fulfillment orchestrators, and personalization modules.

- APIs that needed autoscaling and blue-green deployments.

- Batch processing services that required resource scheduling and monitoring.

To ensure speed, repeatability, and quality in deployments, the platform engineering team:

- Built Helm charts for common service types, standardizing resource definitions, configurations, and secrets management.

- Created CI/CD pipelines in GitHub Actions to automate build, test, and deployment steps for containerized workloads.

- Developed observability templates that instrumented services with logs, metrics, and alerts out of the box.

These tools enabled teams to roll out new microservices in hours instead of weeks and ensured that every deployment followed security, monitoring, and scaling best practices.

This dual approach of serverless for lightweight logic and containers for more robust services offered the best of both worlds. It also nudged teams toward a platform mindset, where infrastructure was treated as a product, and developers were empowered with tools that balanced freedom with responsibility.

Friction with the old ways of working

As the modernization efforts accelerated, Aditya quickly realized that the toughest part was not technology. It was change management.

While the architecture was evolving, not everyone was immediately comfortable with the new direction. Some teams struggled to move from project-based delivery to product-based thinking. Others were unsure how to operate microservices in production, especially with new observability and incident management tools being introduced. For example, QA teams, accustomed to testing monolithic applications in staged environments, found it challenging to adapt to continuous integration pipelines. Even seasoned system admins felt uneasy operating in containerized environments with GitOps-style workflows and shared observability platforms.

So, Aditya kept the transition grounded and focused on learning. He shared architectural blueprints with real-world examples that mapped old workflows to new patterns, making the shift easier to grasp. Internal tech talks and brown-bag sessions showcased early wins, while external experts ran dojos and bootcamps to build hands-on skills. Teams were given time to adapt, there was no pressure for overnight rewrites, just a clear path to evolve safely. Aditya celebrated small wins, like faster deployments or reusable tooling, and most importantly, created psychological safety. Mistakes became learning moments, with teams openly sharing lessons and supporting each other in forums and Slack channels.

Outcome of phase 4

By the end of this phase, the organization had taken a solid step toward building a more modular, event-driven, and API-ready application landscape. The shift from monolithic systems to loosely coupled services gave product teams more flexibility and reduced the strain of cross-team dependencies.

Key outcomes included:

- Faster release cycles and reduced coordination overhead across teams.
- More responsive, real-time workflows across customer and supply chain operations.
- Simplified integration with partners and third-party platforms.
- Greater developer autonomy with standardized environments and pipelines.
- Perhaps the most important shift was culture. Teams had started thinking in services, reacting to events, and collaborating across domains. The technology transformation was becoming a people transformation.

With a more modular and responsive application landscape in place, teams were beginning to think in services, respond to events, and collaborate across domains more naturally. With this new application architecture in place, the spotlight shifted to how these services would be built, secured, and managed at scale. Development teams needed better tooling, automation, and standard practices to move faster without creating chaos.

Phase 5, engineering maturity

With a modern application architecture in place and cloud operations running more predictably, Aditya now turned his attention to how software was being built and delivered inside XYZ Consumer Retail Inc.

While services were becoming more modular and scalable, the engineering practices behind them were still patchy. Teams were using different tools for deployment. Pipelines were managed inconsistently, with several manual steps. Security checks were often treated as a post-go-live formality. Some developers had to raise IT tickets just to provision a testing environment.

All this friction was adding up. Product teams were slowing down, quality was uneven, and incidents were taking longer to resolve. Aditya realized that to scale delivery and maintain agility, engineering needed to mature, and that meant investing in DevSecOps automation, platform consistency, and internal developer experience.

This phase applies the learning from *Chapter 5, Development Practices and Tools*.

Creating a unified CI/CD foundation

Aditya's first priority was to streamline the software delivery process. Teams were using a mix of Jenkins, manual scripts, and third-party tools. There was no clear baseline for how code moved from development to production.

He initiated a company-wide shift to GitHub Actions as the standard CI/CD automation platform across all engineering teams. Every new microservice was required to use automated workflows from day one, covering code builds, test execution, security scans, and multi-environment deployments.

Legacy applications were brought into the GitHub ecosystem gradually. The DevOps team developed and maintained a library of reusable GitHub Actions templates, simplifying onboarding for teams and reducing duplicate effort across projects.

The impact was immediate. Release cycles became faster, more predictable, and easier to audit.

Driving test automation and release quality

To ensure speed did not come at the cost of quality, Aditya made test automation a core engineering priority. Teams integrated unit, integration, and regression tests directly into GitHub Actions workflows.

Each new pull request was automatically validated against a growing library of tests, and build pipelines would fail if quality gates were not met.

Test coverage metrics were visualized in team dashboards, and engineering leads reviewed them regularly during sprint planning.

This shift created a culture of test as you build, reducing post-release bugs and accelerating the feedback loop between development and operations.

Automating infrastructure provisioning

Infrastructure provisioning had long been a bottleneck. Developers were dependent on central IT for creating and configuring environments, leading to delays in testing and deployment.

To eliminate this, Aditya's team standardized on IaC using Bicep and Terraform, and integrated provisioning into GitHub Actions workflows. All infrastructure modules were version-controlled in internal GitHub repositories and published as reusable components.

Developers could now provision dev, test, and even production environments directly through pull requests, triggering automated deployment pipelines with predefined guardrails.

This shift empowered teams to move faster, eliminated waiting periods, and ensured consistent, compliant infrastructure across projects.

Building an internal developer platform

To further simplify the developer experience and reduce cognitive load, Aditya sponsored the creation of an **Internal Developer Platform** (**IDP**) powered by *Backstage*, fully integrated with GitHub Enterprise.

The IDP provided:

- A service catalog linked to GitHub repositories.

- Blueprints for spinning up new microservices from GitHub templates.

- Built-in CI/CD dashboards from GitHub Actions.

- Access to infrastructure modules and deployment pipelines.

- Onboarding guides, secure coding policies, and operational runbooks.

GitHub became the control plane as repositories, permissions, discussions, and automation were all centered there. Developers no longer had to navigate scattered tools or documentation. Adoption spread quickly. Teams began building faster and more consistently, and onboarding new engineers became far easier.

Shifting security left with GitHub Advanced Security

Historically, security reviews happened too late, after the code was merged or deployed. Aditya changed that by embedding GitHub Advanced Security directly into every stage of the developer workflow.

He mandated:

- Code scanning with CodeQL to detect vulnerabilities at the commit and PR level.

- Secret scanning to catch exposed credentials or tokens.

- Dependency scanning to flag vulnerabilities in third-party libraries.

- License compliance checks to avoid usage violations.

- Branch protection rules and required reviews to enforce safe coding practices.

Security alerts surfaced contextually within GitHub so developers could fix issues before merging. This shift empowered teams to take ownership of their security posture.

Security champions were assigned to each squad to guide secure development practices and act as first responders during code reviews.

As a result, vulnerabilities were caught earlier, post-release incidents dropped, and regulatory audits became easier to pass.

Enhancing productivity with GitHub Copilot

To further support engineers, Aditya rolled out GitHub Copilot across development teams.

Initially seen as a coding assistant, Copilot quickly proved to be more than that. Developers used it to write boilerplate logic, generate unit tests, explore APIs, and navigate legacy codebases more confidently. It did not replace engineering effort, but it reduced friction.

Teams reported higher focus, fewer context switches, and improved learning curves for newer developers. In internal surveys, developer satisfaction rose noticeably, and Copilot emerged as one of the most appreciated tools in the engineering toolkit.

Exploring low-code and citizen development

While the core transformation focused on product engineering, Aditya also partnered with business stakeholders to enable low-code solutions.

Using platforms like *Power Apps*, non-technical teams created internal apps for use cases such as leave tracking, performance incentives, and field team surveys. GitHub served as the system of record for version control and approvals, even for low-code apps.

These workflows were integrated into GitHub repositories with simple automation: pull requests for app updates, issue tracking for enhancements, and GitHub Actions to trigger deployments.

This gave business teams speed, while giving IT the governance and visibility it needed.

Outcome of phase 5

By the end of this phase, engineering at XYZ had evolved into a high-velocity, security-conscious, and developer-first function.

Key outcomes included:

- Standardized CI/CD pipelines with GitHub Actions across teams.
- Self-service environment provisioning using GitHub-integrated workflows.
- Embedded security practices via GitHub Advanced Security.
- A unified developer platform that increased reuse and autonomy.
- Productivity gains from GitHub Copilot and citizen developer enablement.

The engineering culture was shifting. Developers felt empowered, security became everyone's responsibility, and cross-functional teams were solving problems faster than ever.

With a stronger engineering foundation in place, Aditya now turned his attention to the next frontier of data. Creating connected, intelligent systems meant building a real-time, scalable, and federated data architecture that could power personalized experiences and dynamic supply chains.

Phase 6, building a modern data architecture

With a modern application stack in place and engineering practices maturing, Aditya now turned his attention to what was possibly the most strategic and complex part of the transformation journey, data.

By now, the organization could launch digital features faster and ship services in weeks instead of quarters. But none of that would matter if the underlying decisions about promotions, pricing, demand planning, or inventory distribution were being made based on outdated, fragmented, or inaccurate data.

What Aditya inherited was a patchwork of legacy data systems. Five different teams maintained their own data lakes. Models were inconsistent. Definitions varied from one department to the next. Reporting pipelines were fragile, breaking quietly and often going unnoticed. Most business decisions were still being supported by spreadsheets, manually compiled, copied across departments, and often out of sync by the time they reached the boardroom.

And so, despite the abundance of data, there was no real-time visibility, no shared truth, and perhaps most importantly very little trust.

Aditya understood that if XYZ Consumer Retail wanted to offer hyper-personalized promotions, respond to regional demand shifts, or make real-time decisions on fulfillment and pricing, they needed to reimagine how data was being captured, processed, governed, and shared across the company.

This was about creating a modern, intelligent data architecture that could scale with the business, power next-gen analytics, and be governed in a way that inspired confidence.

This phase applies the learning from *Chapter 6, Data Architecture and Processing*, and *Chapter 7, Data Strategy and Governance*.

Consolidating the data landscape

Aditya started by mapping the current data estate. There were five separate data lakes across sales, marketing, logistics, finance, and e-commerce, each with its own structure, access rules, and integration logic. Reporting delays were common, and data engineering teams spent more time maintaining fragile pipelines than extracting value from data.

He consolidated these disparate lakes into a unified enterprise-wide lake architecture using Microsoft Fabric's OneLake, which enabled all data domains to operate within a shared, logically centralized foundation. Instead of building bespoke integrations, teams could land raw and curated data into Fabric lakehouses, ready for analytics and reporting.

Aditya's team adopted Microsoft Fabric's integrated Data Factory experience to orchestrate batch and incremental data movement from various sources. This allowed them to create reusable, parameterized pipelines for ingestion from ERP, CRM, and external data providers.

All transformation logic was version-controlled in GitHub repositories, ensuring that data workflows could be peer-reviewed, rolled back, and deployed via CI/CD pipelines. GitHub also managed schema definitions, code reviews, and collaboration between analysts and engineers.

Architecting for hybrid processing, OLTP + OLAP

To support both real-time personalization and historical analytics, Aditya and his team designed a hybrid OLTP and OLAP architecture that could handle both transactional and analytical workloads without duplication or delay.

They started by modernizing the operational data sources:

- **Azure Cosmos DB** was used for high-throughput, globally distributed workloads like order placements, returns, and product browsing behavior.

- **SQL Server workloads**, especially those running on legacy VMs, were migrated to **Azure SQL Managed Instance**, enabling elastic scale and improved security while preserving compatibility.

- Critical Oracle databases handling pricing, finance, and procurement were containerized and moved to Oracle Database Service on Azure, ensuring minimal disruption while benefiting from native integration with Azure services.

- Several open-source databases like *PostgreSQL* and *MySQL*, powering campaign tracking and product catalogs, were migrated to Azure Database for PostgreSQL and Azure Database for MySQL, simplifying operations with fully managed services.

To avoid creating disconnected data marts or heavy ETL layers, Aditya leveraged Microsoft Fabric's near real-time data connectors. These connectors allowed operational data from Cosmos DB, SQL Server, and PostgreSQL to flow directly into Fabric lakehouses with minimal latency. Fabric's native integration ensured that analytical models and dashboards reflected the latest data, sometimes within seconds of the original transaction.

This architecture enabled a wide range of real-time scenarios:

- The pricing team could launch dynamic promotions based on inventory and purchase patterns.

- Store operations could monitor stockouts or overstocks in near real time.

- Marketing analysts could evaluate campaign effectiveness as user engagement data streamed in.

This unlocked new business capabilities-such as enabling the pricing team to adjust discounts in real time based on customer behavior, and allowing the supply chain team to monitor warehouse velocity live.

Enabling real-time streaming and event processing

Aditya recognized that batch processing was not enough. To stay competitive, XYZ needed real-time insights.

The team implemented an event-driven data streaming architecture using Apache Kafka for ingestion and Azure Databricks Structured Streaming for transformation and real-time model scoring.

Some real-world use cases:

- Clickstream data from the digital storefront was streamed into Kafka and enriched in Databricks to trigger real-time product recommendations.

- Point-of-sale updates were streamed to support rolling demand forecasts across micro-markets.

- Logistics feeds from last-mile partners were ingested in real time to optimize delivery routing.

Processed outputs were written into Fabric's lakehouse tables, enabling seamless downstream analysis and reporting through Power BI-without complex ETL chains.

Databricks notebooks were version-controlled in GitHub, and GitHub Actions was used to trigger model training, pipeline deployment, and metadata updates into the data catalog. This automation improved reliability and reduced manual intervention during schema or code changes.

Laying the foundations for federated governance

With more teams consuming and producing data, Aditya knew centralized governance would not scale.

He introduced a Data Mesh approach with domain-oriented data product owners for each business unit. Each product, whether it was daily sales by region or customer churn signals, had a clear owner, SLA, data contract, and audit trail.

Microsoft Purview was implemented as the enterprise-wide data catalog.

It enabled:

- End-to-end data lineage from ingestion to dashboard.
- Clear data ownership and stewardship roles.
- Automated classification and tagging of sensitive data.
- Integration with Azure Policy and RBAC for access control.

Purview was used by analytics teams to discover trusted datasets, by compliance teams to enforce data protection policies, and by engineers to ensure schema changes did not break downstream consumers.

Enhancing data security, observability, and trust

As the data estate grew in scope and criticality, so did the risks. Aditya knew that even the most advanced data architecture could quickly lose credibility if plagued by quality issues, access violations, or undetected pipeline failures. Trust had to be earned from regulators and auditors and from internal users who depended on data to make daily decisions.

He wanted security and governance to be embedded into the foundation of the platform, making it seamless for teams to do the right thing by default.

To do this, he established five foundational pillars:

- **Access control**: Role-based access was enforced across Microsoft Fabric, Cosmos DB, Databricks, and OneLake using Azure Active Directory and integrated policies from Microsoft Purview. Every data product had clear owners and defined access privileges, reducing the risk of over-permissioned users.

- **Encryption**: All data, whether in motion or at rest, was encrypted using enterprise-grade protocols. Keys were centrally managed through Azure Key Vault, ensuring consistent policy enforcement and audit readiness.

- **Monitoring and observability**: Aditya's team instrumented every pipeline, connector, and transformation job with Azure Monitor and Log Analytics. They could now track SLA adherence, pipeline latency, data freshness, and failure rates in real time, allowing proactive resolution before business users even noticed.

- **Data quality**: Checks for schema conformance, null handling, duplicates, and business rule violations were embedded directly into Fabric's Data Factory pipelines and Databricks workflows. These checks ran automatically as part of every job, and failures triggered alerts before flawed data reached downstream systems.

- **Incident management**: Alerts from Azure Monitor were configured to automatically open incident tickets in the operations center whenever a critical job failed, a data quality threshold was breached, or a data source became unreachable. This helped data teams respond quickly and coordinate efficiently during high-impact issues.

Security, lineage, and data quality were not afterthoughts; they were engineered into the platform from the ground up, helping the entire organization build confidence in data as a reliable, governed, and secure business asset.

Outcome of phase 6

By the end of this phase, XYZ Consumer Retail had gone from fragmented data chaos to a unified, intelligent data platform that could keep up with the speed of business.

Key outcomes included:

- A consolidated data estate built on Microsoft Fabric, giving teams a single, governed platform for ingesting, modeling, and analyzing data.

- Real-time data flows from systems like *Cosmos DB*, *SQL Server*, and *Oracle*, enabling dynamic personalization, agile pricing, and timely fulfillment decisions.

- Seamless OLTP and OLAP integration, allowing business leaders to run analytics on live data without slowing down transactional systems.

- A federated data product model with clear ownership, accountability, and agility across business domains.

- Full lineage, access control, and compliance, powered by Microsoft Purview—bringing auditability and reducing the overhead of manual governance.

With clean, current, and connected data available in near real-time, the analytics teams could finally shift from reporting on what happened to predict what was likely to happen next. Aditya was ready to lead XYZ into the next phase of operationalizing AI and advanced analytics at scale.

Phase 7, analytics, AI and insights

With the data platform stabilized and running reliably, Aditya shifted focus to how the business could extract more value from the information flowing through it. Real-time dashboards were now available across departments, and data quality had improved significantly. But even with these foundational changes, most teams were still making decisions based on backward-looking reports.

As expectations grew, different functions started raising specific requirements. The sales team wanted to know which SKUs to prioritize in upcoming promotions. The supply chain team asked for more accurate short-term demand forecasts. Marketing wanted help in identifying high-conversion customer segments and optimizing campaign spend. Finance expected pricing recommendations tied to regional buying behavior. These were clear signals that business teams were ready for more advanced decision support.

Aditya saw that the next phase of the transformation needed to bring analytics and AI into the daily rhythm of the business. With clean, connected data and the right cloud infrastructure in place, the focus now turned to enabling scalable, secure, and outcome-driven use of advanced analytics and machine learning.

This phase applies the learning from *Chapter 8, Advanced Analytics,* and *Chapter 9, Generative AI and Machine Learning.*

Making insights accessible across the business

Aditya's first priority was to ensure that analytics was not limited to a few central analysts or Power BI users. Insights had to reach the people making daily decisions in sales, supply chain, marketing, and store operations. His team focused on embedding analytics into the tools teams already used rather than asking them to open new dashboards.

- Power BI within Microsoft Fabric was used to build domain-specific reports with role-based filters and real-time metrics, served directly inside CRM systems, sales portals, and Microsoft Teams.

- The merchandising team could view sell-through trends by SKU and store cluster, while regional sales managers could compare weekly targets against predicted outcomes.

- Store operations received restock alerts and localized demand anomalies through a simplified mobile interface that pulled insights directly from the data lakehouse.

This created a shift, and analytics was no longer in a report repository. It was available contextually, at the point of action.

Operationalizing predictive models for core scenarios

With analytics delivery in place, Aditya turned to advanced use cases where statistical models could drive measurable improvements.

His data science team collaborated with business functions to shortlist four high-priority scenarios:

- **Personalized offer targeting**: ML models identified customers most likely to respond to specific promotions, enabling smarter allocation of campaign budgets.

- **Demand forecasting**: Forecasting models predicted short-term demand at the SKU x store level, helping reduce overstock and missed sales.

- **Returns risk prediction**: Logistic regression and decision tree models flagged high-risk transactions likely to result in returns.

- **Churn early warning**: Customer behavior clustering helped identify drop-off risk, feeding retention triggers into marketing systems.

These models were developed and deployed using Azure Machine Learning, with GitHub used for version control and pipeline automation. Batch and real-time scoring endpoints were exposed as APIs for integration into downstream applications, like campaign engines, ERP, and retail planning tools.

Each model's performance, accuracy, drift, and latency were monitored continuously, with retraining workflows scheduled based on data changes or business cycles.

Using cognitive services to extend AI capabilities

Not every problem requires a complex, custom-built machine-learning model. In many cases, XYZ Consumer Retail could gain immediate value by applying pre-trained, domain-agnostic AI models to automate and enhance business workflows. Aditya saw this as an opportunity to deliver tangible impact quickly, especially for use cases that had clear ROI and did not justify a large upfront investment in data science resources.

He turned to Azure Cognitive Services, a suite of ready-to-use AI APIs and models that could be easily integrated into applications with minimal overhead.

- Vision APIs were integrated into warehouse and merchandising operations to automate shelf compliance audits, identify missing or misplaced SKUs, and perform product image quality checks. This not only saved inspection time but also improved accuracy and consistency.

- In the call center, speech-to-text capabilities were used to transcribe customer conversations. This allowed supervisors to perform more effective quality audits, enabled faster agent training, and helped surface common pain points voiced by customers.

- Text analytics, including sentiment detection and key phrase extraction, was used to analyze customer feedback across multiple channels, such as surveys, social media, and product reviews. This helped prioritize support tickets, inform product teams about recurring issues, and provide early warning signals for potential brand reputation risks.

What made these capabilities attractive was their ease of use. Development teams could quickly integrate them via simple API calls, and business teams saw results almost immediately. Aditya intentionally positioned these efforts not as long-term AI strategies but as quick wins, solutions that created early momentum, demonstrated AI's value to skeptical stakeholders and allowed the data science team to focus on deeper, domain-specific challenges where custom ML models were truly needed.

Piloting generative AI for knowledge and summarization

As the organization grew more comfortable with predictive analytics and cognitive services, Aditya saw an opportunity to experiment with generative AI to address real inefficiencies in how insights, content, and knowledge were accessed across teams.

Rather than stitching together components manually, his team adopted Azure AI Studio, Microsoft's end-to-end platform for building, testing, and deploying enterprise-grade generative AI applications. This gave them a unified environment to orchestrate the entire lifecycle from prompt engineering and grounding to safety reviews and deployment.

The solution was built using:

- Azure OpenAI Service (GPT-4) as the foundational model.

- **Retrieval-augmented generation (RAG)** pattern to ensure answers were grounded in XYZ's internal data, including BI reports, planning docs, and product catalogs.

- Integrated orchestration and evaluation features in Azure AI Studio, which replaced the need to use separate LangChain setups.

This effort culminated in a Copilot-like assistant embedded into internal tools used by planners, marketers, and field teams. Users could now:

- Ask natural language questions like, `Summarize category performance in North Zone last quarter` or `Why did returns spike for SKU X in January?`

- Auto-generate campaign briefs, pricing insights, or meeting prep notes based on internal reports.

- Request narrative explanations of complex Power BI dashboards without having to interpret filters or KPIs manually.

Built-in capabilities in Azure AI Studio helped the team implement content safety filters, audit logs, prompt evaluations, and responsible AI guardrails, ensuring that outputs remained consistent with enterprise policies, especially for insights used in customer-facing or regulated environments.

This marked a shift from experimentation to real adoption. Teams that had previously relied on BI analysts or PDF reports could now interact directly with business knowledge using plain language, freeing up analyst bandwidth for higher-value work.

Outcome of phase 7

By the end of this phase, analytics and AI were no longer side projects or innovation pilots—they had become embedded into how XYZ Consumer Retail operated across functions. The organization had moved from consuming reports to interacting with live insights, from historical analysis to predictive and generative intelligence.

Key outcomes included:

- Business teams accessed insights in their flow of work, with Power BI dashboards integrated across CRM, planning, and field tools, powered by Microsoft Fabric.

- Machine learning models were running in production, improving precision in offer targeting, demand forecasting, and churn prediction, with measurable improvements in conversion and inventory efficiency.

- Azure Cognitive Services added practical AI use cases in customer support and quality control without requiring custom model development.

- The new AI Copilot, built with Azure AI Studio, enabled teams to ask natural language questions, summarize planning data, and generate content—freeing up time and reducing reliance on manual data extraction.

- A fully operational MLOps framework was now in place, ensuring that models were versioned, monitored, retrained, and governed appropriately.

- Internal awareness and confidence in AI had grown. Teams trusted the insights, engaged with recommendations, and began contributing their own ideas for AI use cases.

Perhaps most importantly, the role of data and AI has shifted from being a specialist function to becoming part of everyday business workflows. Insights were timely, actionable, and aligned with how decisions were made on the ground.

With this momentum, Aditya now turned to the next area of focus: building scalable automation, observability, and operational maturity across the cloud environment, setting the stage for Phase 8, Infrastructure Management.

Phase 8, infrastructure management

With analytics and AI now embedded across workflows, the pace of innovation at XYZ Consumer Retail has accelerated. Teams were launching services faster, experimenting more, and relying heavily on cloud-native infrastructure. But this also meant the environment was growing in complexity.

Aditya began hearing a new set of concerns, not from business stakeholders but from platform and operations teams. Deployments were becoming harder to coordinate. Environment drift was creeping in. Incidents, while fewer, were taking longer to diagnose. Infrastructure costs were rising unpredictably. The question was no longer `Can we deliver fast?` but `Can we deliver fast and reliably?`

It was clear the next phase of the transformation had to focus on automation, observability, and operational consistency to ensure that the foundation could scale securely, sustainably, and with high availability.

This phase applies the learning from *Chapter 10, Automation and Infra Management.*

Standardizing infrastructure with code

Aditya's team started by introducing IaC practices across all environments. While some provisioning scripts had been used earlier, there was no standard or source of truth.

- They adopted Bicep and Terraform for defining Azure resources, including compute, storage, networking, and security policies.

- All environment definitions were moved to GitHub Enterprise repositories, with GitHub Actions used to enforce deployment pipelines, peer reviews, and drift detection.

- Modules were created for commonly used components, AKS clusters, Azure Functions, API Management gateways, which reduced duplication and sped up provisioning for new projects.

This shift eliminated manual provisioning steps, reduced human error, and made infrastructure behavior predictable and auditable.

Implementing observability across the stack

To maintain service quality as workloads grew, Aditya emphasized the importance of end-to-end observability as follows:

- Azure Monitor and Application Insights were used to track application performance, usage patterns, and API latency.

- Log Analytics collected logs and metrics from infrastructure, applications, and data pipelines into a centralized workspace.

- Dashboards were built for each major platform domain, commerce, logistics, personalization, and analytics so that product owners could monitor key health metrics in real time.

- Alerts and auto-remediation scripts were created for common issues, like resource threshold breaches, pipeline failures, and connection timeouts.

This helped the SRE team reduce **mean time to detect** (**MTTD**) and **mean time to resolve** (**MTTR**), while also giving product teams greater visibility into the performance of their services.

Strengthening reliability with SRE principles

To move from reactive incident handling to proactive reliability engineering, Aditya formalized a **site reliability engineering** (**SRE**) framework across critical systems.

Key elements included:

- Defining SLIs, SLOs, and error budgets for key business services (e.g., order placement, offer targeting, last-mile delivery updates).

- Weekly error budget reviews with engineering leads to balance feature velocity and platform stability.

- Blameless postmortems for all critical incidents, with root cause analysis tracked in GitHub Issues.

- Introduction of chaos engineering exercises in non-prod environments to validate failover and redundancy setups.

This not only improved system resilience but also fostered a shared ownership culture between development and operations teams.

Resilience at scale with regional failover readiness

As XYZ Consumer Retail grew, ensuring high availability across regions became critical. Aditya moved beyond standard uptime metrics and focused on building true resilience at scale. Core systems like order processing and inventory were re-architected to run across multiple availability zones, with Azure Site Recovery and geo-redundant storage enabling failover to secondary regions.

To prepare teams for real-world disruptions, Aditya institutionalized quarterly disaster recovery drills using Azure Chaos Studio. These simulations helped fine-tune observability dashboards, alerting thresholds, and runbooks. Infrastructure deployments through GitHub Actions were gated with availability checks, ensuring that every change upheld high-availability standards.

This disciplined, proactive approach shifted the team's mindset from recovery to resilience. With clear processes and well-tested systems, XYZ could now maintain business continuity even during regional outages or service disruptions.

Cost management and resource optimization

As XYZ Consumer Retail's cloud usage expanded, the CFO raised an important concern that cloud spend was accelerating without clear accountability. Aditya knew this was not just a technical optimization issue; it was a business priority that required shared ownership between IT and finance.

To address this, Aditya's team implemented a structured cost management strategy:

- Azure Cost Management and Billing were rolled out to track cloud budgets, allocate costs by the team, and monitor anomalies. This gave leaders real-time visibility into who was consuming what, where costs were trending, and where anomalies were emerging.

- Power BI dashboards were built to provide real-time visibility for business stakeholders, showing spend by application, environment, and business unit.

- Right-sizing and auto-scaling policies were applied across VMs, databases, and compute clusters using Azure Advisor recommendations, ensuring resources matched actual usage.

- Standardized tagging policies were embedded into GitHub IaC workflows to ensure every resource had clear metadata, like project owner, cost center, and environment, for traceability. Non-compliant resources were flagged automatically, helping prevent invisible cost leaks.

- Monthly cost reviews were introduced between IT and finance to review consumption trends, surface optimization opportunities, and tie spend directly to business value. Insights from these meetings fed directly into planning cycles.

- Showback reports were shared with product and business teams, creating awareness and encouraging accountability without introducing penalties.

These actions helped XYZ reduce cloud waste, improve financial predictability, and ensure that every rupee spent on infrastructure was aligned with business priorities without slowing innovation.

Outcome of phase 8

By the end of this phase, XYZ Consumer Retail had built a strong operational backbone to support its growing digital ambitions. Systems were more reliable, environments were fully automated, and teams had clear visibility into platform health and performance.

Key outcomes included:

- All infrastructure provisioned and version-controlled through GitHub-based IaC workflows.

- End-to-end observability dashboards enabled real-time monitoring of both application and infrastructure health.

- SRE practices were adopted, improving incident response and system uptime.

- Standardized tagging, scaling policies, and automation introduced accountability and governance across environments.

- A shift in mindset from reactive incident management to proactive platform reliability and shared ownership.

While the platform was now more secure, stable, and efficient, one area still required focused attention, cost transparency, and financial discipline. As cloud consumption increased with AI workloads, dynamic scaling, and new deployments, business leaders wanted to ensure that every rupee spent was tied to measurable value.

With the technical foundation in place, Aditya's next priority was to embed FinOps practices, creating a shared language between engineering, finance, and business teams to optimize cloud investments and ensure sustainable growth.

Phase 9, cost control and business alignment

With cloud infrastructure automated and systems running reliably, XYZ Consumer Retail was scaling fast, expanding AI workloads, onboarding new digital services, and driving more experimentation across teams. But as usage surged, so did costs.

In a quarterly business review, the CFO flagged a sharp increase in cloud spend. Budgets were being exceeded, forecasts were unreliable, and there was little clarity on which teams or projects were driving the overruns. Engineering had done its part in tagging and automating environments, but there was still a gap: cloud cost visibility had not translated into business accountability.

Aditya recognized the need for a disciplined FinOps practice that aligned engineering velocity with financial control. This was not about limiting innovation. It was about building transparency, predictability, and shared ownership across IT, finance, and business units.

This phase applies the learning from *Chapter 11, FinOps Foundations.*

Building cost transparency across the business

The first step was visibility. Aditya's team created a centralized FinOps dashboard using Azure Cost Management + Power BI, integrating cost data from subscriptions, resource groups, and services.

This dashboard allowed the organization to:

- View spend breakdowns by department, environment, and application.

- Track monthly trends, variances, and forecasted costs.

- Drill down into top consumers across compute, storage, networking, and AI workloads.

- Map costs to business initiatives using Azure tagging policies and resource hierarchies.

These insights were reviewed regularly in business reviews and technology steering committees, helping leaders connect cloud usage to operational goals.

Forecasting, budget controls, and anomaly detection

After gaining visibility into where cloud costs were coming from, Aditya's team turned their attention to building forward-looking controls to detect overspending and help predict and prevent it. The goal was to shift from reactive cost reviews to proactive financial planning.

Key actions included:

- Azure Budgets were set up for all major workloads, with predefined thresholds by team and environment. Automated alerts were sent to cost owners via email and Microsoft Teams when usage approached or exceeded these limits.

- Forecasting models were developed using Microsoft Fabric. These models considered:

    o Historical consumption patterns

    o Seasonal demand shifts

    o Campaign-driven usage spikes

- o Upcoming deployments and feature releases. This helped finance and engineering teams align budgets with actual usage trends instead of relying on static estimates.

- Cost anomaly detection was integrated using Azure Advisor recommendations. Custom dashboards in Microsoft Fabric flagged unusual usage spikes, underutilized resources suddenly turning active, or cost increases outside the norm. Alerts were routed to responsible teams for quick investigation and action.

This created a predictable rhythm of planning, monitoring, and adjusting, which finance stakeholders found far more actionable than post-facto reporting.

Optimizing cloud usage and reducing waste

With visibility and controls in place, the focus shifted to optimization. Aditya's CCoE drove targeted actions such as:

- Rightsizing VMs and databases based on performance telemetry.

- Moving workloads to reserved instances or spot VMs, wherever consistent usage patterns were identified.

- Deallocating idle environments, post-testing, and consolidating underutilized resources.

- Re-evaluating AI model configurations, ensuring cost-effective deployments across inferencing and training pipelines.

Azure Advisor, Azure Monitor, and native usage analytics within Microsoft Fabric helped guide these efforts with data-backed recommendations.

Driving shared accountability

To ensure cost responsibility was embedded in day-to-day operations, Aditya introduced a showback model across departments:

- Business units received monthly summaries of their cloud usage tied to the projects they sponsored.

- No penalties were applied, but units were encouraged to review and optimize their spending.

- IT and finance jointly reviewed consumption patterns, helping prioritize budget allocations based on the value delivered.

Cross-functional governance was formalized, with cloud cost optimization becoming a regular agenda item in steering forums and cost awareness becoming part of DevOps and product management routines.

Outcome of phase 9

By the end of this phase, XYZ Consumer Retail had established a mature, cross-functional approach to cloud financial management, bringing cost transparency, accountability, and operational discipline into the heart of its digital strategy.

Key outcomes included:

- A unified FinOps dashboard mapping cloud spending to business functions and outcomes.
- Improved forecasting accuracy, reducing surprise overruns and enabling better budgeting.
- A 27% reduction in avoidable cloud costs, driven by optimization and accountability.
- Regular governance forums between IT and Finance, creating shared ownership of cloud investments.
- A cultural shift, where cloud spend was not just monitored, it was actively managed as a lever for business performance.

With financial governance now embedded in daily operations, Aditya turned his attention to an even more critical priority of building trust. As AI adoption scaled, the organization needed a stronger posture on security, privacy, and responsible AI.

Phase 10, security, ethics and trust

Security and trust became board-level priorities as XYZ Consumer Retail scaled its cloud footprint, AI models, and data-driven operations. The systems were modern, the insights powerful, but with that power came increased scrutiny.

New regulatory requirements, growing data volumes, and the use of Generative AI in customer-facing workflows triggered critical questions from the CEO, legal counsel, and board audit committee:

- Are we compliant with India's upcoming **Digital Personal Data Protection (DPDP)** Act and global privacy standards?
- Are our AI models explainable, fair, and protected from misuse?
- Can we demonstrate full visibility into how customer data is used across systems?
- Are our cloud identities, endpoints, and APIs secure from breaches?

Aditya knew that security and compliance could not be bolted on at the end. They had to be integrated into every layer of the digital stack, from infrastructure and identity to data governance and AI pipelines. This final phase of transformation was about building a system the organization could trust, and customers could depend on.

This phase applies the learning from *Chapter 12, Security, Privacy, and Ethics.*

Rolling out zero trust across the enterprise

Aditya's security team began by formalizing a Zero Trust architecture across cloud and hybrid systems.

This included:

- **Identity and access management (IAM)**: Enforcing multifactor authentication, just-in-time access, and least privilege principles using Azure Active Directory (Entra ID).

- **Network security**: Replacing implicit network trust with segmented access policies, private endpoints, and conditional access controls.

- **Endpoint protection**: Implementing Microsoft Defender for Endpoint across laptops, mobile devices, and developer machines, with real-time telemetry.

- **Workload identity**: Removing hardcoded credentials in pipelines and replacing them with managed identities for services and APIs.

This reduced the attack surface significantly and ensured every identity, device, and service was continuously validated.

Strengthening data privacy and protection

With large volumes of customer, transaction, and behavioral data now flowing through cloud systems and AI models, Aditya expanded the data protection program with three key components:

- **Data classification and labeling**: Using Microsoft Purview, every dataset was classified based on sensitivity, and access was tiered accordingly (e.g., PII, internal, public).

- **DLP**: DLP policies were applied to prevent leakage of sensitive data in emails, chats, storage, and developer environments.

- **Encryption and key management**: All data was encrypted at rest and in transit, with keys centrally managed via Azure Key Vault.

These efforts ensured compliance readiness and made audits faster, more predictable, and less disruptive.

Implementing responsible AI governance

As AI models and copilots became embedded in planning, support, and marketing workflows, Aditya worked closely with legal, compliance, and product teams to launch a responsible AI governance framework.

Key initiatives included:

- Establishing a Responsible AI Committee to oversee fairness, bias detection, transparency, and usage boundaries of all deployed models.

- Requiring model cards and documentation for each production ML model—explaining the purpose, inputs, outputs, and known limitations.

- Running bias and fairness audits on high-impact models, including offer recommendations and pricing predictions.

- Logging all prompt interactions and outputs for the GenAI copilot in Azure AI Studio, with moderation policies to detect hallucinations or harmful content.

- Defining data minimization rules for AI training datasets, ensuring models learned only from necessary and consented data.

This governance framework helped reduce reputational risk, prepared the organization for future regulation, and aligned AI development with the company's values.

Privacy enhancing technologies for sensitive use cases

In scenarios involving customer profiling, health benefit programs, and location-based analytics, Aditya introduced **privacy enhancing technologies** (**PETs**) to further minimize risk.

This included:

- Synthetic data generation for training ML models without exposing real customer records.

- Differential privacy in analytics dashboards for aggregate metrics at store, region, or category level.

- Data masking and tokenization in datasets used by external partners or shared environments.

These techniques allowed innovation to continue without compromising privacy or compliance.

Outcome of phase 10

By the end of this phase, XYZ Consumer Retail institutionalized trust as a core pillar of its transformation. Security was embedded, compliance was proactive, and responsible AI practices were integrated into the organization's innovation agenda.

Key outcomes included:

- A comprehensive Zero Trust architecture spanning identity, endpoints, networks, and workloads.

- Data protection and privacy measures implemented at scale, with complete lineage tracking and access controls via Microsoft Purview.

- A formal responsible AI governance model ensuring fairness, explainability, and compliance across all deployed models.

- Adoption of PETs to enable safe experimentation with sensitive data.

- Clear improvement in security posture scores, audit preparedness, and executive confidence.

With transformation complete, Aditya had delivered not just scalable platforms and advanced AI, but a foundation of integrity where speed, intelligence, and ethics coexisted. As he looked ahead, the focus shifted once again from transformation to future readiness. How could XYZ stay ahead of the next wave of change?

Phase 11, future readiness

With the core transformation complete, trust embedded, and operations running predictably, Aditya found himself facing a different kind of question of *what's coming next?*

Markets were evolving. Consumer behavior was shifting. Technologies like edge AI, quantum computing, and blockchain were moving out of labs and into real pilots. XYZ Consumer Retail had modernized its systems, but future competitiveness would require continuous sensing, experimentation, and preparedness.

Aditya did not see future-readiness as a one-time investment. He saw it as a capability, something the organization needed to build into its mindset, operating rhythm, and technology strategy.

This phase applies the learning from *Chapter 13, Innovation, and Future Technologies.*

Exploring the edge for real-time local intelligence

XYZ's quick commerce and regional fulfillment network created a natural use case for edge computing. Latency mattered. So did local autonomy.

Aditya's team began piloting Azure Stack Edge at key warehouse and distributor locations. Use cases included:

- **Local inference for inventory scan automation**: Edge devices processed barcode and RFID scans in real-time, enabling immediate stock validation without sending every request to the cloud, improving speed and reducing central processing load.

- **Edge-based camera feeds and AI vision models**: High-resolution image and video analysis was run locally to detect shelf compliance issues, safety violations, and equipment anomalies, triggering on-site alerts without latency delays.

- **Event buffering during connectivity drops**: In semi-connected environments, edge nodes temporarily cached events and synced them with central systems once connectivity was restored, ensuring continuous operations without data loss.

These edge workloads were integrated with the central Fabric-based analytics environment, allowing insights to flow both ways, local to central and vice versa.

Planning for multi-cloud and federated workloads

While Azure served as the primary cloud backbone for most of XYZ Consumer Retail's digital initiatives, Aditya recognized the need for multi-cloud flexibility driven by regulatory requirements in certain markets, the need for disaster recovery diversification, and growing collaboration with global partners using different cloud ecosystems.

Rather than allowing multi-cloud adoption to become ad hoc and fragmented, he took a strategic, policy-driven approach. His architecture team laid down a foundation that enabled cross-cloud consistency while preserving operational clarity and control.

Key initiatives included:

- Deploying Azure Arc to onboard and manage non-Azure resources such as *Kubernetes clusters* running in on-prem or other cloud environments. This gave the operations team a single pane of glass to manage configurations, policies, and monitoring across hybrid and multi-cloud assets.

- Piloting other hyperscale failover for non-critical analytics workloads. This ensured that select Fabric datasets and AI model outputs could be ported and rehydrated on the other cloud platform during planned failover tests, proving that redundancy was more than a diagram.

- Establishing a cloud policy framework that clarified where and when alternate cloud providers could be used. The framework covered data residency rules, approved services per cloud, monitoring standards, and security baselines, so teams had flexibility without sacrificing consistency or compliance.

This strategy created a future-ready posture. Whether due to customer requirements, regulatory shifts, or cost optimization opportunities, XYZ was now positioned to run, monitor, and govern workloads seamlessly, regardless of where they lived.

Embedding sustainability into technology decisions

As AI workloads grew, so did energy consumption. The executive team began asking: *How green is our cloud?* Aditya partnered with the sustainability office to:

- Using the Azure Emissions Impact Dashboard to monitor the carbon footprint of cloud consumption, broken down by project, region, and service type. This gave teams visibility into which workloads were the most energy-intensive and where opportunities for reduction existed.

- Right-sizing AI workloads by optimizing model architecture and resource allocation, ensuring minimal compute was used per inference without compromising performance.

- Reducing data sprawl by re-evaluating retention policies and minimizing redundant data movement, particularly for telemetry, logs, and archival datasets.

- Evaluating sustainable Azure regions and carbon-aware scheduling for batch workloads, allowing teams to run compute jobs when and where the environmental impact was lowest.

Sustainability became a lens through which infrastructure and AI decisions were reviewed.

Experimenting with next-gen technologies

To stay ahead, Aditya set up a Future Tech Lab within the CTO's office, a small team tasked with evaluating and running safe pilots on emerging technologies.

Current pilots included:

- Quantum-safe encryption for customer data archives and compliance records.

- Blockchain-based batch traceability to improve supply chain transparency, especially for regulated SKUs.

- AI agents using small language models for internal automation tasks like data summarization, support triaging, and report generation.

These initiatives were about learning. Each pilot had clear success criteria and a feedback loop into the broader architecture strategy.

Bringing future tech learnings back to the business

Insights and prototypes from the Future Tech Lab did not remain isolated. Aditya set up a quarterly *Tech Futures* showcase, where pilot teams presented outcomes to product owners, architects, and business sponsors.

Select innovations like blockchain-backed traceability or AI agents for internal support were added to upcoming product roadmaps based on feasibility and alignment with business goals. The lab became a bridge between innovation and execution.

Outcome of phase 11

By the end of this phase, XYZ Consumer Retail had extended its transformation journey into a capability for the future.

Key outcomes included:

- Deployment of edge AI pilots that improved responsiveness at the network's edge.
- A multi-cloud foundation that supported flexibility without complexity.
- Clear sustainability metrics to guide cloud and AI decisions.
- Strategic experimentation with quantum-safe encryption and blockchain.
- A future tech lab embedded in the CTO's office, keeping innovation grounded and iterative.

The transformation journey was not a finish line. It was a foundation. And with that, Aditya had helped XYZ not just modernize for today but prepare for the opportunities and disruptions of tomorrow.

Conclusion

In this final chapter, we walked through the transformation journey of an enterprise, end to end. From initial discovery to future readiness, each of the 11 phases demonstrated how thoughtful architecture, disciplined execution, and cross-functional leadership can reshape an organization for the better.

The story of XYZ Consumer Retail and its CTO, Aditya, brought to life the principles, frameworks, and strategies covered throughout this book. It illustrated how vision is translated into action, how systems thinking meets human-centric change, and how modern platforms become catalysts for innovation, trust, and impact.

As you reach the end of this book, take a moment to reflect on where your own journey stands. Whether you are modernizing legacy systems, driving AI adoption, rethinking your data estate, or preparing for what is next, know that you do not need to do everything at once. Start with clarity. Move with purpose. Build coalitions. Above all, transformation should be treated as a continuous capability-building exercise.

Key terms

- **Solution architecture**: A structured approach to designing systems that align technology solutions with business needs.
- **Cloud landing zone**: A pre-configured environment in the cloud that provides governance, security, and networking foundations for workloads.

- **Microservices**: A software architecture style where applications are composed of small, independent services that communicate over APIs.

- **IaC**: The practice of managing and provisioning infrastructure using machine-readable configuration files.

- **CI/CD**: Continuous integration and continuous deployment, automation practices that streamline software delivery and updates.

- **DevSecOps**: The integration of security practices within the DevOps lifecycle to build secure applications by design.

- **Data Lakehouse**: A modern data architecture that combines the scalability of data lakes with the performance and structure of data warehouses.

- **Data Mesh**: A decentralized approach to data architecture where domain-oriented teams own and operate their data as products.

- **MLOps**: A set of practices for deploying, monitoring, and governing machine learning models in production environments.

- **FinOps**: A cultural practice that brings together finance, engineering, and business teams to manage cloud costs and maximize value.

- **Zero Trust**: A security framework that assumes no implicit trust and requires continuous verification of every user and device.

- **Responsible AI**: Principles and practices that ensure AI systems are fair, transparent, explainable, and aligned with ethical standards.

- **Emerging Tech**: New and evolving technologies such as edge computing, quantum computing, blockchain, and sustainable AI.

Join our book's Discord space

Join the book's Discord Workspace for Latest updates, Offers, Tech happenings around the world, New Release and Sessions with the Authors:

https://discord.bpbonline.com

Appendix

Additional Resources for Further Learning

Chapter 1: Introduction to Solution Architecture

- Microsoft Azure Well-Architected Framework: **https://learn.microsoft.com/en-us/azure/architecture/framework/**

- Azure Architecture Center: **https://learn.microsoft.com/en-us/azure/architecture/**

- Microsoft Cloud Design Principles: **https://learn.microsoft.com/en-us/azure/architecture/guide/design-principles/**

- Microsoft Cloud Adoption Framework—Innovate (architecture meets product thinking): **https://learn.microsoft.com/en-us/azure/cloud-adoption-framework/innovate/**

- TOGAF: **https://www.opengroup.org/togaf/**

- AWS Well-Architected Framework: **https://aws.amazon.com/architecture/well-architected/**

- GCP Architecture Framework: **https://cloud.google.com/architecture/framework**

- *Software Architecture in Practice* (Book) by *Len Bass et al.*

- *Software Systems Architecture* (Book) by *Nick Rozanski.*

Chapter 2: Cloud Migration Essentials

- Microsoft Cloud Adoption Framework—Strategy & Plan: **https://learn.microsoft.com/en-us/azure/cloud-adoption-framework/strategy/**

- Azure Cloud Adoption Framework—Migrate: **https://learn.microsoft.com/en-us/azure/cloud-adoption-framework/migrate/**

- Azure Migrate Tool Overview: **https://learn.microsoft.com/en-us/azure/migrate/migrate-overview**

- Microsoft's Cloud Adoption Framework—Organize: **https://learn.microsoft.com/en-us/azure/cloud-adoption-framework/organize/**

- AWS Migration Hub: **https://aws.amazon.com/migration-hub/**

- Google Cloud Migration Center: **https://cloud.google.com/migration-center**

Chapter 3: Operational Excellence in Cloud

- Azure Landing Zones: **https://learn.microsoft.com/en-us/azure/cloud-adoption-framework/ready/landing-zone/**

- Azure Policy (for Policy-as-Code): **https://learn.microsoft.com/en-us/azure/governance/policy/overview**

- Azure Blueprints: **https://learn.microsoft.com/en-us/azure/governance/blueprints/overview**

- Microsoft Defender for Cloud (Governance & Compliance Monitoring): **https://learn.microsoft.com/en-us/azure/defender-for-cloud/defender-for-cloud-introduction**

- AWS Control Tower: **https://aws.amazon.com/controltower/**

- Google Cloud Operations Suite: **https://cloud.google.com/blog/topics/developers-practitioners/introduction-google-clouds-operations-suite**

- CNCF TAG: Cloud Native Security & Governance: **https://github.com/cncf/tag-security**

- OPA: **https://www.openpolicyagent.org/**

Chapter 4: Modern Application Architecture

- Microsoft Azure Container Apps (for microservices/serverless fusion): **https://learn.microsoft.com/en-us/azure/container-apps/overview**

- Microsoft Azure API Management: **https://learn.microsoft.com/en-us/azure/api-management/api-management-key-concepts**

- Microsoft eShopOnContainers reference app: **https://github.com/dotnet/eShop**

- Azure Event Grid Overview: **https://learn.microsoft.com/en-us/azure/event-grid/overview**

- Microsoft Dapr: **https://dapr.io/**

- Domain Driven Design Reference by Eric Evans: **https://domainlanguage.com/ddd/reference/**

- Event-Driven Architecture Guide—AWS: **https://aws.amazon.com/event-driven-architecture/**

- *Kubernetes Patterns* (Book) by *Bilgin Ibryam* and *Roland Huß*:

- 12 Factor App: **https://12factor.net/**

Chapter 5: Development Practices and Tools

- Microsoft DevOps Solution Architecture: **https://learn.microsoft.com/en-us/azure/devops/**

- GitHub Copilot for Enterprise: **https://github.com/features/copilot**

- GitHub Advanced Security & DevSecOps: **https://docs.github.com/en/code-security**

- Microsoft Power Platform Fusion Development: **https://learn.microsoft.com/en-us/power-platform/developer/fusion-development**

- SSDF—NIST: **https://csrc.nist.gov/projects/ssdf**

- *The DevOps Handbook* by *Gene Kim et al*

- Platform Engineering Maturity Model—Humanitec: **https://humanitec.com/whitepapers/state-of-platform-engineering-report-volume-3**

- **Continuous Delivery** (Book) by *Jez Humble* and *David Farley*: **https://continuousdelivery.com/**

Chapter 6: Data Architecture and Processing

- Azure Data Lake Storage Documentation: **https://learn.microsoft.com/en-us/azure/storage/blobs/data-lake-storage-introduction**

- Microsoft Fabric – Lakehouse architecture: **https://learn.microsoft.com/en-us/fabric/data-engineering/lakehouse-overview**

- Azure Cosmos DB (for distributed transactional systems): **https://learn.microsoft.com/en-us/azure/cosmos-db/introduction**

- Azure Stream Analytics: **https://learn.microsoft.com/en-us/azure/stream-analytics/**

- Azure Databricks: **https://learn.microsoft.com/en-us/azure/databricks/**

- *Designing Data-Intensive Applications* (Book) by *Martin Kleppmann*: **https://dataintensive.net/**

- Apache Spark Documentation: **https://spark.apache.org/docs/latest/**

- Confluent Kafka Learning Resources: **https://developer.confluent.io/**

- Snowflake Data Warehouse Docs: **https://docs.snowflake.com/en/user-guide**

Chapter 7: Data Strategy and Governance

- Microsoft Fabric (OneLake + Data Engineering/BI Governance): **https://learn.microsoft.com/en-us/fabric/**

- Azure Data Factory: **https://learn.microsoft.com/en-us/azure/data-factory/introduction**

- Microsoft Fabric—Governance and Compliance: **https://learn.microsoft.com/en-us/fabric/governance/**

- Microsoft Purview (Data Governance Suite): **https://learn.microsoft.com/en-us/azure/purview/overview**

- *Data Mesh Principles* by *Zhamak Dehghani*: **https://martinfowler.com/articles/data-mesh-principles.html**

- Data Fabric Architecture (IBM Resource Center): **https://www.ibm.com/topics/data-fabric**

- Apache Airflow Documentation: **https://airflow.apache.org/**

- EDMC DCAM Data Management Framework: **https://edmcouncil.org/page/DCAM**

- *Fundamentals of Data Engineering* (Book) by *Joe Reis* and *Matt Housley*

Chapter 8: Advanced Analytics

- Microsoft Fabric—Data Science + Real-time Analytics workloads: **https://learn.microsoft.com/en-us/fabric/data-science/data-science-overview**

- Azure Synapse Analytics Docs: **https://learn.microsoft.com/en-us/azure/synapse-analytics/**

- Power BI Guided Learning: **https://learn.microsoft.com/en-us/training/powerplatform/power-bi/**

- Azure Machine Learning Notebooks & Labs: **https://github.com/Azure/MachineLearningNotebooks**
- MIT Applied Data Science Program: **https://professional.mit.edu/course-catalog/applied-data-science-program-leveraging-ai-effective-decision-making**
- *Python for Data Analysis* (Book) by *Wes McKinney*: **https://wesmckinney.com/book/**

Chapter 9: Generative AI and Machine Learning

- Microsoft Learn—Azure AI Studio and OpenAI: **https://learn.microsoft.com/en-us/azure/ai-foundry/azure-openai-in-azure-ai-foundry**
- Responsible AI Toolbox (Microsoft): **https://www.responsibleaitoolbox.ai/**
- Azure AI Content Safety: **https://learn.microsoft.com/en-us/azure/ai-services/content-safety/overview**
- LLMOps with Azure: **https://learn.microsoft.com/en-us/azure/machine-learning/prompt-flow/how-to-end-to-end-llmops-with-prompt-flow?view=azureml-api-2**
- Azure Machine Learning Responsible AI dashboard: **https://learn.microsoft.com/en-us/azure/machine-learning/concept-responsible-ai**
- Microsoft Semantic Kernel (for AI orchestration): **https://github.com/microsoft/semantic-kernel**
- AutoGen by Microsoft Research: **https://github.com/microsoft/autogen**
- Hugging Face Course: **https://huggingface.co/learn**
- *DeepLearning.AI GenAI Courses* by *Andrew Ng*
- LangChain Documentation: **https://docs.langchain.com/**
- PyTorch Documentation: **https://pytorch.org/docs/stable/index.html**

Chapter 10: Automation and Infra Management

- Azure Monitor: **https://learn.microsoft.com/en-us/azure/azure-monitor/overview**
- Azure Chaos Studio: **https://learn.microsoft.com/en-us/azure/chaos-studio/chaos-studio-overview**

- Microsoft Security Architectures: **https://learn.microsoft.com/en-us/azure/architecture/guide/security/security-start-here**

- GitHub Actions for IaC pipelines: **https://docs.github.com/en/actions**

- Azure Bicep Documentation: **https://learn.microsoft.com/en-us/azure/azure-resource-manager/bicep/overview**

- Terraform Learning Resources: **https://developer.hashicorp.com/terraform/tutorials**

- Helm Charts Documentation: **https://helm.sh/docs/**

- Prometheus + Grafana Monitoring: **https://prometheus.io/docs/introduction/overview/**

Chapter 11: FinOps Foundations

- Microsoft FinOps Toolkit (GitHub): **https://github.com/microsoft/finops-toolkit**

- Azure Cost Management and Billing: **https://learn.microsoft.com/en-us/azure/cost-management-billing/**

- Azure Advisor: **https://learn.microsoft.com/en-us/azure/advisor/advisor-overview**

- FinOps Foundation: **https://www.finops.org/**

- AWS Cost Optimization Guide: **https://aws.amazon.com/architecture/cost-optimization/**

- Google Cloud Billing and Budgets: **https://cloud.google.com/billing/docs**

- Cloud Zero Blog (FinOps Best Practices): **https://www.cloudzero.com/blog**

- *Cloud FinOps* (Book) by *J.R. Storment* and *Mike Fuller*

Chapter 12: Security, Privacy, and Ethics

- Microsoft Security Best Practices—Cloud Security Benchmark: **https://learn.microsoft.com/en-us/security/benchmark/azure/**

- Privacy & AI Governance on Microsoft Purview: **https://learn.microsoft.com/en-us/purview/ai-microsoft-purview**

- Microsoft AI Red Teaming Playbook: **https://learn.microsoft.com/en-us/security/ai-red-team/**

- Azure Confidential Ledger (for zero-trust & audit-grade immutability): **https://learn.microsoft.com/en-us/azure/confidential-ledger/**

- Zero Trust Security Model—Microsoft: **https://learn.microsoft.com/en-us/security/zero-trust/**

- Responsible AI Principles—Microsoft: **https://www.microsoft.com/en-us/ai/responsible-ai**

- OWASP Top 10: **https://owasp.org/www-project-top-ten/**

- NIST Cybersecurity Framework: **https://www.nist.gov/cyberframework**

- CIS Benchmarks: **https://www.cisecurity.org/cis-benchmarks/**

Chapter 13: Innovation and Future Technologies

- Microsoft's Industrial IoT reference architecture: **https://learn.microsoft.com/en-us/azure/iot/tutorial-iot-industrial-solution-architecture**

- Azure Sustainability Guidance: **https://azure.microsoft.com/en-us/explore/global-infrastructure/sustainability**

- Microsoft Quantum Learning Resources: **https://azure.microsoft.com/en-in/resources/training-and-certifications/quantum-computing**

- Microsoft Sustainability Calculator: **https://azure.microsoft.com/en-us/blog/microsoft-sustainability-calculator-helps-enterprises-analyze-the-carbon-emissions-of-their-it-infrastructure/**

- Edge Computing on Azure: **https://azure.microsoft.com/en-us/resources/cloud-computing-dictionary/what-is-edge-computing**

- Multi-Cloud Reference Architectures—Azure Arc: **https://learn.microsoft.com/en-us/azure/azure-arc/overview**

- Multi-Cloud Reference Architectures—Google Anthos: **https://cloud.google.com/anthos**

- Multi-Cloud Reference Architectures—AWS Outposts: **https://aws.amazon.com/outposts/**

- Blockchain Developer Portal—Ethereum: **https://ethereum.org/en/developers/**

- Green Software Foundation (Sustainable Computing): **https://greensoftware.foundation/**

Join our book's Discord space

Join the book's Discord Workspace for Latest updates, Offers, Tech happenings around the world, New Release and Sessions with the Authors:

https://discord.bpbonline.com

Index

www.ingramcontent.com/pod-product-compliance
Lightning Source LLC
Chambersburg PA
CBHW061741210326
41599CB00034B/6753